Studies in Mutualist Political Economy

Visit www.booksurge.com to order additional copies.

Studies in Mutualist Political Economy

Kevin A. Carson

2007

Studies in Mutualist Political Economy

Contents

I have criticized the law of Labour
Value with all the severity that a doctrine so utterly false seemed to me
to deserve. It may be that my criticism also is open to many objections.
But one thing at any rate seems to me certain: earnest writers concerned
to find out the truth will not in future venture to content themselves
with asserting the law of value as has been hitherto done.

In future any one who thinks that he can maintain this law will
first of all be obliged to supply what his predecessors have omitted—a
proof that can be taken seriously. Not quotations from authorities; not
protesting and dogmatising phrases; but a proof that earnestly and
conscientiously goes into the essence of the matter. On such a basis no
one will be more ready and willing to continue the discussion than
myself.

—Eugen von Bohm-Bawerk. *Capital and Interest* p. 389.

To my mother, Ruth Emma Rickert, without whose love and support I could never have done this.

Preface

In the mid-nineteenth century, a vibrant native American school of anarchism, known as individualist anarchism, existed alongside the other varieties. Like most other contemporary socialist thought, it was based on a radical interpretation of Ricardian economics. The classical individualist anarchism of Josiah Warren, Benjamin Tucker and Lysander Spooner was both a socialist movement and a subcurrent of classical liberalism. It agreed with the rest of the socialist movement that labor was the source of exchange-value, and that labor was entitled to its full product. Unlike the rest of the socialist movement, the individualist anarchists believed that the natural wage of labor in a free market was its product, and that economic exploitation could only take place when capitalists and landlords harnessed the power of the state in their interests. Thus, individualist anarchism was an alternative both to the increasing statism of the mainstream socialist movement, and to a classical liberal movement that was moving toward a mere apologetic for the power of big business.

Shawn Wilbur has argued that the late-nineteenth century split between individualists and communists in the American anarchist movement (for which the ill-feeling between Benjamin Tucker and Johann Most is a good proxy) left the individualists marginalized and weak. As a result, much of the movement created by Benjamin Tucker was absorbed or colonized by the right. Although there are many honorable exceptions who still embrace the "socialist" label, most people who call themselves "individualist anarchists" today are followers of Murray Rothbard's Austrian economics, and have abandoned the labor theory of value. Had not the anarchism of Tucker been marginalized and supplanted by that of Goldman, it might have been the center of a uniquely American version of populist radicalism. It might have worked out a more elaborate economic theory that was both free market and anti-capitalist, instead of abandoning the socialist label and being co-opted by the Right.

Some self-described individualist anarchists still embrace the socialist aspect of Tucker's thought—Joe Peacott, Jonathan Simcock, and Shawn Wilbur, for example. The Voluntary Cooperation Movement promotes the kinds of mutualist practice advocated by Proudhon. Elements of the nineteenth century radical tradition also survive under other names, in a variety of movements: Georgist, distributist, "human scale" technology, etc. Unfortunately, individualist anarchist economic thought has for the most part been frozen in a time warp for over a hundred years. If the marginalists and subjectivists have not dealt the labor theory of value the final death blow they smugly claim for it, they have nevertheless raised questions that any viable labor theory must answer.

This book is an attempt to revive individualist anarchist political economy, to incorporate the useful developments of the last hundred years, and to make it relevant to the problems of the twenty-first century. We hope this work will go at least part of the way to providing a new theoretical and practical foundation for free market socialist economics.

In Part One, which concerns value theory, we construct the theoretical apparatus for our later analysis. In this section, we attempt to resurrect the classical labor theory of value, to answer the attacks of its marginalist and subjectivist critics, and at the same time to reformulate the theory in a way that both addresses their valid criticisms and incorporates their useful innovations. Part One starts with an assessment of the marginalist revolution and its claims to have demolished the labor theory of value, and then proceeds either to refute these criticisms or to incorporate them.

Part Two analyzes the origins of capitalism in light of this theoretical apparatus; it is an attempt to explicate, if the reader will pardon the expression, the laws of motion of state capitalism—from its origins in statism, through its collapse from the internal contradictions inherent in coercion. We analyze capitalism in the light of individualist anarchism's central insight: that labor's natural wage in a free market is its product, and that coercion is the only means of exploitation. It is state intervention that distinguishes capitalism from the free market.

Part Three, finally, is a vision of mutualist practice, building both on our own previous theoretical analysis, and on the rich history of anarchist thought.

If there is one valuable practical insight in this entire book, it is the realization that coercive state policies are not necessary to remedy the evils of present-day capitalism. All these evils—exploitation of labor, monopoly and concentration, the energy crisis, pollution, waste—result from government intervention in the market on behalf of capitalists. The solution is not more government intervention, but to eliminate the existing government intervention from which the problems derive. A genuine free market society, in which all transactions are voluntary and all costs are internalized in price, would be a decentralized society of human-scale production, in which all of labor's product went to labor, instead of to capitalists, landlords and government bureaucrats.

Some of the material of Parts Two and Three appeared previously in other forms. Chapter Four is a radically expanded and revised version of the subheading "The Subsidy of History" in my pamphlet "The Iron Fist Behind the Invisible Hand," published by Red Lion Press in 2001. Chapter Five is likewise, an expanded version of other sections from the same pamphlet. Chapters Six and Seven are expanded versions of my article "Austrian and Marxist Theories of Monopoly Capitalism: A Mutualist Synthesis." Chapter Eight incorporates some material from the same article, along with the subheading "Political Repression" from "Iron Fist." Chapter Nine includes material from my article "A 'Political' Program for Anarchists."

I welcome any comments, criticism, or suggestions. I can be contacted at this email address: kevin_carson@hotmail.com

Part One
Theoretical Foundations: Value Theory

Chapter One
The Marginalist Assault on Classical Political Economy: An Assessment and Counter-Attack

A. Statement of the Classical Labor Theory of Value

Either the labor theory of value, or, secondarily, some other form of cost theory of value,[1] was common to the classical school of political economy in England.

It was stated by Adam Smith in ambiguous form: "*The real price of everything, what everything really costs to the man who wants to acquire it, is the toil and trouble of acquiring it.... Labour was the first price, the original purchase-money that was paid for all things.*"[2] In the same passage, though, he spoke of the value of a commodity in one's possession as consisting of "*the quantity of the labour which he can command....*" And at other times, he seemed to make the market price of labor the source of its effect on exchange value.

The most clear-cut and effective statement of the labor theory was by David Ricardo, in *Principles of Political Economy and Taxation*: "*The value of a commodity, or the quantity of any other commodity for which it will exchange, depends on the relative quantity of labour which is necessary for its production, and not as the greater or less compensation which is paid for that labour.*"[3] In so defining the doctrine, Ricardo eliminated the confusion between labor as the source of exchange-value and wages as a component of price.

From this principle, it followed that income accruing to the owners of land and capital was a deduction from this exchange-value created by labor, and that wages varied inversely with profit: "*If the corn is to be divided between the farmer and the labourer, the larger the proportion that is given to the latter, the less will remain for the former. So if cloth or cotton goods be divided between the workman and his employer, the larger the proportion given to the former, the less remains for the latter.*"[4]

It was only natural that the emerging socialist movement should seize on the political implications of this conclusion. The school of so-called "Ricardian socialists" in England took just such an inspiration. The greatest of them, Thomas Hodgskin, wrote in *Labour Defended Against the Claims of Capital*, "*Wages vary inversely as profits, or wages rise when profits fall, and profits rise when wages fall; and it is therefore profits, or the capitalist's share of the national produce, which is opposed to wages, or the share of the labourer.*"[5]

Marx, in turn, was inspired by the Ricardian socialist interpretation of classical political economy, as well as by Proudhon. According to Engels, modern socialism was a direct outgrowth of the insights of "bourgeois political economy" on the nature of wages, rent, and profit.

> *Insofar as modern socialism, no matter of what tendency, starts out from bourgeois political economy, it almost without exception takes up the Ricardian theory of value. The two propositions which Ricardo proclaimed in 1817 right at the beginning of his* Principles, *1) that the value of any commodity is purely and solely determined by the quantity of labour required for its production, and 2) that the product of the entire social labor is divided among the three classes: landowners (rent), capitalists (profit), and workers (wages)—these two propositions had ever since 1821 been utilized in England for socialist conclusions, and in part with such pointedness and resolution that this literature, which had then almost been forgotten and was to a large extent only rediscovered by Marx, remained surpassed until the appearance of* Capital.[6]

The actual extent to which Marx's theory of value is a straightforward outgrowth of Ricardo's, and to which it was a preexisting Hegelian philosophy with Ricardian elements grafted on, is an issue in dispute.[7] But for the present purpose, we will treat Marx's theory of value as relevant to our study to the extent that it is amenable to a Ricardian approach.

B. Vulgar Political Economy, Marginalism, and the Issue of Ideological Motivation

Given the fertile ground Ricardo's political economy presented for socialist conclusions, it was naturally seen as problematic by apologists for the newly arisen system of industrial capitalism. Marx made a fundamental distinction, in this regard, between the classical political economists and the "vulgar economists" who came after them. Smith, James Mill and Ricardo had developed their scientific political economy without fear of its revolutionary implications, because industrial capital was still the progressive underdog in a revolutionary struggle against the unearned income of feudal landlords and chartered monopolists.

But that situation came to an end with the capitalists' acquisition of political power.

> *In France and England the bourgeoisie had conquered power* [in the "decisive crisis" year of 1830]. *Thenceforth, the class struggle, practically as well as theoretically, took on more and more outspoken and threatening forms. It sounded the knoll of scientific bourgeois economy. It was thenceforth no longer a question whether this theorem or that was true, but whether it was useful to capital or harmful, expedient or inexpedient, politically dangerous or not. In place of disinterested enquirers, there were hired prize-fighters; in place of genuine scientific research, the bad conscience and the evil intent of apologetic.*[8]

Maurice Dobb, likewise, commented on the transition of political economy from a revolutionary to an apologetic role:

> *As a critique leveled simultaneously against the authoritarianism of an autocratic state and against the privileges and influence of the landed aristocracy Political Economy at its inception played a revolutionary role.... Only later, in its post-Ricardian phase, did it pass over from assault on privilege and restriction to apology for property.*[9]

Although the break was perhaps not as fundamental as the Marxists have made it out to be, there is evidence that at least some of the political economists from the 1830s on, as well as the founders of marginalism, were conscious of the political aspect of the problem. According to Maurice Dobb, the "vulgar political economists" were consciously motivated by apologetic considerations; as an alternative to the mainstream classical school of England, they turned to the subjectivist continental school, which had been influenced by Say's interpretation of Adam Smith.

> *It was against this whole* [Ricardian] *mode of approach that the Senior-Longfield school reacted so strongly—not merely as an inapposite analytical tool..., but against its wider applications and corollaries. In reacting in this way, it was almost inevitable that they should be carried in the wake of (and eventually join) the other and rival tradition deriving from Smith, reinforcing it by so doing. If they are properly described at all as "improvers" or "conciliators", such a term should really be applied to their role in developing* this *Smithian tradition and* not *the Ricardian approach.*[10]

Among the first generation of marginalists, Jevons at least was quite conscious of the political dimension of his anti-Ricardian project. To quote Dobb again, *"...although Menger could be said to have represented this break with classical tradition even more clearly and completely, Jevons was apparently more conscious of the role he was playing in reshunting the 'car of economic science' which Ricardo had so perversely directed 'onto a wrong line.'"*[11]

Dobb considered it telling that the marginalist refinement of subjectivism had been produced near-simultaneously by three different writers, within a decade of the publication of *Capital*. It indicated a prevailing atmosphere of ideological combat, and a vacancy for anti-Marxian polemicists waiting to be filled.

> *It is, at least, a remarkable fact that within ten years of the appearance of the first volume of* Kapital, *not only had the rival utility-principle been enunciated independently by a number of writers, but the new principle was finding a receptivity to its acceptance such as very few ideas of similar novelty can ever have met. If only by the effect of negation, the influence of Marx on the economic theory of the nineteenth century would appear to have been much more profound than it is fashionable to admit....*
>
> *That so many of the economists of the last quarter of the century should have advertised their wares as such an epoch-making novelty, and tilted their lances so menacingly at their forebears, seems to have an obvious, if unflattering explanation: namely, the dangerous use to which Ricardian notions had been recently put by Marx.*[12]

And of the second generation of Austrians, Böhm-Bawerk seemed quite aware, in Dobb's opinion, of the ideological nature of the task before him.

> *It seems clear that Böhm-Bawerk at any rate appreciated the problem which the classical theory had sought to solve. While he is sparing, almost niggardly, in paying tribute to Marx even for formulating the question accurately, there is every indication that he framed his theory directly to provide a substitute answer to the questions which Marx had posed.*[13]

If such speculations on the political motives of the marginalist revolutionaries seem "unflattering," unfair, or ad hominem, it is worth bearing in mind that Böhm-Bawerk himself was not above pointing to the ideological motivations of his predecessors, in language very reminiscent of Marx's dismissal of the "vulgar economists." Even more than grinding his axe against Marx, Böhm-Bawerk seems to have been motivated by a desire to demonstrate the originality of his own views at the expense of previous defenses of interest, like that of Nassau Senior.

> *Senior's Abstinence theory has obtained great popularity among those economists who are favourably disposed to interest. It seems to me, however,*

that this popularity has been due, not so much to its superiority as a theory, as that it came in the nick of time to support interest against the severe attacks that had been made on it. I draw this inference from the peculiar circumstance that the vast majority of its later advocates do not profess it exclusively, but only add elements of the Abstinence theory in an eclectic way to other theories favourable to interest.[14]

Since Böhm-Bawerk was not above such a critique of his own predecessors, we have no obligation to spare him similar treatment, from an excess of chivalry.

It is remarkable, at least, how the cultural atmosphere of the classical liberal mainstream changed from the early nineteenth century on. From a revolutionary assault on the entrenched power of the landed aristocracy and chartered monopolies, by the late nineteenth century it had become an apology for the institutions and interests most closely resembling, in power and privilege, the ruling class of the Old Regime: the large corporations and the plutocracy.

The shift toward reaction was by no means uniform, however. The revolutionary and anti-privilege character of the early movement continued in many strands of liberalism. Thomas Hodgskin, squarely in the classical liberal tradition and also by far the most market-oriented of the Ricardian socialists, criticized the power of the industrial capitalist in language reminiscent of Adam Smith's attack on landlords and mercantilists—and on very much the same principles.

The American school of individualist anarchism, likewise, turned the weapons of free market analysis against the statist props of capitalist privilege. Even Hodgskin's disciple Spencer, usually regarded as a stereotypical apologist for capitalism, at times displayed such tendencies. Henry George and his follower Albert Nock, likewise, turned classical liberalism toward radically populist ends. Our own version of free market socialism, set out in this book, comes from these heirs of the armed doctrine of classical liberalism.

At any rate, regardless of their political motivations, the marginalists performed a necessary role. Their detailed critique of classical political economy pointed out many areas in need of clarification, or of a more explicit philosophical basis. And the marginalist critique, especially that of Böhm-Bawerk, produced genuinely valuable innovations which any viable labor theory of value must incorporate. One such criticism (Böhm-Bawerk's critique of the labor-theory for its lack of an adequate mechanism), and one innovation (the Austrian time preference theory) will be integrated, in the following chapters, into a reworked labor theory of value.

C. The Marginalists versus Ricardo

Although subsequent marginalist criticisms of Ricardo were more thorough, Jevons fired the opening salvo quite dramatically. He explicitly formulated his utility-based theory of value in opposition to the labor theory. In his Introduction to *The Theory of Political Economy*, he wrote:

> Repeated reflection and inquiry have led me to the somewhat novel opinion, that _value depends entirely upon utility_. Prevailing opinions make labour rather than utility the origin of value; and there are even those who distinctly assert that labour is the _cause_ of value. I show, on the contrary, that we have only to trace out carefully the natural laws of the variation of utility, as depending upon the quantity of commodity in our possession, in order to arrive at a satisfactory theory of exchange, of which the ordinary laws of supply and demand are a necessary consequence. This theory is in harmony with facts; and, whenever there is any apparent reason for the belief that labour is the cause of value, we obtain an explanation of the reason. Labour is found often to determine value, but only in an indirect manner, by varying the degree of utility of the commodity through an increase or limitation of the supply.[15]

On the face of it, the bald assertion that utility determines value seems utter nonsense. The only way the supplier of a good can charge according to its utility to the buyer, is if he is in a monopoly situation which enables him to charge whatever the market will bear, without regard to the cost of production. But by qualifying this statement to treat marginal utility as a dependent variable determined by the quantity in our possession, he makes it clear that the influence of value on price assumes a snapshot of the balance of supply and demand in a market *at any given time.* This is also a shortcoming of the Austrian utility theory, as it was developed by Böhm-Bawerk and his Austrian followers, up to the present. Not only did the later Austrians inadequately treat the time dimension, but they were forced to a position of radical skepticism regarding the notions of "equilibrium price," in order to avoid a Marshallian understanding of the dynamic effect of production cost on price, through the effect of market price on supply. To the extent that Jevons admitted the dimension of time, and made supply itself a function of the supplier's response to market price, he was also forced to admit the effect of labor on value "in an indirect manner," in much the same way that Marshall was later to do with his famous scissors.

Böhm-Bawerk was at his best in systematically analyzing the exceptions to the labor-theory and the cost-principle. In so doing, however, he was forced to admit a rough statistical correlation between cost and price in cases of reproducible goods; and in so admitting, he was forced to reduce his argument to quibbling over the required level of generality of a theory of value. So, Böhm-Bawerk having set the terms of discussion, let us proceed to examine his list of exceptions to Ricardo's cost-theory of price. He begins with a general statement of his criticism:

> *Experience shows that the exchange value of goods stands in proportion to that amount of labour which their production costs only in the case of one class of goods, and even then only approximately. Well known as this should be, considering that the facts on which it rests are so familiar, it is very seldom estimated at its proper value. Of course everybody, including the socialist writers, agrees that experience does not entirely confirm the Labour Principle. It is commonly imagined, however, that the cases in which actual facts confirm the labour principle form the rule, and that the cases which contradict the principle form a relatively insignificant exception. This view is very erroneous, and to correct it once and for all I shall put together in groups the exceptions by which experience proves the labour principle to be limited in economic life. We shall see that the exceptions so much preponderate that they scarcely leave any room for the rule.*[16]

As we shall see later, though, it is of questionable value to measure quantitatively the exceptions to the law of value; it makes more sense to treat the effect of cost as a first-order generalization, and then to treat scarcity exceptions as second-order deviations from this generalization. This was the approach of both Ricardo, in treating cost and scarcity as twin principles of value, and Marshall, with his scissors. The longer the time frame, the more cost is shown to be the main influence on the price of goods whose supply can be increased in response to demand, and scarcity rents are shown to be short-term deviations through which the cost-principle works itself out.

The first exception to the labor theory of value Böhm-Bawerk listed was that for scarce goods with an inelastic supply.

> *1. From the scope of the Labour Principle are excepted all "scarce" goods that, from actual or legal hindrances, cannot be reproduced at all, or can be reproduced only in limited amount. Ricardo names, by way of example, rare statues and pictures, scarce books and coins, wines of a peculiar quality, and adds the remark that such goods form only a very small proportion of the goods daily exchanged in the market. If, however, we consider that to this category belongs the whole of the land, and, further, those numerous goods in the production of which patents, copyrights, and trade secrets come into play, it will be found that the extent of these "exceptions" is by no means inconsiderable.*[17]

Goods that are permanently inelastic in supply are, indeed, the most fundamental exception to Ricardo's labor theory of value. Such completely inelastic goods are, however, a relatively minor portion of all commodities. The production of most goods can, eventually, be expanded to a level sufficient to meet demand. For such elastic goods, the only question is the duration required for such adjustment. Böhm-Bawerk addressed that "exception" (not really an exception at all, as we shall see, since it does not in any way violate the correspondence between labor-value and *equilibrium* price) in his fourth point, quoted below. As for the example of rare works of art, etc., Böhm-Bawerk himself admitted that Ricardo had acknowledged them.

The final group of exceptions—land, patents, etc.—deserves close consideration. Böhm-Bawerk lumped together all goods with an inelastic supply, regardless of whether their inelasticity results from "actual or legal hindrances." But the mutualist version of the labor theory of value states that, excepting goods naturally inelastic in supply, profit results from unequal exchange—itself a result of state intervention in the market. To the extent that scarcity of land is natural, and absentee landlord claims are not enforced by the state, economic rent on land is a form of scarcity rent that will prevail under any system. But to the extent that the scarcity is artificial, resulting from government or absentee landlord restrictions on access to vacant land, or landlord rent on those actually occupying and using land, the mutualist contention is that such rent is a deviation from normal exchange-value caused by unequal exchange. Patents, likewise, are such a deviation, being nothing but a monopoly imposed by the state. Such examples, therefore, have no bearing whatsoever on the validity of the labor theory of value.

As his second item in the list of exceptions, Böhm-Bawerk mentioned the product of skilled labor. In the process of his discussion, he ridiculed Marx's attempt to salvage a uniform labor-time standard by reducing skilled labor to a multiple of common labor.[18] In this, Böhm-Bawerk was entirely correct. The validity of this criticism was one factor in our attempt to rework the labor theory of value on the basis of Smith's and Hodgskin's subjective "toil and trouble," in place of Ricardo's and Marx's embodied labor time. This will be discussed in detail in a later chapter.

The third kind of exception, similarly, included "*those goods—-not, it is true, a very important class—that are produced by abnormally badly paid labour.*"[19] But the labor theory of value, as Ricardo formulated it at least, stated that the exchange values of goods were regulated by the quantity of labor embodied in them—not by the wages of labor. And according to the mutualist version of the theory, low wages in relation to the total product of labor are a result of unequal exchange between capital and labor within the production process.

The most important exception, after the first, was the fourth: the fluctuations of commodity prices above and below the axis of their labor-value, in response to changes in supply and demand.

> *4. A fourth exception to the Labour Principle may be found in the familiar and universally admitted phenomenon that even those goods, in which exchange value entirely corresponds with the labour costs, do not show this correspondence at every moment. By the fluctuations of supply and demand their exchange value is put sometimes above, sometimes below the level corresponding to the amount of labour incorporated in them. The amount of labour only indicates the point toward which exchange value gravitates,— not any fixed point of value. This exception, too, the socialist adherents of the labour principle seem to me to make too light of. They mention it indeed, but they treat it as a little transitory irregularity, the existence of which does not interfere with the great "law" of exchange value. But it is undeniable that these irregularities are just so many cases where exchange value is regulated by other determinants than the amount of labour costs. They might at all events have suggested the inquiry whether there is not perhaps a more universal principle of exchange value, to which might be traceable, not only the regular formations of value, but also those formations which, from the standpoint of the labour theory, appear to be "irregular." But we should look in vain for any such inquiry among the theorists of this school.*[20]

In fact, this fourth exception is absolutely devoid of substance, unless one adopts the later Austrian pose of radical epistemological skepticism toward the notion of "equilibrium price." And if, as Böhm-Bawerk said, Ricardo himself admitted the existence of that exception, it can only be deduced that Ricardo did not view it as a fatal flaw in the labor theory. It would seem to follow that Böhm-Bawerk and Ricardo differed in their opinions of the significance of the phenomenon—in which case, Böhm-Bawerk's real task would be to show why Ricardo was mistaken in his views of what constituted an adequate theory.

The labor theory of Ricardo did not just implicitly assume such fluctuation, but depended on it. It was only the process of competition over time, and the response of suppliers and consumers to the fluctuating market price, that continually caused equilibrium price to gravitate around labor value. And Marx said as much explicitly, as we shall see below.

Ricardo for the most part treated "value" and "price" as synonymous, and claimed only that value approximated embodied labor over a period of time. Marx, on the other hand, used "value" in a sense much closer to equilibrium price. Both, then, asserted no more than that the equilibrium price of a good in elastic supply approximates its labor-value. And for both, price fluctuations under the influence of supply and demand were the very mechanism by which the law of value operated.

Finally, Böhm-Bawerk pointed, as a fifth exception, to those cases in which prices "*constantly*" diverged from labor-value, "*and that not inconsiderably*," to the extent that their production "*require*[d] *the greater advance of 'previous' labour....*"[21] If he was referring here to amortization cost of past capital outlays, that presents no problem at all for the labor theory, given its view of capital as accumulated past labor. If he was referring to the problems presented the labor theory of value by capitals of different organic composition and the general rate of profit, an at-length study of that issue is beyond our scope here. Suffice it to say that Ricardo as well as Marx recognized differing capital compositions as a distorting factor; and Marx saw the general rate of profit only as redistributing surplus-value, and thus rendering the operation of the law of value indirect. And from the mutualist point of view, profit and interest are monopoly returns on capital resulting from state intervention in the marketplace; so for mutualism, the rate of profit (excepting the relatively minor part of net profit resulting from time-preference, with which we will deal in Chapter 3) is simply another example of the distortions by which unequal exchange causes a deviation from "normal values."

Böhm-Bawerk summed up all the deviations from the labor principle, and concluded that the labor theory of value

> does not hold at all in the case of a very considerable proportion of goods; in the case of the others, does not hold always, and never holds exactly. These are the facts of experience with which the value theorists have to reckon.[22]

Böhm-Bawerk's straw-man caricature of what the labor theory was intended to demonstrate, certainly, did not hold up at all well under his onslaught. But then, straw-men are deliberately constructed to be knocked down. He would have made as much sense in saying that the law of gravity was invalidated by all the exceptions presented by air resistance, wind, obstacles, human effort, and so forth. The force operates at all times, but its operation is always qualified by the action of *secondary* forces. But it is clear, in the case of gravity, which is the first-order phenomenon, and which are second-order *deviations* from it.

Ricardo's distinction between reproducible and non-reproducible goods, true enough, was misleading. Although goods whose supply is absolutely limited relative to demand are a relatively minor portion of all commodities, it is nevertheless true that even reproducible goods take a greater or lesser period of time for supply to accommodate demand. At any given time, the price of most commodities is probably greater or less than labor-value, as a result of imbalance between supply and demand. It is only over time that price approximates labor-value. So rather than stressing the quantitative insignificance of scarcity deviations from cost, Ricardo would have been more accurate to emphasize the character of such deviations as a secondary phenomenon in the overall process by which equilibrium price approximates labor-value.

But the Austrians were guilty of their own ambiguity. Although Menger and Böhm-Bawerk regarded the influence of production cost as virtually irrelevant in all cases of scarcity, they were unclear exactly what they meant by scarcity.

Menger distinguished economic goods, which were characterized by scarcity, from non-economic goods: *"the difference between economic and non-economic goods is ultimately founded on a difference...in the relationship between requirements for and available quantities of these goods...."*[23] Of non-economic goods, he wrote:

> The relationship responsible for the non-economic character of goods consists in requirements for goods being smaller than their available quantities. Thus there are always portions of the whole supply of non-economic goods that are related to no human need.... Hence no satisfaction depends on our control of any one of the units of a good having non-economic character....[24]

The problem, though, is that goods are almost never "non-economic" in this sense of having no exchange-value whatever. Unless an unlimited supply of a good is located at its point of consumption, and requires no effort to appropriate, it will acquire some value from the effort necessary to transport it to the final user in usable form. Even when a village is surrounded by forest, with no limit on the amount that may be cut by an individual household, firewood has an exchange-value. Even in Cockaigne or Big Rock Candy Mountain, one must make the effort of picking the roast chickens off the bush or dipping the whiskey from the stream.

Menger's disciple, Böhm-Bawerk, likewise made scarcity relative to demand the basis of value. Economic value required *"scarcity as well as usefulness—"*

> not absolute scarcity, but scarcity relative to the demand for the particular class of goods. To put it more exactly: goods acquire value when the whole available stock of them is not sufficient to cover the wants depending on them for satisfaction, or when the stock would not be sufficient without these particular goods.[25]

And this scarcity, as Böhm-Bawerk put it, was a scarcity of "present goods":

> Now it can be shown—and with this we come to the goal of our long inquiry—that the supply of present goods _must_ be numerically less than the demand. The supply, even in the richest nation, is limited by the amount of the people's wealth at the moment. The demand, on the other hand, is practically infinite....[26]

This concept of "scarcity," as used by Menger and Böhm-Bawerk, has three problems. First, as we have already suggested above, making scarcity and utility depend on the balance of demand and "present goods" at the present moment, it ignores the dynamic factor. In taking the balance of supply and demand in a particular market at a particular time as a "snapshot," and deriving value from "utility" in this context, it ignores the effect of short-term price on the future behavior of market actors: the very mechanism through which price is made to approximate cost over time.

Second, it confuses two kinds of scarcity: 1) the kind of scarcity that makes economic goods (i.e., a difficulty of production or appropriation sufficient to require some effort or disutility to acquire them in a usable form); and 2) the kind of scarcity in which a good is in more or less inelastic supply, so that it cannot be produced in quantities proportional to effort. In a sense, the former kind is set up in opposition to a straw man: as we said above, there _are_ virtually no non-economic goods.

And third, the claim that demand is virtually infinite relative to supply is misleading. "Demand" is not an independent variable, but depends on the price at which goods are available. To be "reproducible" in the Ricardian sense, a good need not be reproducible without limit, in any quantities an individual might conceivably be willing to consume of it, if it cost nothing. It has only to be reproducible in the quantities for which there is effective demand at the cost of production. And as we pointed out above, regardless of the degree of elasticity, so long as supply can _eventually_ be adapted to demand, the equilibrium price will approximate the cost of production.

D. Exceptions to the Cost-Principle: The Classicals in Their Own Defense

Since Böhm-Bawerk and others made so much of the various scarcity exceptions to the cost principle, we will examine the treatment of such exceptions in the writings of the classical political economists and socialists themselves. If, as we shall see below, the classicals freely admitted such exceptions, it follows that the marginalists and subjectivists were attacking a straw man; or at the very least, that they had a far different idea of the level of generality necessary for a theory of value.

Although Adam Smith figured much less prominently than Ricardo in subjectivist attacks on the labor and cost theories of value, he still did not entirely escape their attention. So it will be worthwhile to examine statements, in his writing, of exceptions to the cost principle.

Smith treated the fluctuations of price above and below its "natural level," not as violations of his idea of natural price, but as the mechanism by which it was sustained.

The market price of every particular commodity is regulated by the proportion between the quantity which is actually brought to market, and the demand of those who are willing to pay the natural price of the commodity, or the whole value of the rent, labour, and profit, which must be paid in order to bring it thither. Such people may be called the effectual demanders, and their demand the effectual demand; since it may be sufficient to effectuate the bringing of the commodity to market. It is different from the absolute demand. A very poor man may be said in some sense to have a demand for a coach and six...; but his demand is not an effectual demand, as the commodity can never be brought to market in order to satisfy it....

The quantity of every commodity brought to market naturally suits itself to the effectual demand. It is the interest of all those who employ their land, labour, or stock, in bringing any commodity to market, that the quantity never should exceed the effectual demand; and it is the interest of all other people that it never should fall short of that demand.

If, at any time it exceeds the effectual demand, some of the component parts of its price must be paid below their natural rate. If it is rent, the interest of the landlords will immediately prompt them to withdraw a part of their land; and if it is wages or profit, the interest of the labourers in the one case, and of their employers in the other, will prompt them to withdraw a part of their labour or stock from this employment. The quantity brought to market will soon be no more than sufficient to supply the effectual demand. All the different parts of its price will rise to their natural rate, and the whole to its natural price.

If, on the contrary, the quantity brought to market should at any time fall short of the effectual demand, some of the component parts of its price must rise above their natural rate.... [And as a result, factors will enter the market until t]*he quantity brought thither will soon be sufficient to supply the effectual demand. All the different parts of its price will soon sink to their natural rate, and the whole price to its natural price.*

The natural price, therefore, is, as it were, the central price, to which the prices of all commodities are continually gravitating.[27]

Smith, in this analysis, outshone the Austrians on two points. First, he admitted supply as a dynamic factor, rather than treating the balance of supply and demand at any given time outside any larger context. And second, rather than treating demand as absolute, and therefore virtually unlimited compared to supply, he considered only "effectual" demand for a good at its "natural" price. Attention to these two points goes a long way to avoiding the misleading impression of the "utility" theory of value, as baldly stated by the Austrians.

In the same chapter, Smith made a detailed study of the various forms of inelasticity, natural or manmade, which caused price to deviate from cost in the short or long run. Among these he included trade secrets, site advantages of soil, and state-granted monopolies.[28]

The correspondence of actual to natural price, over time, was a function of elasticity of supply. Depending on this variable, prices might approximate costs more or less quickly, or never. Like Ricardo, Smith limited the operation of the cost principle to those cases in which the supply of a good could be increased to meet demand.

> These different sorts of rude produce may be divided into three classes. The first comprehends those which it is scarce in the power of human industry to multiply at all. The second, those which it can multiply in proportion to the demand. The third, those in which the efficacy of industry is either limited or uncertain. In the progress of wealth and improvement, the real price of the first may rise to any degree of extravagance, and seems not to be limited by any certain boundary. That of the second, though it may rise greatly, has, however, a certain boundary beyond which it cannot well pass for any considerable time together. That of the third, though its natural tendency is to rise in the progress of improvement, yet in the same degree of improvement it may sometimes happen even to fall, sometimes to continue the same, and sometimes to rise more or less, according as different accidents render the efforts of human industry...more or less successful.

The first category included those goods which "*nature only produces in certain quantities....*"[29]

As for Ricardo, he made it clear at the outset that his labor theory of exchange-value applied only to those commodities whose supply could be increased in response to demand. (Like the other classical political economists and Marx, he also made utility a criterion for exchange-value—thus dispensing with the favorite "mud pie" red herring of subjectivists.)

> Possessing utility, commodities derive their exchange value from two sources: from their scarcity, and from the quantity of labour required to obtain them.

There are some commodities, the value of which is determined by their scarcity alone. No labour can increase the quantity of such goods, and therefore their value cannot be lowered by an increased supply. Some rare statues and pictures, scarce books and coins, wines of a peculiar quality, which can be made only from grapes grown on a particular soil, of which there is a very limited quantity, are all of this description. Their value is wholly independent of the quantity of labour originally necessary to produce them, and varies with the varying wealth and inclinations of those who are desirous to possess them.

These commodities, however, form a very small part of the mass of commodities daily exchanged in the market. By far the greatest part of those goods which are the objects of desire, are procured by labour, and they may be multiplied... almost without any assignable limit, if we are disposed to bestow the labour necessary to obtain them.

In speaking then of commodities, of their exchangeable value, and of the laws which regulate their relative prices, we mean always such commodities only as can be increased in quantity by the exertion of human industry, and on the production of which competition operates without restraint.[30]

In this passage, Ricardo dealt with goods whose supply is totally inelastic, as exceptions in which exchange-value is determined by scarcity rather than labor. He also mentioned free competition as a requirement for the law of value to operate. These are two of the major exceptions listed by Böhm-Bawerk as damning flaws in Ricardo's system, duly noted by Ricardo and seemingly no great embarrassment to him. Ricardo's main shortcoming in this passage was to treat scarcity and labor as jointly or simultaneously determining factors, rather than treating labor as a primary factor and scarcity rents as secondary deviations from labor-value.

In Chapter 4, Ricardo turned to divergences from labor-value caused by fluctuations in supply and demand—another major exception pointed out by Böhm-Bawerk. Again, such divergences were treated, not as an embarrassing violation of the law of value, but as the mechanism by which it operated.

In the ordinary course of events, there is no commodity which continues for any length of time to be supplied precisely in that degree of abundance, which the wants and wishes of mankind require, and therefore there is none which is not subject to accidental and temporary variations of price.

It is only in consequence of such variations, that capital is apportioned precisely, in the requisite abundance and no more, to the production of the different commodities which happen to be in demand. With the rise or fall of price, profits are elevated above, or depressed below their general level, and capital is either encouraged to enter into, or is warned to depart from the particular employment in which the variation has taken place.[31]

Here he implicitly admitted that the prices of most commodities at any given time are above or below their labor-value, and in the process of moving toward it. Arguably, he did not adequately treat of the degrees of elasticity, and the varying time ranges which were required, as a result, for supply and demand to establish an equilibrium at labor-value. But again, even this was at least implicit in his discussion. It is also clear, from this passage, that Ricardo viewed such oscillations of price as the mechanism by which the law of value operated, rather than as exceptions to it.

Without elaborating on the differing periods of time involved, or the relative speed with which the production of different commodities could be increased, Ricardo wrote in Chapter 30 of "temporary" scarcity rents as existing "for a time," and of production cost "ultimately" regulating price.

> It is the cost of production which must ultimately regulate the price of commodities, and not, as has been so often said, the proportion between the supply and demand: the proportion between the supply and demand may, indeed, for a time, affect the market value of a commodity, until it is supplied in a greater or less abundance, according as the demand may have increased or diminished; but this effect will be only of temporary duration.[32]

Ricardo also wrote of specific kinds of scarcity rent. In Chapter 2, he discussed economic rent to the most fertile tracts of land, owing to the regulation of price by production costs on the least efficient land at the margin of production.[33] In Chapter 27, he expanded the concept to include producer surpluses or quasi-rents in all areas of the economy; for example, he argued that providing artificially cheap wool to half of clothiers would not reduce the retail price, because the price of manufactured goods was "regulated by the cost of...production to those who were the least favoured. Its sole effect...would be to swell the profits of a part of the clothiers beyond the general and common rates of profits.[34] The influence of demand on price, while holding true of all commodities "for a limited period," was true in the long run only of "monopolized commodities."

> Commodities which are monopolized, either by an individual, or by a company, vary according to the law which Lord Lauderdale has laid down: they fall in proportion as the sellers augment their quantity, and rise in proportion to the eagerness of the buyers to purchase them; their price has no necessary connexion with their natural value: but the prices of commodities, which are subject to competition, and whose quantity may be increased in any moderate degree, will ultimately depend, not on the state of demand and supply, but on the increased or diminished cost of their production.[35]

Those who introduced new production technologies might derive temporary producer surpluses, but the general spread of the new technology, spurred by such increased profits, would eventually cause the price to drop to the level of production cost.[36]

Ricardo, in "Notes on Malthus," wrote of the determination of price by cost of production, through the influence of cost on supply, in terms that closely foreshadowed Jevons. Natural price was only "*that price which will repay the wages of labour expended on* [a commodity], *will also afford rent, and profit at their then current rate.*" Those production costs "*would remain the same, whether commodities were much or little demanded, whether they sold at a high or low market price.*" Market prices, true enough, would "*depend on supply and demand*"; but the supply would "*be finally determined by...the cost of production.*"[37]

John Stuart Mill was very much in the Ricardian tradition, in dealing with the effect of cost and scarcity on price. Like Ricardo, he held cost to be the determining factor for reproducible goods.

> 1. *When the production of a commodity is the effect of labour and expenditure, whether the commodity is susceptible of unlimited multiplication or not, there is a minimum value which is the essential condition of its being permanently produced. The value at any particular time is the result of supply and demand; and is always that which is necessary to create a market for the existing supply. But unless that value is sufficient to repay the cost of production...the commodity will not continue to be produced....*

> *When a commodity is not only made by labour and capital, but can be made by them in indefinite quantity, this Necessary Value, the minimum with which the producers will be content, is also, if competition is free and active, the maximum which they can expect....*

> *As a general rule, then, things tend to exchange for one another at such values as will enable each producer to be repaid the cost of production with the ordinary profit....*[38]

> *Adam Smith and Ricardo have called that value of a thing which is proportional to its cost of production, its Natural Value (or its Natural Price). They meant by this, the point about which the value oscillates, and to which it always tends to return; the centre value, towards which, as Adam Smith expresses it, the market value of a thing is constantly gravitating; and any deviation from which is but a temporary irregularity, which, the moment it exists, sets forces in motion tending to correct it....*

> *It is, therefore, strictly correct to say, that the value of things which can be increased in quantity at pleasure, does not depend (except accidentally, and during the time necessary for production to adjust itself,) upon demand and supply; on the contrary, demand and supply depend upon it. There is a*

demand for a certain quantity of the commodity at its natural or cost value,
and to that the supply in the long run endeavours to conform.[39]

Like Smith, Mill divided commodities into three groups, based on their reproducibility. In some cases, there was an *"absolute limitation of the supply,"* owing to the fact that it was *"physically impossible to increase the quantity beyond certain narrow limits."* As examples, he listed the same kinds of commodities as Smith: works of art, and produce grown on specific rare types of soil. Other commodities could be multiplied without limit, given the willingness to incur a certain amount of labor and expense to obtain them. Finally, some commodities could be multiplied indefinitely with sufficient labor and expenditure, *"but not by a fixed amount of labour and expenditure."* Greater levels of output required greater unit costs of production (here he referred mainly to agricultural produce).[40]

Mill was somewhat more explicit than Ricardo in dealing with the time element in determining the *degree* of elasticity. The time period involved in the gravitation of price toward cost depended on the length of time required to adjust production to changes in demand, or to dispose of surplus produce.

> *Again, though there are few commodities which are at all times and for ever unsusceptible of increase of supply, any commodity whatever may be temporarily so.... Agricultural produce, for example, cannot be increased in quantity before the next harvest.... In the case of most commodities, it requires a certain time to increase their quantity; and if the demand increases, then, until a corresponding supply can be brought forward, that is, until the supply can accommodate itself to the demand, the value will so rise as to accommodate the demand to the supply.*[41]

Like Ricardo, Mill believed that price was governed by the cost of production for those producers most unfavorably circumstanced. Those in a more advantageous situation would receive a producer's surplus equivalent to their cost savings. And like Ricardo, he applied the principle not only to economic rent on land, but to quasi-rents on manufactured goods.

> *2. If the portion of produce raised in the most unfavourable circumstances obtains a value proportional to its cost of production; all the portions raised in more favourable circumstances, selling as they must do at the same value, obtain a value more than proportioned to their cost of production.... The owners...of those portions of the produce...obtain a value which yields them more than the ordinary profit. If this advantage depends upon any special exception, such as being free from a tax, or upon any personal advantages, physical or mental, or any peculiar process only known to themselves, or*

upon the possession of a greater capital than other people, or upon various other things which might be enumerated, they retain it to themselves as an extra gain, over and above the general profits of capital, of the nature, in some sort, of a monopoly profit....[42]

4. Cases of extra profit analogous to rent, are more frequent in the transactions of industry than is sometimes supposed. Take the case, for example, of a patent, or exclusive privilege for the use of a process by which cost of production is lessened. If the value of the product continues to persist in the old process, the patentee will make an extra profit equal to the advantage which his process possesses over theirs.[43]

Marx and Engels were in complete agreement with the classical political economists on the role of competition in regulating the law of value. Engels, in his Preface to Marx's *Poverty of Philosophy*, ridiculed the utopian socialist notion of making labor the basis of a medium of exchange. The market forces of supply and demand were needed to inform the producer of the social demand for his product, and to establish the normal amount of social labor necessary for the production of a given commodity. So the deviation of price from value at any given time was not a violation of the law of value, but its driving mechanism.

In present-day capitalist society each individual capitalist produces off his own bat what, how and as much as he likes. The social demand, however, remains an unknown magnitude to him, both in regard to quality, the kind of objects required, and in regard to quantity.... Nevertheless, demand is finally satisfied in way or another, good or bad, and, taken as a whole, production is ultimately geared towards the objects required. How is this evening-out of the contradiction effected? By competition. And how does the competition bring about this solution? Simply by depreciating below their labour value those commodities which by their kind or amount are useless for immediate social requirements, and by making the producers feel...that they have produced either absolutely useless articles or ostensibly useful articles in unusable, superfluous quantity....

....[C]ontinual deviations of the prices of commodities from their values are the necessary condition in and through which the value of the commodities as such can come into existence. Only through the fluctuations of competition, and consequently of commodity prices, does the law of value of commodity production assert itself and the determination of the value of the commodity by the socially necessary labour time become a reality.... To desire, in a society of producers who exchange their commodities, to establish the determination of value by labour time, by forbidding competition to establish this determination of value through pressure on prices in the only way it can be established, is therefore merely to prove that...one has adopted the usual utopian disdain of economic laws.

> *....Only through the undervaluation or overvaluation of products is it forcibly brought home to the individual commodity producers what society requires or does not require and in what amounts.*[44]

Marx made very much the same argument in the main body of *The Poverty of Philosophy*: it was market price that signaled the producer how much to produce, and thus regulated price according to the law of value.

> *It is not the sale of a given product at the price of its cost of production which constitutes the "proportional relation" of supply and demand, or the proportional quota of this product relatively to the sum total of production; it is the variations in demand and supply that show the producer what amount of a given commodity he must produce in order to receive at least the cost of production in exchange. And as these variations are continually occurring, there is also a continual movement of withdrawal and application of capital in the different branches of industry....*
>
> *....Competition implements the law according to which the relative value of a product is determined by the labour time needed to produce it.*[45]

Marx's and Engels' remarks in these passages probably came closer than anywhere else to meeting Bohm-Bawerk's demand for a *mechanism* of the law of value (see Chapter 2 below).

In *Grundrisse*, Marx described the functioning of the law of value through the movement of price in somewhat more dialectical language:

> *The value of commodities determined by labour time is only their average value....*
>
> *The market value of commodities is always different from this average value and always stands either below or above it.*
>
> *The market value equates itself to the real value by means of its continual fluctuations, not by an equation with real value as some third thing, but precisely through continued inequality to itself....*
>
> *Price, therefore, differs from value, not only as the nominal differs from the real; not only by its denomination in gold and silver; but also in that the latter appears as the law of the movements to which the former is subject. But they are always distinct and never coincide, or only quite fortuitously and exceptionally. The price of commodities always stands above or below their value, and the value of commodities itself exists only in the UPS AND DOWNS of commodity prices. Demand and supply continually determine the prices of commodities; they never coincide or do so only accidentally; but*

the costs of production determine for their part the fluctuations of demand and supply.[46]

And such deviations from value included quasi-rents to those who first introduced more efficient methods of production. It was only through the market incentive presented by such quasi-rents, and through the resulting competition, that improved methods were universally adopted and came to define the standard form of production. *"A capitalist working with improved but not as yet generally adopted methods of production sells below the market price, but above his individual price of production; his rate of profit rises until competition levels it out."*[47]

Finally, to bring up the "mud pie" straw-man for another beating, Marx made *socially necessary* labor the regulator of value. The labor theory of value applied only to *commodities*, which were objects of human need. Labor expended in producing goods not demanded, or excess labor wasted in methods of production less efficient than the norm, was a dead loss. It was the function of the market price, in denying payment for such unnecessary labor, that brought the producer into accord with the wishes of society.

> *Each of these units is the same as any other, so far as it has the character of the average labour power of society, and takes effect as such: that is, so far as it requires for producing a commodity no more time than is needed on an average, no more than is socially necessary. The labour time socially necessary is that required to produce an article under the normal conditions of production, and with the average degree of skill and intensity prevalent at the time....*
>
> *We see then that that which determines the magnitude of the value of any article is the amount of labour socially necessary, or the labour time socially necessary for its production.*[48]

The concept of socially necessary labor is the appropriate answer to Böhm-Bawerk's "rare butterfly" challenge to Adam Smith. A rare butterfly that took more effort to capture than a beaver or deer would not carry more exchange-value than those commonly useful items, unless the effectual demand for the butterfly was sufficient to recompense the labor of capturing it. In most cases, therefore, the market for such rare butterflies would consist of rich eccentrics, and the effectual demand for them would support only a small number of laborers. As a result, the market price would inform superfluous butterfly hunters that most of their labor was socially unnecessary, and labor would be withdrawn from such "production" until the price was sufficient to recompense the labor of catching them. The classical political economists and Marxists, as much as Austrians, understood that labor expended on production for which there was no demand was a "sunken cost."

The neo-Ricardian Ronald Meek interpreted the term "value," as Marx used it, to mean something like "equilibrium price" in neoclassical economics.

> It is important to note at the outset that Marx's theory of value, like those of Smith and Ricardo, did not pretend to explain any prices other than those at which "supply and demand equilibrate each other, and therefore cease to act". The prices in which Marx was primarily interested were those which manifested themselves at the point where supply and demand "balanced" or "equilibrated" one another. The very fact that the forces of supply and demand did actually "balance" at this point was taken by Marx as an indication that the level of the equilibrium price could not be adequately explained merely in terms of the interaction of these forces. The relation of supply and demand could certainly explain <u>deviations</u> from the equilibrium price, but it could not explain the level of the equilibrium price itself. It was in fact precisely <u>through</u> fluctuations in "supply and demand" that the law of value operated to determine the equilibrium price.

> "Prices, then, might diverge from values in cases where supply and demand did not "balance"....

> Just as Marx's concept of value involved an abstraction from utility...so the theory of the determination of equilibrium price based upon it involved a similar abstraction from demand. In common with his Classical predecessors, Marx assumed that changes in demand would not in themselves...bring about changes in this long-run equilibrium prices of the commodities concerned. But this is not at all to say that Marx <u>ignored</u> demand. It remained true, as he emphasized, (<u>a</u>) that a commodity had to be in demand before it could possess exchange value; (<u>b</u>) that changes in demand might cause the actual market price of a commodity to deviate from its equilibrium price; (<u>c</u>) that price under conditions of monopoly was "determined only by the eagerness of the purchasers to buy and by their solvency"; and (<u>d</u>) that demand was the main force determining the proportion of the social labour allocated to any given productive sector at any given time.[49]

Of course, as Marshall later pointed out, this irrelevance of demand to equilibrium price was complicated by the fact that the level of effective demand might affect the scale of production, and thereby also affect unit costs of production.

Meek criticized Vilfredo Pareto, in very nearly the same terms as we have criticized Bohm-Bawerk, for his attacks on a straw-man version of Marx's labor theory of value.

> *...all too often the imaginary Marxists with whom Pareto argues are made to put forward interpretations of the labour theory which are suspiciously simple-minded.... [For example] it is easy enough to show that the labour theory does not apply to rare pictures, etc., since (as Pareto well knew) it was never intended to apply to anything other than freely reproducible goods. Nor is it sufficient, when the Marxist characterizes as exceptional the case of the picture whose price increases when its painted becomes famous without anything having happened to the quantity of labour embodied in it, to reply that it is by no means exceptional because the prices of <u>all</u> commodities may vary without anything happening to the quantity of labour embodied in them—e.g., on account of a change in the tastes and incomes of their consumers.*[50]

The proper reply to such criticism, Meek argued, was *"that the long-run equilibrium prices of freely reproducible commodities (as distinct from their day-to-day market prices) will not in fact be affected by a change in demand unless it is accompanied by a change in the conditions of production.*[51]

Finally, since our version of the labor theory of value owes more to Benjamin Tucker than to Marx, it is only appropriate to provide some examples in which Tucker acknowledged "exceptions" to the labor theory. Tucker accepted the existence of short-term quasi-rents on commodities for which demand had increased, or commodities for which new production processes had been introduced. Like the Classicals and Marx, he viewed competition as the mechanism by which price would be reduced to cost, when market entry was free and goods were freely reproducible. *"It is true that the usefulness of* [the laborer's] *product has a tendency to enhance its price; but this tendency is immediately offset, wherever competition is possible,...by the rush of other laborers to create this product, which lasts until the price falls back to the normal wages of labor."*[52]

Tucker also recognized that economic rent on land with advantages in location or fertility would persist, even when absentee landlord rent was abolished. And he likewise viewed producer surpluses resulting from superior innate skill as analogous to economic rent on land, and thus as inevitable even with the abolition of privilege. Although abolishing the land monopoly would reduce rent to *"a very small fraction of its present proportions,"* some would still remain. The *"remaining fraction,"* nevertheless,

> *would be the cause of no more inequality than arises from the unearned increment derived by almost every industry from the aggregation of people or from that unearned increment of superior natural ability which even under the operation of the cost principle, will probably always enable some individuals to get higher wages than the average rate.*[53]

In response to the question of how one could justify the receipt of the equivalent of 500 days' labor, by the possessor of an especially fertile piece of land, for only 300 days of his own, Tucker responded that such justification would be "[p]*recisely as difficult as it would be to show that the man of superior skill (native, not acquired) who produces in the ratio of five hundred to another's three hundred is equitably entitled to this surplus exchange value.*"[54]

Tucker was willing to accept such permanent scarcity rents as necessary evils. He distinguished between competitive disabilities which resulted from "human meddlesomeness," and those which did not.[55] Unlike usury and landlord rent, which resulted from the coercively-maintained legal privilege of owners of capital and land, the remaining forms of producer surplus resulted only from general circumstances or "acts of God," and were therefore not exploitative. The evils involved in creating a coercive mechanism to iron out such inequalities and collect payment from free riders would exceed the evils of the inequalities themselves.

> *To directly enforce equality of material well-being is meddlesome, invasive, and offensive, but to directly enforce equality of liberty is simply protective and defensive. The latter is negative, and aims only to prevent the establishment of artificial inequalities; the former is positive, and aims at direct and active abolition of natural inequalities.*[56]

> *"How are we to remove the injustice of allowing one man to enjoy what another has earned?" I do not expect it ever to be removed altogether. But I believe that for every dollar that would be enjoyed by tax-dodgers under Anarchy, a thousand dollars are now enjoyed by men who have got possession of the earnings of others through special industrial, commercial, and financial privileges granted them by authority in violation of a free market.*[57]

Forcibly charging a man for the producer's surplus resulting from his superior skill or the superior fertility of his land, would be at least as unjust as allowing him to keep it. "*If it is unearned, certainly his neighbors did not earn it.*"[58] "*If the cost principle of value cannot be realized otherwise than by compulsion, then it had better not be realized.*"[59]

E. Generality and Paradigms

Böhm-Bawerk grudgingly admitted a correlation between price and cost: in almost Marshallian terms, he conceded that Ricardo went only "a very little way" too far in downplaying the influence of scarcity, and in overstating the importance of labor as one factor among several.

...the conclusion might very well be drawn that expenditure of labour is one circumstance which exerts a powerful influence on the value of many goods; always remembering that labour is not an ultimate cause—for an ultimate cause must be common to all the phenomena of value—but a particular and intermediate cause....

Ricardo himself only went a very little way over the proper limits. As I have shown, he knew right well that his law of value was only a particular law; he knew, for instance, that the value of scarce goods rests on quite another principle. He only erred in so far as he very much over-estimated the extent to which his law is valid, and practically ascribed to it a validity almost universal. The consequence is that, later on, he forgot almost entirely the little exceptions he had rightly made but too little considered at the beginning of his work, and often spoke of his law as if it were really a universal law of value.[60]

Indeed, but for deviations caused by "friction" and the time element, the correlation between production cost and price would be quite close.

If—what is practically inconceivable—production were carried on in ideal circumstances, unfettered by limitations of place and time, with no friction, with the most perfect knowledge of the position of human wants requiring satisfaction, and without any disturbing changes of wants, stocks, or techniques, than the original productive powers would, with ideal and mathematical exactitude, be invested in the most remunerative employments, and the law of costs, so far as we can speak of such a law, would hold in ideal completeness. The complementary groups of goods from which, in the long-run, the finished good proceeds, would maintain exactly the same value and price at al stages of the process; the commodity would be exactly equal to costs; these costs to their costs, and so on, back to the last original productive powers from which ultimately all goods come.[61]

The assumptions here sound quite similar to the Misesean theoretical construct of the "evenly rotating economy," which we shall discuss below. Böhm-Bawerk went on to elaborate on friction and time as causes for deviation from this ideal model:

The first of these [disturbing causes] *I may call by the general name of Friction. Almost invariably there is some hindrance, great or small, permanent or temporary, to the due investment of the original productive powers in the employments and forms of consumption which are the most remunerative at the time. In consequence the provision for wants, and likewise the prices, are somewhat unsymmetrical. Sometimes it is that individual branches of want are, relatively, more amply supplied than others.... But sometimes it may be that groups of productive materials, successively transformed till they are*

changed at last into the finished commodity, are not equally valued at all stages of the process [here he used the analogy of a stream to illustrate bottlenecks at various stages of the production process]....
In practical life such frictional disturbances are innumerable. At no moment and in no branch of production are they entirely absent. And thus it is that the law of costs is recognized as a law that is only approximately valid; a law riddled through and through with exceptions. These innumerable exceptions, small and great, are the inexhaustible source of the undertakers' profits, but also of the undertakers' losses.

The second disturbing cause is the Lapse of Time—the weeks, months, years which must stretch between the inception of the original productive powers, and the presentation of their finished and final product. The difference of time, in exerting a far-reaching influence on our valuation of goods, makes a normal difference between the value of the productive groups standing at different points of the production process...; and is, therefore, a difference to be kept quite distinct from the unsymmetrical divergences caused by frictional disturbances.[62]

The time element is the subject of Chapter Three below, in which time preference is incorporated into our mutualist version of the labor theory. As for "friction," all scarcity rents can arguably be classed under this heading. And Böhm-Bawerk's treatment of cost and various forms of friction as simultaneously codetermining influences on value is questionable, at best. It is much more useful and informative to treat labor or cost as the primary influence on *normal* value (i.e., equilibrium price given elasticity), and to say that value deviates from this norm to the extent that friction comes into the picture.

Maurice Dobb argued ably that a key difference between the classical political economists and the subjectivists was their opinion on the level of generality necessary for an adequate theory of value. Much of the disagreement over the Ricardian paradigm stems from a difference of opinion on whether the exceptions Ricardo *admitted* to the law of value were sufficient to invalidate it. For Dobb, obviously, the answer was "no."

In *Political Economy and Capitalism*, he detailed the simplifying assumptions of Marx's value theory, and the various exceptions to it resulting from scarcity or differing compositions of capital. These exceptions were "*held to be fatal*" by the marginalists, and were "*the onus of Böhm-Bawerk's criticism of Marx.*"

But all abstractions remain only approximations to reality: this is their essential nature; and it is no criticism of a theory of value merely to say that this is so. Whether such assumptions are permissible or no is a matter of the type of question, the nature of the problem, with which the principle is

*designed to deal. The criticism only becomes valid if it shows that the implicit
assumptions preclude the generalization from sustaining these corollaries
which it is employed to sustain.... It is too seldom remembered to-day that
the concern of classical Political Economy was with what one may term
the "macroscopic" problems of economic society, and only very secondarily
with "microscopic" problems, in the shape of the movements of particular
commodity prices.*

Dobb compared Marx's general law of value, as a first approximation,
and the second approximations adjusting it for deviations resulting
from scarcity and differences in organic composition of capital, to the
successive approximations of the law of projectiles in physics made
necessary by wind resistance and other countervailing influences.[63]

In discussing the proper levels of generality of paradigms, Dobb
mentioned Kuhn's thesis of paradigm shift in science, and the recurring
practice of incorporating rival paradigms as "special theories" within
a larger and more general framework.[64] This model is applicable
here. Marginal utility is quite useful not only in describing the laws of
behavior governing scarcity exceptions to the labor theory of value, but
the laws of behavior governing how much of a commodity is consumed
at its labor value. Marginal utility theory, if incorporated into a labor
theory of value, would be a major improvement in the sophistication
with which the theory explained *how* and *why* the law of value operated
through the subjective perceptions and decisions of concrete human
beings.

For example, Leif Johansen attempted in two articles to show how
marginal utility could be incorporated into a labor theory of value. In
"Marxism and Mathematical Economics," he described the general
terms of such a synthesis:

*The Marxist labor theory of value has been the object of attacks particularly
from the point of view of "marginal utility theory" or "subjective theory of
value," which has been a main component of non-Marxist mathematical
economics. Marxists have usually rejected this whole theory and all
concepts and mathematical arguments introduced in connection with it, as
if acceptance of it, or elements of it, would necessarily imply a rejection of
the labor theory of value. However, this is not so. For goods which can be
reproduced on any scale (i.e. such goods as have been the center of interest of
Marxian value theory) it is very easy to demonstrate that a complete model
still leaves prices determined by the labor theory of value even if one accepts
the marginal utility theory of consumers' behavior.*[65]

Elaborating on this statement in a later article, Johansen described a
model in which prices were determined by the conditions of production,

while "[t]*he marginal utility functions interact with the prices thus given only in determining the quantities to be produced and consumed of the different commodities.*"[66]

In any case, the labor theory of value as we develop it in the next chapter is not an inductive generalization from the empirical data of prices in the market. It is, rather, a law deduced from basic assumptions on the nature of human action, quite similar to those of Mises' praxeology. As Mises wrote, the variables of the market are so many that no laws can be induced from mere observation, without the aid of valid starting assumptions established on an a priori basis. The laws of praxeology were a tool for analyzing market phenomena, not a generalization from them. Like Mises' laws of praxeology, our labor theory of value is not an inductive law of market price, but an a priori assumption in terms of which the observed phenomena of the market make better sense. Starting with our assumptions on the subjective mechanism of human behavior, we can understand *why* equilibrium price will approximate cost. And given this baseline understanding of the primary law of equilibrium price, we can understand *why* price deviates from the cost principle in cases of scarcity.

If an adequate theory of value requires a high degree of predictive value concerning concrete prices, then both the labor theory and subjective theory fall apart equally. On the other hand, if value theory in the sense of an empirical rule for predicting concrete prices is impossible because the variables are too many, then both theories are likewise on equally untenable ground. But like Mises' subjective theory of value, our version of the labor theory is a set of a priori axioms and the deductions from them, which can be used to more usefully interpret market data *after the fact*. Böhm-Bawerk's critiques of Ricardo or Marx, based on the failure of experience to bear them out in all cases, are equally applicable to Mises' theory of value.

The Austrians have made a closely related argument: that equilibrium price is an imaginary construct that can never be observed in the real marketplace. But (as we shall see in a later section of this chapter) this radical epistemological skepticism does not bear much looking into, given the Austrian concept of the "Final State." Any criticism of equilibrium price, as a standpoint from which to examine actual market prices at any given time, applies equally to the "final state" or "final equilibrium." As Mises himself wrote,

> *The specific method of economics is the method of imaginary constructions.*
> *This method is the method of praxeology....*

An imaginary construction is a conceptual image of a sequence of events logically evolved from the elements of action employed in its formation. It is a product of deduction, ultimately derived from the fundamental category of action, the act of preferring and setting aside....

The main formula for designing of imaginary constructions is to abstract from the operation of some conditions present in actual action. Then we are in a position to grasp the hypothetical consequences of the absence of these conditions and to conceive the effects of their existence....

The imaginary construction of a pure or unhampered market economy assumes that there is a division of labor and private ownership (control) of the means of production and that consequently there is market exchange of goods and services. It assumes that the operation of the market is not obstructed by institutional factors.... The market is free; there is no interference of factors, foreign to the market, with prices, wage rates, and interest rates. Starting from these assumptions economics tries to elucidate the operation of a pure market economy. Only at a later stage...does it turn to the study of the various problems raised by interference with the market on the part of government and other agencies employing coercion and compulsion.[67]

Böhm-Bawerk's hypothetical description of a "frictionless" economy, above, can be taken as an early attempt at such an abstract conceptual model. Mises' "final state" was another, a model of the values toward which prices were tending at any time:

The prices of all commodities and services are at any instant moving toward a final state.... However, the changing economy never reaches the imaginary final state. New data emerge again and again and divert the trend of prices from the previous goal of their movement toward a different final state...."[68]

Rothbard developed the concept still further as "final equilibrium." Despite his straw-man caricatures and semantic quibbling with Marshall, it closely resembled Marshall's concept of the "long run."

It is to be distinguished from the market equilibrium prices that are set each day by the action of supply and demand. The final equilibrium state is one which the economy is always tending to approach.... In actual life, however, the data are always changing, and therefore, before arriving at a final equilibrium point, the economy must shift direction, towards some final equilibrium position.

Hence, the final equilibrium position is always changing, and consequently no one such position is ever reached in practice. But even though it is never reached in practice, it has a very real importance. In the first place, it is like the mechanical rabbit being chased by the dog. It is never reached in practice and it is always changing, but it explains the direction in which the dog is moving.[69]

Ah! So Rothbard's objection to the Marshallian "scissors" was Marshall's claim that "equilibrium price" or the "long run" could be reached in practice! Strangely enough, though, I can't recall ever seeing any such claim by Marshall.

We should be careful, by the way, to distinguish the Austrian concepts of "final state" and final "equilibrium" from that of the "Evenly Rotating Economy." Marshall's "long run," although bearing some resemblance to the "final equilibrium," differed fundamentally from the "Evenly Rotating Economy." The latter was an imaginary construct of a static economy from which all change was abstracted. The "long run," on the other hand, was a goal toward which the economy was tending at any given moment <u>through</u> the subjective valuations of market actors and the fluctuations of the market (much like Adam Smith's "natural price").

F. The Marshallian Synthesis

Alfred Marshall, the founder of the so-called neoclassical school, was also the first prominent economist to attempt a reconciliation of Ricardo with the marginalists. Following the Senior-Longfield school, as interpreted by Mill, Marshall treated the "abstinence" of capital (or "waiting") as another form of disutility alongside labor. He thus fused them into a unified subjective theory of "real cost," as the determining factor in supply price. As Mill said, profits were remuneration for the capitalist's abstinence, in the same sense that wages were the remuneration of labor. This Marshallian synthesis adopted virtually the entire apparatus of marginalism, but was much closer in spirit to the cost of production theories of Ricardo and Mill.[70]

In regard to profit as the "cost" of capital, Marshall cast it in subjective terms: the return necessary to persuade the capitalist to bring his capital to market. *"Everyone is aware that no payment would be offered for the use of capital unless some gain were expected from that use...."* In contradiction to the surplus value theory of Rodbertus and Marx, Marshall said that exchange value was the result of both *"labour and waiting."* Marshall distinguished, in much the same terms as Böhm-Bawerk, between *gross* interest, and net interest as the reward for waiting *as such.*[71]

Of this notion of profit or interest as a reward for "abstinence" or "waiting" (or "time preference," as the Austrians preferred to put it), we will have much to say in the next two chapters. Suffice it for the present to say that the market value of abstinence, like the Austrian rate of time preference, varies a great deal with such factors as the distribution of property and the legal disabilities imposed on competition in the capital market.

Marshall recast Ricardo's twin factors of price determination, labor and scarcity, as the two blades of his scissors. *"We might as reasonably dispute whether it is the upper or the underblade of a pair of scissors that cuts a piece of paper, as whether value is governed by utility or cost of production..."*[72] Marshall believed Ricardo had erred in his overemphasis of the importance of cost or supply price at the expense of demand or utility. Regarding Ricardo's neglect of demand, Marshall wrote that it had recently received increased attention as a result of

> *the growing belief that harm was done by Ricardo's habit of laying disproportionate stress on the side of cost of production, when analysing the causes that determine exchange value. For although he and his chief followers were aware that the conditions of demand played as important a part as those of supply in determining value, yet they did not express their meaning with sufficient clearness, and they have been misunderstood by all but the most careful readers.*[73]

As the last phrase suggests, Marshall believed the shortcomings of Ricardian economics were as much the fault of poor interpretation as of the theory itself.

More importantly, Marshall's assertion that demand played "as important a part" as supply was qualified by his understanding of the time factor. For Marshall, the shorter the time period, the more it was possible to treat supply as fixed for the time being; and as a result, the more the blade of scarcity predominated over that of cost. Price was determined, at any given time, by the balance between the demand and supply that actually existed at that moment. As the time factor came into play, and supply could be treated as a dynamic variable, the cost blade gained in ascendancy until, at some hypothetical approach to a "pure" equilibrium price, price approached closer and closer to cost. Marshall concluded that, *"as a general rule, the shorter the period which we are considering, the greater must be the share of our attention which is given to the influence of demand on value; and the longer the period, the more important will be the influence of cost of production on value."*[74]

In describing the hypothetical equilibrium toward which the market tended, Marshall used language quite similar to that of Mises concerning the value of "imaginary constructions":

> *Our first step towards studying the influences exerted by the element of time on the relations between the cost of production and value may well be to consider the famous fiction of the "stationary state" in which those influences would be but little felt; and to contrast the results which would be found there with those in the modern world.*[75]

And, bearing an uncanny resemblance to Böhm-Bawerk, he wrote that short-term prices *"are governed by the relation of demand to stocks actually in the market"* at any given time.[76] Existing stocks of goods are all that are available pending the time lapse required for further production, regardless of demand; and excess goods are a "sunken cost," regardless of demand shortfall.

> *Again, there is no connection between cost of reproduction and price in the cases of food in a beleaguered city, of quinine the supply of which has run short in a fever-stricken island, of a picture by Raphael, of a book that nobody cares to read, of an armour-clad ship of obsolete pattern, of fish when the market is glutted, of fish when the market is nearly empty, of a cracked bell, of a dress material that has gone out of fashion, or of a house in a deserted mining village.*[77]

Production cost is an influence on price only over time, as supply is adjusted in response to effective demand, and supply and demand approach equilibrium.

But as Marshall pointed out, supply is itself a dependent variable: *"the current supply is itself partly due to the action of producers in the past; and this action has been determined on as the result of a comparison of the prices which the expect to get for their goods with the expenses to which they will be put in producing them."*[78] The operation of supply and demand always operated, over time, to bring production into line with effective demand at the cost of production, and thus to equate price with production cost. Demand price was always signaling producers to reduce or increase production, until demand price equaled supply price.

The problem with this simple model, Marshall went on, was that demand and supply schedules were subject to change, so the equilibrium point toward which the market tended was itself in motion.

> *But in real life such oscillations are seldom as rhythmical as those of a stone hanging freely from a string; the comparison would be more exact if the string were supposed to hang in the troubled waters of a mill-race, whose stream was at one time allowed to flow freely, and at another partially cut off.... For indeed the demand and supply schedules do not in practice remain unchanged for a long time together, but are constantly being changed, and every change in them alters the equilibrium amount and the equilibrium price, and thus gives new positions to the centres about which the amount and the price tend to oscillate.*
>
> *These considerations point to the great importance of the element of time in relation to demand and supply....*[79]

But regardless of such complicating factors, it was nevertheless true at any given time that market price was tending toward an equilibrium point at which the producer was just compensated for bringing his goods to market.

> *There is a constant tendency towards a position of normal equilibrium, in which the supply of each of these agents* [i.e., factors of production] *will stand in such a relation to the demand for its services, as to give to those who have provided the supply a sufficient reward for their efforts and sacrifices. If the economic conditions of the country remained stationary sufficiently long, this tendency would realize itself in such an adjustment of supply to demand, that both machines and human beings would earn generally an amount that corresponded fairly with their cost of rearing and training.... As it is, the economic conditions of the country are constantly changing, and the point of adjustment of normal demand and supply in relation to labour is constantly being shifted.*[80]

If Ricardo had overstated his case in one direction, Marshall believed the fathers of the marginal revolution had overstated theirs even further in the opposite direction. Marshall held *"that the foundations of the theory as they were left by Ricardo remain intact; that much has been added to them, and that very much has been built upon them, but that little has been taken from them."*[81]

As for Jevons, not only did he overstate his own doctrine, but it depended on a studious misreading of Ricardo and Mill.

> *There are few writers of modern times who have approached as near to the brilliant originality of Ricardo as Jevons has done. But he appears to have judged both Ricardo and Mill harshly, and to have attributed to them doctrines narrower and less scientific than those which they really held. And his desire to emphasize an aspect of value to which they had given insufficient prominence, was probably in some measure accountable for his saying, "Repeated reflection and inquiry have led me to the somewhat novel opinion that <u>value depends entirely upon utility</u>".... This statement seems to be no less one-sided and fragmentary, and much more misleading, than that into which Ricardo often glided with careless brevity, as to the dependence of value on cost of production; but which he never regarded as more than a part of a larger doctrine, the rest of which he had tried to explain.*

> *Jevons continues:—"we have only to trace out carefully the natural laws of variation of utility as depending upon the quantity of commodity in our possession, in order to arrive at a satisfactory theory of exchange of which the ordinary laws of supply and demand are a necessary consequence.... Labour is found often to determine value, but only in an indirect manner by varying the degree of utility of the commodity through an increase or limitation of the supply." As we shall presently see, the latter of these two statements had been*

> *made before in almost the same form, loose and inaccurate as it is, by Ricardo*
> *and Mill; but they would not have accepted the former statement. For while*
> *they regarded the natural laws of variation of utility as too obvious to require*
> *detailed explanation, and while they admitted that cost of production could*
> *have no effect upon exchange value if it could have none upon the amount*
> *which producers brought forward for sale; their doctrines imply that what is*
> *true of supply, is true <u>mutatis</u> <u>mutandis</u> of demand, and that the utility of a*
> *commodity could have no effect upon its exchange value if it could have none*
> *on the amount which purchasers took off the market....*[82]

Regarding Jevons' seemingly absolutist statement of the determination of price by utility, Marshall pointed out that "*the exchange value of a thing is the same all over a market; but the final degrees of utility to which it corresponds are not equal at any two parts.*" A trading body "*gives up things which represent equal purchasing power to all its members, but very different utilities.*"[83] Marshall had made the same point earlier in the book, using the illustration of a carriage ride: although the marginal utility of a carriage ride may be much greater for a poor than for a rich man; yet the price, in either case, is twopence.[84]

> *It is true that Jevons was himself aware of this; and that his account can*
> *be made consistent with the facts of life by a series of interpretations, which*
> *in effect substitute "demand-price" and "supply-price" for "utility" and*
> *"disutility": but, when so amended, they lose much of their aggressive force*
> *against the older doctrines, and if both are to be held severely to a strictly*
> *literal interpretation, then the older method of speaking, though not perfectly*
> *accurate, appears to be nearer the truth than that which Jevons and some of*
> *his followers have endeavoured to substitute for it.*[85]

In defense of the sophistication of Ricardo's doctrine, as he understood it, Marshall pointed out the statement in Ricardo's letter to Malthus: "*it is supply which regulates value, and supply is itself controlled by comparative cost of production.*" And in his next letter, "*I do not dispute either the influence of demand on the price of corn or on the price of all other things: but supply follows close at its heels and soon takes the power of regulating price in his own hands, and in regulating it he is determined by cost of production.*" He quoted Mill, likewise, to the effect that "*the law of demand and supply...is controlled but not set aside by the law of cost of production, since cost of production would have no effect on value if it could have none on supply.*" Thus, the "revolutionary" doctrine of Jevons, that the influence of cost of production made itself felt through the laws of supply and demand, was part of the doctrine of Ricardo and Mill.[86]

Summing up the conflict between Jevons and the classical political economists, Marshall criticized the former for neglecting the time element to the same degree as had Ricardo: *"For they attempt to disprove doctrines as to the ultimate tendencies...of the relations between cost of production and value, by means of arguments based on the causes of temporary changes, and short-period fluctuations of value."*[87]

As we shall see in the section below, Jevons' overemphasis of the short-term, and his treatment of existing stocks of supply as a static factor at any given time, was almost exactly mirrored by the later Austrians in their criticism of the cost principle.

G. Rothbard versus the Marshallian Synthesis

Murray Rothbard rejected, in the strongest terms, this Marshallian attempt at a synthesis of marginalist innovations with the legacy of Ricardo. And with it, he rejected Marshall's attempted synthesis of labor and waiting as elements of "real cost." To understand why, we must start with Rothbard's distinction between the judging of actions *ex ante* and *ex post*. In judging *ex ante*, an actor determines which future course of action is most likely to maximize his utility. Judgment *ex post*, in contrast, is an assessment of the results of past action. Rothbard denied that "sunken costs" could confer value. *"....cost incurred in the past cannot confer any value...now."*[88] *"It is evident...that once the product has been made, 'cost' has no influence on the price of the product. Past costs, being ephemeral, are irrelevant to present determination of prices...."*[89]

Against the doctrine of classical political economy that *"costs determine price,"* which was *"supposed to be the law of price determination 'in the long run,'"* he argued that *"the truth is precisely the reverse":*

> The price of the final product is determined by the valuations and demands of the consumers, and this price *determines what the cost will be.* Factor payments are the *result* of sales to consumers and *do not determine the latter in advance.* Costs of production, then, are at the mercy of final price, and not the other way around....[90]

A revolutionary doctrine, indeed! Only, on closer inspection, it does not seem so revolutionary after all. And the Marshall and Ricardo to whom Rothbard opposed himself so dramatically, turn out to be gross caricatures. Their statement of the cost principle was nothing so crudely metaphysical as *"the price of the final product is determined by 'costs of production....'"*[91] (Rothbard was, if anything, more charitable than Böhm-Bawerk, who felt compelled to deny that there was power *"in any element of production to infuse value immediately or necessarily into its product."*[92])

Admittedly, too, Rothbard made a half-hearted attempt at fairness, in giving a slightly less cartoonish description of the Marshallian "scissors":

> *Marshall tried to rehabilitate the cost-of-production theory of the classicists by conceding that, in the "short-run," in the immediate market place, consumers' demand rules price. But in the long run, among the important reproducible goods, cost of production is determining. According to Marshall, both utility and money costs determine price, like blades of a scissors, but one blade is more important in the short run, and another in the long run....*

But he immediately proceeded to tear Marshall's doctrine apart—or rather a caricature of it. In this straw-man version of Marshall, a modern counterpart of the scholastic realists of the Middle Ages, the "long run" was a phenomenon with concrete existence.

> *Marshall's analysis suffers from a grave methodological defect—indeed, from an almost hopeless methodological confusion as regards the "short run" and the "long run." He considers the "long run" as actually existing, as being the permanent, persistent, observable element beneath the fitful, basically unimportant flux of market value....*

> *Marshall's conception of the long run is completely fallacious, and this eliminates the whole groundwork of his theoretical structure. The long run, by its very nature, <u>never does</u> <u>and</u> <u>never can</u> <u>exist</u>....*

> *To analyze the determining forces in a world of change, [the economist] must construct hypothetically a world of non-change [i.e., the Evenly Rotating Economy]. This is far different from...saying that the long run exists or that it is somehow <u>more</u> <u>permanently</u> or more persistently existent than the actual market data.... The fact that costs equal prices in the "long run" does not mean that costs will actually equal prices, but that the tendency exists, a tendency that is continually being <u>disrupted</u> in reality by the very fitful changes in market data that Marshall points out.*[93]

(We have already seen, by the way, that Marshall's long-run is not equivalent to the Austrians' hypothetical world of non-change, or ERE, but rather to the Austrian "final equilibrium" *toward which* the economy *tends*, but never approaches).

Compare Rothbard's version of Marshall to what Marshall himself said, as we have already quoted him above:

> *But in real life such oscillations are seldom as rhythmical as those of a stone hanging freely from a string; the comparison would be more exact if the string were supposed to hang in the troubled waters of a mill-race, whose stream was at one time allowed to flow freely, and at another partially cut*

off.... For indeed the demand and supply schedules do not in practice remain unchanged for a long time together, but are constantly being changed, and every change in them alters the equilibrium amount and the equilibrium price, and thus gives new positions to the centres about which the amount and the price tend to oscillate.[94]

There is a constant tendency towards a position of normal equilibrium, in which the supply of each of these agents [i.e., factors of production] *will stand in such a relation to the demand for its services, as to give to those who have provided the supply a sufficient reward for their efforts and sacrifices. If the economic conditions of the country remained stationary sufficiently long, this tendency would realize itself in such an adjustment of supply to demand, that both machines and human beings would earn generally an amount that corresponded fairly with their cost of rearing and training.... As it is, the economic conditions of the country are constantly changing, and the point of adjustment of normal demand and supply in relation to labour is constantly being shifted.*[95]

More important than the deviation of most prices from their normal value, at any given time, is the fact that they will tend toward this value over time if not impeded by monopolistic privilege. As Schumpeter wrote, although there may always be a positive average rate of profit, "[i]*t is sufficient that...the profit of every individual plant is incessantly threatened by actual or potential competition from new commodities or methods of production which sooner or later will turn it into a loss.*" The price trajectory of any particular capital or consumer good, under the influence of competition, will be toward cost: "*for no individual assemblage of capital goods remains a source of surplus gains forever...*"[96] Or in the words of Tucker, "*competition* [is] *the great leveler of prices to the labor cost of production.*"[97]

Setting aside Rothbard's caricature of Marshall's views (i.e., his supposed view of the long-run as actually existing in some real sense, as a static model like the Evenly Rotating Economy), we find that Marshall actually said something quite like what Rothbard said: the price of reproducible goods *tends toward* the cost of production. Equilibrium price and the "long run," like the Austrian "final equilibrium," are not viewed in conceptual realist terms as actually existing *things*. Rather, they are theoretical constructs for making real world phenomena more comprehensible. The Austrian pose of radical skepticism, when it is ideologically convenient, effectively deprives economists of the ability to make useful generalizations about observed regularities in the phenomena of the *real world*.

The problem with Rothbard's critique of Marshall is that it could be applied with almost as much justice to Rothbard himself. For example, Rothbard admitted that cost of production could have an indirect effect on price, through its effect on supply. In his discussion of the distinction between *ex ante* and *ex post* judgments, from which we quoted above, he also proclaimed it *"clear that* [the actor's] *ex post judgments are mainly useful to him in the weighing of his ex ante considerations for future action."*[98] And directly after his statement quoted above that *"'cost' has no influence on the price of the product,"* he went on at greater length:

> That costs do have an influence in production is not denied by anyone. However, the influence is not directly on the price, but on the amount that will be produced or, more specifically, on the degree to which factors will be used.... The height of costs on individual value scales, then, is *one* of the determinants of the quantity, the *stock*, that will be produced. This stock, of course, *later* plays a role in the determination of market price. This, however, is a far cry from stating that cost either determines, or is co-ordinate with utility in determining, price.[99]

But this is almost exactly how Marshall himself explained the action of the cost principle, at length, in his discussion of Jevons' critique of Ricardo, in Appendix I of *Principles of Economics*. Indeed, one can find many passages in the *Principles of Economics* in which Marshall describes the action of cost on price through supply, in language almost identical to that of Rothbard above. Marshall did not claim that the price of a specific present good was mystically "determined" by its past cost of production. He argued, rather, that prices over time tended toward the cost of production *through* the decisions of producers as to whether market prices justified *future* production.

And the Austrians attached some very compromising qualifications to their bald statements that utility determined value, and that final price determined the cost of production. Böhm-Bawerk, in *Positive Theory*, wrote that value was determined by *"the importance of that concrete want...which is least urgent among the wants that are met from the available stocks* of similar goods. [emphasis added]"[100] Rothbard wrote that "[t]*he price of a good is determined by its total stock in existence and the demand schedule for it on the market.* [emphasis added]"[101] Likewise: *"In the real world of immediate market prices,...it is obvious to all that price is solely determined by valuations of stock—by 'utilities'—and not at all by money cost.... [M]ost economists recognize that in the real world (the so-called 'short-run') costs cannot determine price.... [emphasis added]"*[102] This sounds awfully similar, in practice, to Marshall's understanding of the predominance of the "utility" blade of the scissors in the "short run." The difference, as we saw above, was that Rothbard denounced the very idea of the "long run" as utterly meaningless.

Rothbard's qualifications of the utility principle suggest a weakness of the subjective theory of value which we have recurrently pointed to in the sections above: it can be taken literally only to the extent that we ignore the dynamic aspect of supply, and treat the balance between demand and existing stocks of supplies at any point as given, without regard to the time factor.

This is true both of the Austrians' utility theory of value of consumer goods, which assumes fixed stocks at the point of exchange, and of their imputation theory of factor prices, which likewise assumes a fixed stock of higher-order goods. As Dobb criticized the latter,

> *If the situation is handled in terms of concrete capital-goods (dispensing with the <u>genus</u> of "capital" as a supposedly scarce factor), then if these goods are reproducible there should be no reason for any positive rate of profit at all in strictly static conditions. If all inputs other than labour are produced inputs, whence the specific "scarcity" from which profit is supposed to arise? If assumptions of full static equilibrium are consistently adhered to, then production in the capital-goods sector of the economy will tend to be enlarged until the output of goods is eventually adapted to the need for them.... With the supply of them fully adapted to the demand for them for purposes of current replacement, there will no longer be any ground for their prices to be above the (prime) cost of their own current replacement (or depreciation).*[103]

Dobb also wrote of the Austrian "*assumption of <u>given</u> supplies of various factors, with consequential demand-determination of all prices....*"[104] Later in the same work, Dobb remarked on the artificiality of value theories based entirely on the short-term balance of supply and demand:

> *....in order to make such statements, a number of things have to be taken as <u>given</u> (as—to take the extreme case—in all statements about Marshallian "short-period", or quasi-short-period, situations): data that are dependent variables at another, and "deeper", level of analysis....*
>
> *One way of illustrating what is meant when one speaks of contexts in which demand-determined exchange-relations are applicable may be the following. One could suppose that all productive inputs were natural objects available at any given date in given nature-determined amounts [e.g., Marshall's meteoric stones].... But then, of course, the process of production as ordinarily viewed...would be non-existent....*
>
> *To the extent, <u>per contra</u>, that human activity is assigned a major role in the production process and reproducible inputs...replace scarce natural objects, the essentials of the economic problem become different....*
>
> *But if a formal mode of determination in terms of scarcity-relations...can be constructed, and can convey some information, in a situation of naturally-determined means or inputs, why should it not be able to do so in analogous situations where any set of <u>n</u> means or inputs, although not dependent on <u>natural</u> limitations, are necessarily determined as to their supplies in some*

other way?....Indeed, this is quite possible; but...subject to the restrictive condition that the set of $\underline{n}$ means or inputs is already given as __datum__. The restriction is a large one. It excludes from consideration all situations in which these supplies are likely to change (__i.e.__ to change as a "feedback" effect of their prices), and analysis thus restricted can make no pronouncement as to why and how these changes occur or as to their effects—for which reason we spoke of the situations to which such a theory can apply as "quasi-short-period situations".[105]

In *Political Economy and Capitalism*, Dobb wrote in similar terms of the Austrian assumption that, "*in any given set of conditions, the supply of such ultimate productive factors was fixed.*"[106] He qualified this in a footnote by adding, "*Strictly speaking, the Austrians did not assume, or need to assume, that the supply of basic factors of production was unchangeable: merely that the quantity of them was determined by conditions external to the market, and hence could be treated as independent.*"[107] Nevertheless, the practical effect was that, "*[b]eing limited by an unalterable (for the moment) scarcity, these factors, like any commodity, would acquire a price equal to the marginal service which they could render in production: these prices formed the constituent elements of cost.*"[108] This required deliberately abstracting the "theory of value" of factors of production from cost, or any "*characteristics affecting the supply.*"[109]

In addition, the Austrian theory of factor pricing is, in a sense, an elaborate exercise in question-begging. Saying that factors are priced according to their marginal productivity is just another way of saying the price is based on capitalizing expected profit and rent. But the latter quantities, and their natural level in a free market, are precisely the points at issue between the mutualist and Austrian versions of free market theory.

As James Buchanan characterized it, the subjective theory was an attempt to apply the classical theory of value for goods in fixed supply to all goods, both reproducible and not.

The development of a __general__ theory of exchange value became a primary concern. Classical analysis was rejected because it contained two separate models, one for reproducible goods, another for goods in fixed supply. The solution was to claim generality for the simple model of exchange value that the classical writers had reserved for the second category. Exchange value is, in all cases, said the marginal utility theorists, determined by marginal utility, by demand. At the point of market exchange, all supplies are fixed. Hence, relative values or prices are set exclusively by relative marginal utilities.[110]

Marshall believed, by the way, that production cost influenced demand, even in the short run, through buyers' expectations of future changes in price as output increased. For a similar case of the effect of expectations on demand-price, we need go no further than electronic goods. How many people have postponed the purchase of a DVD player in the expectation that they would be produced more cheaply in a year or two?

For the Austrians, by definition, "value" was identical to market price at any given time. "Future price" was indeed subject to change, through producers' reactions to present price; but to go so far as to introduce "equilibrium price" as a useful concept, or to claim a relation between equilibrium price and cost of production, was a no-no. Theoretical constructs are well and good—but only for Austrians.

The Austrian doctrine that utility determines price, if taken literally, is utter nonsense. The doctrine is true only with the qualifications that they, parenthetically, provided: that value is determined without regard to the long run, but only by the existing stocks of supplies in relation to market demand at any given time. And these qualifications, taken with Rothbard's admission that cost of production indirectly affected price through its effects on supply, bring the substance of Rothbard's theory quite close to that of Marshall.

Rothbard's caricature of Marshall closely parallels the straw-man version of classical political economy which Jevons congratulated himself on destroying over a century ago. And Marshall's analysis of the Jevonian critique of Ricardo, which we saw above, could be turned against Rothbard to great effect: if we consider Marshall's actual doctrine, rather than Rothbard's crude parody of it, it is apparent that the two are much closer in substance than Rothbard would admit; but if we are to take the doctrines of either Marshall or Rothbard as lampooned by their enemies—as the bare assertion either that cost "determines" price, or that utility "determines" price—the truth is much closer to the former than to the latter assertion.

Once we take into account changes in supply in response to changes in demand, we end up with a model in which the supply of goods adjusts to demand until the marginal price equals marginal cost; and the supply of factors of production, when it is elastic, will increase until factor prices reflect the cost of providing them. In other words, exactly what Ricardo and the rest of the classical school said.

The subjectivist utility and imputation doctrines, as stated, are true as far as they go; but they depend on taking the statements in other than the ordinary or obvious sense, and attaching special qualifications to them that render them irrelevant to the traditional problems of political economy. Perhaps that's just the point.

NOTES

1. As defined by Ronald Meek, the term "cost theory" includes "*any theory which approaches the problem of the price of a commodity from the angle of the 'costs' (including profits) which have to be covered if it is to be worth a producer's while to carry on producing it. Some 'cost theories' say no more than that the equilibrium price is determined by the cost of production; others go further and seek for an ultimate determinant of the cost of production itself.*" *Studies in the Labour Theory of Value*, 2nd ed. (New York and London: Monthly Review Press, 1956) 77n. In this chapter, the cost of production theory and the labor theory of value are used interchangeably, unless otherwise specified. In mutualist theory, the non-labor components of cost are themselves reducible either to labor-value or to scarcity-rents; the mutualist labor theory of value, therefore, is simply a subspecies of the cost theory that takes it to its logical conclusion.

2. Adam Smith, *An Inquiry Into the Nature and Causes of the Wealth of Nations* (Chicago, London, Toronto: Encyclopedia Britannica, Inc., 1952) 13

3. David Ricardo, *Principles of Political Economy and Taxation*, 3rd ed. (London: John Murray, Albemarle Street, 1821), vol. 1 of Piero Sraffa ed., *The Works and Correspondence of David Ricardo* (Cambridge University Press, 1951) 11.

4. Ibid. p. 35.

5. Thomas Hodgskin, *Labour Defended Against the Claims of Capital* (New York: Augustus M. Kelley, 1963 (1825)) 27-8.

6. Friedrich Engels, "Preface to the First German Edition of *The Poverty of Philosophy* by Karl Marx" (1884), in vol. 26 of Marx and Engels, *Collected Works* (New York: International Publishers, 1990) 279.

7. See, for example, Dirk Struik's "Introduction" to *The Economic and Philosophical Manuscripts of 1844* (New York: International Publishers, 1964); Norman Fischer, "The Ontology of Abstract Labor," *Review of Radical Political Economics* Summer 1982; and E. K. Hunt, "Marx's Concept of Human Nature and the Labor Theory of Value," *Review of Radical Political Economics* Summer 1982.

8. Karl Marx, "Afterword to Second German Edition of *Capital*" (1873), vol. 35 of Marx and Engels, *Collected Works* (New York: International Publishers, 1996) 15.

9. Maurice Dobb, *Political Economy and Capitalism: Some Essays in Economic Tradition* 2nd rev. ed (London: Routledge & Kegan Paul Ltd, 1940, 1960) 53.

10. Maurice Dobb, *Theories of Value and Distribution Since Adam Smith: Ideology and Economic Theory* (Cambridge: Cambridge University Press, 1973) 118.

11. Ibid. 166.

12. Dobb, *Political Economy and Capitalism* 24, 136.

13. Ibid. 24-5.

14. Eugen von Böhm-Bawerk, *Capital and Interest: A Critical History of Economical Theory*, trans. William Smart (New York: Brentanno's, 1922) 286.

15. William Stanley Jevons, *The Theory of Political Economy*, 5th ed. (Kelley & Millman, Inc., 1957) 1-2.

16. Böhm-Bawerk, *Capital and Interest* 383.

17. Ibid. 383-4.

18. Ibid. 384-5.

19. Ibid. 385-6.

20. Ibid. 386.

21. Ibid. 386-7.

22. Ibid. 387.

23. Carl Menger, *Principles of Economics*, trans. James Dingwall and Bert F. Hozelitz (Grove City, PA: Libertarian Press, Inc., 1976) 101.

24. Ibid. 116-7.

25. Eugen von Böhm-Bawerk, *The Positive Theory of Capital*, trans. William Smart (London and New York: MacMillan and Co., 1891) 135-6.

26. Ibid. 332.

27. Smith, *Wealth of Nations* 24.

28. Ibid. 25-6.

29. Ibid. 94-5.

30. Ricardo, *Principles of Political Economy and Taxation* 12.

31. Ibid. 88.

32. Ibid. 382.

33. Ibid. 67-84.

34. Ibid. 364-5.

35. Ibid. 385.

36. Ibid. 386-7.

37. David Ricardo, "Notes on Malthus," qt. in Dobb, *Theories of Value and Distribution* 120.

38. John Stuart Mill, *Principles of Political Economy: With Some of Their Applications to Social Philosophy*, in vol. 3 of *Collected Works of John Stuart Mill* (Toronto: University of Toronto Press, 1965) 471-3.

39. Ibid. 475.

40. Ibid. 464-5.

41. Ibid. 469.

42. Ibid. 490.

43. Ibid. 494-5.

44. Engels, "Preface to the First German Edition of *The Poverty of Philosophy*" 286-7.

45. Karl Marx, *The Poverty of Philosophy*, vol. 6 of Marx and Engels, *Collected Works* (New York: International Publishers, 1976) 134-5.

46. Karl Marx, *Grundrisse*, vol. 28 of Marx and Engels, *Collected Works* (New York: International Publishers, 1986) 75-6.

47. Karl Marx and Friedrich Engels, *Capital* vol. 3, vol. 37 of Marx and Engels, *Collected Works* (New York: International Publishers, 1998) 229.

48. Karl Marx and Friedrich Engels, *Capital* vol. 1, vol. 35 of Marx and Engels, *Collected Works* (New York: International Publishers, 1996) 49.

49. Meek, *Studies in the Labour Theory of Value* 178-9.

50. Ibid. 204-5.

51. Ibid. 205n.

52. Benjamin Tucker, "Why Wages Should Absorb Profits," *Liberty* July 16, 1887, in Benjamin Tucker, *Instead of a Book, By a Man Too Busy to Write One*, Gordon Press Facsimile (New York: 1897/1973) 289-90.

53. Benjamin Tucker, "A Criticism That Does Not Apply," *Liberty* July 16, 1887, in Ibid. 323.

54. Benjamin Tucker, "Protection, and Its Relation to Rent," *Liberty* October 27, 1888, in Ibid. 328, 331.

55. Benjamin Tucker, "Pinney His Own Procrustes," *Liberty* April 23, 1887, in Ibid. 251.

56. Benjamin Tucker, "Liberty and Land," *Liberty* December 15, 1888, in Ibid. 335-6.

57. Benjamin Tucker, "Voluntary Cooperation," *Liberty* May 24, 1890, in Ibid. 105.

58. Benjamin Tucker, "Rent: Parting Words," *Liberty* December 12, 1885, in Ibid. 306.

59. Tucker, "Protection, and Its Relation to Rent" 332.

60. Böhm-Bawerk, *Capital and Interest* 387.

61. Böhm-Bawerk, *Positive Theory of Capital* 233.

62. Ibid. 233-4.

63. Dobb, *Political Economy and Capitalism* 14-7.

64. Dobb, *Theories of Value and Distribution* 10-1.

65. Leif Johansen, "Marxism and Mathematical Economics," *Monthly Review* January 1963 508.

66. Leif Johansen, "Labour Theory of Value and Marginal Utilities," *Economics of Planning* September 1963 100.

67. Ludwig von Mises, *Human Action* (Chicago: Regnery, 1949, 1963, 1966) 236-8.

68. Ibid. 546-7.

69. Murray Rothbard, *Man, Economy, and State: A Treatise on Economic Principles* (Auburn University, Alabama: Ludwig von Mises Institute, 1993) 275-6.

70. Dobb, *Theories of Value and Distribution* 112-3; Meek, *Studies in the Labour Theory of Value* 123, 245-6.

71. Alfred Marshall, *Principles of Economics: An Introductory Volume.* 8th ed. (New York: The MacMillan Company, 1948) 580, 587-8.

72. Ibid. 348.

73. Ibid. 84.

74. Ibid. 349.

75. Ibid. 366.

76. Ibid. 372.

77. Ibid. 402.

78. Ibid. 372.

79. Ibid. 346-7.

80. Ibid. 577.

81. Ibid. 503.

82. Ibid. 817.

83. Ibid. 818.

84. Ibid. 95.

85. Ibid. 818.

86. Ibid. 819.

87. Ibid. 821.

88. Rothbard, *Man, Economy, and State* 239.

89. Ibid. 292.

90. Ibid. 302-3.

91. Ibid. 304.

92. Böhm-Bawerk, *Capital and Interest* 140.

93. Rothbard, *Man, Economy, and State* 305.

94. Marshall, *Principles of Economics* 346-7.

95. Ibid. 577.

96. Joseph Schumpeter, *Ten Great Economists From Marx to Keynes* (New York: Oxford University Press, 1965) 40-1.

97. Benjamin Tucker, "Does Competition Mean War?" *Liberty* August 4, 1888, in Tucker, *Instead of a Book* 405.

98. Rothbard, *Man, Economy, and State* 239.

99. Ibid. 292.

100. Böhm-Bawerk, *Positive Theory of Capital* 148.

101. Murray Rothbard, *Power and Market: Government and the Economy* (Kansas City: Sheed Andrews and Mcmeel, Inc., 1970, 1977) 88-9.

102. Rothbard, *Man, Economy, and State* 303.

103. Dobb, *Theories of Value and Distribution* 205-6.

104. Ibid. 114.

105. Ibid. 179-82.

106. Dobb, *Political Economy and Capitalism* 160.

107. Ibid. 160n.

108. Ibid. 160.

109. Ibid. 140.

110. James Buchanan, *Cost and Choice: An Inquiry in Economic Theory*, vol. 6 *Collected Works* (Indianapolis: Liberty Fund, 1999) 9.

Chapter Two
A Subjective Recasting of the Labor Theory

Eugen von Böhm-Bawerk's critique of the labor theory of value has been the most thorough to date. Many of his criticisms, as we have seen above, were either attacks on straw-men, or based on his own idiosyncratic views about the level of generality necessary for a theory of value. But a few of his criticisms were quite valid.

The most telling of Böhm-Bawerk's criticisms of the classical labor and cost theories of value concerned their lack of an explicit theoretical foundation. Of Rodbertus, for example, he complained that that author was "*content on almost every occasion to assert...in the tone of an axiom*," the proposition that labor creates exchange value. But to justify the proposition Rodbertus appealed only to the authority of Smith and Ricardo.[1] But neither Smith nor Ricardo had "*given any reason for this principle, but simply asserted its validity as something self-explanatory.*"[2]

Böhm-Bawerk cited Smith in particular as an example of this failing. After quoting him on the "*rude state of society*" before the accumulation of capital, in which the quantity of labor "*seem*[ed] *to be*" the only basis for exchange between deer and beaver hunters, Böhm-Bawerk commented:

> In these words also we shall look in vain for any trace of a rational basis for the doctrine. Adam Smith simply says, "seems to be the only circumstance," "should naturally," "it is natural," and so on, but throughout he leaves it to the reader to convince himself of the "naturalness of such judgments—a task...that the critical reader will not find easy.[3]

Certainly Böhm-Bawerk was right in rejecting the process of elimination ("*the logical and systematic processes of distillation*") by which Marx identified embodied labor as the only factor common to commodities, on which their exchange value could be based.[4]

But despite Böhm-Bawerk's criticism, the theoretical basis for the labor theory is implicit in other parts of Marx's work, as well as that of the classical economists. They came very close to formulating it explicitly at times, and often at least suggested it obliquely. In the end, however, they failed to formulate it deliberately and consciously.

In its implicit form, it appears in Adam Smith's work as his "toil and trouble" understanding of the nature of labor. In the time after division of labor but before large-scale accumulation of capital, Smith wrote, all exchanges were exchanges between producers of the surplus products of their respective labor.

> *When the division of labour has been once thoroughly established, it is but a very small part of a man's wants which the produce of his own labour can supply. He supplies the far greater part of them by exchanging that surplus part of the produce of his own labour, which is over and above his own consumption, for such parts of the produce of other men's labour as he has occasion for.*[5]

The "*real price*" of a thing, Smith went on to say, what it "*really costs to the man who wants to acquire it*," was "*the toil and trouble of acquiring it....*"

> *What is bought with money or with goods is purchased by labour as much as what we acquire by the toil of our own body.... Labour was the first price, the original purchase-money that was paid for all things. It was not by gold or silver, but by labour, that all the wealth of the world was originally purchased....*

> *....At all times and places that is dear which it is difficult to come at, or which it costs much labour to acquire; and that cheap which is to be had easily, or with very little labour.*[6]

And Smith made it clear that "toil and trouble" was to be measured from the laborer's subjective standpoint: "*Equal quantities of labour must at all times and in all places have the same value for the labourer. in his normal state of health, strength and activity, and with the average degree of skill that he may possess, he must always give up the same portion of his rest, his freedom, and his happiness.*"[7]

As Maurice Dobb commented, "*Perhaps one could translate this into Marshallian terminology and say that it was equivalent to claiming that labour was the ultimate real cost involved in economic activity.*"[8] Eric Roll called it a "*psychological cost theory of value.*"[9]

The classical political economists occasionally suggested such an understanding of labor, but never developed it systematically. For example, Ricardo at times appeared to recognize a subjective mechanism behind the operation of the cost principle. In language reminiscent of Smith, he wrote:

> *I may be asked what I mean by the word value, and by what criterion I would judge whether a commodity had or had not changed its value. I answer, I know of no other criterion of a thing being dear or cheap but by the sacrifices of labour made to obtain it. Every thing is originally purchased by labour—nothing that has value can be produced without it, and therefore if a commodity such as cloth required the labour of ten men for a year to produce it at one time, and only required the labour of five for the same time to produce it at another it will be twice as cheap....*
>
> *That the greater or less quantity of labour worked up in commodities can be the only cause of their alteration in value is completely made out as soon as we are agreed that all commodities are the produce of labour and would have no value but for the labour expended on them.*[10]

But as to why this should be so, or why commodities should exchange according to the labor *time* required for their production, he did not elaborate.

It is true, as Böhm-Bawerk charged, that the classicals did not elaborate in a sufficiently explicit form, the *reason* that effort translated into exchange value; nevertheless, the rationale should be fairly straightforward on examination. The subjective mechanism for the cost principle is implicitly assumed by the classical economists, to a large extent, because it is rooted in a common sense and self-evident understanding of human nature. The basis of exchange value in the individual's effort lies in the same a priori understanding of human behavior from which Bohm-Bawerk's disciple Mises derived his "praxeology," or science of human action.

The labor theory and cost principle are logically entailed in man's nature as a being who maximizes utility and (more to the point) minimizes disutility. As James Buchanan wrote,

> *Even in so simple a model* [Adam Smith's primitive exchange model of beavers and deer], *why should relative costs determine normal exchange values? They do so because hunters are assumed to be rational utility-maximizing individuals* and *because the positively valued "goods" and the negatively valued "bads" in their utility functions can be identified. If, for any reason, exchange values should settle in some ratio different from that of cost values, behavior will be modified. If the individual hunter knows that he is able, on an outlay of one day's labor, to kill two deer or one beaver, he*

will not choose to kill deer if the price of a beaver is three deer, even should he be a demander or final purchaser of deer alone. He can "produce" deer more cheaply through exchange under these circumstances.... Since all hunters can be expected to behave in the same way, no deer will be produced until and unless the expected exchange value returns to equality with the cost ratio. Any divergence between <u>expected</u> *exchange value and* <u>expected</u> *cost value in this model would reflect irrational behavior on the part of the hunters.*

In this interpretation, the classical theory embodies the notion of opportunity cost. To the hunter at the point of an allocative decision, the cost of a beaver is two deer and the cost of a deer is one-half a beaver. At an expected exchange ratio of one for two, each prospective hunter must be on the margin of indifference. Physical production and production-through-exchange yield identical results. Labor time, the standard for measurement, is the common denominator in which the opportunity costs are computed.[11]

A producer will continue to bring his goods to market only if he receives a price necessary, in his subjective evaluation, to compensate him for the disutility involved in producing them. And he will be unable to charge a price greater than this necessary amount, for a very long time, if market entry is free and supply is elastic, because competitors will enter the field until price equals the disutility of producing the final increment of the commodity.

Such statements require no verification beyond an *a priori* understanding of human nature. Mises himself wrote on the self-evident character of the axioms of praxeology, repeatedly and at length:

[praxeology's] *statements and propositions are not derived from experience. They are, like those of logic and mathematics, a priori. They are not subject to verification or falsification on the ground of experience and facts. They are both logically and temporally antecedent to any comprehension of historical fact.....*

....It [the *a priori*] *refers to the essential and necessary character of the logical structure of the human mind.*

The fundamental logical relations are not subject to proof or disproof. Every attempt to prove them must presuppose their validity. It is impossible to explain them to a being who would not possess them on his own account.... They are ultimate unanalyzable categories. The human mind is utterly incapable of imagining logical categories at variance with them....

Aprioristic reasoning is purely conceptual and deductive. It cannot produce anything else but tautologies and analystic judgments. All its implications are logically derived from the premises and were already contained in them....

All geometrical theorems are already implied in the axioms....
The starting point of praxeology is not a choice of axioms and a decision
about methods of procedure, but reflection about the essence of action....
There is no mode of action thinkable in which means and ends or costs and
proceeds cannot be clearly distinguished and precisely separated. There is
nothing which only approximately or incompletely fits the economic category
of an exchange....[12]

The scope of praxeology is the explication of the category of human action.
All that is needed for the deduction of all praxeological theorems is knowledge
of the essence of human action. It is a knowledge that is our own because
we are men.... No special experience is needed in order to comprehend
these theorems.... The only way to a cognition of these theorems is logical
analysis of our inherent knowledge of the category of action.... Like logic
and mathematics, praxeological knowledge is in us; it does not come from
without.[13]

Similarly, the labor theory of value is based, not on an inductive
generalization from the observed movement of prices, but on an a priori
assumption about *why* price approximates cost, except to the extent to
which some natural or artificial scarcity causes deviations from this
relationship.

But even though the axioms of praxeology are not derived from
historical experience, Mises argued, they are nevertheless useful in
rendering the facts of history intelligible. Studies of economic history

do not deliver bricks for the construction of a posteriori hypotheses and
theorems. On the contrary, they are without meaning if not interpreted in
the light of theories developed without reference to them.... No controversy
concerning the causes of a historical event can be solved on the ground of
an examination of the facts which is not guided by definite praxeological
theories.[14]

So not only does the unique disutility of labor provide a theoretical
basis for a labor theory of value; but economic historians, econometricians,
etc., can make greater sense of the observed movements of price by
using such a labor theory as a paradigm.

The marginalists themselves, both neoclassical and Austrian, have
recognized that labor is a "real cost" in a unique sense. The disutility
of labor, for them, is a basic law of economics. The expenditure of
other factors is limited only by their availability, and by the need to
economize in allocating them to the most productive marginal use.
The only cost in the expenditure of a factor other than labor is an
opportunity cost—the other uses to which it might have been put,
instead. But the expenditure of labor is an absolute cost, regardless of

the quantity available. Or to be more exact, the opportunity cost of an expenditure of labor is not simply the alternative uses of labor, but *non-labor*. The laborer is allocating his time, not just between competing forms of labor, but also between labor and non-labor.

William Stanley Jevons, one of the founders of the marginalist revolution and an originator of the marginalist idea of disutility, explicitly tied the latter to Adam Smith's "toil and trouble." Smith's conception of labor, he wrote, was "*substantially true.*" "*Labour,*" he stated provisionally, "*is the painful exertion which we undergo to ward off pains of greater amount, or to procure pleasures which leave a balance in our favour.*"[15] Faced with questions about the bearing of play and other enjoyable efforts, and of productive labor which was pleasant in its own right, he was forced to define labor more exactly to exclude exertion which was "*completely repaid by the immediate result....*" Labor, to be more exact, was "*any painful exertion of mind or body undergone partly or wholly with a view to future good.*"[16] Thus, it corresponded to what Mises was later to call "extraversive labor." Although even labor undertaken primarily for the sake of the result might be innately pleasurable, additional increments of such labor would cease to provide additional pleasure long before the laborer had satisfied his need for consumption. Even after the laborer had ceased to derive any satisfaction from labor, however, the marginal utility of the product of additional increments of labor would outweigh the marginal disutility of working: "*It is true that labour may be both agreeable at the time and conducive to future good; but it is only agreeable in a limited amount, and most men are compelled by their wants to exert themselves longer and more severely than they would otherwise do.*"[17] The supply of labor was governed by the marginal utility of each increment of wages compared to the marginal disutility of labor.[18]

For Marshall, as for Jevons, unpleasantness was just another quantitative factor alongside the pleasure of work, that entered into the overall calculation of utility vs. disutility. To make the principle clearer, he gave the example of a person working directly for his own consumption:

> *When a boy picks blackberries for his own eating, the action of picking is probably itself pleasurable for a while; and for some time longer the pleasure of eating is more than enough to repay the trouble of picking. But after he has eaten a good deal, the desire for more diminishes; while the task of picking begins to cause weariness, which may indeed be a feeling of monotony rather than of fatigue. Equilibrium is reached when at last his eagerness to play and his disinclination for the work of picking counterbalance the desire for eating.*[19]

Like the earlier Jevons and the later Mises, Alfred Marshall defined labor in terms of its productive character, or its intended results:

> 2. *All labour is directed towards producing some effect. For though some exertions are taken merely for their own sake, as when a game is played for amusement, they are not counted as labour. We may define labour as any exertion of mind or body undergone partly or wholly with a view to some good other than the pleasure derived directly from the work.*[20]

Unlike Jevons, however, Marshall did not limit the term to *painful* exertions.[21]

Eugen von Böhm-Bawerk wrote at length on the distinction between the expenditure of labor as an opportunity cost (common to all expenditures of production factors), and as a positive disutility (unique to labor).

> *The nature of all economic sacrifices that men make consists in some loss of wellbeing which they suffer; and the amount of sacrifice is measured by the amount of this loss. It may be of two kinds: of a positive kind, where we inflict on ourselves positive injury, pain, or trouble; or of a negative kind, where we do without a happiness or a satisfaction which we otherwise might have had. In the majority of economical sacrifices which we make to gain a definite useful end, the only question is about one of these kinds of loss....*
>
> *It is otherwise with the sacrifice of labour. Labour presents two sides to economical consideration. On the one hand it is, in the experience of most men, an effort connected with an amount of positive pain, and on the other, it is a means to the attainment of many kinds of enjoyment. Therefore the man who expends labour for a definite useful end makes on the one hand the positive sacrifice of pain, and on the other, the negative sacrifice of the other kinds of enjoyment that might have been attained as results of the same labour.*[22]

For Böhm-Bawerk, the value of labor was determined either by disutility or by opportunity cost, whichever was greater. But as Buchanan pointed out above, opportunity cost itself was a means (at least in simple commodity exchange) by which the prices of commodities tended to approximate the sacrifice of labor involved in their production.

For all these economists, the disutility of labor was purely quantitative, and could be offset even in the case of extraversive labor by inherent pleasurableness of the work (at least for a time). For all of them, though, labor was also still unique among "factors of production," in that positive disutility entered into the cost-benefit equation at all.

For Mises, unlike the previous thinkers, "extraversive" labor (labor undertaken for the sake of a result rather than for its own sake) possessed an inherent *qualitative* disutility, from the very beginning of a job of work and regardless of the quantity of pleasantness or unpleasantness of it.

> *The expenditure of labor is deemed painful. Not to work is considered a state of affairs more satisfactory than working. Leisure is, other things being equal, preferred to travail. People work only when they value the return of labor higher than the decrease in satisfaction brought about by the curtailment of leisure. To work involves disutility.*
>
> *….For praxeology it is a datum that men are eager to enjoy leisure and therefore look upon their own capacity to bring about effects with feelings different from those with which they look upon the capacity of material factors of production. Man in considering the expenditure of his own labor investigates not only whether there is no more desirable end for the employment of the quantity of labor in question, but no less whether it would not be more desirable to abstain from any further expenditure of labor.*[23]

The idea of labor as disutility has caused some to object that this reflects a crude economic man understanding of human motivation, and ignores the fact that creative labor is an essential part of human nature. Whether man perceives labor as mere travail, or as an expression of his inner nature, depends on the nature of power relations in the production process. For example, Marx objected that Smith's "toil and trouble" view treated the expenditure of labor power "*as the mere sacrifice of rest, freedom, and happiness, and not as at the same time the normal activity of living beings. But then, he has the modern wage labourer in his eye.*"[24]

But disutility, as Mises understood it, was not affected by the joy or tedium of labor. Labor can be especially unpleasant or difficult. But it can also be pleasant. Joy in labor results from the "*expectation of the labor's mediate gratification, the anticipation of the enjoyment of its success and yield*"; it also results from "*the aesthetic appreciation of* [the worker's] *skill and its product*" (i.e., pride in craftsmanship; and finally, joy results from the satisfaction "*of having successfully overcome all the toil and trouble involved.*" But none of these things affects the disutility of labor as such, for the reason that people work for the sake of the mediate gratification provided by labor's product, and not for the pleasure intrinsic to the work itself.[25]

Rothbard, seemingly, shifted back somewhat toward Marshall's position. He treated the disutility of labor as another item on the general scale of pleasantness and tedium.

> *For almost all actors, <u>leisure is a consumers' good</u>, to be weighed in the balance against the prospect of acquiring other consumers' goods, including possible satisfaction from the effort itself. Consequently* [quoting Mises], *"people work only when they value the return of labor higher than the decrease in satisfaction brought about by the decrease in leisure." It is*

possible that included in this "return" of satisfaction yielded by labor may be satisfaction in the labor itself, in the voluntary expenditure of energy on a productive task.... As the quantity of effort increases, however, the utility of the satisfactions provided by labor itself declines, and the utility of the successive units of the final product declines as well....

In some cases, labor itself may be positively disagreeable, not only because of the leisure foregone, but also because of specific conditions attached to the particular labor that the actor finds disagreeable. In these cases, the marginal disutility of labor includes both the disutility due to these conditions and the disutility due to leisure foregone....[26]

Nevertheless, in the next paragraph, Rothbard made it clear that the pleasures of extraversive labor were inseparable from the anticipated utility of the product, and denied that such pleasures would have any utility for the laborer without the product for which the labor was undertaken.

....In cases where the labor itself provides positive satisfactions, however, these are intertwined with and cannot be separated from the prospect of obtaining the final product. Deprived of the final product, man will consider his labor senseless and useless, and the labor itself will no longer bring positive satisfactions. Those activities which are engaged in purely for their own sake are not labor but pure play, consumers' goods in themselves.[27]

Labor is a "cost" in a uniquely positive sense. In comparison, other "costs," like so-called waiting or abstinence, are entirely relative. Indeed, the nature of labor as a unique disutility *implies* that other costs are only relative. The free gifts of nature, and natural processes, have "costs" (aside from the trouble of making them usable) only to the extent that a privileged owner can regulate access to them, and thus charge for something that is not a real cost to him. The "sacrifice" or "cost" entailed in providing natural goods is only such on the assumption of a "natural" state of affairs in which one can control access. The free gifts of nature have exchange value only to the extent that access to them is controlled. As Maurice Dobb wrote,

That labour constitutes a cost in a unique sense was, of course, an assumption. But it was an assumption born of a particular view of what was the essence of the economic problem.... The crux of the economic problem, as this theory represented it, and as it had been traditionally viewed, lay in the struggle of man with nature to wrest a livelihood for himself under various forms of production at various stages of history. As Petty had said, labour is the father, nature the mother of wealth. To this relationship the contrast between human activity and the processes of nature was fundamental....

> *And if we seek to give any quantitative expression to this relationship—to man's mastery over nature—it is hard to see what simple notion one can use other than the expenditure of human energies requisite...to produce a given result.... The essence of value,...by contrast with riches, was conceived to be cost, and the essence of cost to lie in labour, by contrast with nature. Labour, conceived objectively as the output of human energy, was the measure and the essence of Ricardo's "difficulty or facility of production."*[28]

Twentieth century economics has attempted, through the mechanism of opportunity cost, to render all cost entirely subjective.[29] But like Marshall's "abstinence" and "real cost," the opportunity cost of Böhm-Bawerk and Wieser and of the twentieth century Austrian and London School economists is entirely relative to whether one is in a position to charge for something. Unlike labor, which is a positive expenditure of effort or travail, "abstinence" and "opportunity cost" are defined entirely in the context of what one is enabled to charge for access to.

As Dobb explained, there was no limit to "real cost," short of imputing it *"to any means by which an income could be acquired in an exchange society."*[30] He argued that the notion of real cost was rid "of any real content," but was

> *indistinguishable from what later came to be called "opportunity cost"—the cost of sacrificed alternatives (that "arithmetical truism", as Mr. Durbin has called it). Such a quantity by itself affords no explanation, because it is itself not independent, but something dependent on the total situation; and all that has been done by this definition is to shift the inquiry back to the nature of the total situation of which both profit and this so-called "cost" are simultaneously resultant. Whether a person <u>does</u> demand payment for a certain act (i. e. whether it has a "supply-price") depends on whether he <u>can</u> demand payment; and this depends on the total situation of which he is a part. To adopt this criterion is to make the existence or non-existence of a "sacrifice" depend, not on the nature of the action, but on the nature of the circumstances surrounding the individual or class in question. A "sacrifice" can only be incurred in the measure that one has the luxury of alternatives to forego.*[31]

Unlike labor, which is an absolute sacrifice in the sense of the actual expenditure of effort, the "sacrifice" or "opportunity cost" of a capitalist or landlord is only foregoing the further receipt of a good that did not cost him anything, and exists at all only in the context of a set of alternative returns heavily influenced by statist privilege or monopoly.

And as Dobb pointed out, Alfred Marshall admitted as much himself, seeing as he *"defined the term 'waiting' as applying, not to 'abstemiousness', but to the simple fact that 'a person abstained from consuming anything which he had the power of consuming, with the purpose of increasing his resources in the future*." If followed consistently, this principle could produce distinctly absurd results:

> *This seems to imply that the concept was not limited by Senior's qualification, excluding inherited property, and that it could equally well be applied to land—to the fact that a landlord leased his land for cultivation, instead of using it for his own enjoyment or subjecting it to "exhaustive" cultivation himself. In which case, as a category of "real cost", it was clearly so general as to lose any distinctive meaning.*[32]

Such a definition sets aside the question of whether one's control of access to a property or one's acquisition of it is legitimate, and thus whether one has a legitimate right to demand income from it. The only way to address such questions is to go back to the ethical question of what constitutes legitimately acquired property. From the point of view of a mutualist theory of land ownership, by which property rights are established only by occupancy and use, an absentee landlord's claim to compensation for the "sacrifice" of allowing a tenant to use his land is as spurious as a mugger's for the "sacrifice" of not shooting his victim. Even from the standpoint of a Lockean labor standard only for the initial acquisition of property, the overwhelming majority of landlord claims are illegitimate results of statist collusion.

The subjectivists, in other words, treated the existing structure of property rights over "factors" as a given, and proceeded to show how the product would be distributed among these "factors" according to their marginal contribution. By this method, if slavery were still extant, a marginalist might with a straight face write of the marginal contribution of the slave to the product (imputed, of course, to the slave-owner), and of the "opportunity cost" involved in committing the slave to one or another use.

To take Dobb's illustration, "*Suppose that toll-gates were a general institution, rooted in custom or ancient legal right.*"

> *Could it reasonably be denied that there would be an important sense in which the income of the toll-owning class represented "an appropriation of goods produced by others" and not payment for an "activity directed to the production or transformation of economic goods?" Yet toll-charges would be fixed in competition with alternative roadways, and hence would, presumably, represent prices fixed "in an open market...." Would not the opening and shutting of toll-gates become an essential factor of production, according to most current definitions of a factor of production, with as much reason at any rate as many of the functions of the capitalist entrepreneur are so classed to-day? This factor, like others, could then be said to have a "marginal productivity" and its price be regarded as the measure and equivalent of the*

service it rendered. At any rate, where is a logical line to be drawn between toll-gates and property-rights over scarce resources in general?[33]

Or better yet, as Marx had put it almost a century before, *"land becomes personified in the landlord and...gets on its hind legs to demand, as an independent force, its share of the product created with its help. Thus, not the land receives its due portion of the product for the restoration and improvement of its productivity, but instead the landlord takes a share of this product to chaffer away or squander."*[34] The "trinitarian formula" of labor-wages, capital-profit, and land-rent is *"an enchanted, perverted, topsy-turvy world, in which Monsieur le Capital and Madame la Terre do their ghost-walking as social characters and at the same time directly as mere things."*[35]

The point, of course, is not to compare existing property in the means of production to toll-gates, or to slavery. That would be begging the question. The point is that questions of justice in ownership must be addressed *first*.

For the Ricardians, in a sense, distribution was prior to exchange. That is, *"price-relations or exchange-values could only be arrived at after the principle affecting distribution of the total product had been postulated."*[36] The marginalists, on the other hand, subsumed distribution within their price-theory.[37]

> *The change* [of orientation] *was associated...with the drawing of different boundary-lines to the "economic system", as an "isolated system"; so that questions of property-ownership or class relations and conflicts were regarded as falling outside the economist's domain, not directly affecting, in major respects at least, the phenomena and relations with which economic analysis was properly concerned, and belonging instead to the province of the economic historian or the sociologist.*[38]

> [T] *he reduction of distribution to the pricing of productive services or factors had the result of excluding the social circumstances of the individuals (or social groups) associated with the supply of these "services"—even to the extent of dropping from sight the very existence of these individuals.... The extreme case was where given factor-supplies were postulated, and distribution consisted simply of the pricing of n factor inputs.... Hence the illusion of distribution being integrated completely within the exchange-process was at its greatest.*[39]

Of course, the banishment of such "irrelevant," "extra-economic" questions from the purview of economics was, from the marginalist point of view, just another benefit of the new economics as a weapon in the war against socialism. As some Marxist economic historians have pointed out, classical political economy was a revolutionary doctrine.

Smith, Ricardo and Mill all took a jaundiced view of landlords as an essentially parasitic class, whose sole "contribution" to productivity was to be in a position to withhold land from production, and then to allow it to be used by the actually productive. The "productivity" of land was then imputed to its owner. This aspect of classical political economy suggested a possible basis for an analogous radical treatment of interest and profit. The question naturally seemed to suggest itself, of the extra-economic grounds on which capitalists were in a position to control access to capital (i.e., how they came to be in possession of it), and to withhold or release it from production depending on the revenue they derived from it. The heirs of classical political economy were divided on how they reacted to these questions. One school, that of Senior and Longfield, rejected the potentially revolutionary conclusions of Ricardo by setting aside his theory of rent as a parasitic income, and relegating land to the category of another "factor" whose provision entailed a "real cost" to the landlord; in so doing, this school laid the ideological groundwork for marginalism. Another school, that of market-oriented Ricardian socialists like Hodgskin and the American individualists, seized on the radical implications of Ricardo and drew the obvious conclusions. And marginalism, by defining "productivity" simply as the ability to withhold a productive factor from production, set these potentially explosive issues aside.[40]

Any general conception of "real cost" that put the disutility of labor in the same category as a capitalist's "abstention" or "sacrifice," was nonsensical.

> *The statement which the labour-theory implied was that exchange-values bore a certain relation to the output and using-up of human energies, and in doing so provided a term which gave some meaning to the distinction between a gross and a net product and to the concept of surplus, and provided a criterion for differentiating one type of income from another. Thus it is possible in these terms to distinguish exchange-relationships which represent a passing of value-equivalents from those which do not: for instance, the sale of labour-power representing the exchange of income against human energies expended in production, contrasted with the sale of a property-right over the use of scarce resources, representing no such passing of equivalents and constituting an income by no means "necessary" in the fundamental sense in which a subsistence-income to labour is necessary or the return to a machine of a value equal to what the operation of that machine has used up (in a physical sense).[41]*

Dobb himself did not address the crucial issue of whether "scarce resources" were scarce by nature alone, or as a result of State imposed monopoly and privilege as well. If the former, it is only a necessary result of a finite natural order that the first to occupy and use a natural resource should collect some economic rent so long as they use it; if the latter, they are robbers. Under capitalism, distinguished as a system of privilege from a genuine free market, most of the "sacrifices" from which the ruling class derives income presume a set of alternatives that includes, say, controlling access to land one does not use, or controlling access to credit in a seller's market.

Theories of the "productivity" of land and capital, like those of abstinence, are entirely relative, and based on the social convention of imputing their productive qualities to an owner who controls access to them. The "value" created by them is simply a monopoly price paid to their owner. Marx pointed this out at several places in *Theories of Surplus Value*. In the section on Hodgskin, he wrote of the fetishism involved in making the "productivity" of capital a source of exchange-value.

> One can only speak of the _productivity_ of capital if one regards capital as the embodiment of definite social relations of production. But if it is conceived in this way, then the historically transitory character of these relations becomes at once evident....[42]

And in the section on "Revenue and Its Sources," he wrote at much greater length of the fetishistic quality of thought involved in attributing exchange-value to the productivity of land and capital:

> The _land_ or _nature_ as the source of _rent_...is fetishistic enough. But as a result of a convenient confusion of use value with exchange value, the common imagination is still able to have recourse to the productive power of nature itself, which, by some kind of hocus-pocus, is personified in the LANDLORD....[43]

> Thus the participants in capitalist production live in a bewitched world and their own relationships appear to them as properties of things, as properties of the material elements of production. It is however in the last, most derivative forms—forms in which the intermediate stage has not only become invisible but has been turned into its direct opposite—that the various aspects of capital appear as the real agencies and direct representatives of production. Interest-bearing capital is personified in the MONIED capitalist, industrial capital in the INDUSTRIAL CAPITALIST, rent-bearing capital in the LANDLORD as the owner of the land, and lastly, labour in the wage-worker.[44]

The so-called "trinitarian formula" (the division of the product among land, labor and capital according to their "productivity") is utterly erroneous. The natural wage of labor, in a free market, is its product. That is not the same as saying, as do the Austrians, that labor is paid its "marginal product." Their use of the latter expression implies that there is an exchange value, established independently of production cost by utility to the consumer, to which labor "contributes" some portion. Rather, the exchange-value of a good derives from the labor involved in making it; it is the disutility of labor and the need to persuade the worker to bring his services to the production process, unique among all the "factors of production," that creates exchange value.

As Marx said, attributing exchange-value to the productivity of free natural goods, as such, is a confusion of exchange-value with use-value. Use-values have exchange-value only to the extent that it requires some effort to appropriate or modify them. The exchange-value of a pail of water, when access to water is free, is determined by the effort needed to draw the water and carry it to its destination (plus the amortized effort involved in making the pail or earning its purchase price). One can charge for the use-value of the water itself only if one controls the supply. Otherwise a competitor, seeing an opportunity, will enter the market and charge a price closer to his actual effort, until the marginal price is just enough to compensate for the effort of drawing and carrying water.

A producer will be able, in the long run, to pass on only that which is really a cost: the effort entailed in direct production, and that entailed in the purchase of means of production. He will be able to charge for that which is not a genuine cost (i.e., charges for use of capital, based on abstinence, beyond the effort by which it was acquired) only when some form of scarcity rent is involved. Some scarcity rents result from shifts in demand (in which case they will be corrected by market forces and eventually fall to zero). Some scarcity rents result from natural scarcity, like innate skill, and land with above average fertility or site advantage (in which case the scarcity rents are for all intents and purposes permanent). But a great deal of scarcity rent results from the State's intervention to create market entry barriers, or artificially restrict access to the supply of land and capital, so that privileged landlords and capitalists may draw monopoly incomes from land and capital; these scarcity rents will be abolished with the forms of intervention that create them. So all exchange value is reducible to the total subjective effort involved in production, plus scarcity rents. As Benjamin Tucker argued, "*under free competition there is no price where there is no burden.*"[45] And as a corollary, "*is there anything that costs except labor or suffering (another name for labor)?*"[46]

As Ronald Meek pointed out, Smith's and Marx's shared assumptions about labor as a standard of value in simple commodity exchange were hardly arbitrary. Cost price, including both labor expended in direct production and that expended in acquiring the means of production embodied in a commodity, was a natural standard from the viewpoint of artisans.

> ....for the major part of the period of commodity production as a whole, <u>supply prices</u> have in actual fact been directly or indirectly determined by "values" in Marx's sense. And these supply prices are by no means hypothetical: for most of the period of commodity production they have been firmly rooted in the consciousness of the producers themselves. Even in primitive societies one can see the beginnings of the idea that the exchange of commodities "at their values" in the Marxian sense is "the rational way, the natural law of their equilibrium". In quite a few cases, the prices asked and received for commodities in primitive markets are based on production costs.... After a while, the producers of commodities come quite naturally to think of the actual price they happen to receive for their commodity in terms of the extent to which this price deviates from the supply price—i.e., roughly from the <u>value</u> of the commodity in Marx's sense. The value of the commodity, although the market price may not often "tend" to conform to it at any particular stage of development owing to the existence of certain specific forms of monopoly, state interference, etc., characteristic of that stage, is regarded by the producers themselves as a sort of basis from which the deviations caused by these factors may legitimately be measured.

> The idea that the exchange of commodities "at their values" represents the "natural" way of exchanging them was of course often expressed in ethical terms. In other words, it often took the form of an idea concerning the manner in which exchanges <u>ought</u> to be conducted if justice was to be done. But ideas as to what constitutes a "fair" exchange come into men's minds in the first instance from earth and not from heaven. When the small capitalist who is faced with the competition of a powerful monopolist says that he has a right to receive a "fair" profit on his capital, or when the peasant who exchanges his produce for that of a guildsman on disadvantageous terms says that he has a right to receive a "fair" return for his labour, the standard of "fairness" erected by each of the complainants actually has reference to the way in which exchanges <u>would</u> <u>in</u> <u>fact</u> <u>be</u> <u>conducted</u> <u>in</u> <u>the</u> <u>real</u> <u>world</u> if the particular form of monopoly to which he is objecting did not exist. In pre-capitalist times, there must always have been some commodities which were exchanged more or less at their values, and some times and localities in which deviations of price from value were relatively small, so that the "natural" method of exchanging commodities could actually be seen in operation. For obvious reasons, this "natural" method was regarded as the only really "fair" one. Thus the persistence of the concept of a "just price" throughout the major part of the pre-capitalist period seems to me to afford evidence in favour of the objective (and not merely hypothetical) existence of supply prices proportionate to values during that period.

Thus although Adam Smith's picture of an "early and rude state of society" in which deer and beaver hunters exchanged their products strictly in accordance with embodied labour ratios was indeed a "Robinsonade", it did at least contain this element of truth—that in pre-capitalist societies the supply price of a commodity, which had an objective existence even though the actual prices of the majority of commodities usually deviated from their supply prices for one reason or another, could be regarded as directly determined by the value of the commodity.[47]

To go back to the quote from Buchanan above, the view of labor as the basis of "natural price" is logically implied by the nature of man as a utility-maximizing being.

Meek's comments on "just price" theory correspond closely to Tawney's treatment of the prevailing concept of "usury" as it existed in the Middle Ages. Usury, contrary to modern caricature, was not a price above some arbitrarily set "just price," established by scholastic specialists in angelological choreography; it was any form of income extracted from a position of power, in which one was enabled to charge whatever the market would bear.

The essence of the medieval scheme of economic ethics had been its insistence on equity in bargaining—a contract is fair, St. Thomas had said, when both parties gain from it equally. The prohibition of usury had been the kernel of its doctrines, not because the gains of the money-lender were the only species, but because, in the economic conditions of the age, they were the most conspicuous species, of extortion.

In reality, alike in the Middle Ages and in the sixteenth century, the word usury had not the specialized sense which it carries today.... The truth is, indeed, that any bargain, in which one party obviously gained more advantage than the other, and used his power to the full, was regarded as usurious.[48]

It is fair to say that medieval producers, with their concepts of the "just price," had a more common-sensical understanding of reality, than the sophisticates today who set up straw man caricatures of the theory for ridicule. The latter are open to charges of provincialism in time.

The medieval concept of usury corresponds pretty closely to Gary Elkin's use of the term: "*the exaction of tribute for the use of any object whose artificial scarcity and monopolization by an elite class are created and protected by the State.*"[49]

One implication of the subjectively-based LTV, as we have stated it, is the need to abandon embodied labor-time as the basis for quantifying labor. But that standard, as used by Marx and Ricardo, was untenable anyway. Both Marx and Ricardo started from a basic standard of embodied labor-time; they were nevertheless forced to reconcile this with the fact that labor of different intensities, skill, and other qualities, received differing rates of pay. The results were comparable to the elaborate system of epicycles added to Ptolemy's astronomy to make it correspond to the observed facts. What it amounted to, in practice, was that they moved toward a market standard for allocating pay to labor based on its disutility, without explicitly abandoning their labor-time standard.

What both finally wound up with, then, was the principle that, *given* two labors of a certain identical quality, the only basis for comparing them was their respective duration. And it was through the market that the value of various intensities or skills of labor was determined. In practice, the result was something awfully like Smith's "higgling and bargaining of the market" as a mechanism for distributing the produce of labor among laborers. But despite thus robbing labor-time of any practical meaning as a basis for value, they never abandoned it in theory.

Ricardo, for example, in the process of speaking of labor as "*the foundation of all value, and the relative quantity of labour as almost exclusively determining the relative value of commodities*," at the same time acknowledged

> the difficulty of comparing an hour's or a day's labour, in one employment, with the same duration of labour in another. The estimation in which different qualities of labour are held, comes soon to be adjusted in the market with sufficient precision for all practical purposes, and depends much on the comparative skill of the labourer, and intensity of the labour performed.[50]

Marx, likewise, for all intents and purposes backed off from labor-time as an objective measure of value, in denying "*that the days are equivalent, and that the day of one is worth the day of another.*"

> Let us suppose for a moment that a jeweler's day is equivalent to three days of a weaver; the fact remains that any change in the value of jewels relative to that of woven materials, unless it be the transitory result of the fluctuations of demand and supply, must have as its cause a reduction or an increase in the labour time expended in the production of one or the other.... Thus values may be measured by labour time, in spite of the inequality of value of different working days; but to apply such a measure we must have a comparative scale of the different working days: it is competition that sets up this scale.
>
> Is your hour's labour worth mine? That is a question which is decided by competition.[51]

In *A Contribution to the Critique of Political Economy*, Marx argued that labor-time was the only possible measure for comparing different quantities of labor; he argued at the same time that the labor-time standard assumed uniform quality, and that skilled or intense labor could be reduced to "simple labor" by a multiplier system.

> *Just as motion is measured by time, so is labour by <u>labour-time</u>. Variations in the duration of labour are the only possible difference that can occur if the quality of labour is assumed to be given....*

> *....This abstraction, human labour in general, <u>exists</u> in the form of average labour which, in a given society, the average person can perform, productive expenditure of a certain amount of human muscles, nerves, brain, etc. It is <u>simple</u> labour which any average individual can be trained to do and which in one way or another he has to perform.... But what is the position with regard to more complicated labour which, being labour of greater intensity and greater specific gravity, rises above the general level? This kind of labour resolves itself into simple labour; it is simple labour raised to a higher power, so that for example one day of skilled labour may equal three days of simple labour. The laws governing this reduction do not concern us here. It is, however, clear that the reduction is made, for, as exchange-value, the product of highly skilled labour is equivalent, in definite proportions, to the product of simple average labour....*

> *The determination of exchange-value by labour time, moreover, presupposes that the <u>same amount</u> of labour is materialized in a particular commodity..., irrespective of whether it is the work of A or B, that is to say, different individuals expend equal amounts of labour-time to produce use-values which are qualitatively and quantitatively equal. In other words, it is assumed that the labour-time contained in a commodity is the labour-time <u>necessary</u> for its production, namely the labour-time required, under the generally prevailing conditions of production, to produce another unit of the same commodity.*[52]

Marx stated this same principle, in similar terms, in Volume One of *Capital*. And as previously, he appealed to the every day activity of the market as proof that such reductions of complex to simple labor took place.

> *Skilled labour counts only as simple labour intensified, or rather, as multiplied simple labour, a given quantity of skilled being considered equal to a greater quantity of simple labour. Experience shows that this reduction is constantly being made. A commodity may be the product of the most skilled labour, but its value, by equating it to the product of simple unskilled labour, represents a definite quantity of the latter labour alone. The different proportions in which different sorts of labour are reduced to unskilled labour as their standard, are*

> *established by a social process that goes on behind the backs of the producers,*
> *and, consequently, appear to be fixed by custom.*[53]

By subjecting his labor-time standard to skill and intensity multipliers, which were obtained by taking observed market values and then reducing one to a multiple of another, Marx rendered his labor-time standard empirically unfalsifiable. Böhm-Bawerk justly ridiculed Marx for this retreat into circular logic:

> *The naivety of this theoretical juggle is almost stupefying. That a day's*
> *labour of a sculptor may be considered equal to five days' labour of a miner*
> *in many respects—for instance, in money valuation—there can be no doubt.*
> *But that twelve hours' labour of a sculptor actually are sixty hours' common*
> *labour no one will maintain. Now in questions of theory...it is not a matter*
> *of what fictions men may set up, but of what actually is. For theory the day's*
> *production of the sculptor is, and remains, the product of one day's labour,*
> *and if a good which is the product of one day's labour, is worth as much*
> *as another which is the product of five days' labour, men may invent what*
> *fictions they please; there is here an exception from the rule asserted, that*
> *the exchange value of goods is regulated by the amount of human labour*
> *incorporated in them.*[54]

Actually, the variation in the value of the product based on qualities of labor does *not* constitute an exception to the regulation of value by "the amount of human labour incorporated in them," but only indicates that "amount" of labor is not the same as its *duration*.

At any rate, the only way to make such a reduction *without* circularity, by market forces, would be by reference to some feature common to both "complex" and "simple" labor, in terms of which they can be compared on a common scale: i.e., the subjective disutility experienced by laborers as participants in the labor market (including the past disutility involved in learning particular skills). And Marx rejected any such subjective factor as a quantifier of labor.

Since Marx refused to establish the labor theory on any alternative causal mechanism like the psychology of economic actors, he was left as a result with only a general law, unverifiable and asserted in circular form, with no independent reference point to explain it.

Smith, on the other hand, started out with subjective "toil and trouble" as his standard for the labor theory of value. In contrast to Marx, his labor-time standard in the celebrated "deer and beaver" model of primitive exchange was a deliberate simplification; he assumed, for the purpose of illustration, that labor was of equal intensity. But he quickly passed on to the assumption that, while commodities exchanged according to quantity of labor ("[e]*qual quantities of labour, at all times and places, may be said to be of equal value to the labourer*"[55]) quantities of labor were by no means necessarily compared in units of time. And his qualification "*to the labourer*" makes it clear that the laborer's subjective perception of the disutility of labor was the basis of exchange-value.

In a deservedly famous passage, Smith made the "higgling and bargaining" of the market the mechanism by which the comparative value of different acts of labor was established.

> *It is often difficult to ascertain the proportion between two different quantities of labour. The time spent in two different sorts of work will not always alone determine this proportion. The different degrees of hardship endured, and of ingenuity exercised, must likewise be taken into account. There may be more labour in an hour's hard work than in two hour's easy business; or in an hour's application to a trade which it cost ten years' labour to learn, than in a month's industry at an ordinary and obvious employment. But it is not easy to find any accurate measure either of hardship or ingenuity. In exchanging, indeed, the different productions of different sorts of labour for one another, some allowance is commonly made for both. It is adjusted, however, not by any accurate measure, but by the higgling and bargaining of the market, according to that sort of rough equality which, though not exact, is sufficient to carry on the business of common life.*[56]

And note that, unlike Marx, who treated the assignment of value to different qualities of labor as an abstract social process, going on "behind the laborer's back," and without any apparent reference to his desires, Smith made constant reference to such subjective concepts as "hardship," the "long application" or "ease and cheapness" involved in learning a trade, etc.:

> *If the one species of labour should be more severe than the other, some allowance will naturally be made for this superior hardship; and the produce of one hour's labour in the one way may frequently exchange for that of two hours' labour in the other.*

> *Or if the one species of labour requires an uncommon degree of dexterity and ingenuity, the esteem which men have for such talents will naturally give a value to their produce, superior to what would be due to the time employed about it. Such talents can seldom be acquired but in consequence of long application, and the superior value of their produce may frequently be no more than a reasonable compensation for the time and labour which must be spent in acquiring them.*[57]

Unlike Marx's concept of exchange, which can be parodied as an "outward and visible sign" of the mystical phenomenon of social labor, Smith's labor market was the cumulative outcome of countless individual acts of exchange. Smith always went back to the worker's perception, and the need for "compensation" to persuade him, as an economic actor, to bring the product of his labor to market. For Smith, the "higgling and bargaining" of the market would result in wages tending toward a balance between the advantages and disadvantages in various lines of work, so that pay would be distributed according to the net disutility of work.[58]

One assumption not properly addressed by Smith was that, for such "higgling and bargaining" to distribute wages equitably according to laborers' subjective feelings of disutility, they had to be in a position of equality with one another and with their employers. Unequal exchange would force laborers to sell their labor for less than what would be necessary to compensate their disutility in a free market. The intervention of the state, by creating unequal exchange between laborer and capitalist, results in workers selling their labor in a buyer's market, and in Marx's famous difference between the value of labor-power as a commodity and the value of labor's product.

This question was explicitly addressed by Hodgskin, in his own version of the "toil and trouble" standard. In *Labour Defended Against the Claims of Capital*, he argued that the State's interference in the free market, on behalf of employers, was the reason labor received less than its full product in wages. Hodgskin was one of the earliest writers to use the term "capitalism," and may indeed have been the first to coin it. By "capitalism," he meant a system of privilege in which the State enabled the owners of capital to draw monopoly returns on it, in the same sense that the feudal ruling class was able to draw monopoly returns on land; or, as left-Rothbardian Samuel Konkin put it, "Capitalism is state rule by and for those who own large amounts of capital."[59]

But in a genuinely free market, labor would receive its full product in wages. And this product would be distributed among laborers, through the "higgling" process, in accordance to their respective toil and trouble.

> *But though this* [that the whole produce of labor ought to belong to the laborer], *as a general proposition, is quite evident, and quite true, there is a difficulty, in its practical application, which no individual can surmount. There is no principle or rule, as far as I know, for dividing the produce of joint labour among the different individuals who concur in production, but the judgment of the individuals themselves; that judgment depending on the value men may set on different species of labour can never be known, nor can any rule be given for its application by any single person....*

....Wherever the division of labour is introduced..., the judgment of other men intervenes before he labourer can realise his earnings, and there is no longer any thing which we can call the natural reward of individual labour.... Between the commencement of any joint operation,...and the division of its product among the different persons whose combined exertions have produced it, the judgment of men must intervene several times, and the question is, how much of this joint product should go to each of the individuals whose united labours produce it?

I know of no way of deciding this but by leaving it to be settled by the unfettered judgments of the labourers themselves. If all kinds of labour were perfectly free..., there would be no difficulty on this point, and the wages of individual labour would be justly settled by what Dr Smith calls the "higgling of the market."[60]

Of course, this same process applies to the higgling of artisans and independent producers, who exchange their products likewise according to their subjective feelings of disutility. The general principle is that all of society's product, in a free market, will go to labor; and that it will be apportioned among laborers according to their respective toil and trouble. Those who find the average market compensation for a particular form of labor insufficient compensation for their subjective feeling of disutility, will leave it for some other kind of work. And likewise, those who consider the compensation more than sufficient will gravitate toward that kind of work. And the average rate of compensation will thus be adjusted to the level necessary to equate the number of people supplying a particular form of labor to the effective demand at that wage.

Franz Oppenheimer, a later free market socialist, described the process in a slightly different manner: under the inducements of a truly free labor market, labor would distribute itself among employments until incomes became "equal"—in our terms, equal in relation to given quantities of subjectively perceived effort.[61] Oppenheimer, in "A Post-Mortem on Cambridge Economics," quoted with approval Adam Smith's claim that "[t]*he whole of the advantages and disadvantages of the different employments of labour and stock must, in the same neighbourhood, be either perfectly equal or continually tending to equality.*" He also quoted, with like approval, Johann Heinrich von Thuenen's posited equilibrium at which "*labor of equal quality is equally rewarded in all branches of production....*"[62]

The neo-Ricardians Dobb and Meek, among others, have criticized a "toil and trouble" LTV as creating an opening for a Marshallian treatment: that is, consolidating effort with the disutility of "waiting" or "abstinence" as simply one element of "real cost." Ricardo and Marx, in contrast, properly conceived labor objectively as *"the expenditure of a given quantum of human energy,"*[63] Conceived as disutility, however, it was inevitable

> that the very juxtaposition of labour (which Ricardo had always regarded as something objective) and abstinence (which had necessarily to be regarded as something subjective) must have encouraged the growing tendency to conceive economic categories in subjective terms, in abstraction from the relations of production....[64]

And a theory of profits as the reward for "abstinence," to be incorporated into a "real cost" theory, required labor to be recast theoretically in purely subjective terms.

> *"Abstinence"* is capable of being defined, it is true, objectively in terms of the things abstained from; but such abstaining could have no significance as a cost—no more than any other act of free exchange—unless one were to suppose that some special "pain" to the owner was involved in parting with these things. And if "abstinence," as the subjective equivalent of profit, was to be conceived in a psychological sense, then so presumably must labour be: labour as a cost for which wages were paid by being regarded not as a human activity, involving a given expenditure of physical energy, but as the strength of the psychological disinclination to work. Abstraction was to be made of human activity, its characteristics and its relationships, and only the reflection of them in the mind to be taken as the data for economic interpretation.
>
> Already among previous writers there had been signs of an inclination, if shown only in ambiguity, to conceive the notion of "real cost" as something subjective rather than objective. Adam Smith had used the phrase "toil and trouble"....[65]

But on closer inspection, this vulnerability does not exist in any legitimate sense. It would exist only if the marginalists' equation of the capitalist's sacrifice to that of the laborer is a valid one. And labor, we have already seen Dobb himself to have acknowledged, is a "cost" in a unique sense. No system of "real cost" that puts the "sacrifice" or "abstinence" of a capitalist in the same category as positive human effort, can stand up to critical evaluation. Positive human effort is a sacrifice in an absolute sense; whereas the "sacrifices" of the capitalist and landlord are so only in a relative sense.

> The essential dualism of this theory of real cost was admitted by Marshall when, in an article in 1876, he referred to the fact that it was only possible to measure "an effort and an abstinence...in terms of some common unit" through the medium of some artificial mode of measuring them"—namely,

through their market-values.... This difficulty he considered to apply similarly to the measurement of "two diverse efforts". While the difficulty in this latter case is much <u>less</u> than in the case of two quite dissimilar things such as "effort" and "abstinence", it remains a much greater problem when effort is conceived in subjective terms than when it is conceived objectively in terms of output of physical energy.[66]

The treatment of labor as an "output of physical energy" is a recurring theme in Dobb, appearing in several block quotes in this chapter. But he does not say *why* the *"objective output of human energy"* should create exchange value, except for disutility to the laborer.

After all, in the end, what valid basis can any labor theory of value have except the disutility of labor as experienced by the laborer himself? It should be self-evident that the reason labor is unique in creating exchange-value is that the laborer (unlike the land, natural forces, etc.) is unique in having to be persuaded that *it is worth his while* to bring goods to market. To use Dobb's own words in the quote above against him, labor "as a human activity" must be characterized by something more than "a given expenditure of physical energy," since even a lump of coal is capable of the latter. The reason the human demands payment for his "expenditure of physical energy" and the lump of coal doesn't, is that he feels somewhat differently about the expenditure than does the lump of coal.

This relationship between subjective cost as a source of exchange-value, and the resulting lack of exchange-value on the part of natural goods (not counting the effort of appropriation), was widely recognized among the classical political economists. Jean-Baptiste Say, for example, referred to the *"productive agency of natural agents,"* such as the fertility of soil, the biological potential of seed, and the sum total of the *"process performed by the soil, the air, the rain, and the sun, wherein mankind bears no part, but which nevertheless concurs in the new product that will be acquired at the season of harvest...."*[67] But he went on to undercut, in a later passage, any implication this might have for the exchange-value of natural agents as such:

Labour of an unproductive kind, that is to say, such as does not contribute to the raising of the products of some branch of industry or other, is seldom undertaken voluntarily; for labour...implies trouble, and trouble, and trouble so bestowed could yield no compensation or resulting benefit....[68]

This strongly implied that labor was unique, as a factor of production, in the need to be persuaded to contribute its own powers to the production process. And from this, it would seem to follow that natural

agents, which experienced no such disutility and therefore needed no
such persuasion, lacked the basis of exchange-value:

> Of these wants, some are satisfied by the gratuitous agency of natural objects;
> as of air, water, or solar light. These may be denominated <u>natural</u> wealth,
> because they are the spontaneous offering of nature; and as such, mankind is
> not called upon to earn them by any sacrifice or exertion whatever; for which
> reason, they are never possessed of any exchangeable value.[69]

Ricardo made explicit the implications of these latter passages, in
denying that the *"productive agency of natural agents"* was a source of
exchange-value.

> In contradiction to the opinion of Adam Smith, M. Say, in the fourth
> chapter, speaks of the value which is given to commodities by natural agents,
> such as the sun, the air, the pressure of the atmosphere, &c., which are
> sometimes substituted for the labour of man, and sometimes concur with him
> in producing. But these natural agents, though they add greatly to value
> in use, never add exchangeable value...to a commodity: as soon as...you
> oblige natural agents to do the work which was before done by man, the
> exchangeable value of such work falls accordingly.... M. Say constantly
> overlooks the essential difference that there is between value in use, and value
> in exchange.
>
> M. Say accuses Dr. Smith of having overlooked the value which is given to
> commodities by natural agents, and by machinery, because he considered
> that the value of all things was derived from the labour of man; but it does
> not appear to me, that this charge is made out; for Adam Smith nowhere
> undervalues the services which these natural agents and machinery perform
> for us...; but as they perform their work gratuitously, as nothing is paid for
> the use of air, of heat, and of water, the assistance which they afford us adds
> nothing to value in exchange.[70]

Of course, purely natural goods are quite rare. Most gifts of nature
require some human labor to be made usable; and to that extent, they
acquire exchange-value. Even spontaneously arising natural goods like
wild honey, fruit, etc., John Stuart Mill wrote, required *"a considerable
quantity of labour..., not for the purpose of creating, but of finding and
appropriating them. In all but these few...cases, the objects supplied by nature
are only instrumental to human wants, after having undergone some degree of
transformation by human exertion."*[71]

Natural goods do, at times, obtain exchange-value from scarcity
alone, and not just from the labor of alteration or appropriation. Böhm-
Bawerk dismissed as "simply false" Rodbertus' claim that natural goods
did not possess economic value: *"Even purely natural goods have a place in*

economic consideration, provided only they are scarce as compared with the need for them."[72]

John Stuart Mill, earlier, had written of the difference in degree of scarcity between various natural goods, and their resulting economic value:

> *Of natural powers, some are unlimited, others limited in quantity. By an unlimited quantity is of course not meant literally, but practically unlimited: a quantity beyond the use of which can in any, or at least in present circumstances, be made of it. Land is, in some newly settled countries, practically unlimited in quantity: there is more than can be used by the existing population of the country, or by any accession likely to be made of it for generations to come. But even here, land favourably situated with regard to markets or means of carriage, is generally limited in quantity: there is not so much of it as persons would gladly occupy and cultivate, or otherwise turn to use. In all old countries, land capable of cultivation, land at least of any tolerable fertility, must be ranked among agents limited in quantity...*
>
> *.... [S]o long as the quantity of a natural agent is practically unlimited, it cannot, unless susceptible of artificial monopoly, bear any value in the market, since no one will give anything for what can be obtained gratis.*[73]

But that leaves open the question, as Mill's last sentence suggests, of how much of this scarcity is natural, and how much is conventional or legal. (This latter question we will study in much greater depth in our examination, in a later chapter, of the political appropriation of land.) Mill distinguished between natural and artificial scarcity in a hypothetical case involving air:

> *It is possible to imagine circumstances in which air would be a part of wealth.... [I]f from any revolution in nature the atmosphere became too scanty for the consumption, or could be monopolized, air might acquire a very high marketable value. In such a case, the possession of it, beyond his own wants, would be, to its owner, wealth; and the general wealth of mankind might at first sight appear to be increased, by what would be so great a calamity to them. The error would be in not considering, that however rich the possessor of air might become at the expense of the rest of the community, all persons else would be poorer by all that they were compelled to pay for what they had before obtained without payment.*[74]

In any case, the exchange-value accruing to natural goods as such is, along with other scarcity-rents, a secondary deviation from the law of labor-value. In the case of natural resources made artificially scarce by political appropriation, absentee landlordism, etc., it is a state-enforced monopoly income. In the case of natural scarcity of the most fertile land in in the environs of a particular city, it is a spontaneously occurring scarcity rent, like differences in innate skill.

This subjective emphasis of labor as disutility received, at the same time, criticisms from the right. Rothbard treated Marshall's reduction of both labor disutility and "waiting" to the common denominator of "real cost," as an admission that value was purely subjective.

> *This is not to deny...that subjective costs, in the sense of opportunity costs and utilities foregone, are important in the analysis of production. In particular, the disutilities of labor and of waiting—as expressed in the time-preference ratios—determine how much of people's energies and how much of their earnings will go into the production process. This, in the broadest sense, will determine or help to determine the total supply of all goods that will be produced. But these costs are themselves subjective utilities, so that both "blades of the scissors" are governed by the subjective utility of individuals. This is a* <u>monistic</u> *and not a dualistic causal explanation....*
>
> *....The price necessary to call forth a non-specific factor is the highest price this factor can earn elsewhere—an opportunity cost.*[75]

The proper response is, "so what?" There is a great deal of difference between the formulation of a subjective mechanism by which the law of cost operates, and the relegation of value to a purely arbitrary basis on subjective utility. Both Ricardo's and Marx's versions of the labor theory at least implicitly relied on a subjective *mechanism*—after all, as we asked above, why else would labor create exchange-value, except for the fact that the laborer, unlike coal, had to be persuaded to bring his services to market? As for opportunity cost as the basis for the cost-principle, it is worth bearing in mind that "the subjective utility of individuals" is not determined in a vacuum; "the highest price [a] factor can earn elsewhere" is entirely relative, and is conditional on many things, not least among them the existence of monopoly returns enforced by the state.

Böhm-Bawerk himself suggested why a subjective approach to economics was necessary, in his comments on Sombart's contrast between the objective approach of Marx and the subjective approach of the marginalist. Böhm-Bawerk pointed out that "*the knowledge of such an objective connection, without the knowledge of the subjective links which help to form the chain of causation, is by no means the highest degree of knowledge, but that a full comprehension will only be attained by a knowledge of both the internal and external links of the chain.*" The objective and subjective approaches, therefore, were necessarily complementary. And he added, "*as a matter of opinion,*" that *it is just in the region of economics, where we have to deal so largely with conscious and calculated human action, that the first of the two sources of knowledge, the objective source, can at the best contribute a very poor and, especially when standing alone, an altogether inadequate part of the total of attainable knowledge."[76]*

So even Bohm-Bawerk understood that subjective value-judgments were not necessarily arbitrary or independent variables, but could be the mechanism through which objective factors made themselves felt in the market.

Marx himself, Bohm-Bawerk went on to charge, brought in the subjective factor as a mechanism for his labor theory, but did so only unsystematically:

Marx did not hold fast to the "objective" pale. He could not help referring to the motives of the operators as to an active force in his system. He does this pre-eminently by his appeal to "competition." Is it too much to demand that if he introduces subjective interpolations into his system they should be correct, well founded, and non-contradictory?[77]

There was a reason for Marx's ambivalence toward a subjective mechanism. Despite the spuriousness of some Marxist criticism, as we have shown above, a subjective "higgling" basis is indeed vulnerable at first glance to its own charges of unverifiability or circularity. As Dobb pointed out, making subjective disutility, effort or unpleasantness, rather than time, the basis of quantity, would make market price the only objective standard for comparing quantities of labor. Nevertheless, this vulnerability is only apparent. The difference is that, unlike Marx's ratios of simple to complex labor, we are not comparing one set of data to another in a circular process. We are first asserting, on the grounds of an axiomatic understanding of human nature, the basis of all exchange value in subjective effort; deviation from this principle, caused by scarcity rents, are a secondary phenomenon. Once this a priori principle that labor is the basis of exchange value is accepted, we go on to explain why labor's product will be distributed according to the degree of disutility of labor.

Or to approach it from the opposite direction, we can start with the law of cost as the basis of price, and from there systematically eliminate all the subordinate factors that only have a price because of artificial scarcity, leaving only labor as a creator of exchange-value in its own right (at least for the equilibrium prices of goods in elastic supply).

NOTES

1. Eugen von Böhm-Bawerk, *Capital and Interest: A Critical History of Economical Theory*, trans. William Smart (New York: Brentanno's, 1922) 338.

2. Ibid. 376.

3. Ibid. 379-80.

4. Ibid. 382-3; Eugen von Böhm-Bawerk, *Karl Marx and the Close of His System* (published in a single volume with Rudolf Hilferding, *Böhm-Bawerk's Criticism of Marx*) (New York: Augustus M. Kelley, 1945) 68-77.

5. Adam Smith, *An Inquiry Into the Nature and Causes of the Wealth of Nations* (Chicago, London, Toronto: Encyclopedia Britannica, Inc., 1952) 10.

6. Ibid. 13-4.

7. Ibid. 14.

8. Maurice Dobb, *Theories of Value and Distribution Since Adam Smith: Ideology and Economic Theory* (Cambridge: Cambridge University Press, 1973) 48.

9. Eric Roll, *A History of Economic Thought*, 3rd ed. (Englewood, N.J.: Prentice-Hall, Inc., 1956) 159.

10. David Ricardo, "Absolute Value and Exchangeable Value (A Rough Draft)," vol. 4 of Piero Sraffa ed., *The Works and Correspondence of David Ricardo* (Cambridge: Cambridge University Press, 1951) 397.

11. James Buchanan, *Cost and Choice: An Inquiry in Economic Theory*, vol. 6 of *Collected Works* (Indianapolis: Liberty Fund, 1999) 4.

12. Ludwig von Mises, *Human Action* (Chicago: Regnery, 1949, 1963, 1966) 32, 34, 38-40.

13. Ibid. 64.

14. Ibid. 867-8.

15. William Stanley Jevons, *The Theory of Political Economy*, 5th ed. (Kelley & Millman, Inc., 1957) 167.

16. Ibid. 168.

17. Ibid. 168-9.

18. Ibid. 172-4.

19. Alfred Marshall, *Principles of Economics: An Introductory Volume*, 8th ed. (New York: The MacMillan Company, 1948) 330.

20. Ibid. 65.

21. Ibid. 65n.

22. Böhm-Bawerk, *Capital and Interest* 282-3.

23. Mises, *Human Action* 131-2.

24. Karl Marx and Friedrich Engels, *Capital* vol. 1, vol. 35 of Marx and Engels *Collected Works* (New York: International Publishers, 1996)

56n; see also Marx, *Grundrisse*, vol. 28 of Marx and Engels *Collected Works* (New York: International Publishers, 1986) 529-33.

25. Mises, *Human Action* 589-91.

26. Murray Rothbard, *Man, Economy, and State: A Treatise on Economic Principles* (Auburn University, Alabama: Ludwig von Mises Institute, 1993) 38-9.

27. Ibid. 39.

28. Maurice Dobb, *Political Economy and Capitalism: Some Essays in Economic Tradition*, 2nd rev. ed. (London: Routledge & Kegan Paul Ltd, 1940, 1960) 19-20.

29. See Buchanan's *Cost and Choice*, op. cit., for an excellent historical survey of this line of thought.

30. Dobb, *Political Economy and Capitalism* 141-2.

31. Ibid. 147-8.

32. Ibid. 143n.

33. Ibid. 66.

34. Karl Marx and Friedrich Engels, *Capital* vol. 3, vol. 37 of Marx and Engels *Collected Works* (New York: International Publishers, 1998) 811.

35. Ibid. 817.

36. Dobb, *Theories of Value and Distribution* 169.

37. Ibid. 33-4.

38. Ibid. 172-3.

39. Ibid. 175.

40. Dobb, *Political Economy and Capitalism* 49-50.

41. Ibid. 22.

42. Karl Marx, *Theories of Surplus Value*, vol. 32 of Marx and Engels *Collected Works* (New York: International Publishers, 1989) 398.

43. Ibid. 450.

44. Ibid. 514.

45. Benjamin Tucker, "Shall the Transfer Papers Be Taxed?" *Liberty* August 18, 1888, in Benjamin Tucker, *Instead of a Book, By a Man Too Busy to Write One*, Gordon Press Facsimile (New York: 1897/1973) 214.

46. Benjamin Tucker, "Should Labor Be Paid or Not?" *Liberty* April 28, 1888, in Tucker, *Instead of a Book* 403.

47. Ronald Meek, *Studies in the Labour Theory of Value*, 2nd ed. (New York and London: Monthly Review Press, 1956) 294-6.

48. R. H. Tawney, *Religion and the Rise of Capitalism* (New York: Harcourt, Brace and Company, Inc., 1926) 130-1.

49. Gary Elkin, *Mutual Banking*.

50. David Ricardo, *Principles of Political Economy and Taxation*, 3rd ed. (London: John Murray, Albemarle Street, 1821), vol. 1 of Piero

Sraffa, ed., *The Works and Correspondence of David Ricardo* (Cambridge: Cambridge University Press, 1951) 20.

51. Karl Marx, *The Poverty of Philosophy*, vol. 6 of Marx and Engels *Collected Works* (New York: International Publishers, 1976) 126.

52. Karl Marx, *A Contribution to the Critique of Political Economy*, vol. 29 of Marx and Engels *Collected Works* (New York: International Publishers, 1987) 271-3.

53. Marx and Engels, *Capital* vol. 1: 54.

54. Böhm-Bawerk, *Capital and Interest* 384-5; see similar criticism in Böhm-Bawerk, *Karl Marx and the Close of His System*, 80-5.

55. Smith, *Wealth of Nations* 14.

56. Ibid. 13.

57. Ibid. 20.

58. Ibid. 48-9.

59. "Bad Capitalists Good Entrepreneurs," Message 3758 (July 24, 2000) LeftLibertarian@Yahoogroups.com. http://groups.yahoo.com/group/LeftLibertarian/message/3758 Captured August 4, 2004.

60. Thomas Hodgskin, *Labour Defended Against the Claims of Capital* (New York: Augustus M. Kelley, 1963 (1823)) 83-6.

61. Eduard Heimann, "Franz Oppenheimer's Economic Ideas," *Social Research* February 1949 34.

62. Franz Oppenheimer, "A Post Mortem on Cambridge Economics (Part I)," *The American Journal of Economics and Sociology* 1942/43 373-4.

63. Dobb, *Political Economy and Capitalism* 13.

64. Meek, *Studies in the Labour Theory of Value* 246.

65. Dobb, *Political Economy and Capitalism* 140-1.

66. Ibid. 144n.

67. John-Baptiste Say, *A Treatise on Political Economy*, trans. C. R. Prinsep from 4th ed. (Philadelphia: John Grigg, 1827) 14.

68. Ibid. 26.

69. Ibid. 237.

70. Ricardo, *Principles of Political Economy and Taxation* 285-7.

71. John Stuart Mill, *Principles of Political Economy: With Some of Their Applications to Social Philosophy*, vol. 2 of *Collected Works of John Stuart Mill* (Toronto: University of Toronto Press, 1965) 25.

72. Böhm-Bawerk, *Capital and Interest* 338.

73. Mill, *Principles of Political Economy* 29-30.

74. Ibid. 8.

75. Rothbard, *Man, Economy, and State* 307-8.

76. Böhm-Bawerk, *Karl Marx and the Close of His System* 115.

77. Ibid. 116.

Chapter Three
Time Preference and the Labor Theory of Value

In the last chapter, we referred to one valid marginalist criticism of the Labor Theory: its lack of an explicit mechanism. But there is another valid contribution of the marginalists, or more specifically the Austrians, that must be taken into account by any modern Labor Theory, if it is to have any claim to relevance. That contribution is time preference theory.

The principle of time-preference was first stated clearly by Eugen von Böhm-Bawerk. After a painstaking historical survey of past theories of interest—not only the "productivity" and "abstinence" theories of the later classical political economists (or vulgar political economists, as Marx would have it), but the exploitation theories of Rodbertus, Marx, and the other socialists—he set forth his own explanation:

> _The loan is a real exchange of present goods against future goods_.... [P]_resent goods invariably possess a greater value than future goods of the same number and kind, and therefore a definite sum of present goods can, as a rule, only be purchased by a larger sum of future goods. Present goods possess an agio in future goods. This agio is interest. It is not a separate equivalent for a separate and durable use of the loaned goods, for that is inconceivable; it is a part equivalent of the loaned sum, kept separate for practical reasons. The replacement of the capital + the interest constitutes the full equivalent._[1]

This was, he argued, incompatible with the labor theory of value: "_Logically carried out, this_ [the labor theory] _could leave no room for the phenomenon of interest._"[2]

This is as good a place as any, before we go to the more central issues of time-preference's relation to our labor theory developed in this book, to examine another side issue: the extent to which time-preference is mutually exclusive of other defenses of interest and profit, as Austrians have claimed. Böhm-Bawerk, of course, stressed both the uniqueness of his contribution and the inadequacy of earlier attempts to justify interest. He was especially dismissive of Senior's abstinence theory, pointing out that Lasalle was right in arguing

> that the existence and height of interest by no means invariably correspond with the existence and the height of a "sacrifice of abstinence." Interest, in exceptional cases, is received where there has been no individual sacrifice of abstinence. High interest is often got where the sacrifice of the abstinence is very trifling—as in the case of Lasalle's millionaire—and "low interest" is often got where the sacrifice entailed by the abstinence is very great. The hardly saved sovereign which the domestic servant puts in the savings bank bears, absolutely and relatively, less interest than the lightly spared thousands which the millionaire puts to fructify in debenture and mortgage funds. These phenomena fit badly into a theory which explains interest quite universally as a "wage of abstinence."....[3]

In response to the idea that abstinence from consumption was a positive "sacrifice" deserving of compensation in its own right, Böhm-Bawerk proposed this case:

> I work for a whole day at the planting of fruit trees in the expectation that they will bear fruit for me in ten years. In the night following comes a storm and entirely destroys the whole plantation. How great is the sacrifice which I have made…in vain? I think every one will say—a lost day of work, and nothing more. And now I put the question, is my sacrifice in any way greater that the storm does not come, and that the trees, without any further exertion on my part, bear fruit in ten years? If I do a day's work and have to wait ten years to get a return from it, do I sacrifice more than if I do a day's work, and, by reason of the destructive storm, must wait to all eternity for its return?[4]

In response to Cournelle's similar "sacrifice" theory of interest, Böhm-Bawerk joked, "one might say that Cournelle would have had almost as much justification, theoretically speaking, if he had pronounced the bodily labour of pocketing the interest, or of cutting the coupons, to be the ground and basis of interest."[5]

The logical response to Böhm-Bawerk's critique, from the point of view of Marshall's "real cost" theory, is to retreat to defining "sacrifice" in terms of "opportunity cost." And that is exactly what Marshall did, as we saw in the previous chapter: the "sacrifice" of the landlord and capitalist was simply the forebearance to consume what was in one's power to consume. And in denying this opportunity cost as an absolute sacrifice in the same sense as labor, Böhm-Bawerk laid the ground for Dobb's demolition of "abstinence" as a "sacrifice" comparable to labor.

In any case, regardless of its uniqueness as a subjective mechanism, Böhm-Bawerk's time preference theory (that a smaller amount now is worth a greater amount later) bears, in practical terms, a close resemblance to the "abstinence" of Nassau Senior and Alfred Marshall. All these theories amount to ascribing a value-creating quality to time: to make it worth my while to abstain from present consumption, I must receive a greater amount in the future. And all of them are based on some form of pain or hardship entailed in foregoing present for the sake of future consumption. It makes more sense to treat them as a cluster of related theories than as mutually exclusive rivals.

Murray Rothbard, the most famous recent inheritor of the Austrian mantle, was especially prone to blur the distinction between time-preference and "waiting":

> *What has been the contribution of these product-owners, or "capitalists," to the production process? It is this: the saving and restriction of consumption, instead of being done by the owners of land and labor, has been done by the* <u>*capitalists*</u>. *The capitalists originally saved, say, 95 ounces of gold which they could have then spent on consumers' goods. They refrained from doing so, however, and, instead, <u>advanced</u> the money to the original owners of the factors. They <u>paid</u> the latter for their services while they were working, thus advancing them money before the product was actually produced and sold to the consumers. The capitalists, therefore, made an essential contribution to production. They relieved the owners of the original factors from the necessity of sacrificing present goods and waiting for future goods....*
>
> *Even if financial returns and consumer demand are certain, <u>the capitalists are still providing present goods to the owners of labor and land</u> and thus relieving them of the burden of waiting until the future goods are produced and finally transformed into consumers' goods.*[6]

Roger W. Garrison argued, from such evidence, that the concept of "waiting" as a factor of production was compatible with the time-preference of Mises and Rothbard.

> *Neither Mises nor Rothbard has specifically addressed the question of waiting as a factor of production, but passages can be found in the writings of each suggesting that the time-preference view and the waiting-as-a-factor view are to some extent compatible.*[7]

To return to our main line of discussion: there has been a great reluctance among Austrians, generally speaking, to deal explicitly with the comparative roles of time-preference and institutional factors as influences on interest rates, or with the extent to which the steepness of time-preference can be altered by institutional factors. At times, the Austrians explicitly deny that institutional factors have no influence on interest.

For example, Böhm-Bawerk denied that the difference in value between a given amount of money today and the same amount five years from now is, *"as might be thought, a result of social institutions which have created interest and fixed it at 5 per cent."*[8] Time preference alone is the reason for the relative low value of production (future) goods, compared to finished (present) goods:

> *This, and nothing else, is the foundation of the so-called "cheap" buying of production instruments, and especially of labour, which the Socialists rightly explain as the source of profit on capital, but wrongly interpret, in round terms, as the result of a robbery or exploitation of the working classes by the propertied classes.*[9]

At times, however, Böhm-Bawerk moderated this stance with the concession that monopoly and other forms of exploitation might, in certain cases, increase the rate of profit at the expense of labor.

> *Now, of course, the circumstances unfavourable to buyers may be corrected by active competition among sellers.... But, every now and then, something will suspend the capitalists' competition, and then those unfortunates, whom fate has thrown on a local market ruled by monopoly, are delivered over to the discretion of the adversary. Hence direct usury, of which the poor borrower is only too often the victim; and hence the low wages forcibly exploited from the workers....*

> *It is not my business to put excesses like these, where there actually is exploitation, under the aegis of that favourable opinion I pronounced above as to the essence of interest. But, on the other hand, I must say with all emphasis, that what we might stigmatise as "usury" does not consist in the obtaining of a gain out of a loan, or out of the buying of labour, but in the immoderate extent of that gain.... Some gain or profit on capital there would be if there were no compulsion on the poor, and no monopolising of property; and some gain there must be. It is only the height of this gain where, in particular cases, it reaches an excess, that is open to criticism, and, of course, the very unequal conditions of wealth in our modern communities bring us unpleasantly near the danger of exploitation and of usurious rates of interest.*[10]

So here Böhm-Bawerk acknowledged, at least in principle, that institutional factors could affect interest rates, and that the distribution of wealth could affect the steepness of time-preference.

Although he made this concession in principle, Böhm-Bawerk for the most part stuck to an ahistorical treatment of the actual origins of the distribution of wealth, taking as a given that the propertied classes were in a position of having surplus property for investment as a result of their past thrift or productivity. Often he did not address the issue at all, but simply assumed the present distribution of property as his starting point.

> *What, then, are the capitalists as regards the community?—In a word, they are merchants who have present goods to sell. They are the fortunate possessors of a stock of goods which they do not require for the personal needs of the moment. They exchange their stock, therefore, into future goods of some form or another....*[11]

Böhm-Bawerk was far too modest on their behalf, in ascribing this possession of present goods to "fortune." Far from being, as a class, the passive recipients of mere good luck, the capitalists have MADE their own luck. And the history of this, their good fortune, is written in letters of blood and fire.

In keeping with this modesty, Böhm-Bawerk resorted to a Robinsonade on the accumulation of capital.

> *In our science there are three views in circulation as to the formation of capital. One finds its origin in Saving, a second in Production, and a third in both together. Of these the third enjoys the widest acceptance, and it is also the correct one.*[12]

He then illustrated the principle with the example of a solitary man saving the product of his labor and living off the surplus food while he crafted a bow and arrows and other tools. From this island scenario, he went on to society in the large, describing how a nation of ten million saved so many millions of its ten million labor years annually.[13] That those actually deferring consumption from the proceeds of their labor might not be the same ones investing those savings, or reaping the fruits of investment, or that they might have no say in the matter, was an issue set aside entirely—perhaps as complicating the picture unnecessarily.

The propertyless laboring classes, like the capitalists, just happened to be there; perhaps, like Topsy, they "just growed."

> *Over and against this supply of present goods stands, as Demand:—*
> *1. An enormous number of wage-earners who cannot employ their labour remuneratively by working on their own account, and are accordingly, as a body, inclined and ready to sell the future product of their labour for a considerably less amount of present goods....*

2. A number of independent producers, themselves working, who by an advance of present goods are put in a position to prolong the process, and thus increase the productiveness of their personal labour...

3. A small number of persons who, on account of urgent personal wants, seek credit for purposes of consumption, and are also ready to pay an agio for present goods.[14]

It was this inability of the first group to employ their labor remuneratively by working on their own account, Böhm-Bawerk explained, that made them dependent on the capitalist. Their lack of resources to tide them over until the completion of long-term production processes was the "sole" reason for their dependence.

...in the loss of time which is, as a rule, bound up with the capitalist process, lies the sole ground of that much-talked-of and much-deplored dependence of labourer on capitalist.... It is only because the labourers cannot wait till the roundabout process...delivers up its products ready for consumption, that they become economically dependent on the capitalists who already hold in their possession what we have called "intermediate products."[15]

Why the laborers might lack individual or collective property in their means of production, or be unable through cooperative effort to mobilize their own "labor fund" in the production interval, Böhm-Bawerk did not say. Why the capitalists happened to be in possession of so much superfluous wealth, he likewise did not speculate. That the bulk of a nation's productive resources should be concentrated in the hands of a few people, rather than those of the laboring majority, is by no means a self-evident necessity. Böhm-Bawerk himself accepted it as altogether unremarkable. For the cause of such an odd situation, therefore, we will have to look elsewhere than in his work.

The answer lies not in economic theory, but in history. The existing distribution of property among economic classes, about which Böhm-Bawerk was so coy, is the historic outcome of State violence. We shall examine, in a later chapter, the process of primitive accumulation by which the laboring majority has been forcibly robbed of its property in the means of production, transformed into a propertyless laboring class, and since then prevented by law and privilege from obtaining unfettered access to capital.

It will suffice for the moment to say that, although time preference no doubt holds true universally even when property is evenly distributed, the present after-effects of primitive accumulation render time-preference much steeper than it would otherwise be. Time preference is not a constant. It is skewed much more to the present for a laborer without independent access to the means of production, or to subsistence or security. Even the vulgar political economists recognized that the degree of poverty among the laboring classes determined their level of wages, and hence the level of profit.[16]

But what of the residuum of time preference that would exist even in a genuine market economy, without legal privilege to capital, in which the producers retained their own means of production? How can the principle of time preference be reconciled to the labor theory of value?

Even if today's labor is exchanged for tomorrow's labor at a premium, it is still an exchange of labor. Maurice Dobb, for instance, suggested that time-preference might be treated as a scarcity rent on present labor.

> It amounted to an explanation in terms of the relative scarcity, or limited application, of labour applied to particular uses—namely, in the form of stored-up labour embodied in technical processes involving a lengthy "period of production"; a scarcity which persisted by reason of the short-sightedness of human nature. As a result of this under-development of the productive resources, the ownership of money-capital, which in existing society provided the only means by which lengthy production-processes were able to be undertaken, carried with it the power to exact a rent of this scarcity. As a landlord could exact the price of a scarcity imposed by objective nature, so, it would seem, the capitalist could exact the price of a scarcity the subjective nature of man.[17]

Dobb did not made an adequate distinction between the scarcity of present versus future labor that exists naturally as a result of the human preference for present consumption versus postponement; and the artificial scarcity created by a certain class' monopoly of access to the means of production. But even assuming a market economy based on producers' cooperatives, the point is valid. When labor abstains from present consumption to accumulate its own capital, time-preference is simply an added form of disutility of present labor, as opposed to future labor. It is just another factor in the "higgling of the market," by which labor's product is allocated among laborers.

In an economy of distributive property ownership, as would have existed had the free market been allowed to develop without large-scale robbery, time-preference would affect only laborers' calculations of their own present consumption versus their own future consumption. All consumption, present or future, would be beyond question the result of labor. It is only in a capitalist (i.e., statist) economy that a propertied class, with superfluous wealth far beyond its ability to consume, can keep itself in idleness by lending the means of subsistence to producers in return for a claim on future output.

NOTES

1. Eugen von Böhm-Bawerk, *Capital and Interest: A Critical History of Economical Theory*, trans. William Smart (New York: Brentanno's, 1922) 259.

2. Ibid. 269.

3. Ibid. 277.

4. Ibid. 281.

5. Ibid. 303.

6. Murray Rothbard, *Man, Economy, and State: A Treatise on Economic Principles* (Auburn University, Alabama: Ludwig von Mises Institute, 1993) 294-95, 298.

7. Roger W. Garrison, "Professor Rothbard and the Theory of Interest," in Walter Block and Llewellyn H. Rockwell, Jr., eds., *Man, Economy and Liberty: Essays in Honor of Murray N. Rothbard* (Auburn, Ala.: Auburn University Press, 1988) 49.

8. Böhm-Bawerk, *Capital and Interest* 346.

9. Eugen von Böhm-Bawerk, *The Positive Theory of Capital*, trans. William Smart (London and New York: MacMillan and Co., 1891) 301.

10. Ibid. 361.

11. Ibid. 358.

12. Ibid. 100.

13. Ibid. 100-18.

14. Ibid. 330-1.

15. Ibid. 83.

16. Michael Perelman, *Classical Political Economy: Primitive Accumulation and the Social Division of Labor* (Totowa, N.J.: Rowman & Allanheld; London: F. Pinter, 1984, c 1983) 18-9.

17. Maurice Dobb, *Political Economy and Capitalism: Some Essays in Economic Tradition*. 2nd rev. ed. (London: Routledge & Kegan Paul Ltd, 1940, 1960) 154.

Part Two
Capitalism and the State: Past, Present,
and Future

Introduction to Part Two
Exploitation and the Political Means

The question remains: if labor is the source of normal exchange-value for reproducible goods, and the natural wage of labor in a free market is its full product, what is the explanation for profit in "actually existing capitalism"?

A central point of contention between Marx and the utopians was the extent to which the labor theory of value was a description of existing commodity exchange, or a prescription for rules of exchange in a reformed system. Marx criticized the utopians for erecting the law of value into a normative standard for a utopian society, rather than a law descriptive of existing capitalism. For him, the law of value described the process of exchange under capitalism as it was; the law of value was fully compatible with the existence of exploitation. His generalizations about exploitation assumed that commodities were exchanged according to their labor value; far from making profits impossible, exchange according to the law of value was presupposed as the foundation for surplus-value. Profit resulted from the difference in value between labor-power, as a commodity, and the labor-product; this was true even (or rather, especially) when all commodities exchanged at their value.

Some "utopians" (including Proudhon, the Owenites, and some Ricardian socialists), it is true, saw the labor theory as a call for a mandated set of rules (like Labor Notes, or modern proposals for government backing of a LETS system). For these, the law of value ruled out exploitation; but rather than seeing it as an automatically operating law of the market, they saw it as requiring the imposition of egalitarian "rules of the game."

But besides these two opposing theories, there was a possible third alternative that differed significantly from the first two. This third alternative considered all exploitation to be based on force; and the exploitative features of existing society to result from the intrusion of the element of coercion. Unlike utopianism, the third theory treated the law of value as something that operated automatically when not subject to interference. Unlike Marxism, it believed the unfettered operation of the law of value to be incompatible with exploitation. This school included, especially, the market-oriented Ricardian socialist Thomas Hodgskin, and the later individualist anarchists in America; they saw capitalism as exploitative to the extent that unequal exchange prevailed, under the influence of the State. Without such intervention, the normal operation of the law of value would automatically result in labor receiving its full product. For them, exploitation was not the natural outcome of a free market; the difference between the value of labor power as a commodity and the value of labor's product resulted, not from the existence of wage labor itself, but from state-imposed unequal exchange in the labor market. For them, the law of value was both the automatic mechanism by which a truly free market operated, and at the same time incompatible with exploitation.

It followed that the law of value was not something to be surpassed. Unlike the Marxists, who looked forward to an economy of abundance based on a principle of "from each according to his ability, etc.," the individualists and market Ricardians saw the link between effort and reward as fundamental to distributive justice. The defining feature of exploitation was the benefit of one party at the expense of another's labor. As Benjamin Tucker wrote in "Should Labor Be Paid or Not?"

> [Johann] *Most being a Communist, he must, to be consistent, object to the purchase or sale of anything whatever; but why he should particularly object to the purchase and sale of labor is more than I can understand. Really, in the last analysis, labor is the only thing that has any title to be bought or sold. Is there any just basis of price except cost? And is there anything that costs except labor or suffering (another name for labor)? Labor should be paid! Horrible, isn't it? Why, I thought the fact that is not paid was the whole grievance. "Unpaid labor" has been the chief complaint of all Socialists, and that labor should get its reward has been their chief contention. Suppose I had said to Kropotkin that the real question is whether Communism will permit individuals to exchange their labor or products on their own terms. Would then Most have been as shocked?....Yet in another form I said precisely that.*[1]

Given the moral basis of the labor theory of value, as understood by the petty bourgeois socialists, in the principle of self-ownership and ownership of one's labor product, it followed that payment according to work was not a holdover from capitalist society, but the rightful basis of a future socialist order. It was no more acceptable for the collective to appropriate the product of the individual's labor for general use, than for the landlord and capitalist to appropriate it for their own use.

Maurice Dobb, in his introduction to *A Contribution to the Critique of Political Economy*, pointed to the strategic difficulties presented to Marxists by this position. As exemplified by Marx's assertion in *Value, Price and Profit*, Marxists recoiled from the idea that profit was the result of unequal exchange:

> *To explain the general nature of profits, you must start from the theorem that, on an average, commodities are sold at their real value, and that profits are derived from selling them at their values, that is, in proportion to the quantity of labour realised in them. If you cannot explain profit upon this supposition, you cannot explain it at all.*[2]

"The point of this can the better be appreciated," Dobb said,

> *if it is remembered that the school of writers to whom the name of the Ricardian Socialists has been given…, who can be said to have held a "primitive" theory of exploitation, explained profit on capital as the product of superior bargaining power, lack of competition and "unequal exchanges between Capital and Labour" (this bearing analogy with Eugen Dühring's "force theory" which was castigated by Engels). This was the kind of explanation that Marx was avoiding rather than seeking. It did not make exploitation consistent with the law of value and with market competition, but explained it by departures from, or imperfections in, the latter. To it there was an easy answer from the liberal economists and free traders: namely, "join with us in demanding really free trade and then there can be no "unequal exchanges" and exploitation".*[3]

This "easy answer" was exactly the approach taken by Thomas Hodgskin and the individualist anarchists of America. The greatest of the latter, Benjamin Tucker, reproached as merely a "consistent Manchester man," wore that label as a badge of honor.

The great importance of Marx's idea of the difference between the value of labor-power and the value of labor's product, Dobb wrote,

> *lay precisely in its enabling him to show how there could be inequality and non-equivalence in "equivalent exchange"—or exploitation and appropriation of what was created by the producers consistently with the theory of value (i. e., demonstrating how "profits are derived by selling them at their values"). Labour-power, converted into a commodity by the historical process whereby a proletariat was created and from thenceforth freely bought and sold on the*

> *market, acquired a value like other commodities in terms of the amount of*
> *labour that its production (or reproduction) cost.*[4]

This leaves two questions still unresolved: 1) if the "historical process" of primitive accumulation involved the use of force, how essential was force to that process; and if force was essential to the process, does it not follow that past force, as reflected in the present distribution of property, underlies the illusion of "free contract"; 2) how is it possible for employers to consistently pay a price for labor-power less than its product, if labor is free to bargain for the best possible deal? (Recourse to vague ideas of "social power" or "market power," without an explicit examination of their nature, is not a satisfactory explanation.)

Dobb, in *Political Economy and Capitalism*, denied that exploitation of labor could take place through unequal exchange alone, in "an order of free contract." After quoting the same passage from Marx on the assumption of normal exchange values as consistent with exploitation, Dobb went on:

> *Tudor monopolies or feudal liens on the labour of others could no longer*
> *be used to explain how a class drew income without contributing any*
> *productive activity. Gains of chance or of individual "sharp practice" could*
> *exert no permanent influence in a regime of "normal values". Universal and*
> *persistent cheating of the productive by the unproductive seemed impossible*
> *in an order of free contract.*[5]

Of course, this is begging the question. The extent to which the so-called "laissez-faire" era was "an order of free contract" is precisely the point at issue. And Dobb's argument was tautological. By definition, a system of free contract *excludes* unequal exchange enforced by state intervention in the market. To the extent that such politically-enforced unequal exchange prevailed, the economic system was *not* "a regime of 'normal values.'" The questions remain: *to what extent* was the actual economy of the nineteenth century a system of privilege, and a departure from the free market; and *to what extent* was this departure the main cause of profit on capital? Of course, Dobb was right that a general rate of profit could not result from "individual 'sharp practice.'" Such deviations would cancel each other out in an equilibrium economy, like the Austrian entrepreneurial profit. To explain a rate of profit as a general phenomenon, one must have recourse to some *systemic* cause. The Austrians seek it in time preference as a fundamental characteristic of human nature. The mutualists seek it, rather, in systematic state intervention in the market on behalf of privileged interests.

Ronald Meek raised essentially the same question—how the historically universal phenomenon of exploitation could continue to take place in a society in which the sale of labor-power was, ostensibly, regulated by free contract:

> A *"theory of distribution"* which said only that unearned income was the fruit of the surplus labour of those employed in production would hardly qualify as a <u>theory</u> at all.... At the best, such a *"theory"* could be little more than a generalized description of the appropriation by the owners of the means of production, in all types of class society, of the product of the surplus labour of the exploited classes. But surely there are two salient points which a theory of distribution appropriate to our own times should concentrate on explaining: First, how is it that unearned incomes continue to be received in a society in which the prices of the great majority of commodities are determined on an impersonal market by the forces of supply and demand, and in which the relation between the direct producer and his employer is based on contract rather than status? And second, how are the respective shares of the main social classes in the national income determined in such a society? Unless one is content to rely on some sort of explanation in terms of *"force"* or *"struggle"*,...it is impossible to give adequate answers to these questions without basing one's sentiment on a theory of value.[6]

Rather than clarifying such issues, Marxists have (perhaps for good reason) generally been quite ambiguous concerning the relationship between state coercion and economic exploitation. For example, Maurice Dobb wrote vaguely of coercion by "class circumstances" in the absence of legal coercion by the state, avoiding the issue of past force in creating those circumstances or present force in maintaining them:

> Since the proletarian was devoid of land or instruments of production, no alternative livelihood existed for him; and while the legal coercion to work for another was gone, the coercion of class circumstance remained.... [W]ithout the historical circumstance that a class existed which had the sale of its labour-power as a commodity for its only livelihood to confront the capitalist with the possibility of this remunerative transaction, the capitalist would not have been in a position to annex the surplus-value to himself.[7]

And without the state to rob the peasantry of their land, to terrorize the urban proletariat out of organizing, and to legally proscribe alternative working class forms of self-organized credit, this propertyless condition of the working class arguably would never have come about, and would have been unsustainable even after it did come about.

Taking his tautologies and question-begging a step further, Dobb asserted that Pareto's distinction between free exchange and robbery, and the parallel distinction between Pareto-optimality and a zero-sum situation, were meaningless in a "free competitive market."

> *Pareto has pointed to the significant distinction between "activities of men directed to the production or transformation of economic goods", and the appropriation of goods produced by others". Clearly if one views the economic problem simply as a pattern of exchange relations, separated from the social relations of the individuals concerned—treating the individuals who enter into exchange simply as so many x's and y's, performing certain "services", but abstracted from the concrete relation to the means of production...—then Pareto's distinction can have no [?] in a free competitive market. "Appropriation of goods produced by others" can only result from the incursion of monopoly or of extra-economic fraud or force. From the regime of "normal" exchange-values it is excluded by the very definition of a free market.*[8]

Quite right. Zero-sum relations *are* excluded by the very definition of a free market. But the question, again, is *whether* the existing market *is* free or competitive. To abstract production relations and patterns of property ownership from a theory of the exchange process, without first examining the role of coercion in those relations and patterns, is *of course* to render the paradigm irrelevant to the real world. Only when all the data is considered, is it a useful model for evaluating reality. Unfortunately, the more vulgar apologists for capitalism, as well as its more vulgar opponents, share the error of taking the present system as a proxy for the "market." The myth of the nineteenth century, or even the Hoover administration, as a time of "laissez-faire" is cynically adopted by both corporate propagandists and state socialists for their own reasons.

Marx and Engels vacillated a great deal in their analysis of the role of force in creating capitalism, and in their judgment of whether such force had been essential in its rise. In the *Grundrisse*, Marx repeatedly raised the issue of the "pre-bourgeois" or "extra-economic" origins of the capitalist economy, but never with an unambiguous answer. Marx understood that the existing situation, in which a propertyless worker confronted *"the objective conditions of his labour as something separate from him, as capital..., presuppos*[ed]

> an *historical process*, however much capital and wage labour themselves reproduce this relation and elaborate it in its objective scope, as well as in depth. And this historical process, as we have seen, is the history of the emergence of both capital and wage labour.

> In other words, the *extra-economic origin* of property means nothing but the *historical origin* of the bourgeois economy....

> *The original conditions of production cannot* initially be *themselves produced*, cannot be the results of production.... What requires

explanation is not the unity of living and active human beings with the natural, inorganic conditions of their exchange of matter with nature, and their appropriation of nature; nor of course is this the result of an historical process. What we must explain is the separation between these inorganic conditions of human existence and this active being....[9]

Marx ridiculed the idea that the "primitive accumulation" had been accomplished by the diligent and thrifty gradually saving until they had acquired enough capital, and then turning to the laborer with the offer of work:

Nothing is therefore more foolish than to conceive of the original formation of capital as having created and accumulated the objective conditions of production—means of subsistence, raw materials, instruments—and then having offered them to workers stripped of them. For it was monetary wealth which had partly helped to strip of these conditions the labour power of the individuals capable of work. In part this process of separation proceeded without the intervention of monetary wealth. Once the formation of capital had reached a certain level, monetary wealth could insinuate itself as mediator between the objective conditions of life thus become free and the freed but also uprooted and dispossessed living labour powers, and buy the one with the other.[10]

Unfortunately, though, Marx was not explicit on exactly *how* "monetary wealth" did this stripping.

It is clear, however, that Marx understood the origins of the process to be extraordinary, and outside the normal process of exchange; once the process was underway, it was intensified through commodity exchange.

We have thus seen that the transformation of money into capital presupposes an historical process which has separated the objective conditions of labour from, and made them independent of, the worker. Once capital has come into being, the effect of its process is to subject all production to itself, and everywhere to develop and complete the separation between labour and property, between labour and the objective conditions of labour.[11]

The first part of the sentence is a tautology. "Capital," by Marx's definition, is the material conditions of production *not* controlled by labor. So the separation of the means of production from the worker is, *of course*, a precondition of transforming money into capital. But is it a *sufficient* condition? Is the owner of the means of production able to pay labor less than its product, and thus obtain a return on capital, in a genuinely non-coercive exchange process? Is the creation of surplus value inherent in wage labor as such, or does it require the weakened bargaining power resulting from forcible robbery by the state? And can such exploitation continue without the ongoing intervention of the state to handicap labor's bargaining power and enforce unequal exchange?

In *Capital*, Marx was more explicit on the requirement for robbery by actual force, at least to get the ball rolling.

> The dull compulsion of economic relations *completes* [emphasis added] the subjection of the labourer to the capitalist. Direct force, outside economic conditions is of course *still* [emphasis added] used, but only exceptionally. In the ordinary run of things, the labourer can be left to the "natural laws of production," i.e., to his dependence on capital, a dependence springing from, and guaranteed in perpetuity by the conditions of production themselves. *It is otherwise during the historic genesis of capitalist production* [emphasis added]. The bourgeoisie, at its rise, wants and *uses the power of the state* [emphasis added] to "regulate" wages, i.e., to force them within the limits suitable for surplus value making, to lengthen the working day and to keep the labourer himself in the normal degree of dependence. This is an *essential* [emphasis added; cf. Engels' contrary claims in *Anti-Dühring*] element of the so-called primitive accumulation.[12]

First of all, if force was essential to creating the system (and we will see in the chapter on primitive accumulation below the horrifying scale of that force, as described by Marx himself), the fact that it runs in its grooves without further direct intervention does not make the system any less statist in its structure. But in fact, the "conditions of production" require massive state intervention for their continuation; some of the forms of this intervention were described by Benjamin Tucker in his analysis of the alleged "laissez-faire" system of the nineteenth century.

Indeed, Marx himself admitted the more than "exceptional" influence of state policy on the ongoing process of accumulation in his own century. State finance, tariffs, etc., greatly intensified the process above what it would have been in a free market:

> The system of protection was an artificial means of manufacturing manufacturers, of expropriating independent labourers, of capitalizing the national means of production and subsistence, of forcibly abbreviating the transition from the mediaeval to the modern mode of production.[13]

Engels, to render the Marxian theory consistent (and to deflect the strategic threat from the market socialists mentioned above), was forced to retreat on the role of force in primitive accumulation. (And if we take his word on the importance of Marx's input and approval during his writing of *Anti-Dühring*, Marx himself was guilty of similar back-pedaling). In *Anti-Dühring*, Engels vehemently denied that force was necessary at any stage of the process; indeed, that it did little even to further the process significantly.

> *Every socialist worker* [like every British schoolboy?]...*knows quite well that force only protects exploitation, but does not cause it; that the relation between capital and wage labour is the basis of his exploitation, and that this arose by* <u>*purely*</u> *economic causes and* <u>*not at all*</u> *by means of force* [emphasis added].[14]

This raises the question of to what extent the legal system is presupposed in even "purely economic" relations, and whether more than one "purely economic" state of affairs is possible, depending on the degree of such state involvement. For example, are combination laws, laws of settlement, and laws on the issuance of credit without specie backing essential to the process of free exchange itself, or only to the capitalist character of such exchange?

Engels stated the case in even more absolute terms later on, denying that force was necessary (or even especially helpful, apparently) at any stage of the process.

> *...even if we exclude all possibility of robbery, force and fraud, even if we assume that all private property was originally based on the owner's own labour, and that throughout the whole subsequent process there was only exchange of equal values for equal values, the progressive development of production and exchange nevertheless brings us of necessity to the present capitalist mode of production, to the monopolization of the means of production and the means of subsistence in the hands of a numerically small class, to the degradation into propertyless proletarians of the other class, constituting the immense majority, to the periodic alternation of speculative production booms and commercial crises and to the whole of the present anarchy of production. The whole process can be explained by purely economic causes; at no point whatever are robbery, force, the state or political interference of any kind necessary.*[15]

As Dobb suggested in the earlier quote, theories of the role of the state in exploitation were a strategic threat to Marxism. As a leading continental proponent of such a force theory, Dühring presented a threat which could not be ignored. And ironically, even though Marx's own treatment of primitive accumulation was among the most eloquent and incisive ever written, Engels was forced to make a strategic retreat from this treatment in order to maintain a defensible position against the state-centered exploitation theories of Dühring and other thinkers. Indeed, he was forced to deny that the history of primitive accumulation, "written in letters of blood and fire," played any necessary role in the rise of capitalism at all. So to defeat the claims of "consistent Manchesterism," Engels (and by implication Marx) was forced to retreat from the eloquent history, "written in letters of fire and blood," of primitive accumulation in Volume I of *Capital*. Engels resurrected the very same "bourgeois nursery tale" that Marx had put so much effort into killing off.

To counter Dühring's force thesis, Engels had to resort to an incredible mass of sophistry and non sequiturs—not at all a credit to Engels' position, given the utter crankiness of Duhring. In response to Dühring's Robinson Crusoe example, in which Crusoe could only exploit Friday after enslaving him, Engels remarked:

> *The childish example specially selected by Herr Dühring in order to prove that force is "historically the fundamental thing", therefore, proves that force is only the means, and that the aim, on the contrary, is economic advantage. And "the more fundamental" the aim is than the means used to secure it, the more fundamental in history is the economic side of the relationship than the political side.*[16]

So much straw, so little time! The proper initial reaction to this is a resounding "Huh?" Of *course* the use of force is aimed at the benefit of the user—who ever denied it? Who in his right mind would claim that exploitation is motivated by pure E-vill, rather than material gain? And since, by definition, means are always subordinate to ends, the ends are always more fundamental. What has that to do with the question of whether a particular means is necessary to a particular end? The point is that the aim of economic exploitation cannot be accomplished without the means of force. The fact that the goal is exploitation does not change the dependence of exploitation on force.

Next, Engels brought out his big cannon: the forcible exploitation of Friday presupposed preexisting economic means of production!

> *However, let us get back again to our two men. Crusoe, "sword in hand", makes Friday his slave. But in order to manage this, Crusoe needs something else besides his sword. Not everyone can make use of a slave. In order to be able to make use of a slave, one must possess two kinds of things: first, the instruments and material for his slave's labour; and secondly, the means of bare subsistence for him. Therefore, before slavery becomes possible, a certain*

level of production must already have been reached and a certain inequality of distribution must already have appeared....

....The subjugation of a man to make him do servile work, in all its forms, presupposes that the subjugator has at his disposal the instruments of labour with the help of which alone he is able to employ the person placed in bondage, and in the case of slavery, in addition, the means of subsistence which enable him to keep his slave alive. In all cases, therefore, it presupposes the possession of a certain amount of property, in excess of the average. How did this property come into existence? In any case it is clear that it may in fact have been robbed, and therefore may be based on force, *but that this is by no means necessary. It may have been got by labour, it may have been stolen, or it may have been obtained by trade or by fraud. In fact, it must have been obtained by labour before there was any possibility of its being robbed.*[17]

Indeed, "how did this come about?" Where *did* these preexisting means of labor and subsistence come from? Either they are the result of *past* robbery, in which the issue of force is simply regressed another stage; they are the result of past concentration of wealth through a pure market mechanism (a thing to be demonstrated, not assumed); or they are the result of abstention by the capitalist, in the person of Robinson Crusoe. If either of the latter two, it's remarkable that Engels is abandoning the original, violent expropriation process of Marx for the "nursery tale" of peaceful accumulation so beloved of the "vulgar political economists." But if Crusoe did, indeed accumulate the preexisting means of production and subsistence from the action of his labor on nature, this assumption carries certain clear implications. If Friday is not forcibly deprived of similar access to the island's free natural goods (by, e.g., Crusoe acting as absentee landlord over all the natural resources of the island), Crusoe will have to offer him a reward for his labor, at least equal to the likely return on Friday's toil and trouble from duplicating Crusoe's course of labor and abstention. It is the availability of alternatives, and the absence of compulsion, that makes exploitation impossible.

As for the fact that the pre-existing economic means must have been gotten by *someone's* labor, once again, *so what?* Who said that force *created* production? One might as well say that the pre-existence of a host organism negates the principle of parasitism. And Engels himself admitted that the economic means *might* be in the hands of the ruling class as a result of past force. If the means of production under their control may indeed be the result of forcible robbery, what becomes of Engels assertion of these pre-existing means as a telling point against the force theory? In any case, it is quite consistent to posit a process in a series of stages, in which the progressive accumulation of capital, and the increasing exploitation of labor, are a mutually reinforcing synergistic trend, with force as still the primary cause of exploitation. In every case, the accumulated economic means that make heightened exploitation possible are the result of past robbery. As the Hindu theologian said of turtles, it's force all the way down.

In yet another argument which was entirely beside the point, Engels made much of the material prerequisites of force. That sword didn't just fall out of a tree, you know:

> ....*Crusoe enslaved Friday "sword in hand". Where did he get the sword?...* *.[F]orce is no mere act of the will, but requires the existence of very real preliminary conditions before it can come into operation, namely, <u>instruments</u>, the more perfect of which gets the better of the less perfect; moreover..., these instruments have to be produced, which implies that the producer of more perfect instruments of force...gets the better of the producer of the less perfect instruments, and that, in a word, the triumph of force is based on the production of arms, and this in turn on production in general—therefore, on "economic power", on the "economic situation", on the <u>material</u> means which force has at is disposal.*

> ....*[A]nd so once more force is conditioned by the economic situation, which furnishes the means for the equipment and maintenance of the instruments of force.*[18]

For the third time, so what? Engels still did not show that exploitation was inherent in a given level of productive forces, without the use of coercion. He needed to show, not that parasitism depends on the preexistence of a host organism (duh!), but that it cannot be carried out without force. Every increase in economic productivity has created opportunities for robbery through a statist class system; but the same productive technology was always usable in non-exploitative ways. The fact that a given kind of class parasitism presupposes a certain form of productive technology, does not alter the fact that that form of technology has potentially both libertarian and exploitative applications, depending on the nature of the society which adopts it.

Engels, in making such arguments, seems to be ignoring the actual thesis of Dühring (and of Hodgskin and Tucker), that exploitation depends on force, and instead disproving a thesis of his own invention: that the development of productive forces depends on force. "*If, in accordance with Herr Dühring's theory, the economic situation and with it the economic structure of a given country were dependent simply on political force....*"[19] "Economic order" means *what*? Productive technology, or the exploitative use of that technology? The anarchist theory of the state is entirely different from what Engels seems to imply: it holds that the rise of the state is made possible when the development of productive forces by the free labor of the people reaches a point at which they produce a sufficient surplus to support a parasitic ruling class.

As we have already shown, Meek's and Dobb's analyses above beg the question of the extent to which, in fact, economic relations under capitalism (even in the nineteenth century) have been governed by force, and to what extent by uncoerced market exchange. The distinction between the latter-day regime of "free contract," and previous eras of exploitation by naked force, is more apparent than real.

Unlike mainstream libertarians of the right, who typically depict twentieth century state capitalism as a departure from a largely "laissez-faire" nineteenth century idyll, Hodgskin, Tucker et al. were much more thorough-going. It was precisely the capitalism of the nineteenth century that Hodgskin and Tucker described as a statist system of privilege. Although the United States was well into the corporate revolution, and "internal improvements" and railroad subsidies were a large part of national economic life, at the time Tucker wrote, he dealt with these matters almost not at all. The four privileges he attacked—the money and land monopolies, tariffs, and patents—had been an integral part of capitalism from its beginnings. The last-named privileges, tariffs and patents, indeed played a large part in the cartelizing and concentration of the corporate economy during the latter part of the nineteenth century. But Tucker largely neglected their effects on the overall structure of capitalism. So Tucker's critique of capitalism as fundamentally statist was almost completely abstracted from the nascent capitalism of the Gilded Age. The capitalism which Tucker denounced for its statism was, rather, the very capitalism that conventional right-libertarians today point to as a "free market" utopia.

Besides the emergent monopoly capitalism of the late nineteenth century, Tucker's analysis likewise ignored the statist roots of capitalism in the so-called "primitive accumulation" process. Although Tucker treated existing absentee landlordism as a way for the landlord class to live off of other people's labor, he ignored the historical effects of expropriation of the land in initially creating the basic structure of capitalism.

In contrast to the confusion of Marxists as to the role of coercion in exploitation, then, we will proceed from this insight that force is essential to the process, and that the history of the state has been a history of intervention in voluntary relations between human beings in order to benefit one at the expense of another. This is the guiding principle from which Thomas Hodgskin and the American individualist anarchists started. Throughout history, the state has been a means by which the producing classes were robbed of their produce in order to support an idle ruling class. Without state intervention in the marketplace, the natural wage of labor would be its product. It is statism that is at the root of all the exploitative features of capitalism. Capitalism, indeed, only exists to the extent that the principles of free exchange are violated. "Free market capitalism" is an oxymoron.

Thomas Hodgskin, the greatest of the Ricardian socialists, argued that the exploitation of labor in his time resulted from the legal privileges of capitalists and landlords. His was a more radical version of Adam Smith's principle that, when the government undertakes to regulate the relations of masters and workmen, it has the masters for its counselors.

> *Laws being made by others than the labourer, and being always intended to preserve the power of those who make them, their great and chief aim for many ages, was, and still is, to enable those who are not labourers to appropriate wealth to themselves. In other words, the great object of law and of government has been and is, to establish and protect a violation of that natural right of property they are described in theory as being intended to guarantee....*
>
> *Those who make laws, appropriate wealth in order to secure power. All the legislative classes, and all the classes whose possessions depend not on nature, but on the law, perceiving that <u>law</u> alone guarantees and secures their possessions, and perceiving that government as the instrument for enforcing obedience to the law, and thus for preserving their power and possessions, is indispensable, unite one and all, heart and soul to uphold it, and, as the means of upholding it, to place at its disposal a large part of the annual produce of labour....*[20]

Hodgskin followed Ricardo in understanding profit and rent as deductions from a pool of exchange-value created by labor, and thus the livelihoods of capitalists, landlords and church as inversely related to the wages of labor.

> *At present, besides the government, the aristocracy, and the church, the law also protects, to a certain extent, the property of the capitalist, of whom there is somewhat more difficulty to speak correctly than of the priest, because the capitalist is very often a labourer. The capitalist as such, however, whether he be a holder of East India stock, or of a part of the national debt, a discounter of bills, or a buyer of annuities, has no natural right to the large share of the annual produce the law secures to him. There is sometimes a conflict between him and the landowner, sometimes one attains a triumph, and sometimes the*

other; both however willingly support the government and the church; and both side against the labourer to oppress him; one lending his aid to enforce combination laws, while the other upholds game laws, and both enforce the exaction of tithes and of the revenue. Capitalists in general have formed a most intimate union with the landowners, and except when the interest of these classes clash, as in the case of the corn laws, the law is extremely punctilious in defending the claims and exactions of the capitalist.[21]

The effect of these parasitic classes, in living off the produce of labor, was to impoverish the people, discourage industry, and check improvements.

As these people [the great mass of the laboring classes] *are very industrious and very skilful, very frugal and very economical—as their labour pays taxes, tithes, rent, and profit—it cannot be for one moment doubted...that the immediate and proximate cause of their poverty and destitution, seeing how much they labour, and how many people their labour nourishes in opulence, is the law which appropriates their produce, in the shape of revenue, rent, tithes, and profit.*

I also pass by the manner in which the legal right of property operates in checking all improvement.... It is, however, evident, that the labour which would be amply rewarded in cultivating all our waste lands, till every foot of the country became like the garden grounds about London, were all the produce of labour on those lands to be the reward of the labourer, cannot obtain from them a sufficiency to pay profit, tithes, rent, and taxes.[22]

Hodgskin dismissed out of hand the claim that government existed to secure the "general welfare" or to maintain "social order." The intrusion of coercion into the realm of voluntary exchange, rather, *disrupted* the natural social order.

The great object contemplated by the legislator...was to preserve his own power, and the dominion of the law, and with that view to keep in the possession of the landed aristocracy, and the clergy, and the government, all the wealth of society....

Allow me...to notice that the pretexts which the legislator puts forth, about preserving social order, and promoting public good, must not be confounded with his real objects.... If by social order he meant the great scheme of social production, mutual dependence, and mutual service, which grows out of the division of labour, that scheme I will boldly assert the legislator frequently contravenes, but never promotes—that grows from the laws of man's being, and precedes all the plans of the legislator, to regulate or preserve it.[23]

> *The preservation of the power of the unjust appropriators has been called*
> *social order, and mankind have believed the assertion. To maintain their*
> *dominion is the object and aim of all human legislation.*[24]

Although their work preceded that of Pareto, and they did not use
such terms, free market socialists like Hodgskin and Tucker were quite
familiar with the substance of Pareto-optimality and the zero-sum
transaction. In an order of free and voluntary exchange, all transactions
are mutually beneficial to both parties. It is only when force enters the
picture that one party benefits at the expense of the other. Indeed, the
use of force necessarily implies exploitation, since by definition force is
used only to compel one party or the other to do something other than
he would otherwise have done, were he free to maximize his utilities in
the way he saw fit.

Benjamin Tucker wrote of coercion as the fundamental support of
privilege, and of the violence privilege did to the natural harmony of
interests.

> *To-day (pardon the paradox!) society is fundamentally anti-social. The*
> *whole so-called social fabric rests on privilege and power, and is disordered*
> *and strained in every direction by the inequalities that necessarily result*
> *therefrom. The welfare of each, instead of contributing to that of all, as it*
> *naturally should and would, almost invariably detracts from that of all.*
> *Wealth is made by legal privilege a hook with which to filch from labor's*
> *pockets. Every man who gets rich thereby makes his neighbors poor. The better*
> *off one is, the worse the rest are.... The laborer's Deficit is precisely equal to*
> *the Capitalist's Efficit.*
>
> *Now, Socialism wants to change all this. Socialism says that what's one*
> *man's meat must no longer be another's poison; that no man shall be able to*
> *add to his riches except by labor; that in adding to his riches by labor alone no*
> *man makes another man poorer; that on the contrary every man thus adding*
> *to his riches makes every other man richer; that increase and concentration*
> *of wealth through labor tend to increase, cheapen, and vary production; that*
> *every increase of capital in the hands of the laborer tends, in the absence of*
> *legal monopoly, to put more products, better products, cheaper products, and*
> *a greater variety of products within the reach of every man who works; and*
> *that this fact means the physical, mental, and moral perfecting of mankind,*
> *and the realization of human fraternity.*[25]

This line of thought reached full development in the work of Franz
Oppenheimer. Oppenheimer called himself a "liberal socialist": "*a*
socialist in that he regard[ed] *capitalism as a system of exploitation, and capital*
revenue as the gain of that exploitation, but a liberal in that he believ[ed] *in*
the harmony of a genuinely free market." Unlike Marx, who recognized no

legitimate role for monopoly in his theoretical system (which assumed cost price), Oppenheimer blamed exploitation entirely on monopoly and unequal exchange.[26] Profit was a monopoly income, resulting from unequal exchange, accruing to the class which controlled access to the means of production.[27] This control was made possible only by the state.

Oppenheimer contrasted "the State," by which he meant "*that summation of privileges and dominating positions which are brought into being by extra-economic power*," with "Society," which was "*the totality of concepts of all purely natural relations and institutions between man and man....*"[28] He made a parallel distinction between the "economic means" to wealth, i.e., "*one's own labor and the equivalent exchange of one's own labor for the labor of others*," and the "political means": "*the unrequited appropriation of the labor of others....*"[29] The state was simply the "*organization of the political means.*"[30] The state existed for an economic purpose, exploitation, which could not be achieved without force; but it presupposed the pre-existence of the economic means, which had been created by peaceful labor.[31]

Oppenheimer criticized Marx for his confusion in not properly distinguishing between economic purposes and economic means.

> *In the case of a thinker of the rank of Karl Marx, one may observe what confusion is brought about when economic purpose and economic means are not strictly differentiated. All those errors, which in the end led Marx's splendid theory so far away from truth, were grounded in the lack of clear differentiation between the means of economic satisfaction of needs and its end. This led him to designate slavery as an "economic category," and force as an "economic force"—half truths which are far more dangerous than total untruths, since their discovery is more difficult, and false conclusions from them are inevitable.*[32]

We have already seen, in our examination above of Engels argument in *Anti-Dühring*, a clear example of the false conclusions resulting from such confusion.

The economic means to wealth were production and voluntary exchange. The political means were violent robbery.[33] Or, as Voltaire defined it, the state was "*a device for taking money out of one set of pockets and putting it into another.*"[34]

This theory of the state as the agent of exploitation was developed by both Albert J. Nock, and by Murray Rothbard. According to Nock, a Georgist, the state

> *did not originate in the common understanding and agreement of society; it originated in conquest and confiscation. Its intention, far from contemplating*

"freedom and security," contemplated nothing of the kind. It contemplated primarily the continuous economic exploitation of one class by another, and it concerned itself with only so much freedom and security as was consistent with this primary intention.... Its primary function or exercise was...by way of innumerable and most onerous positive interventions, all of which were for the purpose of maintaining the stratification of society into an owning and exploiting class, and a propertyless dependent class.[35]

The positive testimony of history is that the State invariably had its origin in conquest and confiscation.... Moreover, the sole invariable characteristic of the State is the economic exploitation of one class by another. In this sense, every State known to history is a class-State.[36]

Murray Rothbard later used these same principles in his attempted elaboration of Misesean theory, making very much the same substantive points in the language of marginalist economics.

Any exchange in the free market, indeed any action in the free society, occurs because it is expected to benefit each party concerned.... [W]e may say that the free market maximizes social utility, since everyone gains in utility from his free actions.

Coercive intervention, on the other hand, signifies per se that the individual or individuals coerced would not have voluntarily done what they are now being forced to do by the intervener. The person who is being coerced...is having his actions changed by a threat of violence. The man being coerced, therefore, always loses in utility as a result of the intervention....

In contrast to the free market, therefore, all cases of intervention supply one set of men with gains at the expense of another set.[37]

This last was not simply something the state sometimes did, a side-effect of bad policy to be rectified by "good government" or policy "reform." It was the defining characteristic of government.

Rothbard contemptuously dismissed the belief, especially common since democracy has become the dominant legitimizing ideology in most societies, that the state is simply an expression of "*the interests of 'society.'*"

The State is almost universally considered an institution of social service. Some theorists venerate the State as the apotheosis of society; others regard it as an amiable though often inefficient organization for achieving social ends; but almost all regard it as a necessary means for achieving the goals of mankind, a means to be ranged against the "private sector" and often winning in this competition of resources. With the rise of democracy, the identification of the State with society has been redoubled, until it is common to hear sentiments expressed which violate virtually every tenet of reason and common sense: such as "we are the government." The useful collective term "we" has enabled an ideological camouflage to be thrown over the reality of political life. If "we are the government," then anything a government does to an individual is not only just and tyrannical [sic]; it is also "voluntary" on the part of the individual concerned. If the government has incurred a huge public debt which must be paid by taxing one group for the benefit of another, this reality of burden is obscured by saying that "we owe it to ourselves."....

We must therefore emphasize that "we" are not the government; the government is not "us". The government does not in any accurate sense "represents [sic] the majority of the people" but even if it did, even if 70 per cent of the people decided to murder the remaining 30 per cent, this would still be murder, and would not be voluntary suicide on the part of the slaughtered minority. No organicist metaphor, no irrelevant bromide that "we are all part of one another," must be permitted to obscure this basic fact.

If, then, the State is not "us," if it is not "the human family" getting together to solve mutual problems, if it is not a lodge meeting or country club, what is it? Briefly, the State is that organization in society which attempts to maintain a monopoly of the use of force and violence in a given territorial area; in particular, it is the only organization in society that obtains its revenue not by voluntary contribution or payment for services rendered, but by coercion.[38]

The chief act of coercion by which the state exploits labor, as our free market socialist school has understood it, is by restricting, on behalf of a ruling class, the laboring classes' access to the means of production. By setting up such barriers, the ruling class is able to charge tribute in the form of unpaid labor, for allowing access on its own terms. It is only because of the state's enforced separation of labor from the means of production that labor acquires the perverse habit of thinking, not of work as a creative activity performed by the worker with the help of the material prerequisites of production, but of a *job* that he is *given*. Work is not something that one does; it is a boon granted by the ruling class, of its grace.

Our natural resources, while much depleted, are still great; our population is very thin, running something like twenty or twenty-five to the square mile; and some millions of this population are at the moment "unemployed," and likely to remain so because no one will or can "give them work." The point is not that men generally submit to this state of things, or that they accept it as inevitable, but that they see nothing irregular or anomalous about it because of their fixed idea that work is something to be <u>given</u>.[39]

In the chapters of this section, we will proceed in the light of the free market socialist assumption that exploitation is impossible without force, and attempt to demonstrate the extent of such force in "actually existing capitalism." Free market socialists in the Hodgskinian and individualist tradition contend that capitalism has been a radical departure from genuinely free market principles, from its very beginnings. The following chapters will demonstrate the ways in which the state has intervened in the economy from the first beginnings of capitalism. We will begin with the primitive accumulation process, largely neglected by Tucker, in which the laboring classes of the world were robbed of their rightful property in the means of production, and in which the state's coercive means were used to maintain social control over this population. We will continue with the statist features of the so-called "laissez-faire" capitalism of the nineteenth century. We will go on to study the vast expansion of state intervention from the late nineteenth century onward. Finally, we will examine the internal contradictions created by this state intervention in the free market, and the resulting crises of state capitalism.

NOTES

1. Benjamin Tucker, "Should Labor Be Paid or Not?" *Liberty* April 28, 1888, in Benjamin Tucker, *Instead of a Book, By a Man Too Busy to Write One.* Gordon Press Facsimile (New York: 1897/1973) 403.

2. Karl Marx, "Value, Price and Profit," vol. 20 in Marx and Engels *Collected Works* (New York: International Publishers, 1985) 127.

3. Maurice Dobb, Introduction to Karl Marx's *Contribution to the Critique of Political Economy* (New York: International Publishers, 1970) 13.

4. Ibid. 14.

5. Maurice Dobb, *Political Economy and Capitalism: Some Essays in Economic Tradition*, 2nd rev. ed. (London: Routledge & Kegan Paul, Ltd, 1940, 1960) 60.

6. Ronald L. Meek, *Studies in the Labour Theory of Value*, 2nd ed. (New York and London: Monthly Review Press, 1956) 215.

7. Dobb, *Political Economy and Capitalism* 61-2.

8. Ibid. 65.

9. Karl Marx, *Grundrisse*, vol. 28 in Marx and Engels *Collected Works* (New York: International Publishers, 1986) 412-3.

10. Ibid. 432.

11. Ibid. 435.

12. Karl Marx and Friedrich Engels, *Capital* vol. 1, vol. 35 in Marx

and Engels *Collected Works* (New York: International Publishers, 1996) 726.

13. Ibid. 744-5.

14. Friedrich Engels, *Anti-Dühring*, vol. 25 in Marx and Engels *Collected Works* (New York: International Publishers, 1987) 141.

15. Ibid. 151.

16. Ibid. 148.

17. Ibid. 148-9.

18. Ibid. 154.

19. Ibid. 170.

20. Thomas Hodgskin, *The Natural and Artificial Right of Property Contrasted* (London: B. Steil, 1832) 49.

21. Ibid. 53.

22. Ibid. 148-9.

23. Ibid. 77.

24. Ibid. 156.

25. Benjamin Tucker, "Socialism: What It is," *Liberty* May 17, 1884, in Tucker, *Instead of a Book* 361-2.

26. Franz Heimann, "Franz Oppenheimer's Economic Ideas," *Social Research* (New York) (February 1944) 29, 33.

27. Franz Oppenheimer, "A Post Mortem on Cambridge Economics (Part III)," *The American Journal of Economics and Sociology* vol. 3 no. 1 (1944) 117.

28. Franz Oppenheimer, *The State*, trans. By John Gitterman (San Francisco: Fox & Wilkes, 1997) lvi.

29. Ibid. 14.

30. Ibid. 15.

31. Ibid. 15.

32. Ibid. 14.

33. Ibid. 14.

34. Albert Jay Nock, *Our Enemy, the State* (Delavan, Wisc.: Hallberg Publishing Corp., 1983) 74.

35. Ibid. 37.

36. Ibid. 40.

37. Murray Rothbard, *Man, Economy, and State: A Treatise on Economic Principles* (Auburn University, Alabama: Ludwig von Mises Institute, 1993) 768-9.

38. Murray Rothbard, "The Anatomy of the State" *Rampart Journal of Individualist Thought* (Summer 1965), reprinted as pdf file by Libertarian Alliance, www.libertarian.co.uk/lapubs/socin/socin001.pdf Captured August 4, 2004. 1-2.

39. Nock, *Our Enemy, the State* 82n.

Chapter Four
Primitive Accumulation and the Rise of Capitalism

Introduction.

In the Introduction to Part Two, we referred to the "nursery school tale" of primitive accumulation, which has long served the capitalists as a legitimizing myth. In fact, capitalist apologists seldom even address the issue, if they can avoid it. More often, they take the existing distribution of property and economic power as a given. Their most dumbed-down line of argument, typically, simply starts with the unquestioned fact that some people just happen to own the means of production, and that others need access to these means and advances to live on while they work. From this it follows that, if the owners of capital are kind enough to "provide" this "factor of production" for the use of labor, they are entitled to a fair recompense for their "service" or "abstinence."

The inadequacy of this approach should be clear from even the most cursory consideration. An apologist for state socialism might just as easily say, to a free market advocate in a state-owned economy, that he wouldn't have a job if the state didn't "provide" it. An apologist for the manorial economy could likewise admonish the ungrateful peasant that all his labor would avail him nothing without the access to the land that the feudal landlord graciously "provided." The question remains: how did those who control access to the means of production come to be in this position? As Oppenheimer pointed out in his criticism of Marshall, no discussion of the laws governing the distribution of product can be meaningful without first considering the *"primal distribution of the agents (factors) of production...."*[1]

To the extent that they are forced to address this question at all, capitalist apologists fall back on the above-mentioned nursery tale, by which existing class divisions arose naturally from an *"original state of equality,...from no other cause than the exercise of the economic virtues of industry, frugality and providence."* There is, in this process, *"no implication...of any extra-economic power."*[2]

As Marx summarized it, the legend of primitive accumulation was a sort of variation on the fable of the ant and the grasshopper:

> *In times long gone by there were two sorts of people: one, the diligent, intelligent, and, above all, frugal élite; the other, lazy rascals, spending their substance, and more, in riotous living.... Thus it came to pass that the former sort accumulated wealth, and the latter sort had at last nothing to sell except their own skins. And from this original sin dates the poverty of the great majority that, despite all its labour, has up to now nothing to sell but itself, and the wealth of the few that increases constantly although they have long ceased to work. Such insipid childishness is every day preached to us in the defence of property.... In actual history it is notorious that conquest, enslavement, robbery, murder, briefly, force, play the great part.*[3]

Perhaps Engels should have titled his work *Anti-Marx*, instead of *Anti-Dühring*.

Oppenheimer also recounted this edifying fable, in language quite similar to that of Marx. Since, however, Oppenheimer was a free market socialist like Hodgskin and Tucker, he was (unlike Marx and Engels) in no danger of subsequent embarrassment over the implications of rejecting the bourgeois fairy tale.

> *Somewhere, in some far-stretching, fertile country, a number of free men, of equal status, form a union for mutual protection. Gradually they differentiate into property classes. Those best endowed with strength, wisdom, capacity for saving, industry and caution, slowly acquire a basic amount of real or movable property; while the stupid and less efficient, and those given to carelessness and waste, remain without possessions. The well-to-do lend their productive property to the less well-off in return for tribute, either ground-rent or profit, and become thereby continually richer, while the others always remain poor.... The primitive state of free and equal fellows becomes a class State, by an inherent law of development, because in every conceivable mass of men there are, as may readily be seen, strong and weak, clever and foolish, cautious and wasteful ones.*[4]

This ahistorical myth survived the twentieth century, and is still alive and well—at least so long as it is not challenged by the historically literate. It was stated by Mises in *Human Action*:

> *The factory owners did not have the power to compel anybody to take a factory job. They could only hire people who were ready to work for the wages offered*

to them. Low as these wage rates were, they were nonetheless much more than these paupers could earn in any other field open to them.[5]

It can be illustrated by any number of boilerplate articles in *The Freeman: Ideas on Liberty*, debunking the "myth" of dark satanic mills or Third World sweatshops, on the ground that laborers found them preferable to "available alternatives":

But are the "low-wage, non-union" Ecuadorian laborers better off working now for some foreign corporation? Apparently they think so, or else they would have stayed with what they were doing previously. (Would you leave your job for one with less pay and worse conditions?) [Barry Loberfeld. "A Race to the Bottom" (July 2001).]

People line up in China and Indonesia and Malaysia when American multinationals open a factory. And that is because even though the wages are low by American standards, the jobs created by those American firms are often some of the best jobs in those economies. [Russell Roberts. "The Pursuit of Happiness: Does Trade Exploit the Poorest of the Poor?" (September 2001)]

What the Industrial Revolution made possible, then, was for these people, who had nothing else to offer to the market, to be able to sell their labor to capitalists in exchange for wages. That is why they were able to survive at all.... As Mises argues, the very fact that people took factory jobs in the first place indicates that these jobs, however distasteful to us, represented the best opportunity they had. [Thomas E. Woods, Jr. "A Myth Shattered: Mises, Hayek, and the Industrial Revolution" (November 2001)]

In nineteenth-century America, anti-sweatshop activism was focused on domestic manufacturing facilities that employed poor immigrant men, women, and children. Although conditions were horrendous, they provided a means for many of the country's least-skilled people to earn livings. Typically, those who worked there did so because it was their best opportunity, given the choices available....

It is true that the wages earned by workers in developing nations are outrageously low compared to American wages, and their working conditions go counter to sensibilities in the rich, industrialized West. However, I have seen how the foreign-based opportunities are normally better than the local alternatives in case after case, from Central America to Southeast Asia. [Stephan Spath, "The Virtues of Sweatshops" (March 2002)]

The fairy tale was retold recently by Radley Balko, who referred to Third World sweatshops as "*the best of a series of bad employment options available*" to laborers there.[6] Within a couple of days, this piece was recirculated over the "free market" [sic] blogosphere, along with numerous comments to the effect that *"sweatshops are far superior to third-world workers' next best options....,"* or to similar effect.[7]

This school of libertarianism has inscribed on its banner the reactionary watchword: "Them pore ole bosses need all the help they can get." For every imaginable policy issue, the good guys and bad guys can be predicted with ease, by simply inverting the slogan of Animal Farm: "Two legs good, four legs baaaad." In every case, the good guys, the sacrificial victims of the Progressive State, are the rich and powerful. The bad guys are the consumer and the worker, acting to enrich themselves from the public treasury. As one of the most egregious examples of this tendency, consider Ayn Rand's characterization of big business as an "oppressed minority," and of the Military-Industrial Complex as a "myth or worse."

The ideal "free market" society of such people, it seems, is simply actually existing capitalism, minus the regulatory and welfare state: a hyper-thyroidal version of nineteenth century robber baron capitalism, perhaps; or better yet, a society "reformed" by the likes of Pinochet, who played Dionysius to Milton Friedman's and the Chicago Boys' Plato.

Vulgar libertarian apologists for capitalism use the term "free market" in an equivocal sense: they seem to have trouble remembering, from one moment to the next, whether they're defending actually existing capitalism or free market principles. So we get the standard boilerplate by the Adam Smith Institute arguing that the rich can't get rich at the expense of the poor, because "that's not how the free market works"—implicitly assuming that this *is* a free market. When prodded, they'll grudgingly admit that the present system is not a free market, and that it includes a lot of state intervention on behalf of the rich. But as soon as they think they can get away with it, they go right back to defending the wealth of existing corporations on the basis of "free market principles."

The capitalist myth of primitive accumulation cannot stand up either to logic or to the evidence of history; by the two together, it has been smashed beyond recovery. Oppenheimer demonstrated the impossibility of such primitive accumulation by peaceful means. Exploitation could not have arisen in a free society, by the working of the marketplace alone.

> *The proof is as follows: All teachers of natural law, etc., have unanimously declared that the differentiation into income-receiving classes and propertyless classes can only take place when all fertile lands have been occupied. For so long as man has ample opportunity to take up unoccupied land, "no one," says Turgot, "would think of entering the service of another"; we may*

add, "at least for wages, which are not apt to be higher than the earnings of an independent peasant working an unmortgaged and sufficiently large property"; while mortgaging is not possible so long as land is yet free for the working or taking, as free as air and water....

The philosophers of natural law, then, assumed that complete occupancy of the ground must have occurred quite early, because of the natural increase of an originally small population. They were under the impression that at their time, in the eighteenth century, it had taken place many centuries previous, and they naively deduced the existent class aggroupment from the assumed conditions of that long-past point of time.[8]

But on examination, Oppenheimer pointed out, the land could not have been occupied by natural and economic means. Even in the twentieth century, and even in the Old World, the population was not sufficient to bring all arable land into cultivation.[9]

If, therefore, purely economic causes are ever to bring about a differentiation into classes by the growth of a propertyless laboring class, the time has not yet arrived; and the critical point at which ownership of land will cause a natural scarcity is thrust into the dim future—if indeed it can ever arrive.[10]

The land had, indeed, been "occupied"—but not through the economic means of individual appropriation by cultivation. It had been *politically* occupied by a ruling class, acting through the state.

As a matter of fact,...for centuries past, in all parts of the world, we have had a class State, with possessing classes on top and a propertyless laboring class at the bottom, even when population was much less dense than it is to-day. Now it is true that the class State can arise only where all fertile acreage has been <u>occupied</u> completely; and since I have shown that even at the present time, all the ground is not occupied economically, this must mean that it has been occupied politically. Since land could not have acquired "natural scarcity," the scarcity must have been "legal." This means that the land has been preempted by a ruling class against its subject class, and settlement prevented.[11]

Establishing this does not, by any means, depend simply on such deductive arguments. The political preemption of the land is a fact of history. The basic facts, largely beyond serious controversy, are accessible in a large body of secondary works by such radical historians as J.L. and Barbara Hammond, E. G. Hobsbawm, and E. P. Thompson.

Capitalism, arising as a new class society directly from the old class society of the Middle Ages, was founded on an act of robbery as massive as the earlier feudal conquest of the land. It has been sustained to the present by continual state intervention to protect its system of privilege, without which its survival is unimaginable. The current structure of capital ownership and organization of production in our so-called "market" economy, reflects coercive state intervention prior to and extraneous to the market. From the outset of the industrial revolution, what is nostalgically called "laissez-faire" was in fact a system of continuing state intervention to subsidize accumulation, guarantee privilege, and maintain work discipline.

Accordingly, the single biggest subsidy to modern corporate capitalism is the subsidy of history, by which capital was originally accumulated in a few hands, and labor was deprived of access to the means of production and forced to sell itself on the buyer's terms. The current system of concentrated capital ownership and large-scale corporate organization is the direct beneficiary of that original structure of power and property ownership, which has perpetuated itself over the centuries.

A. The Expropriation of Land in the Old World

The term "capitalism" is commonly used, especially on the libertarian right, simply to refer to an economic system based primarily on markets and private property. There is no harm in this; many intellectually honest libertarians (e.g. the Nockians and the Rothbardian Left) distinguish clearly between their "free market capitalism" (much of which is amenable to the free market socialism of Benjamin Tucker), and the "actually existing capitalism" of today's corporate economy. But that is not the meaning of capitalism as the classical socialists used the word. As we have already seen, Thomas Hodgskin used the term "capitalism" to refer, not to a free market, but to a statist system of class rule in which owners of capital were privileged in a manner analogous to the status of landlords under feudalism. For Marx, free markets and private property were not sufficient conditions of capitalism. For example, an economic system in which artisans and peasants owned their means of production and exchanged their labor-products in a free market would not be "capitalism." Capitalism was a system in which markets and private property not only existed, but in which workers did not own the means of production and were forced instead to sell their labor for wages.

For capitalism as we know it to come about, it was essential first of all for labor to be separated from property. Marxians and other radical economists commonly refer to the process as "primitive accumulation"[12]:

> *In themselves money and commodities are no more capital than are the means of production and of subsistence. They want transforming into capital. But this transformation itself can only take place under certain circumstances that centre in this, viz., that two very different kinds of commodity possessors must come face to face and into contact; on the one hand, the owners of money, means of production, means of subsistence...; on the other hand, free labourers, the sellers of their own labour power, and therefore the sellers of labour.... The capitalist system presupposes the complete separation of the labourers from all property in the means by which they can realise their labour.... The process, therefore, that clears the way for the capitalist system, can be none other than the process which takes away from the labourer the possession of his own means of production.... The so-called primitive accumulation, therefore, is nothing else than the historical process of divorcing the producer from the means of production....*[13]

This process did not come about naturally. "*...Nature does not produce on the one side owners of money or commodities, and on the other men possessing nothing but their own labour power.... It is clearly the result of a past historical development, the product of many economic revolutions, of the extinction of a whole series of older forms of social production.*"[14] The means by which it did come about was described by Marx, in perhaps the most eloquent passage in his entire body of work:

> *....[T]hese new freedmen became sellers of themselves only after they had been robbed of all their own means of production, and of all the guarantees of existence afforded by the old feudal arrangements. And the history of this, their expropriation, is written in the annals of mankind in letters of blood and fire.*[15]

That was brought about by expropriating the land, "*to which the* [peasantry] *has the same feudal rights as the lord himself, and by the usurpation of the common lands.*"[16] Although some form of forcible robbery took place in every country in Europe, we focus on Britain as the case most relevant to the origins of industrial capitalism.

To grasp the enormity and wickedness of the process, one must understand that the nobility's rights in land under the manorial economy were entirely a feudal legal fiction deriving from conquest. The peasants who cultivated the land of England in 1650 were descendants of those who had occupied it since time immemorial. By any normally accepted standard of morality, it was their property in every sense of the word. The armies of William the Conqueror, by no right other than force, had compelled these peasant proprietors to pay rent on their own land.

J. L. and Barbara Hammond treated the sixteenth century village and open field system as a survival of the free peasant society of Anglo-

Saxon times, with landlordism superimposed on it. The landlord class saw surviving peasant rights as a hindrance to progress and efficient farming; a revolution in their own power was a way of breaking peasant resistance. Hence the agricultural community was "*taken to pieces...and reconstructed in the manner in which a dictator reconstructs a free government.*"[17]

The first mass expropriation, amounting to about a fifth of the arable land of England, was the Tudor seizure of monastic land and subsequent distribution of it among noble favorites. This was a blow against the laboring classes in two ways: first, because many of the Church's tenants were evicted during the subsequent enclosure process; and second, because income from that land had been the major source of poor relief.

> The suppression of the monasteries, etc., hurled their inmates into the proletariat. The estates of the church were to a large extent given away to rapacious royal favourites, or sold at a nominal price to speculating farmers and citizens, who drove out, en masse, the hereditary subtenants and threw their holdings into one.[18]

The king's men who gobbled up the former property of the monasteries had few qualms about how they treated their new tenants. According to R. H. Tawney,

> Rack-renting, evictions, and the conversions of arable to pasture were the natural result, for surveyors wrote up values at each transfer, and, unless the last purchaser squeezed his tenants, the transaction would not pay.

> Why, after all, should a landlord be more squeamish than the Crown? "Do ye not know," said the grantee of one of the Sussex manors of the monastery of Sion, in answer to some peasants who protested at the seizure of their commons, "that the King's grace hath put down all the houses of monks, friars and nuns? Therefore now is the time come that we gentlemen will pull down the houses of such poor knaves as ye be."

Among the victims, as illustrative cases, were the inhabitants of the village enclosed by the Herbert family to make the park at Washerne; and the tenants of Whitby, whose annual rents were raised from £29 to £64.[19]

The expropriation of the Church destroyed the funding system for the main source of charitable support for the poor and incapacitated. The Tudor state filled the void with its Poor Laws. The effect was as if, in the modern world, the state had expropriated the major property and securities of the charitable foundations, and given them to Fortune

500 corporation; and then created a welfare system at taxpayer expense with incomparably more draconian controls on the poor.[20]

Still another form of expropriation was the enclosure of commons— in which, again, the peasants communally had as absolute a right of property as any defended by today's "property rights" advocates. Enclosures occurred in two large waves: the first, becoming a mighty surge under the Tudors and slowing to a trickle under the Stuarts, was enclosure of land for sheep pasturage. The second, which we will consider below, was the enclosure of open fields for large-scale capitalist farming.

The overall scale of the expropriations was quite massive. The number of tenants dispossessed after the dissolution of the monasteries was 50,000. The area enclosed from 1455-1605 was "some half-million acres." The number dispossessed from enclosed lands between 1455 and 1637 was 30-40,000. *"This may well have represented a figure of over 10 per cent. of all middling and small landholders and between 10 and 20 per cent. of those employed at wages...; in which case the labour reserves thereby created would have been of comparable dimensions to that which existed in all but the worst months of the economic crisis of the 1930's."* Although *"the absolute number of persons affected in each case may seem small by modern standards, the result was large in proportion to the demand for hired labour at the time."*[21] And those peasants not subject to enclosure were victimized by rack-renting and arbitrary fines, which often resulted in their being driven off the land by inability to pay.[22]

The expropriation of Royalist land during the Interregnum followed a similar pattern to that of the monasteries under Henry VIII. Purchasers of confiscated lands, Christopher Hill wrote, *"were anxious to secure quick returns. Those of their tenants who could not produce written evidence of their titles were liable to eviction."*[23] Tenants of sequestered estates complained that the new purchasers *"wrest from the poor Tenants all former Immunities and Freedoms they formerly enjoyed...."*[24]

Another major theft of peasant land was the "reform" of land law by the seventeenth century Restoration Parliament. (The legislation can be assigned more than one date, since like all legislation passed during the Interregnum, it had to be confirmed under Charles II). The landlords' rights in feudal legal theory were transformed into absolute rights of private property; the tenants were deprived of all their customary rights in the land they tilled, and transformed into tenants-at-will in the modern sense.

> *After the restoration of the Stuarts, the landed proprietors carried, by legal means, an act of usurpation, effected everywhere on the Continent without any legal formality. They abolished the feudal tenure of land, i.e., they got*

rid of all its obligations to the State, "indemnified" the State by taxes on the peasantry and the rest of the people, vindicated for themselves the rights of modern private property in estates to which they had only a feudal title, and, finally, passed those laws of settlement which, <u>mutatis mutandis</u>, had the same effects on the English agricultural labourer, as the edict of the Tartar Boris Godunof on the Russian peasantry.[25]

(The effects of the laws of settlement, as a form of social control, will be dealt with below.)

As Christopher Hill put it, "*feudal tenures were abolished upwards only, not downwards*." At the same time that landlords were guaranteed against all uncertainty and caprice from above, the peasants were placed at the absolute mercy of the landlords.

The Act of 1660 insisted that it should not be understood to alter or change any tenure by copyhold. Copyholders obtained no absolute property rights in their holdings, remaining in abject dependence on their landlords, liable to arbitrary death duties which could be used as a means of evicting the recalcitrant. The effect was completed by an act of 1677 which ensured that the property of small freeholders should be no less insecure than that of copyholders, unless supported by written legal title. So most obstacles to enclosures were removed: the agricultural boom of the late seventeenth and eighteenth centuries redounded to the benefit of big landowners and capitalist farmers, not of peasant proprietors.... The century after the failure of the radicals to win legal security of tenure for the small men is the century in which many small landowners were forced to sell out in consequence of rack-renting, heavy fines, taxation and lack of resources to compete with capitalist farmers.[26]

At the same time, all the feudal dues previously paid by the aristocracy as a condition of their ownership, were replaced with taxes on the population at large.

And so the abolition of the military tenures in England by the Long Parliament, ratified after the accession of Charles II, though simply an appropriation of public revenues by the feudal land holders, who thus got rid of the consideration on which they held the common property of the nation, and saddled it on the people at large, in the taxation of all consumers, has long been characterized, and is still held up in the law books, as a triumph of the spirit of freedom. Yet here is the source of the immense debt and heavy taxation of England.[27]

After the "Glorious Revolution," by which the people of England had been freed from the papist tyranny of James II into the tender ministrations of the Whig Oligarchy, yet another reform was introduced.

In a foreshadowing of the misnamed "privatization" of our own day, most of the crown land, rightfully the property of the laboring people of England, was parceled out to the great landlords.

> They inaugurated the new era by practicing on a colossal scale thefts of state lands, thefts that had been hitherto managed more modestly. These estates were given away, sold at a ridiculous figure, or even annexed to private estates by direct seizure.... The Crown lands thus fraudulently appropriated, together with the robbery of the Church estates...form the basis of the today princely domains of the English oligarchy.[28]

In addition to its land "reforms," the Whig parliament under William and Mary introduced the Game Laws as a means of restricting independent subsistence by the laboring classes. Hunting, for the rural population, had traditionally been a supplementary source of food. The 1692 law, in its preamble, specifically referred to the "*great mischief*" by which "*inferior tradesmen, apprentices, and other dissolute persons* [!] *neglect their trades and employments*" in favor of hunting and fishing.[29]

Even after the expropriations of the Tudor and Stuart periods, the dispossession of the peasantry was still incomplete. A significant amount of land still remained in peasant hands under customary forms of ownership, and continued to provide a margin of independence for some. After the Tudor expropriations, many vagabonds migrated into "*such open-field villages as would allow them to squat precariously on the edge of common or waste.*" One seventeenth century pamphleteer noted that "*in all or most towns where the fields lie open and are used in common there is a new brood of upstart intruders as inmates, and the inhabitants of lawful cottages erected contrary to law....*" He referred to the common complaint of employers, that they were "*loyterers who will not usually be got to work unless they may have such excessive wages as they themselves desire.*"[30] Hence, the final expropriation of even these last remaining peasant lands was vital to the full development of capitalism.

The second wave of enclosures, in the eighteenth and nineteenth centuries, was therefore closely connected with the process of industrialization. Not counting enclosures before 1700, the Hammonds estimated total enclosures in the eighteenth and nineteenth centuries at between a sixth and a fifth of the arable land in England.[31] E. J. Hobsbawm and George Rudé, less conservatively, estimated enclosures between 1750 and 1850 alone as transforming "*something like one quarter of the cultivated acreage from open field, common land, meadow or waste into private fields....*"[32] Dobb estimated it as high as a quarter or half of land in the fourteen counties most affected.[33] Of 4000 Private Acts of Enclosure from the early eighteenth century through 1845, two-thirds involved "open fields belonging to cottagers," and the other third involved common woodland and heath.[34]

The Tudor and Stuart enclosures had been carried out by private landlords, on their own initiative, often by stealth. From the eighteenth century on, however, they were carried out by law, through parliamentary "acts of enclosure": "*in other words, decrees by which the landlords grant themselves the people's land as private property...*" Marx cited these acts as evidence that the commons, far from being the "*private property of the great landlords who have taken the place of the feudal lords,*" had actually required "*a parliamentary coup d'etat...for its transformation into private property.*"[35]

The ruling classes saw the peasants' customary right to the land as a source of economic independence from capitalist and landlord, and thus a threat to be destroyed. Mandeville, in *Fable of the Bees*, wrote of the need to keep laborers both poor and stupid, in order to force them to work:

> *It would be easier, where property is well secured, to live without money than without poor; for who would do the work?....As they ought to be kept from starving, so they should receive nothing worth saving. If here and there one of the lowest class by uncommon industry, and pinching his belly, lifts himself above the condition he was brought up in, nobody ought to hinder him;...but it is the interest of all rich nations, that the greatest part of the poor should almost never be idle, and yet continually spend what they get.... Those that get their living by their daily labour...have nothing to stir them up to be serviceable but their wants which it is prudence to relieve, but folly to cure.... To make the society happy and people easier under the meanest circumstances, it is requisite that great numbers of them should be ignorant as well as poor....*[36]

A 1739 pamphlet, quoted by Christopher Hill, warned that the only way to enforce industry and temperance was "*to lay them under the necessity of labouring all the time they can spare from rest and sleep, in order to procure the common necessities of life.*"[37]

These prescriptions for keeping the working classes productive were echoed in a 1770 tract, "Essay on Trade and Commerce":

> *That mankind in general, are naturally inclined to ease and indolence, we fatally experience to be true, from the conduct of our manufacturing populace, who do not labour, upon an average, above four days in a week, unless provisions happen to be very dear.... I hope I have said enough to make it appear that the moderate labour of six days in a week is no slavery.... But our populace have adopted a notion, that as Englishmen they enjoy a birthright privilege of being more free and independent than in any country in Europe. Now this idea, as far as it may affect the bravery of our troops, may be of some use; but the less the manufacturing poor have of it, certainly the better for themselves and for the State. The labouring people should never*

think themselves independent of their superiors.… It is extremely dangerous to encourage mobs in a commercial state like ours, where, perhaps, seven parts out of eight of the whole, are people with little or no property. The cure will not be perfect, till our manufacturing poor are contented to labour six days for the same sum which they now earn in four days.[38]

Enclosure eliminated "*a dangerous centre of indiscipline*" and compelled workers to sell their labor on the masters' terms. Arthur Young, a Lincolnshire gentleman, described the commons as "*a breeding-ground for 'barbarians,' 'nursing up a mischievous race of people'.*" "*[E]very one but an idiot knows,*" he wrote, "*that the lower classes must be kept poor, or they will never be industrious.*" The Board of Agriculture report of Shropshire, in 1794, echoed this complaint: "*the use of common land by labourers operates upon the mind as a sort of independence.*"[39] The *Commercial and Agricultural Magazine* warned in 1800 that leaving the laborer "*possessed of more land than his family can cultivate in the evenings*" meant that "*the farmer can no longer depend on him for constant work.*"[40] Sir Richard Price commented on the conversion of self-sufficient proprietors into "*a body of men who earn their subsistence by working for others.*" As a result there would, "*perhaps, be more labour, because there will be more compulsion to it.*"[41]

The Rev. J. Townsend, worthy man of God, likewise wrote (in "A Dissertation on the Poor Laws, By a Well-Wisher to Mankind") of the benefit of poverty in compelling the poor to labor.

Legal constraint to labour is attended with too much trouble, violence, and noise, creates ill will etc., whereas hunger is not only a peaceable, silent, unremitted pressure, but, as the most natural motive to industry and labour, it calls forth the most powerful exertions.…

It seems to be a <u>law</u> <u>of</u> <u>nature</u> that the poor should be to a certain degree improvident, that there may be always some to fulfill the most servile, the most sordid, and the most ignoble offices in the community. The stock of human happiness is thereby much increased. The more delicate ones are thereby freed from drudgery, and can pursue higher callings etc. undisturbed.[42]

The only humans whose drudgery matters, obviously, are the "more delicate ones" whose "human happiness" is increased by the opportunity to pursue their "higher callings," without the disturbance of having to support themselves by their own labor. The good Reverend was, indeed, a well-wisher of mankind—except, perhaps, for the 95% of it toiling below his threshold of visibility.

The Gloucestershire *Survey* (1807) remarked that among "*the greatest of evils to agriculture would be to place the labourer in a state of independence.*" For as another observer from the same period observed, "*Farmers, like manufacturers, require constant labourers—men who have no other means of support than their daily labour, men whom they can depend on.*"[43]

The Board of Agriculture reports, cited by Christopher Hill, contained enthusiastic praise for the disciplinary effect of enclosures. Enclosure of commons forced laborers *"to work every day in the year."* Children *"*[would]* be put out to labour early."* Most importantly, thanks to the suppression of economic independence, the *"subordination of the lower ranks of society...would be thereby considerably secured."*[44]

Of course, suppression of the means of independent subsistence did not take only the form of land-theft. At times, spinning and weaving in individual cottages was actually prohibited by law, as an interference with the supply of agricultural labor.[45] As Kirkpatrick Sale elaborated on the same theme:

> By the late eighteenth century there were two kinds of machines capable of sophisticated textile production in England. One was a cottage-based, one-person machine built around the spinning jenny, perfected as early as the 1760s; the other was a factory-based, steam-driven machine based on the

> Watts engine and the Arkwright frame, introduced in the 1770s. The choice of which was to survive and proliferate was made not upon the merits of the machines themselves nor upon any technological grounds at all but upon the wishes of the dominant political and economic sectors of English society at the time. The cottage-centered machines, ingenious though they were, did not permit textile merchants the same kind of control over the workforce nor the same regularity of production as did the factory-based machines. Gradually, therefore, they were eliminated, their manufacturers squeezed by being denied raw materials and financing, their operators suppressed by laws that, on various pretexts, made home-production illegal.[46]

Apparently, the recipe for a "free market," as the average vulgar libertarian uses the term, is as follows: 1) first steal the land of the producing classes, by state fiat, and turn them into wage-laborers; 2) then, by state terror, prevent them from moving about in search of higher wages or organizing to increase their bargaining strength; 3) finally, convince them that their subsistence wages reflect the marginal productivity of labor in a "free market."

Marx mocked the bourgeois apologists (in the person of F. M. Eden), usually such zealots for the rights of property, for their blithe acceptance of the past robbery of the working population:

> The stoical peace of mind with which the political economist regards the most shameless violation of the "sacred rights of property" and the grossest acts of violence to persons, as soon as they are necessary to lay the foundations of the capitalist mode of production, is shown by Sir F. M. Eden.... The whole

series of thefts, outrages, and popular misery, that accompanied the forcible expropriation of the people, from the last third of the fifteenth to the end of the eighteenth century, lead him merely to the comfortable conclusion, "The due proportion between arable land and pasture had to be established...."[17]

As always, the passive voice is the last refuge of weasels.

Marx was not the only mocker of the bourgeois nursery tale of primitive accumulation. Albert Jay Nock, that patron saint of the Old Right, also had some sharp words on the subject—not only for the purported apologists of pseudo-"laissez-faire," but for the advocates of state action:

The horrors of England's industrial life in the last century furnished a standing brief for addicts of positive intervention. Child-labour and woman-labour in the mills and mines; Coketown and Mr. Bounderby; starvation wages; killing hours; vile and hazardous conditions of labour; coffin ships officered by ruffians—all these are glibly charged off by reformers and publicists to a regime of rugged individualism, unrestrained competition, and laissez-faire. *This is an absurdity on its face, for no such regime ever existed in England.*

They were due to the State's primary intervention whereby the population of England was expropriated from the land; due to the State's removal of the land from competition with industry for labour. Nor did the factory system and the "industrial revolution" have the least thing to do with creating these hordes of miserable beings. When the factory system came in, those hordes were already there, expropriated, and they went into the mills for whatever Mr. Gradgrind and Mr. Plugson of Undershot would give them because they had no choice but to beg, steal or starve. Their misery and degradation did not lie at the door of individualism; they lay nowhere but at the door of the State.... Our zealots of positive intervention would do well to read the history of the Enclosures Acts and the work of the Hammonds, and see what they can make of them.[18]

Before we close this section, we should consider the claim of some apologists that these acts of expropriation somehow increased "efficiency." Like that of Edens above, such apologies these days often issue from the same figures who are the most scandalized at any threat to the absolute right of private property. Leaving aside the moral illegitimacy of such consequentialist justifications of robbery, it's hard to avoid being amused at the parallelism with Marx and Engels, who, in a distorted version of the Whig theory of history, saw class exploitation and robbery as the necessary means of creating the "productive forces," on the way to the final state of abundance.

As Thomas Fuller scornfully pointed out, an increase in the overall wealth of that mythical being "society" resulting from such robbery did not necessarily translate into an increased quality of life for those robbed. Tell the fenmen, he said,

> *of the great benefit to the public, because where a pike or duck fed formerly, now a bullock or sheep fatted; they will be ready to return that if they be taken in taking that bullock or sheep, the rich owner indicteth them for felons; whereas that pike or duck were their own goods, only for their pains of catching them.*[49]

And even the increased efficiency of production is by no means self-evident. According to Michael Perelman, in cereal farming the spade industry of eighteenth century peasants in Western Europe produced a twenty- to thirty-fold increase on seed-corn, compared to only six-fold by plow cultivation. As for vegetable horticulture, the market gardens of that time compare favorably in output even to the mechanized agriculture of the contemporary United States. One Paris gardener produced 44 tons of vegetables per acre; by way of comparison, in 1979 America, the average output per acre was 15 tons of onions or 8.6 tons of tomatoes (the two most productive crops in terms of weight per unit of area).[50]

Such intensive forms of cultivation were indeed less efficient, if considered in terms of output per man-hour rather than of output per acre. But labor was a commodity in abundant supply; this "superfluous" labor was "freed," by expropriation, from a life of adequate subsistence, in order that it might be allowed to starve without hindrance. As Perelman said, the small-scale cultivation suppressed by the state was "*a viable alternative to wage labor.*"[51] But that was precisely the point. The real "efficiency" aimed at was efficiency in fleecing the producing classes. As we will see later in this chapter, the ruling classes have consistently been willing to adopt less efficient forms of production, in material terms, for the sake of rendering the control of the production process more feasible.

B. Political Preemption of Land in Settler Societies

In the New World as well as the Old, too much comfort or independence on the part of the laboring classes could be a great inconvenience to "the nation" or "the people" (which entities, presumably, did not include the helots who actually produced the things consumed by "the nation" or "the people"). The response of the capitalist (with the power of the state "at his back"), in the colonies as in the Old World, was (as Marx put it) "*to clear out of his way by force, the modes of production and appropriation, based on the independent labour of the producer.*"[52]

Settler societies have always had one disadvantage, from the point of view of the ruling classes: the widespread availability of cheap land. Adam Smith observed that in the North American colonies, where affordable land was readily available, the price of labor was very high because the average laborer preferred independence to employment: *"neither the large wages nor the easy subsistence which that country affords to artificers can bribe him rather to work for other people than for himself."*[53]

E. G. Wakefield, in *View of the Art of Colonization*, wrote of the unacceptably weak position of the employing class in the colonies where self-employment with one's own property was readily available. Labor was scarce even at high wages.[54]

> *In colonies, labourers for hire are scarce. The scarcity of labourers for hire is the universal complaint of colonies. It is the one cause, both of the high wages which put the colonial labourer at his ease, and of the exorbitant wages which sometimes harass the capitalist.*[55]

> *Where land is cheap and all men are free, where every one who so pleases can obtain a piece of land for himself, not only is labour very dear, as respects the labourers' share of the product, but the difficulty is to obtain combined labour at any price.*

This environment also prevented the concentration of wealth, as Wakefield commented: *"Few, even of those whose lives are unusually long, can accumulate great masses of wealth."*[56] As a result, colonial elites petitioned the mother country for imported labor and for restrictions on land for settlement. According to Wakefield's disciple Herman Merivale, there was an *"urgent desire for cheaper and more subservient labourers—for a class to whom the capitalist might dictate terms, instead of being dictated to by them."*[57]

Faced with this situation, the capitalist could resort to one of two expedients. One of them was the use of slave and convict labor, which we will examine in greater detail in a section below. The other was preemption of ownership of the land by the colonial regime. Political preemption of the land was accompanied by a denial of access to ordinary homesteaders—either by pricing land out of their range, or by excluding them altogether. Wakefield suggested that, since *"[i]n the very beginning of a colony, all the land necessarily belongs to the government or is under its jurisdiction,"* the government could remedy the shortage of cheap wage labor by controlling access to the land.[58]

At the same time that it excluded the laboring classes from virgin land, the state in settler societies granted large tracts of land to the privileged classes: to land speculators, logging and mining companies, planters, railroads, etc. Land grants in colonial America were on a scale comparable those of William after the Conquest. Cadwallader Colden, classifying the population in his *State of the Province of New York* (1765), put *"the Proprietors of the Large Tracts of Land"* of 100,000 to above one million acres, at the apex of the social pyramid. According to James Truslow Adams, in *Provincial Society, 1690-1763* (1927), Capt. John Evans, a favorite of Governor Fletcher of New York, was granted *"an area of indeterminate extent of between three hundred and fifty and six hundred thousand acres..."* Although he was later offered £10,000 for this land, his annual quitrent was only twenty shillings (i.e., £1). Governor Bellmont later claimed that almost three-quarters of available land had been granted to thirty persons during Fletcher's term. Lord Courtney, governor from 1702-08, likewise issued large grants often running into the hundreds of thousands of acres, but preferred giving them to companies of land speculators. In New England, in contrast, Adams wrote that the early pattern of land grants to settlers for setting up townships led to more egalitarian patterns of land ownership. Unfortunately, this pattern was later supplanted by large-scale grants of land to speculators, for later sale to settlers, either as individuals or companies.[59]

Such land-grabbing was central to American history from the very beginning, as Albert Jay Nock pointed out: *"....from the time of the first colonial settlement to the present day, America has been regarded as a practically limitless field for speculation in rental values."*[60]

> *If our geographical development had been determined in a natural way, by the demands of use instead of the demands of speculation* [that is, appropriated individually by labor, as Lockeans, Georgists and mutualists agree is just], *our western frontier would not yet be anywhere near the Mississippi River. Rhode Island is the most highly-populated member of the Union, yet one may drive from one end of it to the other on one of its "through" highways, and see hardly a sign of human occupancy.*[61]

One cause of the American Revolution was Britain's *"attempt...to limit the exercise of the political means in respect of rental-values"* (namely, the 1763 prohibition of settlements west of the Atlantic watershed). This prevented preemption of the land by land speculators in league with the state.[62] The mainstream history books, of course, have portrayed this as an offense mainly against the individual homesteader, rather than the big land companies. Many leading figures in the late colonial and early republican period were prominent investors in these land companies: e.g., Washington in the Ohio, Mississippi, and Potomac Companies; Patrick Henry in the Yazoo Company; Benjamin Franklin in the Vandalia Company, etc.[63]

Lest anyone draw the conclusion that the practice of limiting the working population's access to land was a practice only in the periwigged

British Empire of Warren Hastings or Lord North, we should bear in mind that it has been followed in the "new" Empire as well:

> *The apprehension of the same truth* [stated by Wakefield] *has in more recent times led colonial administrators in certain parts of Africa to reduce native tribal reserves and to impose taxation on natives who remain in the reserves, with the object of maintaining a labour supply for the white employer.*[64]

C. Political Repression and Social Control in the Industrial Revolution.

Even after the expropriation of their land, the working class was not sufficiently powerless. The state still had to regulate the movement of labor, serve as a labor exchange on behalf of capitalists, and maintain order. And historically, this function was most vital when the bargaining power of labor threatened to increase: "*one might expect that the efforts of the State in a capitalist society to control wages and to restrict the freedom of movement of the labourer would be greater when the labour reserve was depleted than when it was swollen.*"[65] Thorold Rogers described the law from the Tudor period until the repeal of the Combination Acts in 1824, as

> *a conspiracy...to cheat the English workman of his wages, to tie him to the soil, to deprive him of hope, and to degrade him into irremediable poverty.... For more than two centuries and a half the English law, and those who administered the law, were engaged in grinding the English workman down to the lowest pittance, in stamping out every expression or act which indicated any organized discontent, and in multiplying penalties upon him when he thought of his natural rights.*[66]

As we have seen above, the liquidation of the Church's system of poor relief left a void to be filled by the Tudor state's harsh regulation of the working class. The act of Henry VIII in 1530 licensed beggars who were old or infirm, while providing for the whipping and imprisonment of "sturdy vagabonds." The 27 Henry VIII strengthened the statute with ear-cropping for second offenders, and execution for third. I Edward VI (1547) condemned anyone who refused work as a slave to whoever denounced him. The 1572 act of Elizabeth I prescribed execution of unlicensed beggars on the second offense, unless someone would "take them into service." The statutes were only repealed at the end of the sixteenth century, by 12 Ann, cap. 23, when they had done their work. "*Thus were the agricultural people, first forcibly expropriated from the soil, driven from their homes, turned into vagabonds, and then whipped, branded, tortured by laws grotesquely terrible, into the discipline necessary for the wage system.*"[67]

Queen Anne's repeal of the Tudor legislation did not, by any means, put an end to state-imposed regulation of the working class' movement. The laws of settlement had been created, in the meantime, and were later supplemented by the Combination Laws and the police state of Pitt. The government continued to set maximum wages, as well.

The Act of Settlement dates back to 1662. There had been a great deal of lower class movement during the Interregnum, characterized by the tendency of *"poor people…to settle themselves in those parishes where there is the best stock, the largest commons or wastes to build cottages and the most woods for them to burn or destroy."* As that quote from the preamble might suggest, the Act was intended to remedy such excess mobility. Under its terms, two justices of the peace in each county were empowered to eject any newcomer to a parish without independent means, and return him to his parish of origin. The legislation was explicitly directed against cottagers and squatters in commons, and was evidently followed *"by a destruction of cottages erected in the free times of the interregnum."*[68]

In a quotation earlier in this chapter, Marx referred to the "laws of settlements" as analogous to "the edict of the Tartar Boris Godunov" in their effect on the English working population. Had he been more familiar with events in America at the time he wrote, he might have referred to the Black Codes as a better analogy. Had he lived into the twentieth century, he might have cited the internal passport systems of South Africa or the Soviet Union. The British state's controls on the movement of population, during the Industrial Revolution, were a system of totalitarian control comparable to all these.

Under the Poor Laws and the Laws of Settlement, a member of the English working class was restricted to the parish of his birth, unless an official of another parish granted him a permit to reside there. The state maintained work discipline by keeping laborers from voting with their feet. It was hard to persuade parish authorities to grant a man a certificate entitling him to move to another parish to seek work. Even on the rare occasion when such a certificate was granted, it amounted to a system of peonage in which the worker's continued residence in the new parish was conditioned on maintaining the good will of his employer. Workers were forced to stay put and sell their labor in a buyer's market. Adam Smith ventured that there was *"scarce a poor man in England of forty years of age…who has not in some part of his life felt himself most cruelly oppressed by this ill-contrived law of settlements."*[69]

At first glance this would seem also to be inconvenient for employers in parishes with a labor shortage.[70] Factories were built at sources of water power, generally removed from centers of population. Thousands of workers were needed to be imported from far away. But the state solved the problem by setting itself up as a middleman, and providing labor-poor parishes with cheap surplus labor from elsewhere, depriving workers of the ability to bargain for better terms on their own. This practice amounted, in nearly every sense of the term, to a slave market:

> *No doubt, in certain epochs of feverish activity, the labour market shows significant gaps. In 1834, e.g.. But then the manufacturers proposed to the Poor Law Commissioners that they should send the "surplus population" of the agricultural districts to the north, with the explanation "that the manufacturers would absorb and use it up." "Agents were appointed with the consent of the Poor Law Commissioners.... An office was set up in*

> *Manchester, to which lists were sent of those workpeople in the agricultural districts wanting employment, and their names were registered in books. The manufacturers attended at these offices, and selected such persons as they chose;...they gave instructions to have them forwarded to Manchester, and they were sent, ticketed like bales of goods, by canals, or with carriers, others tramping on the road, and many of them were found on the way lost and half-starved. This system had grown up into a regular trade. This House will hardly believe it, but I tell them that this traffic in human flesh was as well kept up, they were in effect as regularly sold to these...manufacturers as slaves are sold to the cotton grown in the United States."[71]*

There you have it: the Tudor state without the whippings, ear-croppings and executions; the Black Codes without the lynchings.

Child laborers, who were in no position to bargain in any case, were a popular commodity in these poor-house slave markets. According to John Fielden ("The Curse of the Factory System, 1836),

> *In the counties of Derbyshire, Nottinghamshire, and more particularly in Lancashire, the newly invented machinery was used in large factories built on the sides of streams capable of turning the water-wheel. Thousands of hands were suddenly required in these places, remote from towns.... The small and nimble fingers of little children being by very far, the most in request, the custom instantly sprang up of procuring apprentices from the different parish workhouses of London, Birmingham, and elsewhere.[72]*

9.5 ptRelief *"was seldom bestowed without the parish claiming the exclusive right of disposing, at their pleasure, of all the children of the person receiving relief,"* according to the Committee on Parish Apprentices, 1815.[73] Frances Trollope estimated that 200,000 children, altogether, were pressed into factory labor.[74] Even when Poor Law commissioners encouraged migration to labor-poor parishes, they discouraged adult men and *"[p]reference was given to 'widows with large families of children or handicraftsmen...with large families.'"* In addition, the availability of cheap labor from the poor-law commissioners was deliberately used to drive down wages; farmers would discharge their own day-laborers and instead apply to the overseer for help.[75]

Although the Combination Laws theoretically applied to masters as well as workmen, in practice they were only enforced against the latter.[76] "A Journeyman Cotton Spinner"—a pamphleteer quoted by E. P. Thompson[77]—described *"an abominable combination existing amongst the masters,"* in which workers who had left their masters because of disagreement over wages were effectively blacklisted. The Combination Laws required suspects to answer interrogations on oath, empowered magistrates to give summary judgment, and allowed summary forfeiture of funds accumulated to aid the families of strikers.[78] In other words, workers subject to the Combination Law magistrates were deprived of all the common law's due process protections. Workers, far from possessing the much-heralded "rights of Englishmen," were thrown into prerogative courts as arbitrary as Star Chamber.

At the same time, the laws setting maximum rates of pay amounted to a state enforced system of combination for the masters. In Adam Smith's immortal words, "[w]*henever the legislature attempts to regulate the differences between the masters and their workmen, its counselors are always the masters."*[79]

In the mid-19th century, a superficial examiner might conclude, the state's "progressive" reforms finally began to remedy all these evils. But as the historians of corporate liberalism have shown us in regard to the "progressive" reforms of the twentieth century, these "reforms" were in fact undertaken in the interests of the ruling class. Their ameliorating effect on working conditions, to the real but limited extent they occurred, were a side effect of their main purpose of increasing political stability and bringing the working class under more effective social control.[80]

Regarding legislation for the ten-hour day, for example, Marx described it as an attempt by capitalists to regulate the *"greed for surplus labour"*; they served to regulate the economy in the interest of the capitalist class as a whole, in a way that could only be accomplished by acting through the state. With competition unlimited by the state, the issue of working conditions presents a prisoner's dilemma for the individual capitalist; it is in the interest of the capitalist class as a whole that the exploitation of labor be kept to sustainable levels, but in the interest of the individual capitalist to gain an immediate advantage over the competition by working his own labor force to the breaking point. As we shall see in Chapter 6 below on the rise of monopoly capitalism, the real effect of such regulations is to coordinate labor practices through a state-enforced cartel, so that those practices are no longer an issue of competition between firms.

These acts curb the passion of capital for a limitless draining of labour power,
by forcibly limiting the working day by state regulations, made by a state that
is ruled by capitalist and landlord. Apart from the working-class movement
that daily grew more threatening, the limiting of factory labour was dictated
by the same necessity which spread guano over the English fields.[81]

Marx referred, later in the same chapter, to a group of 26 Staffordshire
pottery firms, including Josiah Wedgwood, petitioning Parliament in
1863 for *"some legislative enactment"*; the reason was that competition
prevented individual capitalists from voluntarily limiting the work time
of children, etc., as beneficial as it would be to them collectively: *"Much*
as we deplore the evils before mentioned, it would not be possible to prevent them
by any scheme of agreement between the manufacturers.... Taking all these points
into consideration, we have come to the conviction that some legislative enactment
is wanted." Attempts by employers to limit the workday voluntarily to
nine or ten hours, in their collective interest, always came to nought
because the individual employer found it in his interest to violate the
agreement.[82]

As for trade unions: even after the Combination Laws were repealed
in 1825, the position of workers was different from that of masters in
regard to contract. *"The provisions of the labour statutes as to contracts*
between master and workman, as to giving notice and the like, which only allow
of a civil action against the contract breaking master, but on the contrary permit
a criminal action against the contract-breaking workman, are to this hour (1873)
in full force."[83]

In 1871, trade unions were officially recognized by Act of Parliament.
But another act of the same date (the Act to amend the Criminal Law
relating to Violence, Threats, and Molestation), had the effect that *"the*
means which the labourers could use in a strike or lockout were withdrawn from
the laws common to all citizens, and placed under exceptional penal legislation,
the interpretation of which fell to the masters themselves in their capacity as
justices of the peace."[84] Thus, the state at the same time permitted
collective bargaining, and prohibited collective bargaining outside the
avenues prescribed and regulated by the state. In much the same way,
the great "labor victory" of the Wagner Act was followed, in short order,
by Taft-Hartley, which criminalized most of the tactics by which the CIO
victories of the early Thirties had been won independently of the state.
And in the process, as Hilaire Belloc so brilliantly explained, for the
laborer contract was replaced by status—one step in the retrograde long
march toward industrial enserfment of the wage-earning population.[85]
A comment of Adam Smith a century earlier is worth quoting again:

"Whenever the legislature attempts to regulate the differences between masters and their workmen, its counselors are always the masters."[86]

The working class lifestyle under the factory system, with its new forms of social control, was a radical break with the past. It involved drastic loss of control over their own work. The seventeenth century work calendar had still been heavily influenced by medieval custom. Although there were spurts of hard labor between planting and harvest, intermittent periods of light work and the proliferation of saints days combined to reduce average work-time well below that of our own day. And the pace of work was generally determined by the sun or the biological rhythms of the laborer, who got up after a decent night's sleep, and sat down to rest when he felt like it. The cottager who had access to common land, even when he wanted extra income from wage labor, could take work on a casual basis and then return to working for himself. This was an unacceptable degree of independence from a capitalist standpoint.

> *In the modern world most people have to adapt themselves to some kind of discipline, and to observe other' people's timetables,...or work under other people's orders, but we have to remember that the population that was flung into the brutal rhythm of the factory had earned its living in relative freedom, and that the discipline of the early factory was particularly savage.... No economist of the day, in estimating the gains or losses of factory employment, ever allowed for the strain and violence that a man suffered in his feelings when he passed from a life in which he could smoke or eat, or dig or sleep as he pleased, to one in which somebody turned the key on him, and for fourteen hours he had not even the right to whistle. It was like entering the airless and laughterless life of a prison.*[87]

As Oppenheimer suggested in the quote earlier in this chapter, the factory system could not have been imposed on workers without first depriving them of alternatives, and forcibly denying access to any source of economic independence. No unbroken human being, with a sense of freedom or dignity, would have submitted to factory discipline. Steven Marglin compared the nineteenth century textile factory, staffed by pauper children bought at the workhouse slave market, to Roman brick and pottery factories which were manned by slaves. In Rome, factory production was exceptional in manufactures dominated by freemen. The factory system, throughout history, has been possible only with a work force deprived of any viable alternative.

> *The surviving facts...strongly suggest that whether work was organized along factory lines was in Roman times determined, not by technological considerations, but by the relative power of the two producing classes. Freedmen*

and citizens had sufficient power to maintain a guild organization. Slaves had no power—and ended up in factories.[88]

The problem with the old "putting out" system, in which cottage workers produced textiles on a contractual basis, was that it only eliminated worker control of the product. The factory system, by also eliminating worker control of the production process, introduced the added advantages of discipline and supervision, with workers organized under an overseer.

> *...the origin and success of the factory lay not in technological superiority, but in the substitution of the capitalist's for the worker's control of the work process and the quantity of output, in the change in the workman's choice from one of how much to work and produce, based on his preferences for leisure and goods, to one of whether or not to work at all, which of course is hardly much of a choice.*[89]

Marglin took Adam Smith's classic example of the division of labor in pin-making, and stood it on its head. The increased efficiency resulted, not from the division of labor as such, but from dividing and sequencing the process into separate tasks in order to reduce set-up time. This could have been accomplished by a single cottage workman separating the various tasks and then performing them sequentially (i.e., drawing out the wire for an entire run of production, then straightening it, then cutting it, etc.).

> *without specialization, the capitalist had no essential role to play in the production process. If each producer could himself integrate the component tasks of pin manufacture into a marketable product, he would soon discover that he had no need to deal with the market for pins through the intermediation of the putter-outer. He could sell directly and appropriate to himself the profit that the capitalist derived from mediating between the producer and the market.*[90]

This principle is at the center of the history of industrial technology for the last two hundred years. Even given the necessity of factories for some forms of large-scale, capital-intensive manufacturing, there is usually a choice between alternate productive technologies within the factory. Industry has consistently chosen technologies which de-skill workers and shift decision-making upward into the managerial hierarchy. As long ago as 1835, Dr. Andrew Ure (the ideological grandfather of Taylorism), argued that the more skilled the workman, *"the more self-willed and...the less fit a component of a mechanical system"* he became. The solution was to eliminate processes which required *"peculiar dexterity and steadiness of hand...from the cunning workman"* and replace them by a *"mechanism, so self-regulating, that a child may superintend it."*[91] And the principle has been followed throughout the twentieth century. William Lazonick, David Montgomery, David Noble, and Katherine Stone have produced an excellent body of work on this theme. Even though corporate experiments in worker self-management increase morale and productivity, and reduce injuries and absenteeism beyond the wildest hopes of management, they are usually abandoned out of fear of loss of control.

Christopher Lasch, in his foreword to Noble's *America by Design*, characterized the process of de-skilling in this way:

> *The capitalist, having expropriated the worker's property, gradually expropriated his technical knowledge as well, asserting his own mastery over production....*
> *The expropriation of the worker's technical knowledge had as a logical consequence the growth of modern management, in which technical knowledge came to be concentrated. As the scientific management movement split up production into its component procedures, reducing the worker to an appendage of the machine, a great expansion of technical and supervisory personnel took place in order to oversee the productive process as a whole.*[92]

The expropriation of the peasantry and imposition of the factory labor system was not accomplished without resistance; the workers knew exactly what was being done to them and what they had lost. During the 1790s, when rhetoric from the Jacobins and Tom Paine was widespread among the radicalized working class, the rulers of "the cradle of liberty" lived in terror that the country would be swept by revolution. The system of police state controls over the population resembled an occupation regime. The Hammonds referred to correspondence between north-country magistrates and the Home Office, in which the law was frankly treated *"as an instrument not of justice but of repression,"* and the working classes *"appear[ed]...conspicuously as a helot population."*[93]

> *...in the light of the Home Office papers,...none of the personal rights attaching to Englishmen possessed any reality for the working classes. The magistrates and their clerks recognized no limit to their powers over the freedom and the movements of working men. The Vagrancy Laws seemed to supercede the entire charter of an Englishman's liberties. They were used to put into prison any man or woman of the working class who seemed to the magistrate an inconvenient or disturbing character. They offered the easiest and most expeditious way of proceeding against any one who tried to collect*

money for the families of locked-out workmen, or to disseminate literature that the magistrates thought undesirable.[94]

Peel's "bobbies"—professional law enforcement—replaced the posse comitatus system because the latter was inadequate to control a population of increasingly disgruntled workmen. In the time of the Luddite and other disturbances, crown officials warned that "*to apply the Watch and Ward Act would be to put arms into the hands of the most powerfully disaffected.*" At the outset of the wars with France, Pitt ended the practice of quartering the army in alehouses, mixed with the general population. Instead, the manufacturing districts were covered with barracks, as "*purely a matter of police.*" The manufacturing areas "*came to resemble a country under military occupation.*"[95]

Pitt's police state was supplemented by quasi-private vigilantism, in the time-honored tradition of blackshirts and death squads ever since. For example the "Association for the Protection of Property against Republicans and Levellers"—an anti-Jacobin association of gentry and mill-owners—conducted house-to-house searches and organized Guy Fawkes-style effigy burnings against Paine; "Church and King" mobs terrorised suspected radicals.[96]

Thompson characterized this system of control as "*political and social apartheid,*" and argued that "*the revolution which did not happen in England was fully as devastating*" as the one that did happen in France.[97]

D. Mercantilism, Colonialism, and the Creation of the "World Market"

The discovery of gold and silver in America, the extirpation, enslavement and entombment in mines of the aboriginal population, the beginning of the conquest and looting of the East Indies, the turning of Africa into a warren for the commercial hunting of blackskins, signalised the rosy dawn of the era of capitalist production. These idyllic proceedings are the chief momenta of primitive accumulation. On their heels treads the commercial war of the European nations, with the globe for a theatre....

....The treasures captured outside Europe by undisguised looting, enslavement, and murder, floated back to the mother country and were there turned into capital.[98]

We must find new lands from which we can easily obtain raw materials and at the same time exploit the cheap slave labour that is available from the natives of the colonies. The colonies would also provide a dumping ground for the surplus goods produced in our own factories.[99]

In addition to its transformation of society at home, the state aided the accumulation of capital through mercantilism. The modern "world market" was not created by free market forces. Like capitalist production in Western Europe, it was an artificial creation of the state, imposed by a revolution from above. The world market was established by the European conquest of most of the world, and by the naval supremacy of the Western European powers. Manufacturing to serve a global market was encouraged by state intervention to shut out foreign goods, give European shipping a monopoly of foreign commerce, and stamp out foreign competition by force. Since the process of creating a single world market has been so closely identified, since the mid-seventeenth century, with the hegemony of Great Britain over the other Western European powers, we will focus on British mercantilism and colonial policy in this section. Our survey here is not intended even as a systematic overview of the various subsidiary themes in the evolution of colonialism; as Marx's panoramic quote above suggests, the subject is too broad for us even to touch briefly on all its major sub-topics. The following is only a very uneven look at some of the more interesting aspects of the subject that have especially caught our attention.

The Dutch wars during the Interregnum and the reign of Charles II established England as the dominant mercantile power in the world. The Dutch carrying trade was largely eclipsed, and "*the nucleus of all later settlements in India*" were won from the Dutch. In the process, the value of stock in the East India Company increased nine-fold. The East India Company, established by charter from Cromwell, not only enjoyed close ties to the English state, but acted as proxy for it; it had the financial and military backing of the state behind its rule.[100]

In addition to the naval supremacy arising from those wars, and the Dutch colonies added to English dominions, the British position was further cemented by the Navigation Acts.

> *The imperial monopoly created by the Navigation Acts allowed merchants to buy English and colonial exports cheap and sell them dear abroad, to buy foreign goods cheap and sell them dear in England. This increased merchants' profits, and forced national income from consumption into capital, especially into the artificially stimulated ship-building industry, which boomed. Thanks to new building and prizes captured in war, English shipping tonnage is believed to have more than doubled between 1640 and 1686.*[101]

Trade carried out under such monopoly conditions was a much more lucrative source of accumulation than industry, providing massive sums of capital for investment in the industrial revolution of the late eighteenth century.[102]

Modern exponents of the "free market" generally treat mercantilism as a "misguided" attempt to promote some unified national interest, adopted out of sincere ignorance of economic principles. In fact, the architects of mercantilism knew exactly what they were doing. Mercantilism was extremely efficient for its real purpose: making wealthy manufacturing interests rich at the expense of everyone else. Adam Smith consistently attacked mercantilism, not as a product of economic error, but as a quite intelligent attempt by powerful interests to enrich themselves through the coercive power of the state.

Despite mercantilism's theoretical preoccupation with the balance of trade, its practical concern was with favorable *terms* of trade—buying cheap and selling dear.[103] And this was quite rational, given the existence of captive foreign markets. Modern free trade advocates assume a mythical world of consumer sovereignty, in which domestic capital has no compulsive power over foreign markets. But this is untrue even in today's world, let alone the world of the seventeenth and eighteenth centuries.

> *The reason why an inelastic foreign demand should have been so easily assumed is not at first class clear. A principal reason why they imagined that exports could be forced on other countries at an enhanced price without diminution of quantity was probably because they were thinking, not in terms of nineteenth-century conditions where alternative markets were generally available to a country, but of a situation where considerable pressure, if not actual coercion, could be applied to the countries with whom one did the bulk of one's trade.*[104]

Although opportunities for domestic plunder had been largely exhausted (at least for the time being), the possibilities for naked force in foreign dominions were breathtaking:

> *As regards the internal market, experience had presumably taught* [policy makers] *that such measures* [regulatory rent-seeking and unequal exchange at expense of other capitalists] *could quickly reach a limit, especially when the field was already congested with established privileges and monopolistic regulations. Here there was little chance of a merchant expanding his stint save at the expense of another; and internal trade was consequently regarded as yielding little chance of gain from further regulation. But in virgin lands across the seas, with native populations to be despoiled and enslaved and colonial settlers to be economically regimented, the situation looked altogether different and the prospects of forced trading and plunder must have seemed abundantly rich.*[105]

In their reliance on the state to enforce unequal exchange, the merchant capitalists were acting in the tradition of their ancestors, the oligarchs who had taken over the artisan guilds and towns in the late Middle Ages, and set themselves up as middlemen between the urban craftsmen and the rural peasants.

> *As one writer has said of it, this was the former 'policy of the town writ large in the affairs of State'. It was a similar policy of monopoly to that which at an earlier stage the towns had pursued in their relations with the surrounding countryside, and which the merchants and merchant-manufacturers of the privileged companies had pursued in relation to the working craftsmen.*[106]

Ireland was an early dress rehearsal for a number of atrocious themes that were to recur throughout the history of colonialism. Ireland, during and after Cromwell's conquest, experienced a death-rate comparable to the killing fields of Pol Pot, or of East Timor after Suharto's invasion.

The settler societies of Australia and the New World relied heavily on slave labor of one kind or another. According to Wakefield, when cheap land was available in the colonies, the only way for the capitalist to obtain labor at a profit was to employ convict or slave labor. Although, as we have seen above, Wakefield preferred a government policy of artificially pricing laborers out of the land market, he recognized slavery as a necessary makeshift when labor was scarce relative to land.[107]

As was the case with the use of full-scale terror war to secure control of Ireland and expropriate land from the natives, the large-scale use of slave labor in foreign colonies was pioneered (in British realms at least) by Cromwell. One of the earliest sources of slaves was the defeated Irish people, along with the Protectorate's internal enemies. To be "Barbadoesed" appeared as a new verb, referring to the massive traffic in transported political criminals to that island.

America was built on slave labor. Most people are more or less aware of the importance of African slavery in the New World (as Joshua Gee wrote in 1729, "[a]ll this great increase in our treasure proceeds chiefly from the labour of negroes in the plantations."[108] For that reason, and not to downplay its significance or sheer brutality, we focus here on the coerced labor of convicts and indentured servants, about which much less is generally known. Given the scale of black slavery and of convict and indentured white labor, it is likely that the vast majority of Americans in 1776 were descended from those brought here in chains.

Abbot Smith, a specialist in the history of indentured and convict labor, estimates that one-half to two-thirds of white immigrants to the North American colonies belonged to one of those categories.[109] Although estimates of the extent of such immigration vary, all are quite high. According to Edward Channing's *History of the United States*, 10,000 members of the British underclass were kidnapped for transportation in 1670. A 1680 pamphlet gives the same figure.[110] In Virginia alone, Thomas Wertenbaker estimated anywhere from 1500 to 2000 entered the colony annually from 1635-1705. Indentured labor was the foundation of production in the tobacco colonies throughout the seventeenth century.[111]

From the late seventeenth century on, the tobacco economy shifted to a reliance mainly on black slaves, as a means of social control. The poorly developed legal distinctions between black and white labor, combined with the brutal treatment of both and their close association on the plantations, threatened the planter aristocracy with biracial class solidarity. This threat became concrete from time to time in the form of revolts—especially Bacon's Rebellion, in which white and black laborers together nearly overthrew the colonial government. As a result, the legal status of black slaves was legally formalized in slave codes in the 1670s, and "white skin privilege" and racist ideology were used as a means to divide and rule. The shift to black plantation labor reduced the threat of social war. Even so, indentures and convicts continued to be a major part of the white labor force, and the beginning of large-scale transportation of criminals after 1718 threatened the shaky social peace once more.[112]

As for the eighteenth century, leaving aside voluntary indentures, Arthur Ekirch estimated that "*some 50,000*" convicts were transported from the British Isles.[113] Convict laborers alone represented "*as much as a quarter of all British emigrants to colonial America....*"[114] Lest anyone object that such servitude was involuntary only for those guilty of crimes, we should keep in mind the nature of their offenses. The typical transportee was a petty criminal, "*a young male labourer driven to crime by economic necessity....*" The majority of crimes were theft of property, by members of the classes "*most vulnerable to economic dislocation*"—descendants of the same "sturdy vagabonds" thrown onto the highways by the first large-scale expropriation of the peasantry two centuries before. During economic downturns, an estimated 20-45% of the English populace "*may have lacked the means to buy sufficient bread or otherwise feed themselves.*" Even in comparatively good times, the proportion did not fall below 10%.[115] Gregory King, "the pioneer statistician," estimated that over half of the population earned less than they consumed and were supported by poor rates.[116]

It is also worth bearing in mind that the legal system of that time was in the hands of justices of the peace, who represented the interests of the gentry against the overwhelming majority of the people. And once a pauper entered that legal system, guilt was by no means a necessary condition for transportation. J.P.s assumed the right to sentence to transportation even acquitted persons, if they could not find "*sureties for good behaviour.*"[117]

Another large group who were liable to involuntary transportation without having committed any offense were children. Sir Thomas Smythe and Sir Edwin Sandys, of the Virginia Company, petitioned the Council of London in 1618 to remedy the labor shortage in their American plantation by allowing the transportation of "vagrant" children. According to the terms of the consequent bill, children eight or over were subject to capture and transportation. Boys were liable to sixteen years servitude, and girls to fourteen. The city aldermen were empowered to direct constables to seize children "loitering" on the streets and to commit them to Bridewell prison-hospital pending shipment to America. Besides these "vagrants," children of the indigent were also pressed into service, on pain of cutting off poor relief to recalcitrant parents. Although the bill ostensibly provided land to those who had completed their term of service, a muster of the Virginia colony in 1625 found almost of the 1619 and 1620 transportees still alive.[118]

The rates of death were high for indentured and convict laborers in general, adults as well as children. Beginning with the transatlantic voyage itself, a death rate of 20% was regarded as acceptable, although it was often much higher. The overhead cost of white laborers was much lower than that for African slaves, since the cost of capture was so much lower.[119]

The numbers of indentured servants successfully completing their terms of service and collecting the land guaranteed by law, if any, were likewise small. As was the case with the children in the previous paragraph, only a minority of indentured servants actually collected the land that was guaranteed to them under their contract. In Maryland, for example, of 5000 indentured servants entering that colony from 1670-1680, fewer than 1300 collected their 50 acres. Over 1400 had died in service, and the rest were defrauded.[120] Masters often deliberately worsened conditions of work for indentured laborers toward the end of their terms, in order to induce them to run away and forfeit their land or money. In addition, masters were able to add years to the term of service for relatively minor offenses. Once such offense was marrying without the master's permission, or having children out of wedlock—even when the master was the father. It goes without saying that such children were born into servitude, and stayed there until they reached adulthood. Half of indentured servants, in the colonies taken together, did not survive their term of service.[121]

One of the most lucrative services the state provided for British manufacturing was the suppression of competing production in the colonies.

> *Measures, not only of coercion applied to colonial trade in order that it should primarily serve the needs of the parent country, but also to control colonial production, became a special preoccupation of policy at the end of the seventeenth century and the first half of the eighteenth.... Steps were taken to prohibit the colonial manufacture of commodities which competed with the exportable products of English industry, and to forbid the export of enumerated colonial products to other markets than England.*[122]

Although he was wrong in describing them as "[a]*n essential prerequisite*" for the industrial revolution, Christopher Hill was correct in his assertion that "*large and stable colonial monopoly markets*" were an important means of promoting manufacturing interests.[123]

The conquest of India, where the authorities in India, followed by the destruction of the Bengalese textile industry (makers of the highest quality fabric in the world), was motivated to a large extent by such concerns.[124] Although Bengalese manufacturers had not yet adopted steam-driven methods of production, they likely would have done so, had India remained politically and economically independent. At the time of conquest, as Chomsky describes it,

> *India was comparable to England in industrial development. The conqueror industrialized while Indian industry was destroyed by British regulations and interference.... Had* [such measures] *not been undertaken, Horace Wilson wrote in his* History of British India *in 1826, "the mills of Paisley and Manchester would have been stopped in their outset, and could scarcely have been again set in motion, even by the power of steam. They were created by the sacrifice of Indian manufactures."*

Under British rule, the textile center of Dacca was depopulated from 150,000 to 30,000.[125] Jawaharlal Nehru, in his 1944 work *The Discovery of India*, correlated the level of poverty in the various parts of India with the length of time the British had been there. The once prosperous territory of Bengal, the first to be colonized, is today occupied by Bangladesh and the Calcutta area.[126]

The old mercantilist system having accomplished its mission, by the mid-19th century the official British ideology shifted to "free trade." Free trade ideology has been adopted by the capitalist class, historically, when they were securely in possession of the fruits of past mercantilism, and wished to competing commercial powers from arising in the periphery by the same methods. Of course, the "free trade" actually adopted by Great Britain, as we shall see in Chapter Seven, was much closer to the neo-mercantilist "free trade" of Palmerston than the genuinely liberal free trade of the Cobdenites. Although the U.S., as a latter-day counterpart of Great Britain, is quite vocal in its support of "free trade," the American, German and Japanese industrial systems were created by the same mercantilist policies, with massive tariffs on industrial goods. "Free trade" was adopted by safely established industrial powers, who used "laissez-faire" as an ideological weapon to prevent potential rivals from following the same path of industrialization.

Although we have concentrated in this section on the earlier waves of colonialism and their effects on the formative period of industrial capitalism, the record of enslavement, robbery, and devastation was at least as great under the "New Colonialism" of the late 19th century. Exploitation of the Third World under the latter form of colonialism involved large-scale transfers of wealth to the developed world, and resulted as a consequence in vast super-profits.

In the New as well as the Old Colonialism, a central object of policy was "*to clear out of his way by force, the modes of production and appropriation, based on the independent labour of the producer.*" According to David Korten,

> One of the major challenges faced by colonial administrators was to force those who obtained their livelihoods from their own lands and common areas to give up their lands and labor to plantation development, that is, to make them dependent on a money economy so that their resources, labor, and consumption might yield profits to the colonizers.[127]

This was accomplished first of all by "*dispossessing indigenous communities of the greater part of their traditional territories*": claiming uncultivated or common lands, forests, and grazing lands as property of the colonial administration, and abrogating traditional rights of access; and second, by head taxes to compel subsistence farmers to enter the money economy.

> Throughout the colonies, it became standard practice to declare all "uncultivated" land to be the property of the colonial administration. At a stroke, local communities were denied legal title to lands they had traditionally set aside as fallow and to the forests, grazing lands and streams they relied upon for hunting, gathering, fishing and herding.

> Where, as was frequently the case, the colonial authorities found that the lands they sought to exploit were already "cultivated", the problem was remedied by restricting the indigenous population to tracts of low quality land deemed unsuitable for European settlement. In Kenya, such "reserves" were "structured to allow the Europeans, who accounted for less than one per cent

*of the population, to have full access to the agriculturally rich uplands that
constituted 20 per cent of the country. In Southern Rhodesia, white colonists,
who constituted just five per cent of the population, became the new owners
of two-thirds of the land.... Once secured, the commons appropriated by the
colonial administration were typically leased out to commercial concerns for
plantations, mining and logging, or sold to white settlers.*[128]

The latter theme continued even in post-colonial times, when
corporate agribusiness relied on authoritarian Third World regimes
to evict peasants from land needed for large-scale cash crop
production.[129]

At the same time, to relieve the labor shortage, colonial authorities
(especially in British and French West Africa) resorted to forced labor
to solve the labor shortage. Taxation was found, however, to be a much
more efficient way of accomplishing the same end. In colonial Africa
and Asia, poll taxes or excise taxes on staple commodities were used
to force subsistence farmers to sell their labor in the cash economy in
order to pay them.[130]

Conclusion: "The World We Have Lost"—And Will Regain

Capitalism was not, by any means, a "free market" evolving naturally
or peacefully from the civilization of the high Middle Ages. As
Oppenheimer argued, capitalism as a system of class exploitation was
a direct successor to feudalism, and still displays the birth scars of its
origins in late feudalism.

Romantic medievalists like Chesterton and Belloc recounted a process
in the high Middle Ages by which serfdom had gradually withered away,
and the peasants had transformed themselves into de facto freeholders
who paid a nominal quit-rent. The feudal class system was disintegrating
and being replaced by a much more libertarian and less exploitative
one. Immanuel Wallerstein argued that the likely outcome would have
been "*a system of relatively equal small-scale producers, further flattening out
the aristocracies and decentralizing the political structures.*"[131]

Although such medievalists no doubt idealized that world
considerably, it was still far superior to the world of the sixteenth and
seventeenth centuries. Kropotkin described, in terms evocative of
William Morris, the rich life of the High Middle Ages, "*with its virile
affirmation of the individual, and which succeeded in creating a society through
the free federation of men, of villages and of towns.*"[132] "*In those cities, sheltered
by their conquered liberties, inspired by the spirit of free agreement and of free
initiative, a whole new civilization grew up and flourished in a way unparalleled
to this day.*"[133] The free cities were virtually independent; although the
crown "granted" them a charter in theory, in reality the charter was
typically presented to the king and to the bishop of the surrounding

diocese as a fait accompli, when "*the inhabitants of a particular borough felt themselves to be sufficiently protected by their walls....*"[134]

The technical prerequisites of the industrial revolution had been anticipated by skilled craftsmen in the urban communes, scholars in the universities, and researchers in the monasteries;[135] but the atmosphere of barbarism following the triumph of the centralized state set technical progress back by centuries. The nineteenth century was, in a sense, a technical and industrial "renaissance," built atop the achievements of the High Middle Ages after a prolonged hiatus; but because of the intervening centuries of warfare on society, industrial technology was introduced into a society based on brutal exploitation and privilege, instead of flowering in a society where it might have benefited all.

The Renaissance as it happened, G.K. Chesterton argued, was only an anemic ghost of what it might have been had it taken place under a democracy of guilds and peasant proprietors. Had Wat Tyler and John Ball been successful, Chesterton speculated,

> our country would probably have had as happy a history as is possible to human nature. The Renascence, when it came, would have come as popular education and not the culture of a club of aesthetics. The New Learning might have been as democratic as the old learning in the old days of mediaeval Paris and Oxford. The exquisite artistry of Cellini might have been but the highest grade of the craft of a guild. The Shakespearean drama might have been acted by workmen on wooden stages set up in the street like Punch and Judy, the finer fulfillment of the miracle play as it was acted by a guild.[136]

The real advancement, the real humanism and progress of the High Middle Ages, has been neglected, and the barbarism and regression of the age of the absolute state disguised as a rebirth of civilization. In short, history has been not only rewritten, but stood on its head by the victors.

> How many lies have been accumulated by Statist historians, in the pay of the State, in that period!
>
> Indeed have we not all learned at school for instance that the State had performed the great service of creating, out of the ruins of feudal society, national unions which had previously been made impossible by the rivalries between cities?....
>
> And yet, now we learn that in spite of all the rivalries, medieval cities had already worked for four centuries toward building those unions, through federation, freely consented, and that they had succeeded.[137]

By 1650 the earlier egalitarian trend Wallerstein remarked on had been reversed. In the meantime, what he calls the "capitalist world-system" had been established in response to the crisis of feudalism and rising wages.

The socio-economic crisis weakened the nobility such that the peasants steadily increased their share of the surplus from 1250 to 1450 or 1500.... It was the increase in the standard of living of the lower strata moving in the direction of relative equalization of incomes...that for the upper strata represented the real crisis....

There was no way out of it without drastic social change. This way...was the creation of a capitalist world-system, a _new_ form of surplus appropriation. The replacement of the feudal mode by the capitalist mode was what constituted the seigniorial reaction; it was a great sociopolitical effort by the ruling strata to retain their collective privileges, even if they had to accept a fundamental reorganization of the economy.... There would be some families, it was clear, who would lose out by such a shift; but many would not. Additionally, and most importantly, the principle of stratification was not merely preserved; it was to be reinforced as well.

Does not the discovery that the standard of living of the European lower strata went _down_ from 1500 to at least 1800...demonstrate how successful was the strategy, if such it could be called, of economic transformation?[138]

On this latter point, according to Maurice Dobb, the strategy was successful indeed. In the two centuries before the Tudor dynasty, wages had doubled in terms of wheat. After 1500, they fell more than enough to reverse that gain. Part of this fall in real wages was the result of the price revolution of the 1500s, which amounted to a program of forced investment: "*To the extent that money-wages failed to rise as the commodity price-level rose, all employers and owners of capital were abnormally enriched at the expense of the standard of life of the labouring class.*"[139]

There was, as Wallerstein wrote, "*a reasonably high level of continuity between the families that had been high strata*" in 1450 and 1650. Capitalism, far from being "*the overthrow of a backward aristocracy by a progressive bourgeoisie,*" "*was brought into existence by a landed aristocracy which transformed itself into a bourgeoisie because the old system was disintegrating.*"[140] In *The Modern World-System,* he described the process as one of "*embourgeoisment*" of the nobility[141]—especially in England, where "*the aristocracy to survive had to learn the ways of and partially fuse with the bourgeoisie.*"

As Wallerstein suggested above, some families in the old landed aristocracy lost out; those adaptable elements who survived absorbed large elements of the bourgeoisie into their ranks. The new agricultural class arose in the fifteenth century as a result of the fact that the landed aristocracy had failed to become a caste, and the gentry had failed to become a lesser nobility. In this new class, the old distinction between aristocracy between aristocracy and gentry was losing its significance. Wallerstein cited Perez Zagorin on the tendency for men "*in a position to deploy capital in agriculture, trade, and industry*" to acquire "*the command of social life.*" This combined class, which also included the old merchant oligarchs who were canny enough to invest in modern methods of production, enriched itself at the expense of the increasingly proletarianized peasantry.[142]

Christopher Hill's analysis of the transformation of the landed class parallels that of Wallerstein to a large degree. The great landowners who thrived in the new economy were those who adapted to "*the new society in which money was king.*" The took less interest in court affairs, ostentatious expenditure, and hospitality, and instead turned their attention toward estate management, rack-renting, the leasing of mining rights, etc. By the seventeenth century, the elements of the old landed aristocracy who had been unable to make this transition had largely disappeared. The surviving aristocracy consisted almost entirely of those "*capable of taking advantage of the intellectual and technical revolution in estate management.*"[143]

The Civil War, as Wallerstein understood it, was between the old and the new landed class. The former, the decadent rentier class that infested the royal court, was defeated; the latter went on, as the Whig oligarchy, to achieve political supremacy in 1689.[144] Although the Civil War was followed by a resurgence of the landed interest, this interest consisted of the new capitalist agricultural class: those elements of the old landed aristocracy who had adopted capitalist methods of agricultural production and learned to thrive in a capitalist economy, along with merchant-capitalists, yeomen, and gentry who had had sufficient capital to invest in the capitalist revolution. Wallerstein contrasted this to France, in which the old court aristocracy had retained its supremacy.[145] These points are echoed in part by Arno Mayer,[146] who argued for continuity between the landed aristocracy and the capitalist ruling class.

Some apologists for capitalism try to minimize the continuity between the landed and industrial ruling classes, and stress the plebian origins of industrial capitalists in the nineteenth century. For example:

> *The early industrialists were for the most part men who had their origin in the same social strata from which their workers came. They lived very modestly, spent only a fraction of their earnings for their households and put the rest back into the business. But as the entrepreneurs grew richer, the*

sons of successful businessmen began to intrude into the circles of the ruling class.[147]

As Maurice Dobb pointed out, however, although much of the entrepreneurship of the industrial revolution was indeed carried out by *"new men..., devoid of privilege or social standing,"* they were nevertheless heavily reliant on old money for their investment capital. Although the new industries were, to an extent, built by men from the humble ranks of master craftsmen and yeomen farmers with small savings, the great bulk of capital by which industry was financed came from *"merchant houses and from mercantile centres like Liverpool."* These humble upstarts were able to make money off their own small savings only through the favor and patronage of the old ruling class. *"[A]ntagonism between the older capitalist strata and the nouveaux riches of the new industry never went very deep."*[148]

The investment capital available for the industrial revolution was the accumulated loot from centuries of previous robbery by the ruling class. It was accumulated by the merchant capitalist oligarchies of the late Middle Ages, that took over the democratic guilds and robbed both urban craftsmen and rural peasants through unequal trade. It was accumulated by the mercantilists who carried out a similar policy of unequal exchange on a global scale. It was accumulated by a landed ruling class of capitalist farmers who expropriated the peasantry and became the Whig oligarchy. It was into this old money elite that the new money men of the nineteenth century were co-opted.

But whatever their class origins, the industrial capitalists of the nineteenth century benefited massively from the previous coercion of the landed and mercantilist oligarchies. The prejudicial terms on which the British laboring classes sold their labor were set by the expropriation of their land, and by authoritarian social controls like the Laws of Settlement and the Combination Law. And the favorable terms on which the British textile industry sold its output were set by the role of British armed force in creating the "world market," and suppressing foreign competition.

One might argue that the industrial capitalists were passive beneficiaries of such policies, and played no role in their formation: for example Mises, who portrayed them as offering "salvation" to those reduced to misery by the enclosure movement, a legacy in which they were innocent of any complicity.[149] One might argue that the industrial capitalists would have preferred to operate in an environment where laborers had independent access to the means of production and subsistence, could take work or leave it, and could therefore afford to drive harder bargains in the wage market. One might argue that they would have preferred selling their wares in the face of vigorous competition from Indian and Egyptian textile industry. One might make such arguments, no doubt, and find plenty gullible enough to believe them.

Capitalism has never been established by means of the free market. It has always been established by a revolution from above, imposed by a ruling class with its origins in the Old Regime—or as Christopher Hill or Immanuel Wallerstein might put it, by a pre-capitalist ruling class that had been transformed in a capitalist manner. In England, it was the landed aristocracy; in France, Napoleon III's bureaucracy; in Germany, the Junkers; in Japan, the Meiji. In America, the closest approach to a "natural" bourgeois evolution, industrialization was carried out by a mercantilist aristocracy of Federalist shipping magnates and landlords.[150]

The process by which the high medieval civilization of peasant proprietors, craft guilds and free cities was overthrown, was vividly described by Kropotkin.[151] Before the invention of gunpowder, the free cities repelled royal armies more often than not, and won their independence from feudal dues. And these cities often made common cause with peasants in their struggles to control the land. The absolutist state and the capitalist revolution it imposed became possible only when artillery could reduce fortified cities with a high degree of efficiency, and the king could make war on his own people.[152] And in the aftermath of this conquest, the Europe of William Morris was left devastated, depopulated, and miserable.

> *In the course of the sixteenth century, the modern barbarians were to destroy all that civilization of the cities of the Middle Ages. These barbarians did not succeed in annihilating it, but in halting its progress at least two or three centuries. They launched it in a different direction, in which humanity is struggling at this moment without knowing how to escape.*

> *They subjected the individual. They deprived him of all his liberties, they expected him to forget all his unions based on free agreement and free initiative. Their aim was to level the whole of society to a common submission to the master. They destroyed all ties between men, declaring that the State and the Church alone, must henceforth create union between their subjects; that the Church and the State alone have the task of watching over the industrial, commercial, judicial, artistic, emotional interests, for which men of the twelfth century were accustomed to unite directly.*[153]

> *The role of the nascent State in the sixteenth and seventeenth centuries in relation to the urban centers was to destroy the independence of the cities; to*

*pillage the rich guilds of merchants and artisans; to concentrate in its hands
the external commerce of the cities and ruin it; to lay hands on the internal
administration of the guilds and subject internal commerce as well as all
manufactures, in every detail to the control of a host of officials—and in
this way to kill industry and the arts; by taking over the local militias and
the whole municipal administration, crushing the weak in the interest of the
strong by taxation, and ruining the countries by wars.*

*Obviously, the same tactic was applied to the villages and the peasants.
Once the State felt strong enough it eagerly set about destroying the village
commune, ruining the peasants in its clutches and plundering the common
lands.*[154]

Of course, the urban communes were also subverted from within.
With the help of the rising absolute monarchs, the guilds and towns
were gradually taken over by oligarchies of merchant capitalists and
wholesalers, and transformed from democratic associations of master
craftsmen, into *"close corporations of the richer merchants, which sought to
monopolize wholesale trade"* between town craftsmen and peasants. These
merchant capitalists came to control the town governments as well as
the guilds. The democratic governance of the town communes was
replaced by oligarchy, in which the franchise was increasingly restricted
and public offices formally barred to all but wealthy burghers. These
oligarchs grew rich on unequal exchange, profiting at the expense both
of town laborers and the peasants who bought their goods; craftsmen
were prohibited by law from directly marketing their goods outside the
city walls.[155]

The outcome of the process, both internal subversion and external
assault, was that Europe was spoiled as a conquered territory, and the
people living in it were treated as an occupied enemy. The contrast
between the Europe before and after this spoilation could not have
been greater:

*In the sixteenth century Europe was covered with rich cities, whose artisans,
masons, weavers and engravers produced marvelous works of art; their
universities established the foundations of modern empirical science, their
caravans covered the continents, their vessels ploughed the seas and rivers.*

*What remained two centuries later? Towns with anything from 50,000 to
100,000 inhabitants and which (as was the case of Florence) had a greater
proportion of schools and, in the communal hospitals, beds, in relation to
the population than is the case with the most favored towns today, became
rotten boroughs. Their populations were decimated or deported, the State and*

> *Church took over their wealth. Industry was dying out under the rigorous*
> *control of the State's employees; commerce dead. Even the roads which had*
> *hitherto linked these cities became impassable in the seventeenth century.*[156]

Peter Tosh had a song called "Four Hundred Years." Although the white working class suffered nothing like the brutality of black slavery, there has nevertheless been a "four hundred years" of oppression for all of us under the system of state capitalism established in the sixteenth and seventeenth centuries. Ever since the birth of the first states six thousand years ago, political coercion has allowed one ruling class or another to live off other people's labor. But since the early modern period the system of power has become increasingly conscious, unified, and global in scale. The current system of transnational state capitalism, without rival since the collapse of the soviet bureaucratic class system, is a direct outgrowth of that seizure of power, that revolution from above, "four hundred years" ago. Orwell had it backwards. The past is a "boot stamping on a human face." Whether the future is more of the same depends on what we do now.

Appendix: On the "Necessity" of Primitive Accumulation

A central failing of Marxism (or at least the vulgar variety) has been to treat the evolution of particular social and political forms as natural outgrowths of a given technical mode of production.

> *No social formation is ever destroyed before all the productive forces for which*
> *it is sufficient have been developed, and new superior relations of production*
> *never replace older ones before the material conditions for their existence have*
> *matured within the framework of the old society. Mankind thus inevitably*
> *sets itself only such tasks as it is able to solve, since closer examination will*
> *always show that the problem itself arises only when the material conditions*
> *for its solution are already present or at least in the course of formation. In*
> *broad outline, the Asiatic, ancient, feudal and modern bourgeois modes of*
> *production may be designated as epochs marking progress in the economic*
> *development of society.*[157]

For the Marxists, a "higher" or more progressive form of society could only come about when productive forces under the existing form of society had reached their fullest possible development under that society. To attempt to create a free and non-exploitative society before its technical and productive prerequisites had been achieved would be folly.[158]

According to Marx, the laboring classes were capable, on their own, of achieving only a "petty bourgeois consciousness" (to paraphrase

Lenin). He quoted, with apparent approval, the paternalistic elitist Owen's statement to similar effect:

> *Without large capitals, large establishments would not have been formed; men could not have been trained to conceive the PRACTICABILITY OF EFFECTING NEW COMBINATIONS, IN ORDER TO SECURE A SUPERIOR CHARACTER TO ALL and the production of more wealth annually than all could conceive.*[159]

In other words, workers were too atavistic to perceive the advantages of voluntary cooperation and combination, of pooling their resources for large-scale production, without forward-thinking capitalists knocking their heads together and forcing them to increase the productive forces. By quoting the paternalist Owen with every sign of approval, Marx implied that industrial production was impossible until the producers were robbed of their property in the means of production and driven like beasts into the factories.

This echoed his earlier assertion, in *The Poverty of Philosophy*, that the development of the forces of production was impossible without class antagonism.

> *The very moment civilisation begins, production begins to be founded on the antagonism of orders, estates, classes, and finally on the antagonism of accumulated labour and immediate labour.... No antagonism, no progress.... Till now the productive forces have been developed by virtue of this system of class antagonisms.*[160]

> *In raising such a question* [as that of Proudhon, as to why the English working class had not received all the gains of its 27-fold increase in productivity] *one would naturally be supposing that the English could have produced this wealth without the historical conditions in which it was produced, such as: private accumulation of capital, modern division of labour, automatic workshops, anarchical competition, the wage system— in short, everything that is based upon class antagonism. Now, these were precisely the necessary conditions of existence for the development of productive forces and of the surplus left by labour. Therefore, to obtain this development of productive forces and this surplus left by labour, there had to be classes which profited and classes which decayed.*[161]

Freedom was impossible until slavery had created the material conditions for it. Indeed, Engels put it in so many words, praising the "progressive" achievements of slavery and successive forms of class exploitation as necessary preconditions of socialism (much as Christian theologians praise the *felix culpa*, or "happy sin" of Adam, for making possible the beatific state of redeemed humanity).

> *It was slavery that first made possible the division of labour between
> agriculture and industry on a larger scale, and thereby also Hellenism, the
> flowering of the ancient world.. Without slavery, no Greek state, no Greek art
> and science; without slavery, no Roman Empire. But without the basis laid
> by Hellenism and the Roman Empire, also no modern Europe. We should
> never forget that our whole economic, political and intellectual development
> presupposes a state of things in which slavery was as necessary as it was
> universally recognized. In this sense we are entitled to say: Without the
> slavery of antiquity no modern socialism.*[162]

That the working classes' own forms of self-organization could not
have been the basis for industrialization, went without saying:

> *Glassworks, papermills, ironworks, etc., cannot be organized on guild
> principles. They require mass production; sale in a general market; monetary
> wealth on the part of the entrepreneur.... [U]nder the old property and
> production relations these conditions cannot be brought together.*[163]

So industrial production, by definition, is something that cannot be
freely organized by producers. Hell on earth is historically necessary.

A simple exchange economy, in which labor owned its means
of production, was unable to move beyond petty industry of its own
volition.

> *This mode of production* [petty industry] *presupposes parceling of the
> soil, and scattering of the other means of production. As it excludes the
> concentration of these means of production, so also it excludes cooperation,
> division of labor within each separate process of production, the control over,
> and the productive application of, the forces of Nature by society, and the
> free development of the social productive powers. It is compatible only with a
> system of production, and a society, moving within narrow and more or less
> primitive bounds. To perpetuate it would be, as Pecqueur rightly says, "to
> decree universal mediocrity."*[164]

The obvious question that springs to mind is, "Why?" Why could not
an artisans' guild function as a means of mobilizing capital for large-
scale production, the same as a corporation? Why could not the peasants
of a village cooperate in the purchase and use of mechanized farming
equipment? Perhaps because, in the absence of a "progressive" ruling
class, they just couldn't get their minds right. Or maybe just because.

The anarchist position, in contrast, is that exploitation and class rule
are not inevitable at any time; they depend upon intervention by the
state, which is not at all necessary. Just social and economic relations
are compatible with any level of technology; technical progress can be
achieved and new technology integrated into production in any society,

through free work and voluntary cooperation. Likewise, any technology is amenable to either libertarian or authoritarian applications, depending on the nature of the society into which it is integrated.

All the technical prerequisites for steam engines had been achieved by the skilled craftsmen of the High Middle Ages. As Kropotkin wrote,

> *Once the great discoveries of the fifteenth century were made, especially that of the pressure of the atmosphere, supported by a series of advances in natural philosophy—and they were made under the mediaeval city organization,—once these discoveries were made, the invention of the steam-motor, and all the revolution which the conquest of a new power implied, had necessarily to follow. If the mediaeval cities had lived to bring their discoveries to that point, the ethical consequences of the revolution effected by steam might have been different; but the same revolution in technics and science would have inevitably taken place. It remains, indeed, an open question whether the general decay of industries which followed the ruin of the free cities, and was especially noticeable in the first part of the eighteenth century, did not considerably retard the appearance of the steam-engine as well as the consequent revolution in arts.*[165]

Had not the expropriation of the peasantry and the crushing of the free cities taken place, a steam powered industrial revolution would still have taken place—but the main source of capital for industrializing would have been in the hands of the democratic craft guilds. The market system would have developed on the basis of producer ownership of the means of production. Had not Mesopotamian and Egyptian elites figured out six thousand years ago that the peasantry produced a surplus and could be milked like cattle, free people would still have exchanged their labor and devised ways, through voluntary cooperation, to make their work easier and more productive. Parasitism is not necessary for progress.

If anything, primitive accumulation hindered the cause of industrial progress at least as much as it helped it. Rather than furthering the cause of innovation that would not otherwise have taken place, it is more accurate to say that primitive accumulation *created* a situation in which the working class could be motivated only by compulsion. *Given* the separation of labor from capital, the only means to industrialize and adopt large-scale production was by impoverishing labor until its only choice lay between accepting work on any terms offered, and starvation. This is not to say that industrialization could only have occurred under these circumstances—only that the wage system, once created, was limited to the possibilities set by its own inner logic.

The separation of labor from capital, as has been true of so many aspects of state capitalism, led to irrationality. Laborers were deprived of the intrinsic motivation to increase the efficiency and productivity of their work methods, which would have existed in an economy of worker-owned and -organized production. The disutilities and benefits of labor not being fully internalized by the laborer, the owners of capital could not find a sufficient labor force willing to work.

In fact, the ruling class did not simply impose from above a revolution that could not otherwise have occurred. Rather, it preempted all alternative possibilities for industrialization from below. To the extent that the only source of investment capital for machine production came from above, it is because the mercantile interests controlling the guilds and towns had made it impossible for the laboring class to achieve the same results by horizontal association, and by mobilizing and pooling their own credit. As we saw above, the mass of investment capital used in the industrial revolution came from the merchant capitalists, who had taken it from the direct producers by robbery. In such a zero-sum situation, the laboring classes necessarily had fewer reserves at their own disposal. At the same time, the democratic qualities of the guilds were actively suppressed, and rendered incapable of serving as a vehicle for craftsmen to mobilize their own capital from below.

It is in this context that we should consider the extended passages in the *Grundrisse* on the role of usury and merchant capital in preparing the way for capitalism. The merchant oligarchies, with the help of the state, were able to preempt, crowd out, or suppress the self-organization of credit and to prohibit direct trade between producers and consumers, while amassing to themselves large masses of merchant capital through state-enforced monopoly. It was only as a result of this legacy that merchant capital was able to take control of the supply of raw materials for artisan labor, to control the wholesale marketing of its products, and thus to organize production under the putting-out system.

NOTES

1. Franz Oppenheimer, "A Post Mortem on Cambridge Economics (Part II)," *The American Journal of Economics and Sociology* 2:4 (1943) 533.

2. Franz Oppenheimer, *The State*, trans. By John Gitterman (San Francisco: Fox & Wilkes, 1997) li-lii.

3. Karl Marx and Friedrich Engels, *Capital* vol. 1, vol. 35 of Marx and Engels *Collected Works* (New York: International Publishers, 1996) 704-5.

4. Oppenheimer, *The State* 5-6.

5. Ludwig von Mises, *Human Action* (Chicago: Regnery, 1949, 1963, 1966) 619-20.

6. Radley Balko, "Third World Workers Need Western Jobs," Fox News. Com May 6, 2004. http://www.foxnews.com/story/0,2933,119125,00. htm Captured May 6, 2004.

7. Art Carden, "Sweatshops," Mises Economics Blog, May 6, 2004. http://www.mises.org/blog/archives/001956.asp#more Captured May 6, 2004.

8. Oppenheimer, *The State* 6.

9. Ibid. 7-8.

10. Ibid. 8.

11. Ibid. 8.

12. The term "primitive accumulation" (or "original accumulation"), was originally used by the classical economists in reference to the process by which, in the mists of time, capital had been originally accumulated by an owning class distinct from laborers (Adam Smith's "accumulation of stock"); it was assumed to have been the result of success in the marketplace. Marx used the term ironically, standing it on its head. The term, succinctly, referred to "an accumulation not the result of the capitalist mode of production, but its starting point." Marx and Engels, *Capital* vol. 1 704.

13. Marx and Engels, *Capital* vol. 1 705-6.

14. Ibid. 179-80.

15. Ibid. 706.

16. Ibid. 709.

17. J. L. and Barbara Hammond, *The Village Labourer (1760-1832)* (London: Longmans, Green & Co., 1913) 27-8, 35-6.

18. Marx and Engels, *Capital* vol. 1 711.

19. R. H. Tawney, *Religion and the Rise of Capitalism* (New York: Harcourt, Brace and Company, Inc., 1926) 120.

20. Frances Fox Piven and Richard Cloward, *Regulating the Poor* (New York: Vintage Books, 1971, 1993) 3-42.

21. Maurice Dobb, *Studies in the Development of Capitalism* (London: Routledge & Kegan Paul, Ltd, 1963) 224-5, 224-5n.

22. Immanuel Wallerstein, *The Modern World System, Part I* (New York: Academic Press, 1974) 251n.

23. Christopher Hill, *The Century of Revolution: 1603-1714* (New York: W. W. Norton & Co., Inc., 1961) 147.

24. Dobb, *Studies in the Development of Capitalism* 172.

25. Marx and Engels, *Capital* vol. 1 713.

26. Christopher Hill, *Reformation to the Industrial Revolution, 1603-1714.* Vol. 2 of Pelican History of Great Britain (London: Penguin Books, 1967) 116.

27. Henry George, *Progress and Poverty* (New York: Walter J. Black, 1942) 320.

28. Marx and Engels, *Capital* vol. 1 714.

29. Michael Perelman, *Classical Political Economy: Primitive Accumulation and the Social Division of Labour* (Totowa, N.J.: Rowman & Allanheld; London: F. Pinter, 1984, c 1983) 48-9.

30. Dobb, *Studies in the Development of Capitalism* 226; *Considerations Concerning Common Fields and Enclosures* (1653), in Ibid. 226.

31. The Hammonds, *Village Labourer* 42.

32. E. J. Hobsbawm and George Rudé, *Captain Swing* (New York: W.W. Norton & Company Inc., 1968) 27.

33. Dobb, *Studies in the Development of Capitalism* 227.

34. "Development as Enclosure: The Establishment of the Global Economy," *The Ecologist* (July/August 1992) 133.

35. Marx and Engels, *Capital* vol. 1 715.

36. Qt. In Ibid. 610.

37. Hill, *Reformation to the Industrial Revolution* 275.

38. Marx and Engels, *Capital* vol. 1 231.

39. Perelman, *Classical Political Economy* 38.

40. E. P. Thompson, *The Making of the English Working Class* (New York: Vintage, 1963, 1966) 219-20, 358.

41. Marx and Engels, *Capital* vol. 1 716.

42. Karl Marx, *A Contribution to the Critique of Political Economy*, vol. 3 of Marx and Engels *Collected Works* (New York: International Publishers, 1998) 205.

43. Dobb, *Studies in the Development of Capitalism* 222.

44. Hill, *Reformation to the Industrial Revolution* 222.

45. Trevor Ashton, *An Economic History of England: the 18th Century* (London: University Paperbacks, 1972) 115, qt. in Perelman, *Classical Political Economy* 38.

46. Kirkpatrick Sale, *Human Scale* (New York: Coward, McCann & Geoghegan, 1980) 162.

47. Marx and Engels, *Capital* vol. 1 717-8.

48. Albert Jay Nock, *Our Enemy, the State* (Delavan, Wisc.: Hallberg Publishing Corp., 1983) 106n.

49. Hill, *Reformation to the Industrial Revolution* 121.

50. Perelman, *Classical Political Economy* 41-2.

51. Ibid. 42.

52. Marx and Engels, *Capital* vol. 1 752.

53. Adam Smith, *An Inquiry Into the Nature and Causes of the Wealth of Nations* (Chicago, London, Toronto: Encyclopedia Britannica, Inc. 1952).

54. E. G. Wakefield, *A View of the Art of Colonization*. Reprints of Economic Classics (New York: Augustus M. Kelley, 1969 (1849)) 166.

55. E. G. Wakefield, *England and America* II:5, qt. in Marx and Engels, *Capital* vol. 1 755.

56. Wakefield, *England and America* I:131, qt. in ibid. 756-7.

57. Herman Merivale, *Lectures on Colonisation and Colonies*, qt. in Ibid. 757.

58. Wakefield, *View of the Art of Colonization* 332-3.

59. Gary B. Nash, *Class and Society in Early America* (Englewood Cliffs, N.J.: Prentice-Hall, Inc., 1970) 23, 33, 46.

60. Nock, *Our Enemy, the State* 67.

61. Ibid. 67n.

62. Ibid. 69.

63. Ibid. 71.

64. Dobb, *Studies in the Development of Capitalism* 222.

65. Ibid. 23-4.

66. *Six Centuries of Work and* Wages, qt. in Ibid. 233.

67. Marx and Engels, *Capital* vol. 1 723-6.

68. Hill, *Reformation to the Industrial Revolution* 141-2.

69. Smith, *Wealth of Nations* 59-61.

70. Ibid. 60.

71. Marx and Engels, *Capital* vol. 1 273; all material in quotes is from Ferrand's Speech in the House of Commons, April 27, 1863.

72. Qt. in ibid 746.

73. J. L. and Barbara Hammond, *The Town Labourer (1760-1832)* (London: Longmans, Green & Co., 1917) 1:44, 147.

74. Michael A. Hoffman II, *They Were White and They Were Slaves: The Untold History of the Enslavement of Whites in Early America.* 4th ed. (Dresden, N.Y.: Wiswell Ruffin House, 1992) 16.

75. Thompson, *Making of the English Working Class* 223-4.

76. Smith, *Wealth of Nations* 61; Hammonds, *Town Labourer* 1:74.

77. Thompson, *Making of the English Working Class* 199-202.

78. The Hammonds, *Town Labourer* 123-7.

79. Smith, *Wealth of Nations* 61.

80. See Piven and Cloward, *Regulating the Poor,* on how these purposes were served by 20th century welfare and labor legislation.

81. Marx and Engels, *Capital* vol. 1 247.

82. Ibid. 276n.

83. Ibid. 729.

84. Ibid. 729-30.

85. Hilaire Belloc, *The Servile State* (Indianapolis: Liberty Classics, 1913, 1977).

86. Smith, *Wealth of Nations* 61.

87. Hammonds, *Town Labourer* 1:33-4.

88. Steven A. Marglin, "What Do Bosses Do? The Origins and Functions of Hierarchy in Capitalist Production—Part I" *Review of Radical Political Economics* (Summer 1974) .

89. Ibid.

90. Ibid.

91. Andrew Ure, *Philosophy of Manufactures*, in Thompson, *Making of the English Working Class* 360.

92. David Noble, *America by Design: Science, Technology, and the Rise of Corporate Capitalism* (N.Y.: Alfred A. Knopf, 1977) xi-xii.

93. Hammonds, *Town Labourer* 72.

94. Ibid. 80.

95. Ibid. 91-2.

96. "Planting the Liberty Tree," Chapter Five of Thompson, *Making of the English Working Class.*

97. Ibid. 197-8.

98. Marx and Engels, *Capital* vol. 1 741.

99. Cecil Rhodes, qt. In "Development as Enclosure" 134.

100. Hill, *Reformation to the Industrial Revolution* 129.

101. Ibid. 127.

102. Ibid. 128.

103. Dobb, *Studies in the Development of Capitalism* 202.

104. Ibid. 203-4.

105. Ibid. 210.

106. Ibid. 206.

107. Wakefield, *A View of the Art of Colonization* 324-6.

108. Hill, *Reformation to the Industrial Revolution* 185.

109. James G. Leyburn, *The Scotch-Irish* (Chapel Hill, N.C.: University of North Carolina Press, 1962) 176.

110. Hoffman, *They Were White and They Were Slaves* 55, 77.

111. Thomas Wertenbaker, *The First Americans: 1607-1690* (Chicago: Quadrangle Books, 1971) 24-5.

112. A. Roger Ekirch, *Bound for America: The Transportation of British Convicts to the Colonies, 1718-1775* (Oxford, UK: Clarendon Paperbacks, 1987) 134-40.

113. Ibid. 1.

114. Ibid. 27.

115. Ibid. 55, 58.

116. Richard Hofstadter, *America at 1750: A Social Portrait* (New York: Vintage Books, 1973) 34-5.

117. Hill, *Reformation to the Industrial Revolution* 143.

118. Hoffman, *They Were White and They Were Slaves* 72-3.

119. Ibid. 80.

120. Ibid. 85-6.

121. Ibid. 85-90.

122. Dobb, *Studies in the Development of Capitalism* 205.

123. Hill, *Reformation to the Industrial Revolution* 191.

124. Ibid. 191.

125. Noam Chomsky, *World Orders Old and New* (New York: Columbia University Press, 1998) 115.

126. Noam Chomsky, *Keeping the Rabble in Line* (Monroe, Maine: Common Courage Press, 1994) 87.

127. David Korten, *When Corporations Rule the World* (West Hartford, Conn.: Kumarian Press, 1995; San Francisco, Calif.: Berrett-Koehler Publishers, Inc., 1995) 252.

128. "Development as Enclosure" 134.

129. Ibid. 138-9.

130. Ibid. 135-7.

131. Immanuel Wallerstein, *Historical Capitalism* (London, New York: Verso, 1983) 41-2.

132. Peter Kropotkin, *The State: Its Historic Role*, http://dwardmac. pitzer.edu/Anarchist_Archives/kropotkin/state/state_toc.html Captured November 12, 2003. Sec. IV.

133. Ibid. Sec. V.

134. Ibid. Sec. IV.

135. See Jean Gimpel, *The Medieval Machine: The Industrial Revolution of the Middle Ages* (New York: Penguin, 1977); also Peter Kropotkin, *Mutual Aid: A Factor of Evolution* (New York: Doubleday, Page & Co., 1909) 297-8.

136. G. K. Chesterton, *A Short History of England* (New York: John Lane Company, 1917) 163-4.

137. Kropotkin, *The State* Sec. VII.

138. Immanuel Wallerstein, *The Modern World System, Part II* (New York: Academic Press, 1980) 31.

139. Dobb, *Studies in the Development of Capitalism* 235-6.

140. Wallerstein, *Historical Capitalism* 105-6.

141. Wallerstein, *The Modern World System, Part I* 62, 286.

142. Ibid. 245-6, 256; Perez Zagorin, "The Second Interpretation of the English Revolution," *Journal of Economic History* (September 3, 1959) qt. in ibid. 256.

143. Hill, *Reformation to the Industrial Revolution* 50.

144. Wallerstein, *The Modern World-System, Part I* 283.

145. Ibid. 290.

146. Arno Mayer, *The Persistence of the Old Regime*

147. Mises, *Human Action* 622.

148. Dobb, *Studies in the Development of Capitalism* 22, 277-8.

149. Mises, *Human Action* 620.

150. Michael Harrington, *The Twilight of Capitalism* (Simon and Schuster, 1976)

151. Kropotkin, *Mutual Aid* 215-22, 226-7, 230

152. See, for example, John S. Pettingill, "Firearms and the Distribution of Income: A Neoclassical Model," *Review of Radical Political Economics* (Summer 1981) 1-10.

153. Kropotkin, *The State* Sec. VI.

154. Ibid. Sec. VIII.

155. Dobb, *Studies in the Development of Capitalism* 88-124.

156. Kropotkin, *The State* Sec. VII.

157. Marx, *A Contribution to the Critique of Political Economy* 263.

158. In fairness, Michael Harrington argued that that work was a deliberate simplification and did not do justice to the complexity of Marx's thought as a whole. *Twilight of Capitalism* 37-41.

159. *Six Lectures at Manchester*, qt. in Karl Marx, *Grundrisse*, vol. 29 of Marx and Engels *Collected Works* (New York: International Publishers, 1987) 99.

160. Karl Marx, *The Poverty of Philosophy*, vol. 6 of Marx and Engels *Collected Works* (New York: International Publishers, 1976) 132.

161. Ibid. 159.

162. Friedrich Engels, *Anti-Dühring*, vol. 25 of Marx and Engels *Collected Works* (New York: International Publishers, 1987) 168.

163. Marx, *Grundrisse* 435.

164. Marx and Engels, *Capital* vol. 1 749.

165. Kropotkin, *Mutual Aid* 297.

Chapter Five
The State and Capitalism in the "Laissez-Faire" era.

The nineteenth century is commonly described, alike by paternalistic liberals and social democrats, and by the kinds of vulgar "libertarians" who engage mainly in pro-corporate apologetics, as an age of "laissez-faire." But to use such a term in reference to that period is an utter travesty. We have already seen, in our previous chapter on primitive accumulation, how the capitalism of the nineteenth century reflected the violent reconstruction of society by a statist revolution from above. In addition, it was of the allegedly "laissez-faire" nineteenth century that Benjamin Tucker wrote, when he identified the four great forms of legal privilege on which capitalism, as a statist system of exploitation, depended. We will examine those four privileges, central to the structure of "laissez-faire" capitalism, in this chapter. In addition, we will examine a fifth form of state intervention largely ignored by Tucker, even though it was central to the development of capitalism throughout the nineteenth century: transportation subsidies.

Both state socialists and corporate welfare queens, for nearly identical reasons, have a common interest in maintaining the myth of the laissez-faire nineteenth century. The advocates of the regulatory-welfare state must pretend that the injustices of the capitalist economy result from the unbridled market, rather than from state intervention in the market; otherwise, they could not justify their own power as a remedy. The apologists of big business, on the other hand, must pretend that the regulatory-welfare state was something forced on them by anti-business ideologues, rather than something they themselves played a central role in creating; otherwise their worst fears might be realized, and the interventionist state might actually be pruned back. "Laissez-faire" is, therefore, what Albert Jay Nock called it: an "impostor term."[1]

The horrors of England's industrial life in the last century furnish a standing brief for addicts of positive intervention. Child-labour and woman-labour in the mills and mines; Coketown and Mr. Bounderby; starvation wages; killing hours; vile and hazardous conditions of labour; coffin ships officered by ruffians—all these are glibly charged off by reformers and publicists to a regime of rugged individualism, unrestrained competition, and laissez-faire. This is an absurdity on its face, for no such regime ever existed in England. They were due to the State's primary intervention whereby the population of England was expropriated from the land; due to the State's removal of land from competition with industry for labour.... Adam Smith's economics are not the economics of individualism; they are the economics of landowners and mill-owners.[2]

A. Tucker's Big Four: The Land Monopoly.

Tucker classified, as one of the four forms of monopoly, the *state's enforcement of "land titles which do not rest upon personal* occupancy and cultivation."[3] A great deal of material that he would have included under this heading has already been treated, instead, as part of our analysis of primitive accumulation in the last chapter. That material will not be duplicated; for purposes of the present chapter, it will suffice to point out that the seizure and monopoly of land by the ruling classes in the early days of capitalism has ongoing effects today.

The primitive accumulation described in the previous chapter was only one example of a general historical phenomenon: as the Georgists Oppenheimer and Nock pointed out, the state has, throughout history, made exploitation possible by politically controlling access to the land. The latter, referring to Wakefield's frank ruling class perspective on the land monopoly, commented that "*economic exploitation is impracticable until expropriation from the land has taken place.*"[4] Henry George's brief survey, in *Progress and Poverty*, of ruling classes' encroachments on the peasantry's land, is a good introduction. Livy's history of the Roman republic, for example, is dominated by the struggle between the plebians and the patrician landlords. The great landed estates of the aristocracy were carved out of the public domain, originally the common property of the entire Roman people.[5]

The system of land tenure in medieval Europe was established, likewise, by the seizure of land by the feudal ruling classes. By political means, they claimed legal property in the lands already occupied and worked by the peasantry, and compelled them to pay rent on their own land. By political means, likewise, they claimed ownership of vacant lands, and controlled access to it without themselves ever directly occupying or working it. As Adam Smith wrote, "*A great part of them was uncultivated; but no part of them, whether cultivated or uncultivated, was left without a proprietor. All of them were engrossed, and the greater part by a few great proprietors.*" [6]

This evil was in the process of being remedied in the late Middle Ages. By means such as tenure in copyhold, western Europe was evolving toward a system in which the peasant was a de facto owner, required to pay only a nominal quit-rent set by custom; after that nominal rent was paid, he could treat the land in practice as his own. Had that system been allowed to develop without violence, Europe today might be a continent of small proprietors. But as we saw in the previous chapter, that was not to be.

This last, however, has already been dealt with. In this chapter we examine statist forms of property in land as a general phenomenon. Although the primitive accumulation already recounted is regarded as unjust by all major libertarian theories of property (at least to the extent that they acknowledge its occurrence), these theories are not by any means agreed on what the proper basis of ownership might be. Our next order of business, therefore, is a comparative survey of the major theories of property in land.

The bare principle of private property in land does not carry with it, of any necessity, any particular set of rules of land tenure. Nozick pointed out that any theory of "justice in holdings" must include three major topics: 1) a theory of "*the original acquisition of holdings, the appropriation of unheld things*"; 2) "*the transfer of holdings from one person to another*"; and 3) "*principles governing how a person may divest himself of a holding, passing it into an unheld state.*"[7] Or as Tucker put it, "*The question is not whether we should be able to sell or acquire in 'the open market' anything which we rightfully possess, but how we come into rightful possession.*"[8] Free market liberals are divided among themselves on how to answer this question.

There are three main rival theories of justice in holdings among free market libertarians—the Lockean, the Georgist, and the mutualist— with Lockeanism predominating. As Bill Orton has characterized their differences, the three schools agree fairly closely on the acquisition of property (i.e., by labor homesteading), but differ considerably on their rules for transfer and abandonment.[9] All three schools agree that the only legitimate way of appropriating unowned land is homesteading by direct, personal occupation and alteration of it: as Locke put it, by admixture of labor.

In contradistinction to Lockeans, Georgists and mutualists agree in seeing the land, in some sense, as a common patrimony which cannot be permanently alienated from the commons in fee simple. Both differ from the Lockeans on the extent to which appropriation by admixture of labor permanently removes land from this common patrimony. Both groups view the common rights of mankind to the land as inalienable, and the individual's possessory or usufructory right to be in some sense a stewardship on behalf of the general human community. The Georgists, however, attribute to the community a more active role in exercising its ultimate property rights over the commons than do the mutualists, and treat the community as joint owners of the commons in a more active sense. The mutualists, on the other hand, tend to see unoccupied land simply as an unowned commons over which mankind's ultimate ownership rights are latent, and which the individual is free to use as he sees fit without accounting to any proxy for collective rights; but the latent common right of the rest of mankind prohibits the individual from claiming more land than he can personally use at the expense of the common interest, and requires that his possessory title revert to the commons when he ceases to occupy and use the land. In regard to the theoretical status of land, therefore, mutualists and individualists have more in common with each other than with the Lockeans.

Regarding practical treatment of existing land titles, on the other hand, Georgists and mainstream Lockeans have more in common with each other, and mutualists (and to some extent radical Lockeans) are the odd man out. Mutualists and (among Lockeans) the left-Rothbardians, agree that any current titles to land not established by such labor-appropriation are invalid, and that land held by such title should be regarded as unowned and open to appropriation by the first homesteader to mix his labor with it. Lockeans on the more mainstream libertarian right are more willing to accept existing property titles as valid on conventional or positivistic grounds, in the interest of stability. Georgists regard the injustice by which existing titles were acquired as relatively insignificant; the proper remedy is not to nullify existing land titles but, through community collection of rent, to nullify the unjust benefits of holding such titles. The Georgist remedy of the single tax, to a large extent, presupposes a market in land values that deals with titles and transfers in more or less Lockean terms.

On how land, once acquired by admixture of labor, is to be transferred, and on what constitutes abandonment, the three schools differ radically. The Lockeans believe that land, once justly appropriated from an unowned state, may be given away, sold, or rented by the rightful owner, and that ownership is maintained regardless of whether the original owner retains possession or rents it to another occupant. Given the justice of the existing land title, a new owner may establish legitimate ownership by a simple transfer of title, regardless of whether he personally occupies and uses the land. Direct occupancy and use is necessary only for initial appropriation, not for subsequent transfers of ownership. Georgists, besides agreeing with the Lockeans on initial appropriation, are also generally accepting of Lockean standards of transfer, so long as the principle of community collection of ground rent is followed.

Mutualists, however, advocate a much different standard for establishing ownership during subsequent transfers. For mutualists, occupancy and use is the only legitimate standard for establishing ownership of land, regardless of how many times it has changed hands. An existing owner may transfer ownership by sale or gift; but the new owner may establish legitimate title to the land only by his own occupancy and use. A change in occupancy will amount to a change in ownership. Absentee landlord rent, and exclusion of homesteaders from vacant land by an absentee landlord, are both considered illegitimate by mutualists. The actual occupant is considered the owner of a tract of land, and any attempt to collect rent by a self-styled landlord is regarded as a violent invasion of the possessor's absolute right of property.

None of these alternative sets of rules for property allocation is self-evidently right. No ownership claim can be deduced logically from the principle of self-ownership alone, without the *"overlay' of a property system,"* or a system of *"allocation rules."*[10] No such system, whether Lockean, Georgist, or Mutualist, can be proved correct. Any proof requires a common set of allocation rules, and a particular set of allocation rules for property can only be established by social consensus, not by deduction from the axiom of self-ownership.[11] (However, since all three traditions deduce their theory of appropriation by homesteading from the principle of self-ownership, in so similar a manner, it might be more accurate to say that the labor theory of appropriation common to the different overlays is more plausibly deducible from self-ownership, and less dependent on convention than the rules concerning transfer and abandonment.)

In any case, there is a great deal of practical overlap in their positions. For one thing, the "stickiness" of property is a matter of degree:

> *In both systems* [i.e., "sticky" (Lockean) and "non-sticky" (socialist/usufruct)], *in practice there are well-known exceptions. Sticky property systems recognize abandonment and salvage; usufruct allows for people to be absent for some grace period without surrendering property, and of course allows trade. You might even see the two systems as a continuum from high to low threshold for determining what constitutes "abandonment."*[12]

Or as Orton put it elsewhere, stickiness is a matter of degree, rather than a qualitative difference between capitalist and socialist property. They are *"the same thing...with different parameters"* for the length of time necessary to establish abandonment.[13]

For another, since the three systems agree on the standard of legitimacy for appropriating unowned property, much existing property is illegitimate from all three perspectives, to the extent that a large portion was acquired by means other than personal use. Murray Rothbard, for example, pointed to the illegitimacy of most historic land appropriation, even by Lockean standards:

> *How will an individual's title to the nature-given factor be determined? If Columbus lands on a new continent, is it legitimate for him to proclaim all the new continent his own, or even that sector "as far as his eye can see"? Clearly, this would not be the case in the free society that we are postulating. Columbus or Crusoe would have to <u>use</u> the land, to "cultivate" it in some way, before he could be asserted to own it.... If there is more land than can be used by a limited labor supply, then the unused land must simply remain unowned until a first user arrives on the scene. Any attempt to claim a new resource that someone does not use would have to be considered invasive of the property right of whoever the first user will turn out to be.*[14]

Rothbard later argued in *Power and Market* that land appropriated by a mere grant from the state was a grant of monopoly power analogous to that of a feudal landlord, enabling the holder of the title to charge a tax or rent on the first legitimate appropriator of the land, and force him to pay tribute for the right to occupy it.

> *Problems and difficulties arise whenever the "first-user, first-owner" principle is <u>not</u> met. In almost all countries, <u>governments</u> have laid claim to ownership of new, unused land. Governments could never own original land <u>on the free market</u>. This act of appropriation by the government already sows the seeds for distortion of market allocations when the land goes into use. Thus, suppose that the government disposes of its unused public lands by selling them at auction to the highest bidder. Since the government has no valid property claim to ownership, neither does the buyer from the government. If the buyer, as often happens, "owns" but does not use or settle the land, then he becomes a <u>land speculator</u> in a pejorative sense. For the true user, when he comes along, is forced either to rent or buy the land from the speculator, who does not have valid title to the area. He cannot have valid title because his title derives from the State, which also did not have valid title in the free-market sense....*[15]

The same was true of feudal appropriation of land in older settled areas:

> *The affinity of rent and taxation is even closer in the case of "feudal" land grants. Let us postulate a typical case of feudal beginnings: a conquering tribe invades a territory of peasants and sets up a State to rule them. It <u>could</u> levy taxes and support its retinue out of the proceeds. But it could also do something else, and it is important to see that there is no essential difference between the two. It could parcel out all of the land as individual grants of "ownership" to each member of the conquering band. Then, instead of or in*

addition to one central taxing agency, there would be a series of regional rent collecting agencies. But the consequences would be exactly the same.[16]

Clearly, the agreed-upon labor standard of appropriation still leaves much to convention: How much labor is required to appropriate how much land? Is it necessary to physically alter or use every square foot in a parcel of land one claims? Can appropriation by labor take place through the hired labor of others, or is it by personal appropriation only? The exclusion of the state from appropriating land through the labor of its "servants" might also, it seems, exclude the indirect appropriation of land by the labor of those in a private capitalist's hire. The labor standard, depending on the strictness of its interpretation, would mean that a housing development belonged to the construction workers who built it, and not to the contractor who bought the land and hired the labor. Even so, the Lockean standard of labor appropriation rules out a great deal of what Jerome Tucille called "land-grabbism, " or climbing a mountain and claiming all the land you can see,[17] and goes a long way toward remedying the evils associated by Georgists and mutualists with landlordism as such.

> *Under a "first-user, first-owner" regime, the Georgists would be wrong in asserting that no labor had been mixed with nature-given land to justify private ownership of sites. For them, land could not be owned unless it were first used and could be originally appropriated for ownership only to the extent that it was so used. The "mixing" of labor with nature may take the form of draining, filling, clearing, paving, or otherwise preparing the site for use. Tilling the soil is only one possible type of use. The use claim to the land could be certified by courts if any dispute over its ownership arose....*

> *....[S]ome of the charges that Georgists have leveled against land speculation are true, not because land speculation is bad per se, but because the speculator came to own the land, not by valid title, but via the government, which originally arrogated title to itself. So now the purchase price (or alternatively, the rent) paid by the would-be user really does become the payment of a tax for permission to use the land....*[18]

According to Mises, large-scale landlordism has always been the result of state-created land monopolies, and not of aggregation of small parcels of land by market processes.

> *Nowhere and at no time has the large-scale ownership of land come into being through the working of economic forces in the market. It is the result of military and political effort. Founded by violence, it has been upheld by violence and by that alone. As soon as the latifundia are drawn into the sphere of market transactions they begin to crumble, until at last they*

disappear completely. Neither at their formation or in their maintenance have economic causes operated. The great landed fortunes did not arise through the economic superiority of large-scale ownership, but by violent annexation outside the area of trade.... The non-economic origin of landed fortunes is clearly revealed by the fact that, as a rule, the expropriation by which they have been created in no way alters the manner of production. The old owner remains on the soil under a different legal title and continues to carry on production.[19]

Although the expression "bourgeois nursery tale" does not appear anywhere in the quote above, the import is just as clear as if it did.

In addition to the three schools' agreement on the moral illegitimacy of much existing property in land, there is also much agreement among them, as well, on the exploitative consequences of statist land appropriation. Oppenheimer argued that the monopoly of land by big landlords contributed to the system of unequal exchange by which all labor was exploited—not just the agricultural laborer or peasant, but the industrial worker as well.

The exchange economy becomes perverted by a compromise with the slave economy. In the "pure economy" no one could dream of appropriating more land than he and his family could till; such appropriation presupposes a slave system. Yet the exchange economy did tolerate great landed property, that economic institution of the political means, as legitimate and on an equal footing with property arising from work personally done. In the hybrid system which combines the transformed feudal system with the exchange economy—this is the definition of capitalism—harmony is distorted by two interrelated effects of great landed (feudal) property: the countryside's purchasing power for urban products is weakened by exploitation and ensuing inefficiency; and the urban labor market is flooded, and wages pressed down, by the slaves or serfs or agricultural workers who escape from pressure into the freedom of the cities. In a harmonious system, where the land is not appropriated, an urban worker would demand and get as much as he could otherwise receive as an independent peasant on free land; in the hybrid structure the wage is pressed down to that of an agricultural serf. This makes urban capital property a means of exploitation alongside great landed property: the propertyless suffers a deduction from his original wage, the product of his work, to the profit of the big owners.[20]

Rothbard also pointed to the exploitative effect of state land monopoly, which resulted in raising the rents of land in use and lowering wage rates.

Government sale of "its" unused land to speculators, therefore, restricts the use of new land, distorts the allocation of resources, and keeps land out of use that would be employed were it not for the "tax" penalty of paying a purchase price or rent to the speculator. Keeping land out of use raises the marginal value product and the rents of remaining land and lowers the marginal value product of labor, thereby lowering wage rates.[21]

More specifically, "conservation" laws played a key role in the land monopoly by forcibly withholding resources from the market, and thus raising the price of the resources land-owners *did* sell. It served exactly the same function as output restrictions in any other kind of monopoly.

Conservation laws, therefore, must also be looked upon as grants of monopolistic privilege. One outstanding example is the American government's policy, since the end of the nineteenth century, of "reserving" vast land tracts of the "public domain"—i.e., the government's land holdings.... Forests, in particular, have been reserved, ostensibly for the purpose of conservation. What is the effect of withholding huge tracts of timberland from production? It is to confer a monopolistic privilege, and therefore a restrictionist price, on competing private lands and on competing timber.[22]

But that is telling only half the story. In addition to withholding land from production, the state gives favored capitalists *preferential access* to it. Huge tracts of land are leased to timber, petroleum, mining, and ranching interests, at politically determined rates. For example, most of the devastation of giant redwoods in the Pacific Northwest takes place on land owned by the government, and is only profitable because the lumber companies do not have to buy the land in a competitive market. Likewise, the debate over drilling in ANWAR is not about *selling* the land to oil companies. It's about giving them preferential access, denied to ordinary citizens, and letting them pay a sweetheart price for the privilege.[23]

These two aspects, withholding and preferential access, sometimes dovetailed nicely. The main beneficiaries of conservation policy were "*the land-grant Western railroads*" and existing timber owners. The railroads' land grants had included not only the rights of way for their roads, but fifteen-mile swaths on either side of the line as well. By charging settlers for homesteading rights, including the most desirable commercial properties in the new railroad towns, the railroads obtained a large income from land speculation, in addition to their primary business of actually operating railroads. Government conservation policies further increased the price of the railroads' land holdings, and along with it added even more to their income from land speculation. The value of timber land, likewise, was raised by the withholding of land. The railroad and timber industries, consequently, were large contributors to the conservation movement.[24]

Besides the sheer injustice involved in statist land theft, and the ongoing exploitation of the producing classes by parasitic landlords, it has been a great drag on progress. This was true of the feudal system of land ownership in the Old World. Property in land not being in the hands of those who worked it, neither the landlord nor the peasant had an incentive for improving it.

> *It seldom happens that a great proprietor is a great improver...To improve land with profit, like all other commercial projects, requires an exact attention to small savings and small gains of which a man born to a great fortune...is seldom capable. The situation of such a person naturally disposes him to attend to ornament which pleases his fancy than to profit for which he has so little occasion.... He embellishes perhaps four or five hundred acres in the neighbourhood of his house, at ten times the expense which the land is worth after all his improvements; and finds that if he was to improve his whole estate in the same manner, and he has little taste for any other, he would be a bankrupt before he finished the tenth part of it....*
>
> *But if great improvements are seldom to be expected from great proprietors, they are least of all to be expected when they employ slaves for their workmen.... A person who can acquire no property, can have no other interest but to eat as much, and to labour as little as possible. Whatever work he does beyond what is sufficient to purchase his own maintenance can be squeezed out of him by violence only, and not by any interest of his own.*[25]

Even among peasants not reduced to serfdom or villeinage, who only paid a portion of their produce as rent and kept the rest, the rents reduced the marginal incentive to labor or to improve the land.[26] As evidence for these claims, Smith challenged the reader to compare the condition of great estates in the same family for generations, to that of the estates of small proprietors in the same neighborhood.[27]

We proceed now to a more detailed account of the unique tenets of the mutualist position on land tenure. Tucker's "occupancy and use" standard of ownership was directly influenced by the land theory of J.K. Ingalls in the United States; but its antecedents went back much further—at least to Godwin and Proudhon.

The Ricardian socialist Hodgskin, in *The Natural and Artificial Right of Property Contrasted*, seemed in many places to identify the natural right with direct cultivation; his distinction bore a striking resemblance to Nock's later distinction between "labour-made" and "law-made" property:[28]

> *In all these circumstances which in relation to the right of property may be considered as the leading objects of legislation, I see no particular guarantee*

or protection of the natural right of property.... To those by whose combined labour the ground is cultivated, and the harvest gathered in, nature gives every sheaf and every stalk which they choose to collect; the law, however, takes almost the whole of it away.[29]

Never has the law employed any means whatever to protect the property nature bestows on individuals; on the contrary, it is a great system of means devised to appropriate in a peculiar and unjust manner the gifts of nature. It exacts a revenue for the government,—it compels the payment of rent,—it enforces the giving of tithes, but it does not ensure to labour its produce and its reward.[30]

In contrasting the class nature of the natural and artificial rights, Hodgskin tended to identify the former with the peasant, and the latter with the landlord, in ways that would certainly make a modern libertarian-lite like (say) Milton Friedman nervous: "*The right of property, which is now arming the land-owner and the capitalist against the peasant and the artizan, will, in truth, be the one great subject of contention for this and the next generation....*"[31] He went so far as to describe the state as the organized power of the landowners, and the guarantor of their right to possess the land without actually cultivating it:

Among the legislative classes embodied into, and constituting the government, we must place the landed aristocracy. In fact, the landed aristocracy and the government are one—the latter being nothing more than the organized means of preserving the power and privileges of the former.... His [the landowner's] *right to possess the land, not to possess the produce of his own labour, is as admirably protected as can be effected by the law. Another must not even walk on it, and all the wild animals and fruit it bears are said by the law to be his. Nature makes it a condition of man having land, that he must occupy and cultivate it, or it will yield nothing.... The mere landowner is not a labourer, and he never has been even fed but by violating the natural right of property. Patiently and perseveringly, however, has the law endeavoured to maintain his privileges, power, and wealth.*[32]

Still, in fairness, we should add that Hodgskin's position is ambiguous. It is difficult at times, in a country like Britain with so much feudal baggage in its present distribution of land ownership, to distinguish between criticism of the landed aristocracy and criticism of absentee ownership as such, or between taxation and rent. To assume that he identified rent with taxation in all circumstances, as did Tucker, is begging the question.

The passages above do seem to imply, though, that cultivation is an ongoing title to the land and its produce even in the present, and not merely a means of initially appropriating it. But most of the large land-holdings in England at the time fall under the condemnation of Lockeans (especially left-Rothbardians), as well.

Hodgskin cited a very radical version of Locke on the labor theory of appropriation, in language that might suggest to some a fairly literal interpretation of the need to work the land.

> He [Locke] *says accurately, "as much land as a man tills, plants, and improves, cultivates, and can use, the product of so much is his property."—*
> *"This is the measure of property in land, which nature has well set by the extent of man's labour, and the conveniences of life; no man's labour could subdue or appropriate all, not could his enjoyment consume more than a small part, so that it would be impossible in this way to intrench on the right of another, or acquire to himself a property to the injury of his neighbours."*
> *Unfortunately, however, this admirable principle has not the smallest influence over legislators in dealing out that which, by the bye, is not theirs, the land of new colonies....*
>
> *There are many things about the right of property in land...which ought to be deeply meditated by those who...aspire to influence the opinions and the destinies of their fellow men. You must be sensible, for example, that the quantity of land necessary for each individual, according to the principle just quoted from Mr. Locke, must vary with the qualities and situation of the soil with the skill and knowledge of the people; and, in short, with the successive changes in the condition of mankind.... In the multiplication of mankind,...in improvements in skill and knowledge, as well as in diversities of soil and climate, we find principles which continually modify the appropriation of land, and alter the quantity to which a man can properly devote his labour.*[33]

Shortly thereafter, in a rather dense passage, Hodgskin cast doubt on whether the supervisory labor of a gentleman-farmer with several farms was a sufficient natural title to his property, or whether the size conducive to optimal efficiency of such a large enterprise had any bearing on the size which an individual could appropriate by natural means:

> *Perhaps you may suppose, that the collecting of many small farms into the hands of one farmer,—a process which for some years was going on in this country* [with a little help, as we have seen—K.C.], *though it appears now to have stopped,—is an exception to these remarks. I am speaking, however, of the quantity of land from which increasing skill obtains a sufficient quantity of subsistence, and of the decreasing surface to which, as labour becomes skilful, it will be necessarily confined, not of the quantity of land which a capitalist, or farmer, commanding the service of any given number of labourers, finds it at present most convenient to hire. The size farms ought to be of, in the present condition of society, is quite a distinct*

question from the quantity of land necessary to supply an individual with the means of subsistence, and therefore determining the natural right of property in land....[34]

Any consequentialist argument concerning the restraint this "natural right of property in land" might exert on the economies of scale can be answered, obviously, with a denial that ownership by "a capitalist," as in "the present condition of society," is the only means by which "any given number of labourers" can combine their efforts in a common enterprise.

But then, Locke was himself ambiguous; he (and especially his Proviso) have been put to much more radical uses than many modern Lockeans would approve.

J.K. Ingalls, probably the strongest direct influence on Tucker's land theory, called for "*repealing all laws in regard to land ownership, leaving 'occupancy and use' as it was originally, the only title to land.*"[35] Like the later Georgist Franz Oppenheimer, he saw history in terms of "*the courses by which man's natural birthright in the soil has been usurped in every land by a domineering class who, sooner or later, sought the cover of pretended law to sanction unlawful acts, so that they might enjoy quiet possession of dominion obtained by violence.*"[36] Absolute dominion over the land, to the exclusion of the rest of mankind, was possible only through the coercive power of the state, established through "the law of the stronger" or "the rights of the victor"—essentially the same thing described by Oppenheimer as "the political means."[37]

Ingalls, like Henry George, emphasized the original practice, common to all human societies, of treating land as a communal property to be assigned to individual cultivators only on a usufructory basis. Even under the usurpations of landlords, for most of the state's history, the peasant commune's subjection to the landed aristocracy was still collective. The peasantry continued, in medieval Europe, in Russia, in India, etc., to cultivate the land in common, and to pay tribute to the state or the landlord as a community.[38]

As described in the Introduction to Part II of this work, the mutualist theory of exploitation emphasizes the role of privilege in restricting labor's access to the means of production, and compelling labor, through the process of unequal exchange, to pay tribute to the owning classes by accepting less than its product as a wage. Ingalls' work on landlordism is an excellent case study of the operation of this principle as it relates specifically to land. Ingalls quoted Adam Smith on the labor-product as the natural wage of labor, in the days before appropriation of land. He contrasted this to Ricardo's subsistence theory of wages, in which the price of labor was determined by the cost of reproduction.

The difference between the two, as Ingalls saw it, resulted from the control of land by the landlord rather than the cultivator.[39] Or, as we have suggested earlier, Marx's distinction between the price of labor power and the value of the labor-product holds good only after the laboring classes have been deprived of their property in the means of production. The price of labor-power is determined by its reproduction cost, not as an inherent quality of wage-labor, but only where labor is sold in a regime of unequal exchange.

A return on land or capital, as such, could exist only through privilege. Only through the state's legal privileging of the ownership of capital and labor, was it possible for the capitalist or landlord to charge labor a tribute for access to the means of production, and thus to obtain a cumulative increase over time.[40] The expansion of capital through the magic of compound interest is not, as the Marxists believe, a property of the market. The natural law of the market is for labor to receive its full product. And although he wrote in a time before the marginalists had fully explained the principle of labor's disutility, Ingalls implicitly assumed the principle. In terms quite similar to our own analysis in Chapter 2, Ingalls contrasted the normal price of a commodity in a free market (a price just sufficient to compensate labor for the disutility of its work), with the monopoly rents accruing to the owners of capital or land without regard to their real costs or disutility in acquiring them:

> When a man buys a coat or a dinner, he regards it as of sufficient value to pay its fair price, without any consideration as to whether it will enable him to earn an income without work. And this is true of nearly everything consumed by individual men and their families, or by the world generally. It is only the trader, the banker, or landlord who measures price by the profit, interest, or rent it will exploit.[41]

In other words, as we stated in Chapter 2, the power to receive a rent on capital or land without earning it through labor can only enter the calculation of "opportunity cost" by which net profit and rent are calculated, only when the state has first made possible such an unearned rent through its enforcement of legal privilege.

Ingalls, like Tucker, devoted a great deal of energy to countering the theories of Henry George. Like Tucker, he minimized the importance of economic rent as such and saw it as a mere side-effect of the general phenomenon of landlord rent—in his words, economic rent "*could hardly form a serious difficulty were occupancy made the sole title to land.*"[42] Indeed, he went beyond Tucker in his denial that economic rent would exist without landlordism:

Instead of analyzing rent, he [George] *seems to regard it as a mysterious power which creates value independent of labor, and as something which he can tax to any degree without taking from the natural wages of labor; whereas, it is wholly due to exclusive land ownership, as he himself frequently asserts....*

According to Ricardo, rent is not an arbitrary tribute levied upon industry by usurped rights, but merely the excess of product, of the best land over the poorest, as the latter shall come into cultivation or other use under the exigencies of increasing population.... While land is under exclusive dominion it [the Ricardian theory of differential rent] *may serve in a certain way to explain how the rent rate is determined as between particular lands. But this is by no means the limit of its use by the followers of Ricardo, among whom Mr. George must be included. The inference is always sought to be carried that it also reveals an economic law under which only rent is developed. It assumes that rent does not arise until increase of population forces the use of less productive soils. In fact, the operation is directly the reverse of this.*[43]

Ingalls, in making such a bald assertion, indeed went too far. He virtually admitted as much himself, in conceding that a producer's surplus would exist for owners of superior land even in a regime of occupancy-based ownership: "*The man with land of easier tillage, or more productive soil, will be able, doubtless, to obtain the same price for his grain or fruits as the man with poorer soil and shorter crops.*"[44]

Still, Ingalls did make a good case for the contention that the evils of differential rent were exacerbated by landlord rent, and partially derived from it. For example, he wrote, absentee landlordism itself compelled the cultivation of marginal land to a degree that would not occur were all vacant land open to cultivation, and thus increased the differential between the best and worst land under cultivation.[45]

He also pointed out the fact, commonly neglected in the simplified explanations of Ricardo's rent theory, that land was amenable to a number of different uses, and that a parcel of land that was of inferior quality for producing one crop might be of better than average quality for a different crop. The sorting out of land for its most productive use, among a variety of competing uses, would tend to reduce the differential in productivity between sites.[46] In addition, the original quality of unimproved land was comparatively less important, by a considerable degree, than the improvements introduced by the labor of the cultivator (e.g., manuring and crop rotation), in determining its fertility. George had argued, in different passages of *Progress and Poverty*, that increases in population both increased rent by bringing less productive land under cultivation, and made marginal land more productive than before by the application of human labor—two contradictory tendencies.[47]

These arguments, indeed, robbed the Georgist theory of differential rent of much of its force—but only to the extent that the Georgist theory was based on differences in fertility of soil. But the Georgist treatment of rent concerned not only differences in fertility, but site advantages as well. On producers' surpluses accruing to the occupants of land more favorably situated in relation to its market, Ingalls had little or nothing to say. But even though Ingalls did not directly address this point, absentee landlordism has an effect in this regard as well in promoting differential rent. The rent accruing to land with site advantages is artificially increased by the ability of landlords to keep vacant urban land out of the market. The phenomenon is analogous to the one described above, regarding the withholding of more fertile land from cultivation by absentee landlords, in increasing the differential rent of land in superior locations.

As Tucker stated it, the principle of occupancy tenure required the protection "*of all people who desire to cultivate land in the possession of whatever land they cultivate, without distinction between the existing classes of landlords, tenants, and laborers, and the positive refusal of the protecting power to lend its aid to the collection of any rent whatsoever....*" This system was to be brought about by the refusal of ordinary people to pay rent or taxes, thus "*compel*[ling] *the State to repeal all the so-called land titles now existing.*"[48]

As Bill Orton argued in the quotes above, no "overlay" of land tenure rules can be deduced self-evidently from the right of self-ownership; further, no system of transfer and abandonment rules can be logically derived even from an agreed labor standard of appropriation. We can, however, evaluate the various sets of rules on prudential or consequentialist grounds, insofar as they promote other shared values, or promote results conducive to commonly accepted standards of fairness. In my opinion, the mutualist system of occupancy-and-use tenure has an advantage over both orthodox Lockean and Georgist systems, in the fairness of its operation.

Both the mutualist and Georgist systems, unlike the Lockean system, deal with the unique scarcity of land, characterized by the saying that "they ain't making any more of it"; both deal with the ethical objection to drawing an income from withholding a resource that one did not create with one's own labor. Lockeans sometimes respond that the same argument applies to *all* the matter one reworks by one's labor, and indeed to the very atoms in the laborer's own body. The problem with this response is that the atoms in raw materials can be renewed and recombined, and (given a long enough time frame) reproduced in response to virtually any level of demand. The same is not true of the available space in a property *site* (leaving aside quibbles about marsh reclamation, ocean-farming, space colonies, etc.). Put in a more sophisticated form, the argument to land scarcity is not so much that land isn't the creation of human labor, but that available site area is fixed (or virtually fixed) for a particular area. Even given quibbles about marsh reclamation, etc., the supply of site area is extremely inelastic in the face of demand, in comparison to the supply of movable goods.

At the same time, mutualism has an advantage over Georgism in that it recognizes an absolute individual right of property, so long as it is established and maintained only by personal occupancy. The Georgists, in claiming the right to tax increases in land value, claim a right by "the community" to penalize the occupant for the actions of his neighbors, over which he has no control. My neighbors, in claiming the right to tax me for increases in the value of my land resulting from activities they undertook on their own behalf, resemble the men on the make who wash windshields at intersections, and then demand payment for this unsolicited "service."

Besides the inconsistency of this claim with normally accepted notions of fairness, it has additional practical difficulties. For one, it requires some form of coercive apparatus to assess and collect rent on behalf of "the community"—unlike mutualism, which simply requires voluntary associations to defend the occupant in his possession. (In fairness, though, according to the Georgist property rights "overlay," this isn't coercive in the sense of initiating force, because ultimate property rights are located in the community and the community is simply regulating access to its own commons.) In addition, by funding social services out of rent, rather than user fees, Georgism fails to address the irrationalities produced by divorcing cost from price. Georgists are prone to exaggerate the number of public goods or "territorial monopolies"—assuming that any exist at all. It is conducive to economic efficiency that if any service can be funded by user fees, it should be. The cost of the residuum of public goods, assuming there are any, is likely to be of insufficient cost to soak up all the land-rent collected.

Tucker's version of mutualist land tenure leaves some questions open, or at least inadequately answered. Perhaps the most important was raised by "Egoist," in correspondence with *Liberty*. Egoist pointed out the seeming contradiction between wage labor and occupancy-based ownership: *"....if production is carried on in groups, as it now is, who is the legal occupier of the land? The employer, the manager, or the ensemble of those engaged in the co-operative work? The latter appearing the only rational answer...."*[49] Tucker, unfortunately, did not respond to this particular item in Egoist's letter, and therefore we cannot be sure how he would have dealt with this issue. It is, clearly, something that can be answered only at least as much by local social consensus as by logical deduction from principle.

Another question only partially answered is that of economic rent. Tucker gave little attention to issues of economic rent from superior fertility or site advantage. He believed that absentee landlord rent far outweighed it in importance, and that it could be safely left alone so long as landlordism was abolished.

It was Oppenheimer, ironically a Georgist, who demonstrated why most rent deriving from site and fertility advantage would be relatively insignificant in a system of occupancy and use tenure. Oppenheimer, like Tucker, admitted that rent might accrue to land from advantages in fertility or location, without resulting from any exploitative relationship existing. But while the holders of such land might have to work less for the same income, he believed the forces of the market would still prevent large concentrations of wealth resulting from the holding of superior land. Oppenheimer regarded rent per acre as less important than the total rent accruing to a single owner.

> *Oppenheimer goes so far as to assert that in a system where unused land is freely accessible, rent cannot survive. Rent-bearing land would be partitioned through inheritance; while land that did not bear rent would remain unpartitioned in the hands of one heir, the other heirs taking new lands. Thus the sizes of properties would be in inverse proportion to their rent capacity, and the smaller a property the more intensively it would be cultivated until rents were eliminated by diminishing returns.*[50]

Still, this is relevant mainly to differential rent based on superior location or fertility of land—not to scarce natural resources like minerals.

As we have seen, arguments for the superiority of one set of property rules over another can be established only on consequentialist grounds (i.e., on the basis of prudential assessments of how they lead to results consistent with commonly accepted ideas of "fairness"), and not deduced from principle. Any decentralized, post-state society, following the collapse of central power, is likely to be a panarchy characterized by a wide variety of local property systems. For them to coexist peacefully, all three property systems must reflect the understanding of their most enlightened proponents. Those favoring each of the property system must be willing to admit that it is not self-evidently true, or at least be willing to acquiesce to the system favored by majority consensus in each particular area.

Bill Orton, who favors Lockean (or "sticky") property, has made some provocative observations on how property metasystems have coexisted in the past, and speculations on how they are likely to do in the future. The three major metasystems we have examined in this section are agreed that aggression is bad. The reason they come into conflict is that they differ greatly in how they define "aggression." Accusations of aggression or initiation of force, according to Orton, result from conflicting property overlays. *"Liberty (and initiation of force) is defined in terms of property rights...."*[51]

> *....(almost) <u>nobody</u> claims to initiate force. When people accuse others of different political persuasions of initiating force, they are using their own property overlay, their own standard of property. Judged from <u>his</u> <u>own</u> property overlay, he is not initiating force at all. E.g., if you favor sticky property, then squatting is a no-no. If you favor possession property, squatting is just fine. The conception of "force" is different, due to the differing system of property.*[52]

In the past, proponents of one or the other metasystem have often been lacking in the forbearance needed to coexist peacefully with other property systems. And today, many libertarian socialists and anarcho-capitalists see the very existence of other property systems as an affront.

> *Yes, there are some anarcho-socialists who would attack people who use sticky property, and there are some anarcho-capitalists who would attack people who use usufruct property. If you don't believe this last, look back at comments related to aboriginal peoples—you see claims that it's okay to loot their hunting grounds because...they don't have deeds, they don't recognize private ownership of land, etc. But ownership is objective—it doesn't matter if they recognize it. They've either separated it from the [unowned] commons, mixed their labor and personality with it..., or they haven't.*[53]

> *Saying "all market anarchists" are tolerant of usufruct arrangements is grossly mistaken. People on this very board have "justified" US grabs of Indian land on the basis of arguments like: they didn't recognize sticky property, they didn't officially claim it, so they have no property rights." Other rabid quasi-Randroids deem usufruct "collectivist" arrangements as downright evil, and to be obliterated. Make no mistake, there do exist many intolerant market anarchists.*[54]

Orton expressed hope for peaceful coexistence of property systems, after "separation of property and state":

If ancapistan turned anti-capitalist, I probably wouldn't notice. I believe that without a State capitalism and socialism are harmonious and non-conflicting. Sure, you may call it a syndical or mutual, while I call it a firm with restricted transfer of ownership. You may call it a commune while I call it a household. Whatever.

Of course, hypothesizing that everyone will have the same economic ideology after separation of Econ and State is like saying that everyone will become atheist after separation of Church and State. No, just as there are various religions and denominations and cults with disestablishment, similarly there will be all sorts of economic arrangements with statelessness. There will be more, not fewer, economic experiments, just as the number of religious cults proliferated. Thus, the answer to your question will most likely turn out to be: Move to the next block, or a mile down the road, or simply change the people you deal with.

But the main answer would be: Who cares? The commies look just like capitalists to me. Who cares about the economic school of the guy who grows your potatoes or bakes your bread?[55]

I've come to the conclusion that both socialists and capitalists would benefit from a stateless society. Even if there is predominance of one form or the other, I think it would be easy and mellow to start a minority enclave. Certainly a damn sight easier than going up against a State! But I seriously doubt that any particular property form will dominate. There'll be every kind of property arrangement that you can imagine, and many more you can't. When religion was disestablished, when it went anarchist, did everyone become an atheist? Did the Catholic Church, or any other church or religion dominate?[56]

The coexistence of different systems of property in a panarchy would require an agreement by all parties to respect the rules established by majority consensus in each area, along with an arbitration system for disputes:

> *Now, for the dispute at hand* [between syndicalist workers and a dispossessed capitalist], *the property theories of the disputants are different, so "who is the aggressor" is at issue. By the usufruct theory, the returning capitalist is the aggressor; by the sticky theory the syndicalist workers are the aggressors. There can be no internal theoretical resolution.*
>
> *To avoid violence, some kind of moderation or arbitration is almost certainly necessary. The disputants could agree upon a wise arbiter, one without bias for or against either type of property system, to settle the issue. E.g. Wolf De Voon, who has made it clear that he thinks property amounts more or less to what the neighbors will allow. He would probably judge based on local custom and expectations of the parties involved. E.g. If the factory were located in an area where sticky property dominates, where the capitalist had*

reasonable expectation of sticky ownership, where the local people expect the same, and the syndicalist workers came in from a 'foreign' culture expecting to pull a fast one, then he'd probably judge in favor of the capitalist. OTOH If the factory were located in an area where usufruct dominates, and virtually all the locals expect and act in accordance with usufruct, and the capitalist, representing the 'foreign' culture, was trying to pull a property coup, then he would probably rule in favor of the syndicalist workers.

Neither property system can be proved to be correct. Proof requires agreement on a set of axioms. Capitalists and syndicalists don't agree on the axioms concerning property, so proof is impossible. So it's force or arbitration, and we all know which is better in the long run.[57]

B. Tucker's Big Four: The Money Monopoly.

In every system of class exploitation, a ruling class controls access to the means of production in order to extract tribute from labor. The landlord monopoly, which we examined in the last section, is one example of this principle. And until the nineteenth century, the control of land was probably the single most important form of privilege by which labor was forced to accept less than its product as a wage. But in industrial capitalism, arguably, the importance of landlordism has been surpassed in importance by the money monopoly. Under that latter form of privilege, the state's licensing of banks, capitalization requirements, and other market entry barriers enable banks to charge a monopoly price for loans in the form of usurious interest rates. Thus, labor's access to capital is restricted, and labor is forced to pay tribute in the form of artificially high interest rates.

Individualist anarchists like William Greene[58] and Benjamin Tucker viewed the money monopoly as central to the capitalist system of privilege. As Tucker pointed out, the capitalist bank, in the case of a secured "loan," does not in fact lend anything. The banker *"invests little or no capital of his own, and therefore, lends none to his customers, since the security which they furnish him constitutes the capital upon which he operates...."*[59] What the banker actually does is perform the simple service of making the "borrower's" property available in a liquid form. And because of the state's laws, which restrict the performance of this "service" to those with enough available capital to meet its capitalization requirements, he is able to charge a usurious price for it.

The process of obtaining a banking charter from the government, either federal or state, was described by Karl Hess and David Morris in *Neighborhood Power*:

First, one gets a certificate which gives permission to raise capital for the bank and outlines what conditions need to be met in order to receive a charter. Step

*two is getting the charter after having met the conditions. The conditions
are numerous, but the most important one is that a given amount of deposit
capital must be raised in a specific period of time. In order to get permission
to raise capital a group must prove that there is a reason to have another
bank, that it can serve a necessary function, and that it has a viable chance
of succeeding.*[60]

In a genuinely free banking market, any voluntary grouping of
individuals could form a cooperative bank and issue mutual bank notes
against any form of collateral they chose, with acceptance of these
notes as tender being a condition of membership. Tucker and Greene
usually treated land as the most likely form of collateral, but at one
point Greene speculated that a mutual bank might choose to honor
not only marketable property as collateral, but the *"pledging...[of]
future production."*[61] But assuming that the mutual bank limited itself to
rendering liquid the property of its members, there would be, strictly
speaking, "*no borrowing at all*":

*The so-called borrower would simply so change the face of his own title as
to make it recognizable by the world at large, and at no other expense than
the mere cost of the alteration. That is to say, the man having capital or
good credit, who...should go to a...bank...and procure a certain amount of
its notes by the ordinary process of mortgaging property or getting endorsed
commercial paper discounted, would only exchange his own personal credit...
for the bank's credit, known and receivable for products delivered throughout
the State, or the nation, or perhaps the world. And for this convenience
the bank would charge him only the labor-cost of its service in effecting
the exchange of credits, instead of the ruinous rates of discount by which,
under the present system of monopoly, privileged banks tax the producers of
unprivileged property out of house and home.*[62]

Were the property owned by the working class freed up for
mobilization as capital by such means, and the producers allowed to
organize their own credit without hindrance, the resources at their
disposal would be enormous. As Alexander Cairncross observed, "*the
American worker has at his disposal a larger stock of capital at home than in the
factory where he is employed....*"[63]

Abundant cheap credit would drastically alter the balance of power
between capital and labor, and returns on labor would replace returns
on capital as the dominant form of economic activity. According to
Robinson,

*Upon the monopoly rate of interest for money that is...forced upon us by law,
is based the whole system of interest upon capital, that permeates all modern
business.*

With free banking, interest upon bonds of all kinds and dividends upon stock would fall to the minimum bank interest charge. The so-called rent of houses...would fall to the cost of maintenance and replacement.

All that part of the product which is now taken by interest would belong to the producer. Capital, however...defined, would practically cease to exist as an income producing fund, for the simple reason that if money, wherewith to buy capital, could be obtained for one-half of one per cent, capital itself could command no higher price.[64]

And the result would be a drastically improved bargaining position for tenants and workers against the owners of land and capital. According to Gary Elkin, Tucker's free market anarchism carried certain inherent libertarian socialist implications:

It's important to note that because of Tucker's proposal to increase the bargaining power of workers through access to mutual credit, his so-called Individualist anarchism is not only compatible with workers' control but would in fact promote it. For if access to mutual credit were to increase the bargaining power of workers to the extent that Tucker claimed it would, they would then be able to (1) demand and get workplace democracy, and (2) pool their credit buy and own companies collectively.[65]

Given the worker's improved bargaining position, "*capitalists' ability to extract surplus value from the labor of employees would be eliminated or at least greatly reduced.*"[66] As compensation for labor approached value-added, returns on capital were driven down by market competition, and the value of corporate stock consequently plummeted, the worker would become a de facto co-owner of his workplace, even if the company remained nominally stockholder-owned.

Near-zero interest rates would increase the independence of labor in all sorts of interesting ways. For one thing, anyone with a twenty-year mortgage at 8% now could, in the absence of usury, pay it off in ten years. Most people in their 30s would own their houses free and clear. Between this and the nonexistence of high-interest credit card debt, two of the greatest sources of anxiety to keep one's job at any cost would disappear. In addition, many workers would have large savings ("go to hell money"). Significant numbers would retire in their forties or fifties, cut back to part-time, or start businesses; with jobs competing for workers, the effect on bargaining power would be revolutionary.

Under industrial capitalism, Tucker argued, the money monopoly reinforced the monopoly of land and capital. Site rent, as such, depended mainly on the enforcement of absentee land titles. The availability of all vacant land for homesteading would cause ground rent, as such to fall to zero through competition. But in built-up areas, the value of improvements and buildings outweighed that of the site itself. And the availability of interest-free credit would, likewise by competition, would cause house rent to fall to zero. Nobody would pay rent on a house when he could get the wherewithal, interest free, to build one of his own. And by the same token, nobody would accept significantly less than his labor product in return for the use of the means of production, when he and his fellow workers could mobilize the interest-free capital to buy their own. "*In this situation,*" as Gary Elkin wrote, "*it would be absurd for workers to pay someone else (i.e. a capitalist) more for the use of tools and equipment than a fee equal to their depreciation and maintenance costs plus the cost of the taxes (if any) and utilities involved in housing them.*"[67]

In addition to all this, central banking systems perform an additional service to the interests of capital. First of all, a major requirement of finance capitalists is to avoid inflation, in order to allow predictable returns on investment. This is ostensibly the primary purpose of the Federal Reserve and other central banks. But at least as important is the role of the central banks in promoting what they consider a "natural" level of unemployment—until the 1990s around six per cent. The reason is that when unemployment goes much below this figure, labor becomes increasingly uppity and presses for better pay and working conditions and more autonomy. Workers are willing to take a lot less crap off the boss when they know they can find a job at least as good the next day. On the other hand, nothing is so effective in "getting your mind right" as the knowledge that people are lined up to take your job.

The Clinton "prosperity" was a seeming exception to this principle. As unemployment threatened to drop below the four per cent mark, a minority of the Federal Reserve agitated to raise interest rates and take off the "inflationary" pressure by throwing a few million workers on the street. But as Greenspan testified before the Senate Banking Committee, the situation was unique. Given the degree of job insecurity in the high-tech economy, there was "[a] *typical restraint on compensation increases.*" In 1996, even with a tight labor market, 46% of workers at large firms were fearful of layoffs—compared to only 25% in 1991, when unemployment was much higher.

> The reluctance of workers to leave their jobs to seek other employment as the labor market tightened has provided further evidence of such concern, as has the tendency toward longer labor union contracts. For many decades, contracts rarely exceeded three years. Today, one can point to five- and six-year contracts—contracts that are commonly characterized by an emphasis on job security and that involve only modest wage increases. The low level of work stoppages of recent years also attests to concern about job security.[68]

Thus the willingness of workers during the Clinton "boom" to trade off smaller increases in wages for greater job security seems to be reasonably well documented. For the bosses, the high-tech economy is the next best thing to high unemployment for keeping our minds right. "Fighting inflation" translates operationally to increasing job insecurity and making workers less likely to strike or to look for new jobs.

C. Tucker's Big Four: Patents.

Although Tucker included patents and tariffs among his big four privileges, he approached them in a largely individualistic manner, as a source mainly of monopoly prices to the consumer. He ignored, for the most part, the effects of patents and tariffs on business structure, and their role in promoting cartelization in the late nineteenth century. Patents and tariffs, along with transportation subsidies (a form of government intervention that Tucker ignored in his own time) together laid the foundation in the late nineteenth century for what was to become twentieth century monopoly capitalism.

The patent privilege has been used on a massive scale to promote concentration of capital, erect entry barriers, and maintain a monopoly of advanced technology in the hands of western corporations. It is hard even to imagine how much more decentralized the economy would be without it.

Although right-libertarians of all stripes are commonly stereotyped as apologists for big business, Murray Rothbard was not shy about denouncing patents as a fundamental violation of free market principles:

> The man who has not bought a machine and who arrives at the same invention independently, will, on the free market, be perfectly able to use and sell his invention. Patents prevent a man from using his invention even though all the property is his and he has not stolen the invention, either explicitly or implicitly, from the first inventor. Patents, therefore, are grants of exclusive monopoly privilege by the State and are invasions of property rights on the market.[69]

It is sometimes argued, in response to attacks on patents as monopolies, that "all property is a monopoly." True, as far as it goes; but property in land, even when based on occupancy alone, is a monopoly by the nature of the case. A parcel of land can only be occupied and used by one owner at a time, because it is finite. By nature, two people cannot occupy the same physical space at the same time. "Intellectual property," in contrast, is an artificial monopoly on the right to perform a certain action—to arrange material elements or symbols in a particular configuration—which is not otherwise restricted of necessity to one person at a time. And unlike property in tangible goods and land, the defense of which is a necessary outgrowth of the attempt to maintain possession, enforcement of "property rights" in ideas requires the invasion of someone else's space.

> [E]*veryone's property right is defended in libertarian law without a patent. If someone has an idea or plan and constructs an invention, and it is stolen from his house, the stealing is an act of theft illegal under general law. On the other hand, patents actually invade the property rights of those independent discoverers of an idea or an invention who made the discovery after the patentee....*
> *Patents, therefore, invade rather than defend property rights.*[70]

Patents make an astronomical price difference. Until the early 1970s, for example, Italy did not recognize drug patents. As a result, Roche Products charged the British national health a price over 40 times greater for patented components of Librium and Valium than charged by competitors in Italy.[71]

Patents suppress innovation as much as they encourage it. Chakravarthi Raghavan pointed out that research scientists who actually do the work of inventing are required to sign over patent rights as a condition of employment, while patents and industrial security programs prevent sharing of information, and suppress competition in further improvement of patented inventions.[72] Rothbard likewise argued that patents eliminate "*the competitive spur for further research*" because incremental innovation based on others' patents is hindered, and because the holder can "*rest on his laurels for the entire period of the patent,*" with no fear of a competitor improving his invention. And they hamper technical progress because "*mechanical inventions are discoveries of natural law rather than individual creations, and hence similar independent inventions occur all the time. The simultaneity of inventions is a familiar historical fact.*"[73]

The intellectual property regime under the Uruguay Round of GATT goes far beyond traditional patent law in suppressing innovation. One benefit of traditional patent law, at least, was that it required an invention under patent to be published. Under U.S. pressure, however, "trade secrets" were included in GATT. As a result, governments will be required to help sup- press information not formally protected by patents.[74]

And patents are not necessary as an incentive to innovate. According to Rothbard, invention is motivated not only by the quasi-rents accruing to the first firm to introduce an innovation, but by the threat of being surpassed in product features or productivity by its competitors. "*In active competition...no business can afford to lag behind its competitors. The reputation of a firm depends upon its ability to keep ahead, to be the first in the market with new improvements in its products and new reductions in their prices."* [75]

This is borne out by F. M. Scherer's testimony before the FTC in 1995.[76] Scherer spoke of a survey of 91 companies in which only seven *"accorded high significance to patent protection as a factor in their R & D investments."* Most of them described patents as *"the least important of considerations."* Most companies considered their chief motivation in R & D decisions to be *"the necessity of remaining competitive, the desire for efficient production, and the desire to expand and diversify their sales."* In another study, Scherer found no negative effect on R & D spending as a result of compulsory licensing of patents. A survey of U.S. firms found that 86% of inventions would have been developed without patents. In the case of automobiles, office equipment, rubber products, and textiles, the figure was 100%.

The one exception was drugs, in which 60% supposedly would not have been invented. I suspect either self-deception or disingenuousness on the part of the respondents, however. For one thing, drug companies get an unusually high portion of their R & D funding from the government, and many of their most lucrative products were developed entirely at government expense. And Scherer himself cited evidence to the contrary. The reputation advantage for being the first into a market is considerable. For example in the late 1970s, the structure of the industry and pricing behavior was found to be very similar between drugs with and those without patents. Being the first mover with a non-patented drug allowed a company to maintain a 30% market share and to charge premium prices.

The injustice of patent monopolies is exacerbated by government funding of research and innovation, with private industry reaping monopoly profits from technology it didn't spend a penny to develop. In 1999, extending the research and experimentation tax credit was, along with extensions of a number of other corporate tax preferences, considered the most urgent business of the Congressional leadership. Hastert, when asked if any elements of the tax bill were essential, said: *"I think the* [tax preference] *extenders are something we're going to have to work on."* Ways and Means Chair Bill Archer added, *"before the year is out...we will do the extenders in a very stripped down bill that doesn't include anything else."* A five-year extension of the research and experimentation credit (retroactive to 1 July 1999) was expected to cost $13.1 billion. (That credit makes the effective tax rate on R & D spending less than zero).[77]

The Government Patent Policy Act of 1980, with 1984 and 1986 amendments, allowed private industry to keep patents on products developed with government R & D money—and then to charge ten, twenty, or forty times the cost of production. For example, AZT was developed with government money and in the public domain since 1964. The patent was given away to Burroughs Wellcome Corp.[78]

As if the deck were not sufficiently stacked already, the pharmaceutical companies in 1999 actually lobbied Congress to extend certain patents by two years by a special act of private law.[79]

Patents have been used throughout the twentieth century "*to circumvent antitrust laws*," according to David Noble. They were "*bought up in large numbers to suppress competition*," which also resulted in "*the suppression of invention itself.*"[80] Edwin Prindle, a corporate patent lawyer, wrote in 1906:

> *Patents are the best and most effective means of controlling competition. They occasionally give absolute command of the market, enabling their owner to name the price without regard to the cost of production.... Patents are the only legal form of absolute monopoly.*[81]

The exchange or pooling of patents between competitors, historically, has been a key method for cartelizing industries. This was true especially of the electrical appliance, communications, and chemical industries. G. E. and Westinghouse expanded to dominate the electrical manufacturing market at the turn of the century largely through patent control. In 1906 they curtailed the patent litigation between them by pooling their patents. G.E., in turn (later to become the patriarchal see of Gerard Swope), had been formed in 1892 by consolidating the patents of the Edison and Thomson-Houston interests.[82] AT&T also expanded "*primarily through strategies of patent monopoly.*" The American chemical industry was marginal until 1917, when Attorney-General Mitchell Palmer seized German patents and distributed them among the major American chemical companies. Du Pont got licenses on 300 of the 735 patents.[83]

Patents are also being used on a global scale to lock the transnational corporations into a permanent monopoly of productive technology. The single most totalitarian provision of the Uruguay Round is probably its "industrial property" provisions. GATT has extended both the scope and duration of patents far beyond anything ever envisioned in original patent law. In England, patents were originally for fourteen years—the time needed to train two journeymen in succession (and by analogy, the time necessary to go into production and reap the initial profit for originality). By that standard, given the shorter training times required today, and the shorter lifespan of technology, the period of monopoly should be shorter. Instead, the U.S. seeks to extend them to fifty years.[84] According to Martin Khor Kok Peng, the U.S. is by far the most absolutist of the participants in the Uruguay Round. Unlike the European Community, and for biological processes for animal and plant protection.[85]

The provisions for biotech are really a way of increasing trade barriers, and forcing consumers to subsidize the TNCs engaged in agribusiness. The U.S. seeks to apply patents to genetically-modified organisms, effectively pirating the work of generations of Third World breeders by isolating beneficial genes in traditional varieties and incorporating them in new GMOs—and maybe even enforcing patent rights against the traditional variety which was the source of the genetic material. For example Monsanto has attempted to use the presence of their DNA in a crop as prima facie evidence of pirating—when it is much more likely that their variety cross-pollinated and contaminated the farmer's crop against his will. The Pinkerton agency, by the way, plays a leading role in investigating such charges—that's right, the same folks who have been breaking strikes and kicking organizers down stairs for the past century. Even jack-booted thugs have to diversify to make it in the global economy.

The developed world has pushed particularly hard to protect industries relying on or producing "generic technologies," and to restrict diffusion of "dual use" technologies. The U. S.-Japanese trade agreement on semi-conductors, for example, is a *"cartel-like, 'managed trade' agreement."* So much for "free trade."[86]

Patent law traditionally required a holder to work the invention in a country in order to receive patent protection. U.K. law allowed compulsory licensing after three years if an invention was not being worked, or being worked fully, and demand was being met "to a substantial extent" by importation; or where the export market was not being supplied because of the patentee's refusal to grant licenses on reasonable terms.[87]

The central motivation in the GATT intellectual property regime, however, is to permanently lock in the collective monopoly of advanced technology by TNCs, and prevent independent competition from ever arising in the Third World. It would, as Martin Khor Kok Peng writes, *"effectively prevent the diffusion of technology to the Third World, and would tremendously increase monopoly royalties of the TNCs whilst curbing the potential development of Third World technology."* Only one percent of patents worldwide are owned in the Third World. Of patents granted in the 1970s by Third World countries, 84% were foreign-owned. But fewer than 5% of foreign-owned patents were actually used in production. As we saw before, the purpose of owning a patent is not necessarily to use it, but to prevent anyone else from using it.[88]

Raghavan summed up nicely the effect on the Third World:

> *Given the vast outlays in R and D and investments, as well as the short life cycle of some of these products, the leading Industrial Nations are trying to prevent emergence of competition by controlling...the flows of technology to others. The Uruguay round is being sought to be used to create export monopolies for the products of Industrial Nations, and block or slow down the rise of competitive rivals, particularly in the newly industrializing Third*
>
> *World countries. At the same time the technologies of senescent industries of the north are sought to be exported to the South under conditions of assured rentier income.*[89]

Corporate propagandists piously denounce anti-globalists as enemies of the Third World, seeking to use trade barriers to maintain an affluent Western lifestyle at the expense of the poor nations. The above measures—trade barriers—to permanently suppress Third World technology and keep the South as one big sweatshop, give the lie to this "humanitarian" concern. This is not a case of differing opinions, or of sincerely mistaken understanding of the facts. Setting aside false subtleties, what we see here is pure evil at work—Orwell's "boot stamping on a human face forever." If any architects of this policy believe it to be for general human well-being, it only shows the capacity of ideology to justify the oppressor to himself and enable him to sleep at night.

D. Tucker's Big Four: Tariffs

As with patents, we are interested here in the aspects of tariffs that Tucker neglected: their effect in promoting the cartelization of industry. In the next chapter, on the rise of monopoly capitalism, we will see the full-blown effects of what Schumpeter called "export-dependent monopoly capitalism." That term refers to an economic system in which industry cartelizes behind the protection of tariff barriers; sells its output domestically for a monopoly price significantly higher than market-clearing level, in order to obtain super-profits at the consumer's expense; and disposes of its unsellable product abroad, by dumping it below cost if necessary.

The tariff was commonly called "the mother of trusts" by the populists of a century ago, because of the way it facilitated collusion between large domestic producers and the creation of oligopolies. Mises, in *Human Action*, described the dependence of cartels on tariff barriers (especially interacting with other state-enforced monopolies like patents). Of course, in keeping with his usual "pro-business" emphasis, Mises treated the large industrial firms, at worst, as passive beneficiaries of a state protectionist policy aimed primarily at raising the wages of labor. This parallels his view of the early industrial capitalists, and their non-implication in the primitive accumulation process, in the previous chapter.

According to Kolko's account in *The Triumph of Conservatism*, the large trusts at the turn of the twentieth century were not able to maintain their market share against more efficient smaller firms. The stabilization of most industries on an oligopoly pattern was possible, in the end, only with the additional help of the "Progressive" Era's anti-competitive regulations. The fact that the trusts were so unstable, despite the cartelizing effects of tariffs and patents, speaks volumes about the level of state intervention necessary to maintain monopoly capitalism. But without the combined influence of tariffs, patents, and railroad subsidies, it is unlikely they would have been able to make even a credible attempt to organize such trusts in the first place.

E. Infrastructure

One form of contemporary government intervention that Tucker almost entirely ignored was transportation subsidies. This seems odd at first glance, since "internal improvements" had been a controversial issue throughout the nineteenth century, and were a central part of the mercantilist agenda of the Whigs and the Gilded Age GOP. Indeed, Lincoln announced the beginning of his career with a "short but sweet" embrace of Henry Clay's program: a national bank, a high tariff, and internal improvements. This neglect, however, was in keeping with Tucker's inclination. He was concerned with privilege primarily as it promoted monopoly profits through unfair exchange at the individual level, and not as it affected the overall structure of production. The kind of government intervention that James O'Connor was later to write about, that promoted accumulation and concentration by directly subsidizing the operating costs of big business, largely escaped his notice.

At the end of the previous section, we noted that the failure of the trust movement reflected the insufficiency of railroad subsidies, tariffs and patents alone to maintain stable monopoly power. But without the government-subsidized "internal improvements" of the nineteenth century, it is doubtful that most national-scale industrial firms would even have existed, let alone been able to make attempts at collusion.

Adam Smith argued over two hundred years ago for the fairness of internalizing the costs of transportation infrastructure through user fees.

It does not seem necessary that the expense of those public works should be defrayed from that public revenue, as it is commonly called, of which the collection and application is in most countries assigned to the executive power. The greater part of such public works may easily be so managed as to afford a particular revenue sufficient for defraying their own expense, without bringing any burden upon the general revenue of society....

When the carriages which pass over a highway or a bridge, and the lighters which sail upon a navigable canal, pay toll in proportion to their weight or their tonnage, they pay for the maintenance of those public works exactly in proportion to the wear and tear which they occasion of them. It seems scarce possible to invent a more equitable way of maintaining such works. This tax or toll too, though it is advanced by the carrier, is finally paid by the consumer, to whom it must always be charged in the price of the goods....

It seems not unreasonable that the extraordinary expense which the protection of any particular branch of commerce may occasion should be defrayed by a moderate tax upon that particular branch; by a moderate fine, for example, to be paid by the traders when they first enter into it, or, what is more equal, by a particular duty of so much percent upon the goods which they either import into, or export out of, the particular countries with which it is carried on.[90]

But that's not the way things work under what the neoliberals like to call "free market capitalism." Spending on transportation and communications networks from general revenues, rather than from taxes and user fees, allows big business to "externalize its costs" on the public, and conceal its true operating expenses. Chomsky described this state capitalist underwriting of shipping costs quite accurately:

One well-known fact about trade is that it's highly subsidized with huge market-distorting factors.... The most obvious is that every form of transport is highly subsidized.... Since trade naturally requires transport, the costs of transport enter into the calculation of the efficiency of trade. But there are huge subsidies to reduce the costs of transport, through manipulation of energy costs and all sorts of market-distorting functions.[91]

Every wave of concentration of capital in the United States has followed a publicly subsidized infrastructure system of some sort. The national railroad system, built largely on free or below-cost land donated by the government, was followed by concentration in heavy industry, petrochemicals, and finance. Albert Nock ridiculed the corporate liberals of his time, who held up the corruption of the railroad companies as examples of the failure of "rugged individualism" and "laissez-faire."

It is nowadays the fashion, even among those who ought to know better, to hold "rugged individualism" and laissez-faire responsible for the riot of stock-waterings, rebates, rate-cutting, fraudulent bankruptcies, and the like, which prevailed in our railway-practice after the Civil War, but they had no more to do with it than they have with the precession of the equinoxes. The fact is that our railways, with few exceptions, did not grow up in response to any actual economic demand. They were speculative enterprises enabled by State intervention, by allotment of the political means in the form of land-grants and subsidies; and of all the evils alleged against our railway-practice, there is not one but what is directly traceable to this primary intervention.[92]

The modern telecommunications system goes back to the Bell Patent association, organized in 1875; the various Bell systems were consolidated as AT&T in 1900. Without the government's enforcement of its huge arsenal of patents on virtually every aspect of telephony, a centralized communications infrastructure would have been impossible on anything like the present scale.[93] And that is leaving out entirely the role of government franchises and right-of-way grants in the rise of the AT&T monopoly.

The next major transportation projects were the national highway system, starting with the system of designated national highways in the 1920s and culminating with Eisenhower's interstate system; and the civil aviation system, built almost entirely with federal money. The result was massive concentration in retail, agriculture, and food processing.

The most recent such project was the infrastructure of the worldwide web, originally built by the Pentagon. It permits, for the first time, direction of global operations in real time from a single corporate headquarters, and is accelerating the concentration of capital on a global scale. To quote Chomsky again, "*The telecommunications revolution...is... another state component of the international economy that didn't develop through private capital, but through the public paying to destroy themselves....*"[94]

The centralized corporate economy depends for its existence on a shipping price system which is artificially distorted by government intervention. To fully grasp how dependent the corporate economy is on socializing transportation and communications costs, imagine what would happen if truck and aircraft fuel were taxed enough to pay the full cost of maintenance and new building costs on highways and airports; and if fossil fuels depletion allowances were removed. The result would be a massive increase in shipping costs. Does anyone seriously believe that Wal-Mart could continue to undersell local retailers, or corporate agribusiness could destroy the family farm?

It is fallacious to say that state-subsidized infrastructure "creates efficiencies" by making possible large-scale production for a national market. The fact that a large, centralized infrastructure system can only come about when the state subsidizes or organizes it from above, or that such state action causes it to exist on a larger scale than it otherwise would, indicates that the transaction costs are so high that the benefits *are not worth it* to people spending their own money. There is no demand for it by consumers willingly spending their own money, at the actual costs of providing the services, risks and all, without state intervention.

If production on the scale promoted by infrastructure subsidies were actually efficient enough to compensate for *real* distribution costs, the manufacturers would have presented enough effective demand for such long-distance shipping at actual costs to pay for it without government intervention. On the other hand, an apparent "efficiency" that presents a positive ledger balance only by shifting and concealing real costs, is no "efficiency" at all. Costs cannot be destroyed. Shifting them does not make them any less of a cost—it only means that, since they aren't being paid by the beneficiary of the service, he profits at someone else's expense. There Ain't No Such Thing As A Free Lunch.

Intellectually honest right-libertarians freely admit as much. For example, Tibor Machan wrote in *The Freeman* that

> *Some people will say that stringent protection of rights* [against eminent domain] *would lead to small airports, at best, and many constraints on construction. Of course—but what's so wrong with that?*

> *Perhaps the worst thing about modern industrial life has been the power of political authorities to grant special privileges to some enterprises to violate the rights of third parties whose permission would be too expensive to obtain. The need to obtain that permission would indeed seriously impede what most environmentalists see as rampant—indeed reckless—industrialization.*

> *The system of private property rights—in which...all...kinds of...human activity must be conducted within one's own realm except where cooperation from others has been gained voluntarily—is the greatest moderator of human aspirations.... In short, people may reach goals they aren't able to reach with their own resources only by convincing others, through arguments and fair exchanges, to cooperate.*[95]

NOTES

1. Albert Jay Nock, *Our Enemy, the State* (Delevan, Wisc.: Hallberg Publishing Corp., 1983) 97.
2. Ibid. 106n.

3. Benjamin Tucker, "State Socialism and Anarchism," in Benjamin Tucker, *Instead of a Book, by a Man Too Busy to Write One*. Gordon Press Facsimile (New York: Gordon Press, 1897, 1973) 12.

4. Nock, *Our Enemy, the State* 41n.

5. Henry George, *Progress and Poverty* (New York: Walter J. Black, 1942) 312; Joshua King Ingalls, *Social Wealth: The Sole Factors and Exact Ratios in Its Acquirement and Apportionment* (New York: Social Science Publishing Co., 1885) 145-50.

6. Adam Smith, *An Inquiry Into the Nature and Causes of the Wealth of Nations* (Chicago, London, Toronto: Encyclopedia Britannica, Inc., 1952) 165.

7. Robert Nozick, *Anarchy, State, and Utopia* (U.S.A.: Basic Books, 1974) 150-1.

8. Benjamin Tucker, "An Alleged Flaw in Anarchy," in Tucker, *Instead of a Book* 212.

9. "Re: On the Question of Private Property," August 26, 2003. http://anti-state.com/forum/index.php?board=6;action=display;threa did=6726;start=20 Captured April 30, 2004.

10. Bill Orton, "Cohen's Argument," Free-Market.Net forums, January 1, 2001 http://www.free-market.net/forums/main0012/ messages/807541545.html Captured April 30, 2004.

11. Orton, "Re: On the Question of Private Property," Anti-State. Com Forum, August 30, 2003. http://www.antistate.com/forum/index. php?board=6;action=display;threadid=6726;start=20 Captured April 30, 2004.

12. Bill Orton, "Yet Another Variation," Anti-State.Com Forum, December 7, 2003. http://anti-state.com/forum/index.php?board=1;a ction=display;threadid=7965;start=0 Captured April 30, 2004.

13. Bill Orton, "Property (Wolf De Voon)," Anti-State.Com Forum, July 07, 2003, http://anti-state.com/forum/index.php?board=2;action =display;threadid=6072;start=0 Captured April 30, 2004.

14. Murray Rothbard, *Man, Economy, and State: A Treatise on Economic Principles* (Auburn University, Alabama: Ludwig von Mises Institute, 1993) 147.

15. Murray Rothbard, *Power and Market: Government and the Economy* (Kansas City: Sheed Andrews and Mcmeel, Inc., 1970, 1977) 132.

16. Ibid. 133.

17. Jerome Tuccille, "Bits and Pieces," *The Libertarian Forum* (November 1, 1970) 3.

18. Rothbard, *Power and Market* 131-2.

19. Ludwig von Mises, *Socialism* (New York: Yale University Press, 1951) 375.

20. Edward Heimann, "Franz Oppenheimer's Economic Ideas," *Social Research* (New York) (February 1944) 28.

21. Rothbard, *Power and Market* 132-3.

22. Ibid. 68.

23. See Bernie Jackson, "The Fine Art of Conservation," *The Freeman: Ideas on Liberty* (October 1998).

24. Rothbard, *Power and Market* 70.

25. Smith, *Wealth of Nations* 166-7.

26. Ibid. 168.

27. Ibid. 167.

28. Nock, *Our Enemy, the State* 80.

29. Thomas Hodgskin, *The Natural and Artificial Right of Property Contrasted* (London: B. Steil, 1832) 53-4.

30. Ibid. 55-6.

31. Ibid. 15.

32. Ibid. 52.

33. Ibid. 61-3.

34. Ibid. 67.

35. Ingalls, *Social Wealth* 287.

36. Ibid. 139.

37. Ibid. 133.

38. Ibid. 133.

39. Ibid. 132.

40. Ibid. 248-9.

41. Ibid. 252.

42. Ibid. 74.

43. Ibid. 68-9.

44. Ibid. 74.

45. Ibid. 69.

46. Ibid. 71.

47. Ibid. 71-2.

48. Benjamin Tucker, "The Land for the People," *Liberty* June 22, 1882, in Tucker, *Instead of a Book* 299-300.

49. Benjamin Tucker, "The Distribution of Rent," *Liberty* February 23, 1884, in Tucker, *Instead of a Book* 340.

50. Heimann, "Franz Oppenheimer's Economic Ideas" 30.

51. Bill Orton, "Property and Panarchy," Free-Market.Net Forum, December 28, 2000. http://www.free-market.net/forums/main0012/messages/408156009.html Captured April 30, 2004.

52. Orton, "Cohen's Argument."

53. Bill Orton, "Which is MORE important—market or anarchy?" Anti-State.Com Forum, August 23, 2003. http://anti-state.com/forum/index.php?board=1;action=display;threadid=6721;start=20 Captured April 30, 2004.

54. Bill Orton, "Re: Anarch-Socialism," Anti-State.Com Forum, April 1, 2004. http://anti-state.com/forum/index.php?board=6;action=display;threadid=9256;start=120 Captured April 30, 2004.

55. Bill Orton, "Re: Poll: What if An-capistan turned anti-capitalist?" Anti-State.Com Forum, January 31, 2003. http://anti-state.com/forum/index.php?board=1;action=display;threadid=8702;start=140 Captured April 30, 2004.

56. Orton, "Re: Yet Another Variation..." Antistate.Com Forum, December 8, 2003. http://www.antistate.com/forum/index.php?board=1;action=display;threadid=7965;start=20 Captured April 30, 2004.

57. Orton, "Re: On the Question of Private Property," Anti-State. Com Forum, August 30, 2003. http://anti-state.com/forum/index.php?board=6;action=display;threadid=6726;start=20 Captured April 30, 2004.

58. William B. Greene, *Mutual Banking.* Gordon Press Facsimile (New York: Gordon Press, 1849, 1974).

59. Benjamin Tucker, "Economic Hodge-Podge," *Liberty* October 8, 1887, in Tucker, *Instead of a Book* 206.

60. Karl Hess and David Morris, *Neighborhood Power: The New Localism* (Boston: Beacon Press, 1975) 81.

61. Greene, *Mutual Banking* 73.

62. Benjamin Tucker, "Apex or Basis," *Liberty* December 10, 1881, in Tucker, *Instead of a Book* 194.

63. Alexander Cairncross, "Economic Schizophrenia," *Scottish Journal of Political Economy* (February 1950), qt. in Michael Perelman, *Classical Political Economy: Primitive Accumulation and the Social Division of Labor* (Totowa, N.J.: Rowman & Allanheld; London: F. Pinter, 1984, c 1983) 27.

64. J. B. Robertson, *The Economics of Liberty* (Minneapolis: Herman Kuehn, 1916) 80-1.

65. Gary Elkin. "Benjamin Tucker—Anarchist or Capitalist?" http://flag.blackened.net/daver/anarchism/tucker/an_or_cap.html Captured October 28, 2003.

66. Elkin. "Mutual Banking." The original that Elkin posted on the web is down, but it is available in a post cached at alt.philosophy.debate, Jul 12, 1999. http://groups.google.com/groups?q=%22gary+elkin%22+%22mutual+banking%22&hl=en&lr=&ie=UTF-8&oe=UTF-8&safe=

off&selm=37897B99.1B1E%40columbia-center.org&rnum=7&filter=0 Captured May 15, 2004.

67. Ibid.

68. "Testimony of Chairman Alan Greenspan". U. S. Senate Committee on Banking, Housing, and Urban Affairs. 26 February 1997. http://www.federalreserve.gov//boarddocs/hh/1997/february/testimony/htm Captured May 1, 2001.

69. Rothbard, *Man, Economy, and State* 655.

70. Rothbard, *Power and Market* 71.

71. Chakravarthi Raghavan, *Recolonization: GATT, the Uruguay Round & the Third World* (Penang, Malaysia: Third World Network, 1990) 124.

72. Ibid. 118.

73. Rothbard, *Man, Economy, and State* 655, 658-9.

74. Raghavan, *Recolonization* 122.

75. Rothbard, *Power and Market* 74.

76. *Hearings on Global and Innovation-Based Competition*. FTC, 29 November 1995. http://www.ftc.gov/opp/gc112195.pdf Captured May 1, 2001.

77. Citizens for Tax Justice. "GOP Leaders Distill Essence of Tax Plan: Surprise! It's Corporate Welfare" 14 September 1999. http://www.ctj.org/pdf/corp0999.pdf Captured May 1, 2001.

78. Chris Lewis, "Public Assets, Private Profits," *Multinational Monitor*, in *Project Censored Yearbook 1994* (New York: Seven Stories Press, 1994).

79. Benjamin Grove. "Gibbons Backs Drug Monopoly Bill," *Las Vegas Sun* 18 February 2000. http://www.ahc.umn.edu/NewsAlert/Feb00/022100NewsAlert/44500.htm Captured May 1, 2001.

80. David Noble, *America by Design: Science, Technology, and the Rise of Corporate Capitalism* (New York: Alfred A. Knopf, 1977) 84-109.

81. Ibid. 90.

82. Ibid. 92.

83. Ibid. 10, 16.

84. Raghavan, *Recolonization* 119-20.

85. Martin Khor Kok Peng, *The Uruguay Round and Third World Sovereignty* (Penang, Malaysia: Third World Network, 1990) 28.

86. Dieter Ernst, *Technology, Economic Security and Latecomer Industrialization*, in Raghavan, *Recolonization* 39-40.

87. Ibid. 120, 138.

88. Martin Khor Kok Peng, *The Uruguay Round and Third World Sovereignty* 29-30.

89. Raghavan, *Recolonization* 96.

90. Smith, *Wealth of Nations* 315, 319.

91. Noam Chomsky, "How Free is the Free Market?" *Resurgence* no. 173. http://www.oneworld.org/second_opinion/chomsky.html Captured May 1, 2001.

92. Nock, *Our Enemy, the State* 102.

93. Noble, *America by Design* 91-2.

94. Noam Chomsky, *Class Warfare: Interviews with David Barsamian* (Monroe, Maine: Common Courage Press, 1996) 40.

95. Tibor Machan, "On Airports and Individual Rights," *The Freeman: Ideas on Liberty* (February 1999) 11.

Chapter Six
The Rise of Monopoly Capitalism

Introduction.

Although the state capitalism of the twentieth century (as opposed to the earlier misnamed "laissez faire" variant, in which the statist character of the system was largely disguised as a "neutral" legal framework) had its roots in the mid-nineteenth century, it received great impetus as an elite ideology during the depression of the 1890s. From that time on, the problems of overproduction and over-accumulation, the danger of domestic class warfare, and the need for the state to solve them, figured large in the perception of the corporate elite. The unregulated market was increasingly viewed as destructive and inefficient. The shift in elite consensus in the 1890s (toward corporate liberalism and foreign commercial expansion) was as profound as that of the 1970s, when reaction to wildcat strikes, the "crisis of governability," and the looming "capital shortage" led the power elite to abandon corporate liberalism in favor of neo-liberalism.

Martin Sklar commented that the "corporate reconstruction of American capitalism" that arose out of the Depression of the 1890s was as fundamental a revolution in American life as had been the Civil War and Reconstruction.

> *Yet, for all the bitter and angry conflict it generated and for all its rapidity and hugeness of scale, it proceeded relatively peacefully and within the framework of the existing political institutions. How come?*
>
> *....Unlike the great sociopolitical crisis of the 1850s and 1860s, which was resolved by a national reconstruction that required a civil war and revolution,*

the corporate reconstruction required neither civil war nor revolution, but rather political reorganization and reform.[1]

The answer to Sklar's question, in my opinion, is that the corporate reconstruction of the 1890s took place without violent political transformation precisely because the "civil war and revolution" of 1861-77 had already established all the political prerequisites for a peaceful corporate reconstruction of the economy. The withdrawal and subsequent political transformation of the South, followed by the ascendancy of the "redeemers," with their national-capitalist orientation, gave the Republicans uncontested political terrain and a free hand to impose the full Whig economic agenda. The corporate economy was made possible by high industrial tariffs and the full-scale subsidy of "internal improvements"—along with corporate personhood, "substantive due process," and the rest of the legal regime growing out of the Fourteenth Amendment. The creation of the latter legal regime was analogous, on a smaller scale, to the legal regime of Bretton Woods and GATT that provided a political structure for global capitalism after WWII.

The rise of an economy dominated by firms operating on a continental scale, and of industries in which a relative few firms predominated, was not an outgrowth of the 1890s. It evolved over the previous two or three decades, as a result of the Whig-Republican triumph of 1861-77. And the economic crises of the 1890s, to which full-blown corporatism was a response, were themselves a result of the destabilizing tendencies of the previous corporate evolution. The growing geographic scale, centralization, and levels of accumulation characteristic of American business organization during the previous decades culminated in the full-blown crisis of over-accumulation and under-consumption of the 1890s.

As Martin Sklar himself pointed out, the process of "industrial concentration," which he distinguished from corporate reconstruction, had been going on for some time before the 1890s. And the 1880s were a decade of unprecedented accumulation that continued into the crisis decade of the '90s.[2] The crisis of the 1890s was the outcome of this concentration and over-accumulation; but they, in turn, were the result of the Whig-Republican state capitalist intervention, and not of the "unregulated" or "competitive" market.

The American ruling class, therefore, was wrong in seeing the crises of overproduction and surplus capital as "*natural or inevitable outgrowths of a market society.*"[3] Nevertheless, from the Depression of the 1890s onward, through most of the Twentieth Century, corporatist solutions to these crisis tendencies dominated the state's economic policy. But every subsequent corporatist measure, adopted to solve the previous problems of over-accumulation, itself further exacerbated the problems of over-accumulation.

> *But corporate reorganization on a large scale of operations was not by itself a solution of the problem of the surplus. It intensified the problem in certain decisive ways: It raised prices, or made them less elastic, and thereby limited demand in relation to capacity; it restricted the flow of savings into competitive investment, but at the same time it facilitated the concentrated accumulation of investment funds in corporate treasuries, and it mobilized investment funds through the creation of organized capital markets for negotiable securities and through the activity of investment banking houses and trust companies, which grew in number and size with the emergence of corporate capitalism. The corporate reorganization may be said to have treated, without curing, the malady of "overproduction" from the diagnostic standpoint of the capitalist property system; precisely in so doing, it reinforced the tendency toward oversaving and the generation of surplus capital, in the absence of vigorous international expansion of the investment system. It thereby made the disposal of the surplus and access to growing international investment outlets an all the more urgent question of policy both in the private sector and in government.[4]*

The ultimate result was a spiral into further statism, culminating in the corporatism of the New Deal and the permanent war economy of WWII and the Cold War.

In the realm of foreign policy, the problem of over-accumulation and under-consumption led to the regime known as "export-dependent monopoly capitalism," relying on what William A. Williams called a policy of "Open Door Empire." We will study the history of monopoly capitalism as it affected U.S. foreign policy in Chapter 7.

The state's remedies to the crisis of over-accumulation and under-consumption (primarily Keynesian demand-management, corporatist labor policy and the welfare state) themselves lead to opposing crisis tendencies: the crisis of under-accumulation and the fiscal crisis of the state. The ways in which these conflicting crisis tendencies interact, and their likely final outcome, are the subject of Chapter 8.

The primary subject matter of this chapter is the rise of monopoly capitalism itself, and the state's policies for cartelizing the economy. The effects of the state's subsidies and regulations are 1) to encourage creation of production facilities on such a large scale that they are not viable in a free market, and cannot dispose of their full product domestically; 2) to promote monopoly prices above market clearing levels; and 3) to set up market entry barriers and put new or smaller firms at a competitive disadvantage, so as to deny adequate domestic outlets for investment capital. The result is a crisis of overproduction and surplus capital, and a spiraling process of increasing statism as politically connected corporate interests act through the state to resolve the crisis. The best single analysis of this process I am aware of is Joseph Stromberg's in "The Role of State Monopoly Capitalism in the American Empire"[5]

A. Liberal Corporatism, Regulatory Cartelization, and the Permanent Warfare State.

Stromberg's argument, to which we are heavily indebted, is based on Murray Rothbard's Austrian theory of regulatory cartelization. Economists of the Austrian school, especially Rothbard and his followers on the Rothbardian left, have taken a view of state capitalism in many respects resembling that of the New Left. That is, both groups portray it as a movement of large-scale, organized capital to obtain its profits through state intervention into the economy, although the regulations entailed in this project are usually sold to the public as "progressive" restraints on big business. This parallelism between the analyses of the New Left and the libertarian Right was capitalized upon by Rothbard in his own overtures to the Left. In such projects as his journal *Left and Right*, and in the anthology *A New History of Leviathan* (co-edited with New Leftist Ronald Radosh), he sought an alliance of the libertarian Left and Right against the corporate state.

Rothbard treated the "war collectivism" of World War I as a prototype for twentieth century state capitalism. He described it as

> *a new order marked by strong government, and extensive and pervasive government intervention and planning, for the purpose of providing a network of subsidies and monopolistic privileges to business, and especially to large business, interests. In particular, the economy could be cartelized under the aegis of government, with prices raised and production fixed and restricted, in the classic pattern of monopoly; and military and other government contracts could be channeled into the hands of favored corporate producers. Labor, which had been becoming increasingly rambunctious, could be tamed and bridled into the service of this new, state monopoly-capitalist order, through the device of promoting a suitably cooperative trade unionism, and by bringing the willing union leaders into the planning system as junior partners.*[6]

This view of state capitalism, shared by New Leftists and Rothbardians alike, flies in the face of the dominant American ideological framework. Before we can analyze the monopoly capitalism of the twentieth century, we must rid ourselves of this pernicious conventional wisdom, common to mainstream left and right. Both mainline "conservatives" and "liberals" share the same mirror-imaged view of the world (but with "good guys" and "bad guys" reversed), in which the growth of the welfare and regulatory state reflected a desire to restrain the power of big business. According to this commonly accepted version of history, the Progressive and New Deal programs were forced on corporate interests from outside, and against their will. In this picture of the world, big government is a populist "countervailing power" against the "economic royalists." This picture of the world is shared by Randroids and Chicago boys on the right, who fulminate against "looting" by "anti-capitalist" collectivists; and by NPR liberals who confuse the New Deal with the Second Advent. It is the official ideology of the publick skool establishment, whose history texts recount heroic legends of "trust buster" TR combating the "malefactors of great wealth," and Upton Sinclair's crusade against the meat packers. It is expressed in almost identical terms in right-wing home school texts bemoaning the defeat of business at the hands of the collectivist state, or describing the New Deal as an example of the masses voting themselves largesse from the public treasury.

The conventional understanding of government regulation was succinctly stated by Arthur Schlesinger, Jr., the foremost spokesman for corporate liberalism: *"Liberalism in America has ordinarily been the movement on the part of the other sections of society to restrain the power of the business community."*[7] Mainstream liberals and conservatives may disagree on who the "bad guy" is in this scenario, but they are largely in agreement on the anti-business motivation. For example, Theodore Levitt of the *Harvard Business Review* lamented in 1968: *"Business has not really won or had its way in connection with even a single piece of proposed regulatory or social legislation in the last three-quarters of a century."*[8]

The problem with these conventional assessments is that they are an almost exact reverse of the truth. The New Left has produced massive amounts of evidence to the contrary, virtually demolishing the official version of American history. (The problem, as in most cases of "paradigm shift," is that the consensus reality doesn't know it's dead yet). Scholars like James Weinstein, Gabriel Kolko and William Appleman Williams, in their historical analyses of "corporate liberalism," have demonstrated that the main forces behind both Progressive and New Deal "reforms" were powerful corporate interests. The following is intended only as a brief survey of the development of the corporate liberal regime, and an introduction to the New Left (and Austrian) analysis of it.

Despite Schlesinger's aura of "idealism" surrounding the twentieth century welfare/regulatory state, it was in fact pioneered by the Junker

Socialism of Prussia—the work of that renowned New Age tree-hugger, Bismarck. The mainline socialist movement at the turn of the century (i.e., the part still controlled by actual workers, and not coopted by Fabian intellectuals) denounced the tendency to equate such measures with socialism, instead calling it "state socialism"—state intervention in the economy on behalf of the capitalists. The *International Socialist Review* in 1912, for example, warned workers not to be fooled into identifying social insurance or the nationalization of industry with "socialism." Such state programs as workers' compensation, old age and health insurance, were only measures to strengthen and stabilize capitalism. And nationalization simply reflected the capitalist's realization "*that he can carry on certain portions of the production process more efficiently through <u>his</u> government than through private corporations..... Some muddleheads find that will be Socialism, but the capitalist knows better.*"[9] Friedrich Engels had taken the same view of public ownership:

> At a further stage of evolution this form [the joint-stock company] *also becomes insufficient: the official representative of capitalist society—the state—will ultimately have to undertake the direction of production. This necessity for conversion into state property is felt first in the great institutions for intercourse and communication—the post office, the telegraphs, the railways.*[10]

The rise of "corporate liberalism" as an ideology at the turn of the twentieth century was brilliantly detailed in James Weinstein's *The Corporate Ideal in the Liberal State.*[11] It was reflected in the so-called "Progressive" movement in the U.S., and by Fabianism, the closest British parallel. The ideology was in many ways an expression of the world view of "New Class" apparatchiks, whose chief values were planning and the cult of "professionalism," and who saw the lower orders as human raw material to be managed for their own good. This class is quite close to the social base of the Insoc movement that Orwell described in *1984*:

> The new aristocracy was made up for the most part of bureaucrats, scientists, technicians, trade-union organizers, publicity experts, sociologists, teachers, journalists, and professional politicians. These people, whose origins lay in the salaried middle class and the upper grades of the working class, had been shaped and brought together by the barren world of monopoly industry and centralized government.[12]

The key to efficiency, for the New Class, was to remove as much of life as possible from the domain of "politics" (that is, interference by non-professionals) and to place it under the control of competent authorities. "Democracy" was recast as a periodic legitimation ritual, with the individual returning between elections to his proper role of sitting down and shutting up. In virtually every area of life, the average citizen was to be transformed from Jefferson's self-sufficient and resourceful yeoman into a client of some bureaucracy or other. The educational system was designed to render him a passive and easily managed recipient of the "services" of one institution after another. In every area of life, as Ivan Illich wrote, the citizen/subject/resource was taught to *"confuse process and substance."*

> *Health, learning, dignity, independence, and creative endeavor are defined as little more than the performance of the institutions which claim to serve these ends, and their improvement is made to depend on allocating more resources to the management of hospitals, schools, and other agencies in question.*

As a corollary of this principle, the public was taught to *"view doctoring oneself as irresponsible, learning on one's own as unreliable, and community organization, when not paid for by those in authority, as a form of aggression or subversion."*[13]

This general phenomenon, in which passive human raw material was managed by "service" bureaucracies, was described by Edgar Friedenberg as the "conscript clientele."

> *Although they are called "clients," members of conscript clienteles are not regarded as customers by the bureaucracies that service them since they are not free to withdraw or withhold their custom or to look elsewhere for service. They are treated as raw material that the service organization needs to perform its social function and continue its existence. It does not take many hours of observation—or attendance—in a public school to learn, from the way the place is actually run, that the pupils are there for the sake of the school, not the other way around....*

> [Public school spending] *is money spent providing goods and services to people who have no voice in determining what those goods and services shall be or how they shall be administered; and those who have no lawful power to withhold their custom by refusing to attend even if they and their parents feel that what the schools provide is distasteful or injurious. They are provided with textbooks that, unlike any other work, from the Bible to the sleaziest pornography, no man would buy for his personal satisfaction. They are, precisely, not "trade books"; rather, they are adopted for the compulsory use of hundreds of thousands of other people by committees, no member of which would have bought a single copy for his own library.*

Although Friedenberg treated public schools as the most obvious example of a conscripted clientele, they were by no means the only member of that class: "*Ultimately, bureaucracies with conscript clienteles become real clients of one another, mutually dependent for referral of cases. They create conditions in one system that generate clients for another....*" For example, the schools process human raw material to be taken over by the "human resources" bureaucracies of private industry (with the transition made as seamless as possible by the school-to-work movement), or by the bureaucracies of the welfare state and prison-industrial complex.[14]

Although the corporate liberal ideology is associated with the New Class world view, it intersected in many ways with that of "enlightened" employers who saw paternalism as a way of getting more out of workers. Much of corporate leadership at the turn of the century

> revealed a strikingly firm conception of a benevolent feudal approach to the firm and its workers. Both were to be dominated and co-ordinated from the central office. In that vein, they were willing to extend...such things as new housing, old age pensions, death payments, wage and job schedules, and bureaus charged with responsibility for welfare, safety and sanitation.[15]

The New Class mania for planning and rationality was reflected within the corporation in the Taylorist/Fordist cult of "scientific management," in which the workman was deskilled and control of the production process was shifted upward into the white collar hierarchy of managers and engineers.[16]

This new intersection of interests between the progressive social planners and corporate management was reflected, organizationally, in the National Civic Federation, whose purpose was to bring together the most enlightened and socially responsible elements of business, labor, and government.[17] If, as Big Bill Haywood said of the I.W.W.'s founding convention, that body was "the Continental Congress of the working class," then the NCF was surely the Continental Congress of the New Class. The themes of corporate liberalism, as David Noble described them, were "*cooperation rather than conflict, the natural harmony of interest between labor and capital, and effective management and administration as the means toward prosperity and general welfare.*"[18]

The New Class intellectuals, despite their prominent role in formulating the ideology, were co-opted as a decidedly junior partner of the corporate elite. As Hilaire Belloc and William English Walling perceived, "Progressives" and Fabians valued regimentation and centralized control much more than their allegedly "socialist" economic projects. They recognized, for the most part, that expropriation of the capitalists was impossible in the real world. The large capitalists, in turn, recognized the value of the welfare and regulatory state for maintaining social stability and control, and for making possible the political extraction of profits in the name of egalitarian values. The result was a devil's bargain by which the working class was guaranteed a minimum level of comfort and security, in return for which the large corporations were enabled to extract profits through the state. Of the "Progressive" intellectual, Belloc wrote:

> *Let laws exist which make the proper housing, feeding, clothing, and recreation of the proletarian mass be incumbent on the possessing class, and the observance of such rules be imposed, by inspection and punishment, upon those whom he pretends to benefit, and all that he really cares for will be achieved.*[19]

The New Class, its appetite for power satiated with petty despotisms in the departments of education and human services, was put to work on its primary mission of cartelizing the economy for the profit of the corporate ruling class. Its "populist" rhetoric was harnessed to sell state capitalism to the masses. Those overeducated yahoos admirably served their masters in the capacity of useful idiots.

But whatever the "idealistic" motivations of the social engineers themselves, their program was implemented to the extent that it furthered the material interests of monopoly capital. Kolko used the term "political capitalism" to describe the general objectives big business pursued through the "Progressive" state:

> *Political capitalism is the utilization of political outlets to attain conditions of stability, predictability, and security—to attain rationalization—in the economy. Stability is the elimination of internecine competition and erratic fluctuations in the economy. Predictability is the ability, on the basis of politically stabilized and secured means, to plan future economic action on the basis of fairly calculable expectations. By security I mean protection from the political attacks latent in any formally democratic political structure. I do not give to rationalization its frequent definition as the improvement of efficiency, output, or internal organization of a company; I mean by the term, rather, the organization of the economy and the larger political and social spheres in a manner that will allow corporations to function in a predictable and secure environment permitting reasonable profits over the long run.*[20]

From the turn of the twentieth century on, there was a series of attempts by corporate leaders to create some institutional structure by which price competition could be regulated and their respective market shares stabilized. *"It was then,"* Paul Sweezy wrote, *that U.S. businessmen learned the self-defeating nature of price-cutting as a competitive weapon and started the process of banning it through a complex network of laws (corporate and regulatory), institutions (e.g., trade associations), and conventions (e.g., price leadership) from normal business practice.[21]*

But merely private attempts at cartelization before the Progressive Era—namely the so-called "trusts"—were miserable failures, according to Kolko. The dominant trend at the turn of the century—despite the effects of tariffs, patents, railroad subsidies, and other existing forms of statism—was competition. The trust movement was an attempt to cartelize the economy through such voluntary and private means as mergers, acquisitions, and price collusion. But the over-leveraged and over-capitalized trusts were even less efficient than before, and steadily lost market share at the hands of their smaller, more efficient competitors. Standard Oil and U.S. Steel, immediately after their formation, began a process of eroding market share. In the face of this resounding failure, big business acted through the state to cartelize itself—hence, the Progressive regulatory agenda. "*Ironically, contrary to the consensus of historians, it was not the existence of monopoly that caused the federal government to intervene in the economy, but the lack of it.*"[22]

The FTC and Clayton Acts reversed this long trend toward competition and loss of market share and made stability possible.

The provisions of the new laws attacking unfair competitors and price discrimination meant that the government would now make it possible for many trade associations to stabilize, for the first time, prices within their industries, and to make effective oligopoly a new phase of the economy.[23]

The Federal Trade Commission created a hospitable atmosphere for trade associations and their efforts to prevent price cutting.[24] The two pieces of legislation accomplished what the trusts had been unable to: it enabled a handful of firms in each industry to stabilize their market share and to maintain an oligopoly structure between them. This oligopoly pattern has remained stable ever since.

It was during the war [i.e. WWI] that effective, working oligopoly and price and market agreements became operational in the dominant sectors of the American economy. The rapid diffusion of power in the economy and relatively easy entry [i.e., the conditions the trust movement failed to suppress] virtually ceased. Despite the cessation of important new legislative enactments, the unity of business and the federal government continued throughout the 1920s and thereafter, using the foundations laid in the Progressive Era to stabilize and consolidate conditions within various industries. And, on the same progressive foundations and exploiting the experience with the war agencies, Herbert Hoover and Franklin Roosevelt later formulated programs for saving American capitalism. The principle of utilizing the federal government to stabilize the economy, established in the context of modern industrialism during the Progressive Era, became the basis of political capitalism in its many later ramifications.[25]

In addition, the various safety and quality regulations introduced during this period also had the effect of cartelizing the market. They served essentially the same purpose as the later attempts in the Wilson war economy to reduce the variety of styles and features available in product lines, in the name of "efficiency." Any action by the state to impose a uniform standard of quality (e.g. safety), across the board, necessarily eliminates safety as a competitive issue between firms. Thus, the industry is partially cartelized, to the very same extent that would have happened had all the firms in it adopted a uniform level of quality standards, and agreed to stop competing in that area. A regulation, in essence, is a state-enforced cartel in which the members agree to cease competing in a particular area of quality or safety, and instead agree on a uniform standard. And unlike non-state-enforced cartels, which are unstable, no member can seek an advantage by defecting. Similarly, the provision of services by the state (R&D funding, for example) removes them as components of price in cost competition between firms, and places them in the realm of guaranteed income to all firms in a market alike. Whether through regulations or direct state subsidies to various forms of accumulation, the corporations act through the state to carry out some activities jointly, and to restrict competition to selected areas.

And Kolko provided abundant evidence that the main force behind this entire legislative agenda was big business. The Meat Inspection Act, for instance, was passed primarily at the behest of the big meat packers. In the 1880s, repeated scandals involving tainted meat had resulted in U.S. firms being shut out of several European markets. The big packers had turned to the U.S. government to conduct inspections on exported meat. By carrying out this function jointly, through the state, they removed quality inspection as a competitive issue between them, and the U.S. government provided a seal of approval in much the same way a trade association would—but at public expense. The problem with this early inspection regime was that only the largest packers were involved in the export trade; mandatory inspections therefore gave a competitive advantage to the small firms that supplied only the domestic market. The main effect of Roosevelt's Meat Inspection Act was to bring the small packers into the inspection regime, and thereby end the competitive disability it imposed on large firms. Upton Sinclair simply served as an unwitting shill for the meat-packing industry.[26] This pattern was repeated, in its essential form, in virtually every component of the "Progressive" regulatory agenda.

The same leitmotif reappears in the New Deal. The core of business support for the New Deal was, as Ronald Radosh described it, "*leading moderate big businessmen and liberal-minded lawyers from large corporate enterprises.*"[27] Thomas Ferguson and Joel Rogers described them more specifically as "*a new power bloc of capital-intensive industries, investment banks, and internationally oriented commercial banks.*"[28]

Labor was a relatively minor part of the total cost package of such businesses; at the same time, capital-intensive industry, as Galbraith pointed out in his analysis of the "technostructure," depended on long-term stability and predictability for planning high-tech production. Therefore, this segment of big business was willing to trade higher wages for social peace in the workplace.[29] The roots of this faction can be traced to the relatively "progressive" employers described by James Weinstein in his account of the National Civic Federation at the turn of the century, who were willing to engage in collective bargaining over wages and working conditions in return for uncontested management control of the workplace.[30]

This attitude was at the root of the Taylorist/Fordist social contract, in which the labor bureaucrats agreed to let management manage, so long as labor got an adequate share of the pie.[31] Such an understanding was most emphatically in the interests of large corporations. The sitdown movement in the auto industry and the organizing strikes among West coast longshoremen were virtual revolutions among rank and file workers on the shop floor. In many cases, they were turning into regional general strikes. The Wagner Act domesticated this revolution and brought it under the control of professional labor bureaucrats.

Industrial unionism, from the employer's viewpoint, had the advantage over craft unionism of providing a single bargaining agent with which management could deal. One of the reasons for the popularity of "company unions" among large corporations, besides the obvious advantages in pliability, was the fact that they were an alternative to the host of separate craft unions of the AFL. Even in terms of pliability, the industrial unions of the Thirties had some of the advantages of company unions. By bringing collective bargaining under the aegis of federal labor law, corporate management was able to use union leadership to discipline their own rank and file, and to use the federal courts as a mechanism of enforcement.

> *The New Dealers devised...a means to integrate big labor into the corporate state. But only unions that were industrially organized, and which paralleled in their structure the organization of industry itself, could play the appropriate role. A successful corporate state required a safe industrial-union movement to work. It also required a union leadership that shared the desire to operate the economy from the top in formal conferences with the leaders of the other functional economic groups, particularly the corporate leaders. The CIO unions...provided such a union leadership.*[32]

Moderate members of the corporate elite also gained reassurance from the earlier British experience in accepting collective bargaining. Collective bargaining did not affect the distribution of wealth, for one thing: "*Labor gains were made due to the general growth in wealth and at the expense of the consumer, which would mean small businessmen, pensioners, farmers, and nonunionized white collar employees.*" (Not to mention a large contingent of unskilled laborers and lumpenproles without bargaining leverage against the employing classes). And the British found that firms in a position of oligopoly, with a relatively inelastic demand, were able to pass increased labor costs on to the consumer at virtually no cost to themselves.[33]

The Wagner Act served the central purposes of the corporate elite. To some extent it was a response to mass pressure from below. But the decision on whether and how to respond, the form of the response, and the implementation of the response, were all firmly in the hands of the corporate elite. According to Domhoff (writing in *The Higher Circles*), "*The benefits to capital were several: greater efficiency and productivity from labor, less labor turnover, the disciplining of the labor force by labor unions, the possibility of planning labor costs over the long run, and the dampening of radical doctrines.*"[34] James O'Connor described it this way: "*From the standpoint of monopoly capital the main function of unions was...to inhibit disruptive, spontaneous rank-and-file activity (e.g., wildcat strikes and slowdowns) and to maintain labor discipline in general. In other words, unions were...the guarantors of 'managerial prerogatives.'*"[35] The objectives of stability and productivity were more likely to be met by such a limited Taylorist social compact than by a return to the labor violence and state repression of the late nineteenth century.

In *The Power Elite and the State*, Domhoff put forth a slightly more nuanced thesis.[36] It was true, he admitted, that a majority of large corporations opposed the Wagner Act as it was actually presented. But the basic principles of collective bargaining embodied in it had been the outcome of decades of corporate liberal theory and practice, worked out through policy networks in which "progressive" large corporations had played a leading role; the National Civic Federation, as Weinstein described its career, was a typical example of such networks. The motives of those in the Roosevelt administration who framed the Wagner Act were very much in the mainstream of corporate liberalism. Although they may have been ambivalent about the specific form of FDR's labor legislation, Swope and his corporate fellow travelers had played the major role in formulating the principles behind it. Whatever individual business leaders thought of Wagner, it was drafted by mainstream corporate lawyers who were products of the ideological climate created by those same business leaders; and it was drafted with a view to their interests. Although it was not accepted by big business as a whole, it was largely the creation of representatives of big business interests whose understanding of the act's purpose was largely the same as those outlined in Domhoff's quote above from *The Higher Circles*. And although it was designed to contain the threat of working class power, it enjoyed broad working class support as the best deal they were likely to get. Finally, the southern segment of the ruling class was willing to go along with it because it specifically exempted agricultural laborers.

Among the other benefits of labor legislation, corporate interests are able to rely on the state's police powers to impose an authoritarian character on labor relations. In the increasingly statist system, Bukharin pointed out in his analysis of state capitalism almost a century ago,

> *workers* [become] *formally* <u>*bonded*</u> *to the imperialist state. In point of fact, employees of state enterprises even before the war were deprived of a number of most elementary rights, like the right to organise, to strike, etc.... With state capitalism making nearly every line of production important for the state, with nearly all branches of production directly serving the interests of war, prohibitive legislation is extended to the entire field of economic activities. The workers are deprived of the right to move, the right to strike, the right to belong to the so-called "subversive" parties, the right to choose an enterprise, etc. They are transformed into bondsmen attached, not to the land, but to the plant.*[37]

The relevance of this line of analysis to America can be seen with a cursory look at Cleveland's response to the Pullman strike, the Railway Labor Relations Act and Taft-Hartley (which, in James O'Connor's words, "included a ban on secondary boycotts and hence tried to 'illegalize' class solidarity...")[38], and Truman's and Bush's threats to use soldiers as scabs in, respectively, the steelworkers' and longshoremen's strikes.

The Social Security Act was the other major part of the New Deal agenda. In *The Higher Circles*, Domhoff described its functioning in language much like his characterization of the Wagner Act. Its most important result *from the point of view of the power elite was a restabilization of the system. It put a floor under consumer demand, raised people's expectations for the future and directed political energies back into conventional channels.... The wealth distribution did not change, decision-making power remained in the hands of upper-class leaders, and the basic principles that encased the conflict were set forth by moderate members of the power elite.*[39]

In his later work *The Power Elite and the State*, Domhoff undertook a much more thorough analysis, with a literature review of his structuralist Marxists critics, that essentially verified his earlier position.[40]

The New Deal and Great Society welfare state, according to Frances Piven and Richard Cloward, served a similar function to that of Social Security: it blunted the danger of mass political radicalism resulting from widespread homelessness and starvation. In addition, it also provided social control by bringing the underclass under the supervision of an army of intrusive, paternalistic social workers and welfare case workers.[41] And like Social Security, it put a floor on aggregate demand.

To the extent that the welfare and labor provisions of FDR's New Deal have benefited average people, the situation resembles a parable of Tolstoy's:

I see mankind as a herd of cattle inside a fenced enclosure. Outside the fence are green pastures and plenty for the cattle to eat, while inside the fence there is not quite grass enough for the cattle. Consequently, the cattle are tramping underfoot what little grass there is and goring each other to death in their struggle for existence.

I saw the owner of the herd come to them, and when he saw their pitiful condition he was filled with compassion for them and thought of all he could do to improve their condition.

So he called his friends together and asked them to assist him in cutting grass from outside the fence and throwing it over the fence to the cattle. And that they called Charity.

Then, because the calves were dying off and not growing up into serviceable cattle, he arranged that they should each have a pint of milk every morning for breakfast.

Because they were dying off in the cold nights, he put up beautiful well-drained and well-ventilated cowsheds for the cattle.

Because they were goring each other in the struggle for existence, he put corks on the horns of the cattle, so that the wounds they gave each other might not be so serious. Then he reserved a part of the enclosure for the old bulls and cows over 70 years of age.

In fact, he did everything he could think of to improve the condition of the cattle, and when I asked him why he did not do the one obvious thing, break down the fence, and let the cattle out, he answered: "If I let the cattle out, I should no longer be able to milk them."[42]

The capitalist supporters of the welfare state are like an enlightened farmer who understands that his livestock will produce more for him, in the long run, if they are well treated.

Hilaire Belloc speculated that the industrial serfdom in his Servile State would only be stable if the State subjected the unemployable underclass to "corrective" treatment in forced labor camps, and forced everyone even marginally employable into a job, as a deterrent to deliberate parasitism or malingering. Society would *"find itself"* under the *"necessity,"*

when once the principle of the minimum wage is conceded, coupled with the principle of sufficiency and security, to control those whom the minimum wage excludes from the area of normal employment.[43]

This society would be organized on the pattern of Anthony Burgess' squalid and decaying welfare state, in which "everyone not a child, or with child, must be employed." But Belloc's speculation was not idle; since Fabians like the Webbs and H.G. Wells had proposed just such labor camps for the underclass in their paternalistic utopia.[44]

Although we are still far from a formal requirement to be either employed or subjected to remedial labor by the State, a number of intersecting State policies have that tendency. For example, the imposition of compulsory unemployment insurance, with the State as arbiter of when one qualifies to collect:

A man has been compelled by law to put aside sums from his wages as insurance against unemployment. But he is no longer the judge of how such sums shall be used. They are not in his possession.... They are in the hands of a government official. "Here is work offered you at twenty-five shillings a week. If you do not take it, you certainly shall not have a right to the money you have been compelled to put aside. If you will take it the sum shall still stand to your credit, and when next in my judgment your unemployment is not due to your recalcitrance and refusal to labor, I will permit you to have some of your money: not otherwise."[45]

Still another measure with this tendency is "workfare," coupled with subsidies to employers who hire the underclass as peon labor. Vagrancy laws and legal restrictions on jitney services, self-built temporary shelters, etc., serve to reduce the range of options for independent subsistence. And finally, the prison-industrial complex, as "employer" for the nearly half of its "clients" guilty of only consensual market transactions, is in effect a forced labor camp absorbing a major segment of the underclass.

The culmination of FDR's state capitalism was (of course) the military-industrial complex which arose from World War II, and has continued ever since. It has since been described as "military Keynesianism," or a "perpetual war economy." A first step in realizing the monumental scale of the war economy's effect is to consider that the total value of plant and equipment in the United States increased by about two-thirds (from $40 to $66 billion) between 1939 and 1945, most of it a taxpayer "gift" of forced investment funds provided to the country's largest corporations.[46] Profit was virtually guaranteed on war production through "cost-plus" contracts.[47] In addition, 67% of federal R&D spending was channeled through the 68 largest private laboratories (40% of it to the ten largest), with the resulting patents being given away to the companies that carried out the research under government contract.[48]

Demobilization of the war economy after 1945 very nearly threw the overbuilt and government-dependent industrial sector into a renewed depression. For example, in *Harry Truman and the War Scare of 1948,* Frank Kofsky described the aircraft industry as spiraling into red ink after the end of the war, and on the verge of bankruptcy when it was rescued by Truman's new bout of Cold War spending on heavy bombers.[49]

The Cold War restored the corporate economy's heavy reliance on the state as a source of guaranteed sales. Charles Nathanson argued that *"one conclusion is inescapable: major firms with huge aggregations of corporate capital owe their survival after World War II to the Cold War...."*[50] For example, David Noble pointed out that civilian jumbo jets would never have existed without the government's heavy bomber contracts. The production runs for the civilian market alone were too small to pay for the complex and expensive machine tools. The 747 is essentially a spin-off of military production.[51]

The heavy industrial and high tech sectors were given a virtually guaranteed outlet, not only by U.S. military procurement, but by grants and loan guarantees for foreign military sales under the Military Assistance Program. Although apologists for the military-industrial complex have tried to stress the relatively small fraction of total production represented by military goods, it makes more sense to compare the volume of military procurement to the amount of idle capacity. Military production runs amounting to a minor percentage of total production might absorb a major part of total excess production capacity, and have a huge effect on reducing unit costs. Besides, the rate of profit on military contracts tends to be quite a bit higher, given the fact that military goods have no "standard" market price, and the fact that prices are set by political means (as periodic Pentagon budget scandals should tell us).[52]

But the importance of the state as a purchaser was eclipsed by its relationship to the producers themselves, as Charles Nathanson pointed out. The research and development process was heavily militarized by the Cold War "military-R&D complex." Military R&D often results in basic, general use technologies with broad civilian applications. Technologies originally developed for the Pentagon have often become the basis for entire categories of consumer goods.[53] The general effect has been to "*substantially* [eliminate] *the major risk area of capitalism: the development of and experimentation with new processes of production and new products.*"[54]

This is the case in electronics especially, where many products originally developed by military R&D "*have become the new commercial growth areas of the economy.*"[55] Transistors and other forms of miniaturized circuitry were developed primarily with Pentagon research money. The federal government was the primary market for large mainframe computers in the early days of the industry; without government contracts, the industry might never have had sufficient production runs to adopt mass production and reduce unit costs low enough to enter the private market. And the infrastructure for the worldwide web itself was created by the Pentagon's DARPA, originally as a redundant global communications system that could survive a nuclear war. Any implied commentary on the career of Bill Gates is, of course, unintended.

Overall, Nathanson estimated, industry depended on military funding for around 60% of its research and development spending; but this figure is considerably understated by the fact that a significant part of nominally civilian R&D spending is aimed at developing civilian applications for military technology.[56] It is also understated by the fact that military R&D is often used for developing production technologies (like automated control systems in the machine tool industry) that become the basis for production methods throughout the civilian sector.

Seymour Melman described the "permanent war economy" as a privately-owned, centrally-planned economy that included most heavy manufacturing and high tech industry. This *"state-controlled economy"* was based on the principles of *"maximization of costs and of government subsidies."*[57]

> It can draw on the federal budget for virtually unlimited capital. It operates in an insulated, monopoly market that makes the state-capitalist firms, singly and jointly, impervious to inflation, to poor productivity performance, to poor product design and poor production managing. The subsidy pattern has made the state-capitalist firms failure-proof. That is the state-capitalist replacement for the classic self-correcting mechanisms of the competitive, cost-minimizing, profit-maximizing firm.[58]

B. Power Elite Theory.

The state capitalism of the twentieth century differed fundamentally from the misnamed "laissez-faire" capitalism of the nineteenth century in two regards: 1) the growth of direct organizational ties between corporations and the state, and the circulation of managerial personnel between them; and 2) the eclipse of surplus value extraction from the worker through the production process (as described by classical Marxism), by the extraction of "super-profits" a) from the consumer through the exchange process and b) from the taxpayer through the fiscal process.

Although microeconomics texts generally describe the functioning of supply and demand curves as though the nature of the market actors were unchanged since Adam Smith's day, in fact the rise of the large corporation as the dominant type of economic actor has been a revolution as profound as any in history. It occurred parallel to the rise of the "positive" state (i.e., the omnicompetent, centralized regulatory state) in the nineteenth and early twentieth century. And, vitally important to remember, the two phenomena were mutually reinforcing. The state's subsidies, privileges and other interventions in the market were the major force behind the centralization of the economy and the concentration of productive power. In turn, the corporate economy's need for stability and rationality, and for state-guaranteed profits, has been the central force behind the continuing growth of the leviathan state.

The rise of the centralized state and the centralized corporation has created a system in which the two are organizationally connected, and run by essentially the same recirculating elites (a study of the careers of David Rockefeller, Averell Harriman, or Robert McNamara should be instructive on the last point). This phenomenon has been most ably described by the "power elite" school of sociologists, particularly C. Wright Mills and G. William Domhoff.

According to Mills, the capitalist class was not supplanted by a "managerial revolution," as James Burnham had claimed; but the elite's structure was still most profoundly affected by the corporate revolution. The plutocracy ceased to be a social "class" in the sense described by Marx: an autonomous social formation or amorphous mass of wealthy families, perpetuated largely through family lines of transmission and informal social ties, with its organizational links of firm ownership clearly secondary to its existence in the "social" realm. The plutocracy were no longer just a few hundred rich families who happened to invest their old money in one firm or another. Rather, Mills described it as "*the managerial reorganization of the propertied classes into the more or less unified stratum of the corporate rich.*"[59] Rather than an amorphous collection of wealthy families, in which legal claims to an income from property were the defining characteristic, the ruling class came to be defined by the organizational structure through which it gained its wealth. It was because of this new importance of the institutional forms of the power structure that Mills preferred the term "power elite" to "ruling class": "*'Class' is an economic term; 'rule' a political one. The phrase, 'ruling class,' thus contains the theory that an economic class rules politically.*"[60]

Domhoff, who retained more of the traditional Marxist idea of class than did Mill, described the situation in this way:

> *The upper class as a whole does not do the ruling. Instead, class rule is manifested through the activities of a wide variety of organizations and institutions. These organizations and institutions are financed and directed by those members of the upper class who have the interest and ability to involve themselves in protecting and enhancing the privileged social position of their class. Leaders within the upper class join with high-level employees in the organizations they control to make up what will be called the power elite. This power elite is the leadership group of the upper class as a whole, but it is not the same thing as the upper class, for not all members of the upper class are members of the power elite and not all members of the power elite are part of the upper class. It is members of the power elite who take part in the processes that maintain the class structure.*[61]

While Mills virtually replaced the traditional idea of a ruling class with that of the transcendent power elite, Domhoff saw the power elite as an action arm of the upper class; this action arm incorporated both elements of the upper class itself, who were active in business and government, and their managerial servants.[62]

In language quite similar to that of Domhoff, Martin Sklar described the "corporate reconstruction of American capitalism," as it affected the nature of the ruling class, in this way:

> *It was characteristic of the transition from competitive to corporate capitalism in the United States that although no family alliances and family-based wealth continued to be no less important than before, the families actively involved in engineering the transition shifted their base of income, power, and prestige from the proprietary enterprise to the bureaucratic corporation, usually multifunctional and multilocational in operation, and to the diversified investment portfolio.*[63]

Because of the corporate reorganization of the ruling class, senior corporate management has been incorporated as junior partners in the power elite. Contrary to theories of the "managerial revolution," senior management is kept firmly subordinated, through informal social ties and the corporate socialization process, to the goals of the owners. Even a Welch or Eisner understands that his career depends on being a "team player," and the team's objectives are set by the Rockefellers and Du Ponts.[64] The corporate reorganization of the economy has led to permanent organizational links between large corporations, government agencies, research institutions, and foundation money, and resulted in the plutocracy functioning *organizationally* on a class-wide basis.[65]

The power elite theory of Mills and Domhoff had been anticipated, in many ways, by Bukharin. He wrote, in language that prefigured Mills, of intersecting corporate and state elites:

> *With the growth of the importance of state power, its inner structure also changes. The state becomes more than ever before an "executive committee of the ruling classes." It is true that state power always reflected the interests of the "upper strata," but inasmuch as the top layer itself was a more or less amorphous mass, the organised state apparatus faced an unorganised class (or classes) whose interests it embodied. Matters are totally different now. The state apparatus not only embodies the interests of the ruling classes in general, but also their collectively expressed will. It faces no more atomised members of the ruling classes, but their organisations. Thus the government is de facto transformed into a "committee" elected by the representatives of entrepreneurs' organizations, and it becomes the highest guiding force of the state capitalist trust.*[66]

In a passage that could have been written by Mills, Bukharin described the rotation of personnel between "private" and "public" offices in the interlocking directorate of state and capitalist bureaucracies:

The bourgeoisie loses nothing from shifting production from one of its hands into another, since present-day state power is nothing but an entrepreneurs' company of tremendous power, headed even by the same persons that occupy the leading positions in the banking and syndicate offices.[67]

It is the common class background of the state and corporate elites, and the constant circulation of them between institutions, that underscores the utter ridiculousness of controlling corporate power through such nostrums as "clean election" reforms. The promotion of corporate aims by high-level policy makers is the result mainly, not of soft money and other forms of cartoonishly corrupt villainy, but of the policy makers' cultural background and world view. Mills commented ironically on the "pitiful hearings" on confirmation of corporate leaders appointed to government office:

The revealing point...is not the cynicism toward the law and toward the lawmakers on the middle levels of power which they display, nor their reluctance to dispose of their personal stock. The interesting point is how impossible it is for such men to divest themselves of their engagement with the corporate world in general and with their own corporations in particular. Not only their money, but their friends, their interests, their training—their lives in short—are deeply involved in this world.... The point is not so much financial or personal interests in a given corporation, but identification with the corporate world.[68]

Although the structuralist Marxists have created an artificial dichotomy between their position and that of institutional elitists like Mill and Domhoff,[69] they are entirely correct in pointing out that the political leadership does not have to be subject, in any crude way, to corporate control. Instead, the very structure of the corporate economy and the situations it creates compel the leadership to promote corporate interests out of perceived "objective necessity." Given not just the background and assumptions of the policy elite, but the dependence of political on economic stability, policies that stabilize the corporate economy and guarantee steady output and profits are the only imaginable alternatives. And regardless of how "progressive" the regulatory state's ostensible aims, the organizational imperative will make the corporate economy's managers and directors the main source of the processed data and technical expertise on which policy makers depend.

The public's control over the system's overall structure, besides, is severely constrained by the fact that people who work inside the corporate and state apparatus inevitably have an advantage in time, information, attention span, and agenda control over the theoretically "sovereign" outsiders in whose name they act. The very organs of cultural reproduction—the statist school system, the corporate press, etc.— shape the public's "common sense" understanding of what is possible, and what is to be relegated to the outer darkness of "extremism." So long as wire service and network news foreign correspondents write their copy in hotel rooms from government handouts, and half the column inches in newspapers are generated by government and corporate public relations departments, the "moderate" understanding will always be conditioned by institutional culture.

In making use of the "Power Elite" model of Mills and Domhoff, one must be prepared to counter the inevitable "tinfoil hat" charges from certain quarters. Power Elite theory, despite a superficial resemblance to some right-wing conspiracy theories, has key differences from them. The latter take, as the primary motive force of history, personal cabals united around some esoteric or gratuitously evil ideology.[70] Now, the concentration of political and economic power in the control of small, interlocking elites, is indeed likely to result in informal personal ties, and therefore to have as its side-effect sporadic conspiracies (Stinnett's *Day of Deceit* theory of Pearl Harbor is a leading example). But such conspiracy is not necessary to the working of the system—it simply occurs as a secondary phenomenon, and occasionally speeds up or intensifies processes that happen for the most part automatically. Although the CFR is an excellent proxy for the foreign policy elite, and some informal networking and coordination of policy no doubt get done through it, it is essentially a secondary organization, whose membership are *ex officio* representatives of the major institutions regulating national life. The primary phenomenon is the institutional concentration of power that brings such people into contact with each other, in the first place, in their official capacities.

C. Monopoly Capital and Super-Profits.

We now proceed to the second difference between twentieth century monopoly capitalism and earlier variants of capitalism: the growth of surplus value extraction through exchange. In the "monopoly capitalism" model of Paul Baran and Paul Sweezy, the central figures in the *Monthly Review* group, the corporate system can maintain stable profit levels by passing its costs on to the consumer. The increased labor costs of unionized heavy manufacturing are paid, ultimately, by the non-cartelized sectors of the economy (the same is true of the corporate income tax and the rest of the burden of "progressive" taxation, although the authors do not mention it in this context). Capitalism is no longer predominantly, as Marx had assumed in the nineteenth century, a system of competition. As a result, the large corporate sector of the economy becomes immune to Marx's law of the falling tendency of the rate of profit.[71]

> *The crucial difference between* [competitive capitalism and monopoly capitalism] *is well known and can be summed up in the proposition that under competitive capitalism the individual enterprise is a "price taker," while under monopoly capitalism the big corporation is a "price maker."* [72]

Direct collusion between the firms in an oligopoly market, whether open or hidden, is not required. "Price leadership," although the most common means by which corporations informally agree on price, is only one of several.

> *Price leadership...is only the leading species of a much larger genus.... So long as some fairly regular pattern is maintained such cases may be described as modified forms of price leadership. But there are many other situations in which no such regularity is discernible: which firm initiates price changes seems to be arbitrary. This does not mean that the essential ingredient of tacit collusion is absent. The initiating firm may simply be announcing to the rest of the industry, "We think the time has come to raise (or lower) the price in the interest of all of us." If the others agree, they will follow. If they do not, they will stand pat, and the firm that made the first move will rescind its initial price change. It is this willingness to rescind if an initial change is not followed which distinguishes the tacit collusion situation from a price-war situation. So long as firms accept this convention...it becomes relatively easy for the group as a whole to feel its way toward the price which maximizes the industry's profit.... If these conditions are satisfied, we can safely assume that the price established at any time is a reasonable approximation of the theoretical monopoly price."* [73]

In this way, the firms in an oligopoly market can jointly determine their price very much as would a single monopoly firm. The resulting price surcharge passed on to the consumer is quite significant. According to an FTC study in the 1960s, "*if highly concentrated industries were deconcentrated to the point where the four largest firms control 40% or less of an industry's sales, prices would fall by 25% or more.*"[74]

This form of tacit collusion is not by any means free from breakdowns. When one firm develops a commanding lead in some new process or technology, or acquires a large enough market share or a low enough cost of production to be immune from retribution, it may well initiate a war of conquest on its industry.[75] Such suspensions of the rules of the game are identified, for example, with revolutionary changes like Wal-Mart's blitz of the retail market. But in between such disruptions, oligopoly markets can often function for years without serious price competition. As mentioned above, the Clayton Act's "unfair competition" provisions were designed to prevent the kind of catastrophic price wars that could destabilize oligopoly markets.

The "monopoly capital" theorists introduced a major innovation over classical Marxism by treating monopoly profit as a surplus extracted from the consumer in the exchange process, rather than from the laborer in the production process. This innovation was anticipated by the Austro-Marxist Hilferding in his description of the super profits resulting from the tariff:

> The productive tariff thus provides the cartel with an extra profit over and above that which results from the cartelization itself, and gives it the power to levy an indirect tax on the domestic population. This extra profit no longer originates in the surplus value produced by the workers employed in cartels; nor is it a deduction from the profit of the other non-cartelized industries. It is a tribute exacted from the entire body of domestic consumers.[76]

Baran and Sweezy were quite explicit in recognizing the central organizing role of the state in monopoly capitalism. They described the political function of the regulatory state in ways quite similar to Kolko:

> Now under monopoly capitalism it is as true as it was in Marx's day that the "executive power of the...state is simply a committee for managing the common affairs of the entire bourgeois class." And the common affairs of the entire bourgeois class include a concern that no industries which play an important role in the economy and in which large property interests are involved should be either too profitable or too unprofitable. Extra large profits are gained not only at the expense of consumers but also of other capitalists (electric power and telephone service, for example, are basic costs of all industries), and in addition they may, and at times of political instability do, provoke demands for genuinely effective antimonopoly action [They go on to point out agriculture and the extractive industries as examples of the opposite case, in which special state intervention is required to increase the low profits of a centrally important industry].... It therefore becomes a state responsibility under monopoly capitalism to insure, as far as possible, that prices and profit margins in the deviant industries are brought within the general run of great corporations.

> This is the background and explanation of the innumerable regulatory schemes and mechanisms which characterize the American economy today.... In each case of course some worthy purpose is supposed to be served—to protect consumers, to conserve natural resources, to save the family-size farm—but only the naive believe that these fine sounding aims have any more to do with the case than the flowers that bloom in the spring.... All of this is fully understandable once the basic principle is grasped that under

> *monopoly capitalism the function of the state is to serve the interests of monopoly capital....*
>
> *Consequently the effect of government intervention into the market mechanism of the economy, whatever its ostensible purpose, is to make the system work more, not less, like one made up exclusively of giant corporations acting and interacting* [according to a monopoly price system]....[77]

It is interesting, in this regard, to compare the effect of antitrust legislation in the U.S. to that of nationalization in European "social democracies." In most cases, the firms affected by both policies involve centrally important infrastructures or resources, on which the corporate economy as a whole depends. Nationalization in the Old World is used primarily in the case of energy, transportation and communication. In the U.S., the most famous antitrust cases have been against Standard Oil, AT&T, and Microsoft: all cases in which excessive prices in one firm could harm the interests of monopoly capital as a whole. And recent "deregulation," as it has been applied to the trucking and airline industries, has likewise been in the service of those general corporate interests harmed by monopoly transportation prices. In all these cases, the state has on occasion acted as an executive committee on behalf of the entire corporate economy, by thwarting the mendacity of a few powerful corporations.

D. Socialization of Costs as a Form of Cartelization.

The common thread in all these lines of analysis is that an ever-growing portion of the functions of the capitalist economy have been carried out through the state. According to James O'Connor, state expenditures under monopoly capitalism can be divided into "social capital" and "social expenses."

> *Social capital is expenditures required for profitable private accumulation; it is indirectly productive (in Marxist terms, social capital indirectly expands surplus value). There are two kinds of social capital: social investment and social consumption (in Marxist terms, social constant capital and social variable capital).... Social investment consist of projects and services that increase the productivity of a given amount of laborpower and, other factors being equal, increase the rate of profit.... Social consumption consists of projects and services that lower the reproduction costs of labor and, other factors being equal, increase the rate of profit. An example of this is social insurance, which expands the productive powers of the work force while simultaneously lowering labor costs. The second category, social expenses, consists of projects and services which are required to maintain social harmony—to fulfill the state's "legitimization" function.... The best example*

is the welfare system, which is designed chiefly to keep social peace among unemployed workers.[78]

According to O'Connor, such state expenditures counteract the falling general rate of profit that Marx predicted. Monopoly capital is able to externalize many of its operating expenses on the state; and since the state's expenditures indirectly increase the productivity of labor and capital at taxpayer expense, the apparent rate of profit is increased.

Unquestionably, monopoly sector growth depends on the continuous expansion of social investment and social consumption projects that in part or in whole indirectly increase productivity from the standpoint of monopoly capital. In short, monopoly capital socializes more and more costs of production.[79]

O'Connor listed several of the main ways in which monopoly capital externalizes its operating costs on the political system:

Capitalist production has become more interdependent—more dependent on science and technology, labor functions more specialized, and the division of labor more extensive. Consequently, the monopoly sector (and to a much lesser degree the competitive sector) requires increasing numbers of technical and administrative workers. It also requires increasing amounts of infrastructure (physical overhead capital)—transportation, communication, R&D, education, and other facilities. In short, the monopoly sector requires more and more social investment in relation to private capital.... The costs of social investment (or social constant capital) are not borne by monopoly capital but rather are socialized and fall on the state.[80]

As suggested already by our reference above to O'Connor, these forms of state expenditure have the practical effect of promoting several of the "counteracting influences" to the declining rate of profit that Marx described in Volume 3 of *Capital*. The second such influence Marx listed, for example, was the "depression of wages below the value of labor power." Through welfare, taxpayer-funded education, and other means of subsidizing the reproduction cost of labor-power, the state reduces the minimum sustainable cost of labor-power that must be paid by employers. This is true, likewise, of Marx's third influence: the "cheapening of the elements of constant capital." The state, by subsidizing many of the operating costs of large corporations, artificially shifts their balance sheet further into the black. The fourth influence listed, "relative overpopulation," is promoted by state subsidies to the adoption of capital-intensive forms of production and to the education of technically skilled manpower at government expense—with the effect of artificially increasing the supply of labor relative to demand, and thus reducing its bargaining power in the labor market.[81]

We should briefly recall here our examination above of how such socialization of expenditures serves to cartelize industry. By externalizing such costs on the state, through the general tax system, monopoly capital removes these expenditures as an issue of competition between individual firms. It is as if all the firms in an industry formed a cartel to administer these costs in common, and agreed not to include them in their price competition. The costs and benefits are applied uniformly to the entire industry, removing it as a competitive disadvantage for some firms.

Although it flies in the face of "progressive" myth, big business is by no means uniformly opposed to national health insurance and other forms of social insurance. Currently, giant corporations in the monopoly capital sector are the most likely provide private insurance to their employees; and such insurance is one of the fastest-rising components of labor costs. Consequently, firms that are already providing this service at their own expense are the logical beneficiaries of a nationalized system. The effect of such a national health system would be to remove the cost of this benefit as a competitive disadvantage for the companies that provided it. Even if the state requires only large corporations in the monopoly sector to provide health insurance, it is an improvement of the current situation, from the monopoly capital point of view: health insurance ceases to be a component of price competition among the largest firms. A national health system provides a competitive advantage to a nation's firms at the expense of their foreign competitors, who have to fund their own employee health benefits—hence, American capital's hostility to the Canadian national health, and its repeated attempts to combat it through the WTO. The cartelizing effects of socializing the costs of social insurance, likewise, was one reason a significant segment of monopoly capital supported FDR's Social Security agenda.

Daniel Gross, although erroneously treating it as a departure from the alleged traditional big business hostility to the welfare state, has made the same point about more recent big business support of government health insurance.[82] Large American corporations, by shouldering the burden of health insurance and other employee benefits borne by the state in Europe and Japan, are at a competitive disadvantage both against companies there and against smaller firms here.

Democratic presidential candidate Dick Gephart, or rather his spokesman Jim English, admitted to a corporate liberal motivation for state-funded health insurance in his 2003 Labor Day address. Gephart's proposed mandatory employer coverage, with a 60% tax credit for the cost, would (he said) eliminate competition from companies that don't currently provide health insurance as an employee benefit. It would also reduce competition from firms in countries with a single-payer system.[83]

Another "progressive" cause du jour, the reform of corporate governance, likewise serves elite interests. It's odd that so much of the populist outrage against corporations these days is focused, not on billionaire stockholders, but on their hired help. It's a misguided populism that buys into the misleading "pension fund socialism" or "people's capitalism" image of stock ownership. Although stock is indeed distributed more widely, a great majority of it is still owned by a fairly small fraction of the population. So all the agitation to rein in the misbehavior of senior management, supposedly on behalf of the average working Joe whose 401k is tanking, is a con job. The main effect of "corporate accountability" legislation is to protect the assets of David Rockefeller and his ilk against depreciation through white collar crime.

The level of technical training necessary to keep the existing corporate system running, the current level of capital intensiveness of production, and the current level of R&D efforts on which it depends, would none of them pay for themselves on a free market. The state's education system provides a technical labor force at public expense, and whenever possible overproduces technical specialists on the level needed to ensure that technical workers are willing to take work on the employers' terms. On this count, O'Connor quoted Veblen: the state answers capital's *"need of a free supply of trained subordinates at reasonable wages..."*[84] Starting with the Morrill Act of 1862, which subsidized agricultural and mechanical colleges, the federal government has underwritten a major part of the reproduction costs of technical labor.[85] In research and development, likewise, federal support goes back at least to the agricultural and experiment stations of the late nineteenth century, created pursuant to the Hatch Act of 1887.[86]

The state's cartelization and socialization of the cost of reproducing a technically sophisticated labor force, and its subsidies to R&D, make possible a far higher technical level of production than would support itself in a free market. The G.I. Bill was an integral part of the unprecedentedly high scale of state capitalism created during and after WWII.

Technical-administrative knowledge and skills, unlike other forms of capital over which private capitalists claim ownership, cannot be monopolized by any one or a few industrial-finance interests. The discoveries of science and technology spill over the boundaries of particular corporations and industries, especially in the epoch of mass communications, electronic information processing, and international labor mobility. Capital in the form of knowledge resides in the specialized skills and abilities of the working class itself. In the context of a free market for laborpower…no one corporation or industry or industrial-finance interest group can afford to train its own labor force or channel profits into the requisite amount of R&D. Patents afford some protection, but there is no guarantee that a particular corporation's key employees will not seek positions with other corporations or industries. The cost of losing trained laborpower is especially high in companies that employ technical workers whose skills are specific to particular industrial process— skills paid for by the company in question. Thus, on-the-job training (OJT) is little used not because it is technically inefficient…but because it does not pay.

Nor can any one corporation or industrial-finance interest afford to develop its own R&D or train the administrative personnel increasingly needed to plan, coordinate, and control the production and distribution process. In the last analysis, the state is required to coordinate R&D because of the high costs and uncertainty of getting utilizable results.[87]

At best, from the point of view of the employer, the state creates a "reserve army" of scientific and technical labor—as William Appleman Williams described it, the elite has *"seen to it that experts are a glut on the market."*[88] At worst, when there is a shortage of such labor, the state at least absorbs the cost of producing it and removes it as a component of private industry's production costs. In either case, *"the greater the socialization of the costs of variable capital, the lower will be the level of money wages, and…the higher the rate of profit in the monopoly sector."*[89] And since the monopoly capital sector is able to pass its taxes onto the consumer or to the competitive capital sector, the effect is that *"the costs of training technical laborpower are met by taxes paid by competitive sector capital and labor."*[90]

The "public" schools' curriculum can much more justly be described as servile than liberal education. Its objective is a human product which is capable of fulfilling the technical needs of corporate capital and the state, but at the same time docile and compliant, and incapable of any critical analysis of the system of power it serves. The public educationist movement and the creation of the first state school systems, remember, coincided with the rising factory system's need for a work force that was trained in obedience, punctuality, and regular habits. Technical competence and a "good attitude" toward authority, combined with twelve years of conditioning in not standing out or making waves, were the goal of the public educationists.

Even welfare expenses, although O'Connor classed them as a

completely unproductive expenditure, are in fact another example of the state underwriting variable capital costs. Some socialists love to speculate that, if it were possible, capitalists would lower the prevailing rate of subsistence pay to that required to keep workers alive only when they were employed. But since that would entail starvation during periods of unemployment, the prevailing wage must cover contingencies of unemployment; otherwise, wages would be less than the minimum cost of reproducing labor. Under the welfare state, however, the state itself absorbs the cost of providing for such contingencies of unemployment, so that the uncertainty premium is removed as a component of wages in Adam Smith's "higgling of the market."

And leaving this aside, even as a pure "social expense," the welfare system acts primarily (in O'Connor's words) to *"control the surplus population politically."*[91] The state's subsidies to the accumulation of constant capital and to the reproduction of scientific-technical labor provide an incentive for much more capital-intensive forms of production than would have come about in a free market, and thus contribute to the growth of a permanent underclass of surplus labor;[92] the state steps in and undertakes the minimum cost necessary to prevent large-scale homelessness and starvation, which would destabilize the system, and to maintain close supervision of the underclass through the human services bureaucracy.[93]

The general effect of the state's intervention in the economy, then, is to remove ever increasing spheres of economic activity from the realm of competition in price or quality, and to organize them collectively through organized capital as a whole.

We have, in this chapter, made a partial study of the problem of over-accumulation, and of the intensification of state capitalism in response to that crisis. In the following chapter, we will examine another response to the same crisis, the policy of foreign imperialism to dispose of surplus production abroad. And in Chapter Eight, we will see that these state capitalist policies not only intensify the problem of over-accumulation, but at the same time create contrary crisis tendencies toward under-accumulation; so that state capitalism is constantly balanced on a razor's edge between crises of over- and under-accumulation.

NOTES

1. Martin Sklar, *The Corporate Reconstruction of American Capitalism, 1890-1916: The Market, the Law, and Politics* (Cambridge, New York and Melbourne: Cambridge University Press, 1988) 20-1.

2. Ibid. 44.

3. Joseph Stromberg, "The Role of State Monopoly Capitalism in the American Empire," *Journal of Libertarian Studies* (Summer 2001) 64. Available online at http://www.mises.org/journals/jls/15_3/15_3_3.pdf Captured October 28, 2003.

4. Sklar, *Corporate Reconstruction of American Capitalism* 72-3.

5. See note 3 above.

6. Murray Rothbard, "War Collectivism in World War I," in Murray Rothbard and Ronald Radosh, eds., *A New History of Leviathan: Essays on the Rise of the American Corporate State* (New York: E. P. Dutton & Co., Inc., 1972) 66-7.

7. Arthur Schlesinger, Jr., *The Age of Jackson* (Boston: Houghton-Mifflin, 1946) 505.

8. "Why Business Always Loses," qt. in G. William Domhoff, *The Higher Circles: The Governing Class in America* (New York: Vintage Books, 1971) 157.

9. Robert Rives La Monte, "You and Your Vote," *International Socialist Review* XIII, No. 2 (August 1912); "Editorial," *International Socialist Review* XIII, No. 6 (December 1912).

10. Friedrich Engels, *Anti-Dühring*, vol. 25 of Marx and Engels *Collected Works* (New York: International Publishers, 1987) 265.

11. James Weinstein, *The Corporate Ideal in the Liberal State: 1900-1918* (Boston: Beacon Press, 1968).

12. George Orwell, *1984*. Signet Classics reprint (New York: Harcourt Brace Jovanovich, 1949, 1981) 169.

13. Ivan Illich, *Deschooling Society* (1970) 1-3. Online edition, http://philosophy.la.psu.edu/illich/deschool/intro.html Captured October 15, 2003.

14. Edgar Z. Friedenberg, *The Disposal of Liberty and Other Industrial Wastes* (Garden City, N.Y.: Anchor, 1976) 2-6.

15. William Appleman Williams, *The Contours of American History* (Cleveland and New York: The World Publishing Company, 1961) 382.

16. There is a large body of historical and industrial engineering work on this theme. See, for example: Harry Braverman, *Labor and Monopoly Capital: The Degradation of Work in the Twentieth Century*, 25th Anniversary Edition (New York: Monthly Review Press, 1998); William Lazonick, *Business Organization and the Myth of the Market Economy* (New York: Cambridge University Press, 1991); William Lazonick, *Competitive Advantage on the Shop Floor* (New York: Cambridge University Press, 1990); Steven A. Marglin, "What Do Bosses Do? The Origins and Functions of Hierarchy in Capitalist Production—Part I" *Review of Radical Political Economics* 6:2 (Summer 1974); David Montgomery, *The Fall of the House of Labor* (New York: Cambridge University Press, 1979); David Montgomery,

Workers Control in America (New York: Cambridge University Press, 1979); David F. Noble, *America by Design: Science, Technology, and the Rise of Corporate Capitalism* (New York: Alfred A. Knopf, 1977); David F. Noble, *Forces of Production: A Social History of Industrial Automation* (New York: Alfred A. Knopf, 1984).

17. See James Weinstein, *The Corporate Ideal in the Liberal State: 1900-1918* (Boston: Beacon Press, 1968).

18. Noble, *America by Design* 181.

19. Hilaire Belloc, *The Servile State* (Indianapolis: Liberty Classics, 1913, 1977) 146-7.

20. Gabriel Kolko, *The Triumph of Conservatism: A Reinterpretation of American History 1900-1916* (New York: The Free Press of Glencoe, 1963) 3.

21. Paul M. Sweezy, "Competition and Monopoly," *Monthly Review* (May 1981) 1-16.

22. Kolko, *Triumph of Conservatism* 5.

23. Ibid. 268.

24. Ibid. 275.

25. Ibid. 287.

26. Ibid. 98-108.

27. Ronald Radosh, "The Myth of the New Deal," in Rothbard and Radosh, eds., *A New History of Leviathan* 154-5.

28. Thomas Ferguson and Joel Rogers. *Right Turn* (New York: Hill and Wang, 1986), p. 46; this line of analysis is pursued more intensively in Thomas Ferguson, *Golden Rule: The Investment Theory of Party Competition and the Logic of Money-Driven Political Systems* (Chicago: University of Chicago Press, 1995).

29. Ferguson, *Golden Rule* 117 et seq.; John Kenneth Galbraith, *The New Industrial State* (New York: Signet Books, 1967) 25-37, 258-9, 274, 287-9.

30. Weinstein, *Corporate Ideal in the Liberal State*, esp. the first two chapters.

31. Montgomery, *Workers' Control in America* 49-57.

32. Radosh, "The Myth of the New Deal" 178-9, 181.

33. Domhoff, *Higher Circles* 223.

34. Ibid. 225.

35. James O'Connor, *The Fiscal Crisis of the State* (New York: St. Martin's Press, 1973) 23.

36. G. William Domhoff, *The Power Elite and the State: How Policy is Made in America* (New York: Aldine de Gruyter, 1990) 65-105.

37. Nikolai Bukharin. *Imperialism and World Economy,* Chapter XIII, online edition http://www.marxists.org/archive/bukharin/works/1917/imperial/ Captured October 15, 2003.

38. James O'Connor, *Accumulation Crisis* (Oxford: Basil Blackwell Ltd, 1984) 75.

39. Domhoff, *Higher Circles* 218.

40. Domhoff, *Power Elite and the State* 44-64.

41. Frances Fox Piven and Richard Cloward, *Regulating the Poor* (New York: Vintage Books, 1971, 1993).

42. Leo Tolstoy, "Parable" http://www.geocities.com/glasgowbranch/parable.html Captured June 5, 2002.

43. Belloc, *Servile State* 189.

44. John P. McCarthy, *Hilaire Belloc: Edwardian Radical* (Indianapolis: Liberty Press, 1978) Chapter 6.

45. Belloc, *Servile State* 190-1.

46. C. Wright Mills, *The Power Elite* (Oxford and New York: Oxford University Press, 1956, 2000) 101.

47. David W. Eakins, "Business Planners and America's Postwar Expansion," in David Horowitz, ed., *Corporations and the Cold War* (New York and London: Monthly Review Press, 1969) 148.

48. G. William Domhoff, *Who Rules America?* (Englewood Cliffs, N.J.: Prentice-Hall, 1967) 121.

49. Frank Kofsky, *Harry S. Truman and the War Scare of 1948* (New York: St. Martin's Press, 1993).

50. Charles E. Nathanson, "The Militarization of the American Economy," in Horowitz, ed., *Corporations and the Cold War* 214.

51. Noble, *America by Design* 6-7.

52. Nathanson, "The Militarization of the American Economy" 208.

53. Ibid. 208.

54. Ibid. 230.

55. Ibid. 230.

56. Ibid. 222-5.

57. Seymour Melman, *The Permanent War Economy: American Capitalism in Decline* (New York: Simon and Schuster, 1974) 11.

58. Ibid. 21.

59. Mills, *Power Elite* 147.

60. Ibid. 277n.

61. G. William Domhoff, *Who Rules America Now?* (Prospect Heights, Ill.: Waveland Press, 1983, 1997) 2.

62. Domhoff, *Who Rules America?* 9-10.

63. Sklar, *Corporate Reconstruction of American Capitalism* 27.

64. Mills, *Power Elite* 118-146; see also material on corporate socialization in William M. Dugger, *Corporate Hegemony* (Westport, Conn.: Greenwood Press, 1989).

65. Mills, *Power Elite* 147-70.

66. Bukharin, *Imperialism and World Economy* Chapter XI.

67. Ibid. Chapter XIII.

68. Mills, *Power Elite* 285.

69. For an excellent summary of the structuralists' differences with corporate liberals and elite theorists, see G. William Domhoff, *Power Elite and the State*, op. cit., pp. 1-44. The rest of the book is a series of case studies, with literature reviews of structuralist and state autonomist interpretations, of the major regulatory initiatives of the twentieth century.

70. See Domhoff's chapter on right-wing conspiracy theory, "Dan Smoot, Phyllis Schlafly, Reverend McBirnie, and Me" in *Higher Circles* 281-308.

71. Paul Baran and Paul Sweeny, *Monopoly Capitalism: An Essay in the American Economic and Social Order* (New York: Monthly Review Press, 1966) 72, 77.

72. Ibid. 53-4.

73. Ibid. 61-2.

74. Mark J. Green, et al., eds., *The Closed Enterprise System*. Ralph Nader's Study Group Report on Antitrust Enforcement (New York: Grossman Publishers, 1972) 14.

75. Baran and Sweezy, *Monopoly Capital* 63, 68-9.

76. Rudolf Hilferding, *Finance Capital*. Ed. and trans. By Tom Bottom ore (London and Boston: Routledge & Kegan Paul, 1910, 1981) 308.

77. Baran and Sweezy, *Monopoly Capital* 64-6.

78. O'Connor, *Fiscal Crisis of the State* 6-7.

79. Ibid. 24.

80. Ibid. 24.

81. Karl Marx and Friedrich Engels, *Capital* vol. 3, vol. 37 of Marx and Engels *Collected Works* (New York: International Publishers, 1998) 234-5.

82. Daniel Gross, "Socialism, American Style: Why American CEOs covet a massive European-style social-welfare state" *Slate* Aug. 1, 2003 http://slate.msn.com/id/2086511/

83. C-SPAN, September 1, 2003.

84. O'Connor, *Fiscal Crisis of the State* 111.

85. Noble, *America by Design* 24 et seq.

86. Ibid. 132.

87. O'Connor, *Fiscal Crisis of the State* 112.

88. William Appleman Williams, "A Profile of the Corporate Elite," in Rothbard and Radosh, eds., *New History of Leviathan* 5.

89. O'Connor, *Fiscal Crisis of the State* 124.

90. Ibid. 160.

91. Ibid. Ibid. 69.

92. Ibid. 161.

93. Piven and Cloward, *Regulating the Poor.*

Chapter Seven
Monopoly Capitalism and Imperialism

Introduction: Elite Reaction to Crisis (with Digression on Maldistribution of Income)

William Appleman Williams summarized the lesson of the 1890s in this way: "*Because of its dramatic and extensive nature, the Crisis of the 1890's raised in many sections of American society the specter of chaos and revolution.*"[1] American economic elites saw it as the result of overproduction and surplus capital, and believed it could be resolved only through access to a "new frontier." Without state-guaranteed access to foreign markets, output would be too far below capacity, unit costs would be driven up, and unemployment would reach dangerous levels.

The seriousness of the last threat was underscored by the radicalism of the Nineties. The Pullman Strike, Homestead, and the formation of the Western Federation of Miners (precursor to the IWW) were signs of dangerous levels of labor unrest and class consciousness. Coxey's Army marched on Washington, a small foretaste of the kinds of radicalism that could be produced by unemployment. The anarchist movement had a growing foreign component, more radical than the older native faction, and the People's Party seemed to have a serious chance of winning national elections. At one point Jay Gould, the mouthpiece of the robber barons, was threatening a capital strike (much like those in Venezuela recently) if the populists came to power. In 1894 businessman F. L. Stetson warned, "*We are on the edge of a very dark night, unless a return of commercial prosperity relieves popular discontent.*"[2]

We should note, in passing, that from a mutualist perspective the roots of over-accumulation go much deeper than Stromberg's description of cartelization under monopoly capitalism. The origin of overproduction and over-accumulation lies in the legal privileges of "laissez-faire" capitalism, described under the headings of Tucker's "Big Four" in the last chapter.

J.A. Hobson, in his brilliant chapter on "The Economic Taproot of Imperialism," ascribed the problem to mal-distribution of purchasing power. Ever greater incomes had been concentrated in the hands of the plutocracy, who were unable to dispose of it on any conceivable amount of luxury; the result was that "*a process of automatic saving set in...*" This had the effect of exacerbating the problem of excess capital accumulation, expanding production facilities still further to produce even more output for which there was no demand. "*The power of production has far outstripped the actual rate of consumption....*"[3] The excess of accumulation and shortfall in demand, by disrupting the circuit of capital and creating what Marx called a crisis of realization, led to a worsening business cycle.

In response to his rhetorical question of *why* over-saving and under-consumption occurred, and consumption failed to keep pace with productive capacity, Hobson pointed to the social system.

> But it may be asked, "Why should there be any tendency to over-saving? why should the owners of consuming power withhold a larger quantity for savings than can be serviceably employed?" Another way of putting the same question is this, "Why should not the pressure of present wants keep pace with every possibility of satisfying them? The answer to these pertinent questions carries us to the broadest issue of the distribution of wealth. If a tendency to distribute income or consuming power according to needs is operative, it is evident that consumption would rise with every rise of producing power, for human needs are illimitable, and there could be no excess of saving. But it is quite otherwise in a state of economic society where distribution has no fixed relation to needs, but is determined by other conditions which assign to some people a consuming power vastly in excess of needs or possible uses, while others are destitute of consuming power enough to satisfy even the full demands of physical efficiency.[4]

Over-saving results almost entirely from the surplus income of the rich.[5]

The question remains, what is the reason for this mal-distribution of income? Hobson approached, without ever reaching, an adequate explanation.

> The over-saving which is the economic root of Imperialism is found by analysis to consist of rents, monopoly profits, and other unearned or excessive elements of income, which, not being earned by labour of head or hand, have no legitimate <u>raison d'être</u>. Having no natural relation to effort of production, they impel their recipients to no corresponding satisfaction of

consumption: they form a surplus wealth, which, having no proper place in the normal economy of production and consumption, tends to accumulate as excessive savings.[6]

Hobson proposed, in response to this deficiency, what would later be called a Keynesian solution:

Let any turn in the tide of politico-economic forces divert from these owners their excess of income and make it flow, either to the workers in higher wages, or to the community in taxes, so that it will be spent instead of being saved...there will be no need to fight for foreign markets or foreign areas of investment....

Where the distribution of incomes is such as to enable all classes of the nation to convert their felt wants into an effective demand for commodities, there can be no over-production, no under-employment of capital and labour, and no necessity to fight for foreign markets.[7]

Hobson's reference to the divorce of consumption from the effort of production might have been written by Tucker. The natural wage of labor, when the state does not specially privilege ownership of land and capital, is its product. When labor receives its full product in payment for work done, the disutility of labor is directly related to its product by market price. The laborer is able to decide how much to work, based on how much he wants to consume—and to cease work when his needs are met. Whatever savings are made reflect the worker's own decision to work less in the future, either by living off present savings or by investing them in more efficient production. No superfluity is ever created. But under the capitalist system of privilege, the divorce of effort from consumption results in the same irrationality as any other violation of the cost principle that governs free markets. Because the disutility and the benefit of labor are not both fully internalized by the laborer, he is unable to govern productive output in relation to consumption. The laborer produces a surplus because the market relation between effort and consumption is distorted, and he does not receive the market signal to stop work when he had met his own needs. Because labor pays tribute for access to the means of production, the total output necessary to receive a given level of consumption is always greater than the amount consumed; meanwhile the rentier classes collect a surplus income for which they did not labor. The producing classes therefore create a surplus, not for their own consumption, but to be piled up by a privileged class that cannot possibly dispose of it all.

In the end, Hobson failed to isolate the "taproot" of this phenomenon. His analysis repeatedly grazed the true nature of the problem, without ever directly hitting it. The problem is not the failure to distribute income according to "need," but according to work: labor does not receive its full product as a wage. And the solution is not the Keynesian redistribution of income by the state from rich to poor, but an end to the state's existing redistribution of income from poor to rich. Thomas Hodgskin had stuck nearer the real root of the problem a couple of generations earlier:

> *The wants of individuals which labour is intended to gratify, are the natural guides to their exertions. The instant they are compelled to labour for others, this guide forsakes them, and their exertions are dictated by the greed and avarice, and false hopes of their masters. The wants springing from our organization, and accompanying the power to labour, being created by the same hand which creates and fashions the whole universe,...it is fair to suppose that they would at all times guide the exertions of the labourer, so as fully to ensure a supply of necessaries and conveniences, and nothing more.... By this system* [of the avarice and greed of masters] *the hand is dissevered from the mouth, and labour is put in motion to gratify vanity and ambition, not the natural wants of animal existence. When we look at the commercial history of our country, and see the false hopes of our merchants and manufacturers leading to periodical commercial convulsions, we are compelled to conclude, that they have not the same source as the regular and harmonious external world. Capitalists have no guide to their exertions, because nature rejects and opposes their dominion over labour. Starts of national prosperity, followed by bankruptcy and ruin, have the same source then as fraud and forgery. To our legal* [as opposed to natural] *right of property we are indebted for those gleams of false wealth and real panic, which have so frequently shook, to its centre, the whole trading world.*[8]

The concentration of the economy in corporate form, in subsequent years, only intensified these inherent tendencies toward crisis.

Nevertheless, despite their faulty understanding of the reasons for the crisis, both business and government resounded with claims that U.S. productive capacity had outstripped the domestic market's ability to consume, and that the government had to take active measures to obtain outlets. We proceed to a brief survey of typical remarks from business and government leaders in the years following the depression of the 1890s. In reading the quotes over the next few pages, it's worth bearing in mind that they are not the ravings of Marxist ideologues; they are, rather, the measured reflections of sound, conservative businessmen. The theory of imperialism was the creation, not of Lenin, but of corporate leaders.

In 1897 NAM president Theodore C. Search said, *"Many of our manufacturers have outgrown or are outgrowing their home markets, and the expansion of our foreign trade is our only promise of relief."*[9] In the same year,

Albert J. Beveridge proclaimed: *"American factories are making more than the American people can use; American soil is producing more than they can consume. Fate has written our policy for us; the trade of the world must and shall be ours."*[10] As the State Department's Bureau of Foreign Commerce put it in 1898,

> It seems to be conceded that every year we shall be confronted with an increasing surplus of manufactured goods for sale in foreign markets if American operatives and artisans are to be kept employed the year around. The enlargement of foreign consumption of the products of our mills and workshops has, therefore, become a serious problem of statesmanship as well as of commerce.[11]

In 1900, former Secretary of State John W. Foster wrote, *"it has come to be a necessity to find new and enlarged markets for our agricultural and manufactured products. We cannot maintain our present industrial prosperity without them."*[12]

Ohio governor McKinley emerged as spokesman for this new American consensus, proposing a combination of protective tariffs and reciprocity treaties to open foreign markets to American surplus output with help from the state.[13] As keynote speaker at an organizational meeting of the National Association of Manufacturers in 1895, he said:

> We want our own markets for our manufactures and agricultural products.... [W]e want a foreign market for our surplus products.... We want a reciprocity which will give us foreign markets for our surplus products, and in turn that will open our markets to foreigners for those products which they produce and we do not.[14]

The imperialism of McKinley and Roosevelt, and the resulting Spanish-American War, were outgrowths of this orientation. They were not, however, the only or obvious form of state policy for securing foreign markets. Much more typical of U.S. policy, in the coming years, was the orientation outlined in John Hay's *Open Door Notes* (the first was written in 1899), which Williams called "Open Door Empire."

A. "Open Door Imperialism" Through the 1930s.

Open Door imperialism consisted of using U.S. political power to guarantee access to foreign markets and resources on terms favorable to American corporate interests, without relying on direct political rule. Its central goal was to obtain for U.S. merchandise, in each national market, treatment equal to that afforded any other industrial nation. Most importantly, this entailed active engagement by the U.S.

government in breaking down the imperial powers' existing spheres of economic influence or preference. The result, in most cases, was to treat as hostile to U.S. security interests any large-scale attempt at autarky, or any other policy whose effect was to withdraw a major area from the disposal of U.S. corporations. When the power attempting such policies was an equal, like the British Empire, the U.S. reaction was merely one of measured coolness. When it was perceived as an inferior, like Japan, the U.S. resorted to more forceful measures, as events of the late 1930s indicate. And whatever the degree of equality between advanced nations in their access to Third World markets, it was clear that Third World nations were still to be subordinated to the industrialized West in a collective sense. Indeed, one might think that Kautsky had the Open Door in mind in formulating his theory of "ultra-imperialism," in which the developed capitalist nations cooperated to exploit the Third World collectively.[15]

This Open Door system was the direct ancestor of today's neoliberal system, which is falsely called "free trade" in the apologetics of court intellectuals. It depended on active management of the world economy by dominant states, and continuing intervention to police the international economic order and enforce sanctions against states which did not cooperate. Woodrow Wilson, in a 1907 lecture at Columbia University, said:

> *Since trade ignores national boundaries and the manufacturer insists on having the world as a market, the flag of his nation must follow him, and the doors of the nations which are closed must be battered down.... Concessions obtained by financiers must be safeguarded by ministers of state, even if the sovereignty of unwilling nations be outraged in the process. Colonies must be obtained or planted, in order that no useful corner of the world may be overlooked or left unused. Peace itself becomes a matter of conference and international combinations.*[16]

Wilson warned during the 1912 election that *"Our industries have expanded to such a point that they will burst their jackets if they cannot find a free* [i.e., guaranteed by the state] *outlet to the markets of the world."*[17]

In a 1914 address to the National Foreign Trade Convention, Secretary of Commerce Redfield followed very nearly the same theme:

> *...we have learned the lesson now, that our factories are so large that their output at full time is greater than America's market can continuously absorb. We know now that if we will run full time all the time, we must do it by reason of the orders we take from lands beyond the sea. To do less than that means homes in America in which the husbands are without work; to do that means factories that are shut down part of the time.*[18]

Under the Open Door system, the state and its loans were to play a central role in the export of capital. The primary purpose of foreign loans, historically, has been to finance the infrastructure which is a prerequisite for the establishment of enterprises in foreign countries. As Edward E. Pratt, chief of the Bureau of Foreign and Domestic Commerce, said in 1914:

> ...we can never hope to realize the really big prizes in foreign trade until we are prepared to loan capital to foreign nations and to foreign enterprise. The big prizes...are the public and private developments of large proportions,... the building of railroads, the construction of public-service plants, the improvement of harbors and docks,...and many others which demand capital in large amounts.... It is commonly said that trade follows the flag. It is much more truly said that trade follows the investment or the loan.[19]

It was, however, beyond the resources of individual firms or venture capitalists, or of the decentralized banking system, to raise the sums necessary for these tasks. One purpose of creating a central banking system (the Federal Reserve Act, 1914) was to make possible the large-scale mobilization of investment capital for overseas ventures. Under the New Deal, the mobilization began to take the form of direct state loans.[20] The state's financial policies, besides promoting the accumulation of capital for foreign investment, also underwrite foreign consumption of U.S. produce. As John Foster Dulles said in 1928, "*We must finance our exports by loaning foreigners the where-with-all to pay for them....*"[21] These two functions were perfected in the Bretton Woods system after WWII.

B. The Bretton Woods System: Culmination of Open Door Empire

The second Roosevelt's administration saw the guarantee of American access to foreign markets as vital to ending the Depression and the threat of internal upheaval that went along with it. Assistant Secretary of State Francis Sayre, chairman of Roosevelt's Executive Committee on Commercial Policy, warned: "*Unless we can export and sell abroad our surplus production, we must face a violent dislocation of our whole domestic economy.*"[22] FDR's ongoing policy of Open Door Empire, faced with the withdrawal of major areas from the world market by the autarkic policies of the Greater East Asia Co-Prosperity Sphere and Fortress Europe, led to American entry into World War II, and culminated in the postwar establishment of what Samuel Huntington called a "system of world order" guaranteed both by global institutions of economic governance like the IMF, and by a hegemonic political and military superpower.

In 1935, a War Department memorandum described the emerging Japanese threat in primarily economic terms. Japanese hegemony over

Asia, it warned, would have "*a direct influence on those people of Europe and America who depend on trade and commerce with this area for their livelihood.*" Germany, likewise, was defined as an "aggressor" because of its trade policies in Latin America.[23]

After the fall of western Europe in the spring of 1940, Assistant Secretary of State Breckinridge Long warned that "*every commercial order will be routed to Berlin and filled under its orders somewhere in Europe rather than in the United States,*" resulting in "*falling prices and declining profits here and a lowering of our standard of living with the consequent social and political disturbances.*"[24]

Beginning in the Summer of 1940, the CFR and State Department undertook a joint study to determine the minimum portion of the world the U.S. would have to integrate with its own economy, in order to provide sufficient resources and markets for economic stability; it also explored policy options for reconstructing the postwar world.[25] The study group found that Germany's continental system was far more self-sufficient in resources, and more capable of autarky, than was the United States. The U.S. economy could not survive in its existing form without access to the resources and markets not only of the Western Hemisphere, but of the British Empire and Far East (together called the Grand Area). But the latter region was rapidly being incorporated into Japan's economic sphere of influence. FDR made the political decision to contest Japanese power in the Far East, and if necessary to initiate war. In the end, however, he successfully maneuvered Japan into firing the first shot.[26] The American policy that emerged from these struggles was one of securing control over the markets and resources of the global "Grand Area" through institutions of global economic governance, reflected in the postwar Bretton Woods system.

The problem of access to foreign markets and resources was central to U.S. policy planning for a postwar world. Given the structural imperatives of "export dependent monopoly capitalism," the fear of a postwar depression was a real one. The original drive toward foreign expansion at the end of the nineteenth century reflected the fact that industry, with state capitalist encouragement, had expanded far beyond the ability of the domestic market to consume its output. Even before World War II, the state capitalist economy had serious trouble operating at the level of output needed for full utilization of capacity and cost control. Military-industrial policy during the war greatly exacerbated the problem of over-accumulation, increasing the value of plant and equipment by two-thirds at taxpayer expense. The end of the war, if followed by the traditional pattern of demobilization, would result in a drastic reduction in orders to this overbuilt industry at the same time that over ten million workers were dumped back into the civilian labor force. And four years of forced restraints on consumption had created a vast backlog of savings with no outlet in the already overbuilt domestic economy.

In November 1944, Dean Acheson addressed the Congressional committee on Postwar Economic Policy and Planning. He stressed the consequences if the war were be followed by a slide back into depression: *"it seems clear that we are in for a very bad time, so far as the economic and social position of the country is concerned. We cannot go through another ten years like the ten years at the end of the twenties and the beginning of the thirties, without having the most far-reaching consequences upon our economic and social system."* The problem, he said, was markets, not production. *"You don't have a problem of production.... The important thing is markets. We have got to see that what the country produces is used and is sold under financial arrangements which make its production possible."* Short of the introduction of a command economy, with controls over income and distribution to ensure the domestic consumption of all that was produced, Acheson said, the only way to achieve full output and full employment was through access to foreign markets.[27]

A central facet of postwar economic policy, as reflected in the Bretton Woods agencies, was state intervention to guarantee markets for the full output of U.S. industry and profitable outlets for surplus capital. The World Bank was designed to subsidize the export of capital to the Third World, by financing the infrastructure without which Western-owned production facilities could not be established there. According to Gabriel Kolko's 1988 estimate, almost two thirds of the World Bank's loans since its inception had gone to transportation and power infrastructure.[28] A laudatory Treasury Department report referred to such infrastructure projects (comprising some 48% of lending in FY 1980) as "externalities" to business, and spoke glowingly of the benefits of such projects in promoting the expansion of business into large market areas and the consolidation and commercialization of agriculture.[29]

Besides the benefit of building *"an internal infrastructure which is a vital prerequisite for the development of resources and direct United States private investments,"* such banks (because they must be repaid in U.S. dollars) require the borrowing nations *"to export goods capable of earning them, which is to say, raw materials...."*[30]

The International Monetary Fund was created to facilitate the purchase of American goods abroad, by preventing temporary lapses in purchasing power as a result of foreign exchange shortages. It was *"a very large international currency exchange and credit-granting institution that could be drawn upon relatively easily by any country that was temporarily short of any given foreign currency due to trade imbalances."*[31]

The Bretton Woods system by itself, however, was not nearly sufficient to ensure the levels of output needed to keep production facilities running at full capacity, or to absorb excess investment funds. First the Marshall Plan, and then the permanent war economy of the Cold War, came to the rescue.

The Marshall Plan was devised in reaction to the impending economic slump predicted by the Council of Economic advisers in early 1947 and the failure of Western Europe *"to recover from the war and take its place in the American scheme of things."* Undersecretary of State for Economic Affairs Clayton declared that the central problem confronting the United States was the disposal of its *"great surplus."*[32] Dean Acheson defended the Marshall Plan in a May 1947 address:

> *The extreme need of foreign countries for American products is likely...to continue undiminished in 1948, while the capacity of foreign countries to pay in commodities will be only slightly increased.... What do these facts of international life mean for the United States and for United States foreign policy?...the United States is going to have to undertake further emergency financing of foreign purchases if foreign countries are to continue to buy in 1948 and 1949 the commodities which they need to sustain life and at the same time rebuild their economies....*[33]

One New Deal partisan implicitly compared foreign economic expansion to domestic state capitalism as analogous forms of surplus disposal: *"it is as if we were building a TVA every Tuesday."*[34]

The permanent war economy, however, had another advantage over projects like the TVA that produced use-value for the civilian population: since it did not produce consumer goods, it did not add to the undisposable surplus or compete with the output of private capital in consumer markets. In the apt words of Immanuel Goldstein: *"Even when weapons of war are not actually destroyed, their manufacture is still a convenient way of expending labor power without producing anything that can be consumed."* War is a way of *"shattering to pieces, or pouring into the stratosphere, or sinking in the depths of the sea,"* excess output and capital.[35]

Besides facilitating the export of goods and capital, the Bretton Woods agencies play a central role in the discipline of recalcitrant regimes. There is a considerable body of radical literature on the Left on the use of debt as a political weapon to impose pro-corporate policies (e.g., the infamous "structural adjustment program") on Third World governments, analogous to the historic function of debt in keeping miners and sharecroppers in their place.[36] Cheryl Payer compared

Third World debt to individual debt peonage, in that the aim of the latter was *"neither to collect the debt once and for all, nor to starve the employee to death, but rather to keep the labourer permanently indentured through his debt to his employer...."*[37] David Korten argued, likewise:

> The very process of the borrowing that created the indebtedness that gave the World Bank and the IMF the power to dictate the policies of borrowing countries represented an egregious assault on the principles of democratic accountability. Loan agreements, whether with the World Bank, the IMF, other official lending institutions, or commercial banks, are routinely negotiated in secret between banking officials and a handful of government officials—who in many instances are themselves unelected and unaccountable to the people on whose behalf they are obligating the national treasury to foreign lenders. Even in democracies, the borrowing procedures generally bypass the normal appropriation processes of democratically elected legislative bodies.
>
> Thus, government agencies are able to increase their own budgets without legislative approval, even though the legislative body will have to come up with the revenues to cover repayment. Foreign loans also enable governments to increase current expenditures without the need to raise current taxes—a feature that is especially popular with wealthy decision makers. The same officials who approve the loans often benefit directly through participation in contracts and "commissions" from grateful contractors. The system creates a powerful incentive to over-borrow.[38]

Another way the Bretton Woods agencies exercise political power over recalcitrant regimes is the punitive withholding of aid. This powerful political weapon has been used at times to undermine elective democracies whose policies fell afoul of corporate interests, and to reward compliant dictatorships. For example, the World Bank refused to lend to the Goulart government in Brazil; but following the installation of a military dictatorship by the 1964 coup, the Bank's lending averaged $73 million a year for the rest of the decade, and reached almost a half-billion by the mid-70s. Chile, before and after the Pinochet coup, followed a similar pattern.[39] Or as Ambassador Korry warned, in the latter-day equivalent of a papal interdict, *"Not a nut or bolt shall reach Chile under Allende. Once Allende comes to power we shall do all within our power to condemn Chile and all Chileans to utmost deprivation and poverty."*[40]

Cheryl Payer's *The Debt Trap* is an excellent historical survey of the use of debt crises to force countries into standby arrangements, precipitate coups, or provoke military crackdowns. In addition to their use against Goulart and Allende, as mentioned above, she provides case studies of the Suharto coup in Indonesia and Marcos' declaration of martial law in the Philippines. Walden Bello, in *Development Debacle*,[41] goes into much greater depth on the Philippines specifically, based on extensive documentation of World Bank collaboration with Marcos in support of the authoritarian crackdown preceding his austerity programs.

Among the many features of the so-called structural adjustment program, mentioned above, the policy of "privatization" (by selling state assets to "latter-day Reconstructionists," as Sean Corrigan says below) stands out. Joseph Stromberg described the process, as it has been used by the Iraq Provisional Authority, as "*funny auctions, that amounted to new expropriations by domestic and foreign investors....*" Such auctions of state properties will "*likely lead...to a massive alienation of resources into the hands of select foreign interests.*"[42]

The promotion of unaccountable, technocratic Third World governments, insulated from popular pressure and closely tied to international financial elites, has been a central goal of Bretton Woods agencies since World War II.

> *From the 1950s onwards, a primary focus of* [World] *Bank policy was "institution-building", most often taking the form of promoting the creation of autonomous agencies within governments that would be continual World Bank borrowers. Such agencies were intentionally established to be independent financially from their host governments, as well as minimally accountable politically—except, of course, to the Bank.*[43]

The World Bank created the Economic Development Institute in 1956 specifically to enculture Third World elites into the values of the Bretton Woods system. It offered a six-month course in "the theory and practice of development," whose 1300 alumni by 1971 included prime ministers, ministers of planning, and ministers of finance.[44]

> *The creation of such patronage networks has been one of the World Bank's most important strategies for inserting itself in the political economies of Third World countries. Operating according to their own charters and rules (frequently drafted in response to Bank suggestions), and staffed with rising technocrats sympathetic, even beholden, to the Bank, the agencies it has funded have served to create a steady, reliable source of what the Bank needs most—bankable loan proposals. They have also provided the Bank with critical power bases through which it has been able to transform national economies, indeed whole societies, without the bothersome procedures of democratic review and discussion of the alternatives.*[45]

Despite the vast body of scholarly literature on the issues discussed in this passage, perhaps the most apt description of it was a pithy comment by a free market libertarian, Sean Corrigan:

> *Does he* [Treasury Secretary O'Neill] *not know that the whole IMF-US Treasury carpet-bagging strategy of full-spectrum dominance is based on promoting unproductive government-led indebtedness abroad, at increasingly usurious rates of interest, and then—either before or, more often these days,*

after, the point of default—bailing out the Western banks who have been the agents provocateurs of this financial Operation Overlord, with newly-minted dollars, to the detriment of the citizenry at home?

Is he not aware that, subsequent to the collapse, these latter-day Reconstructionists must be allowed to swoop and to buy controlling ownership stakes in resources and productive capital made ludicrously cheap by devaluation, or outright monetary collapse?

Does he not understand that he must simultaneously coerce the target nation into sweating its people to churn out export goods in order to service the newly refinanced debt, in addition to piling up excess dollar reserves as a supposed bulwark against future speculative attacks (usually financed by the same Western banks' lending to their Special Forces colleagues at the macro hedge funds)—thus ensuring the reverse mercantilism of Rubinomics is maintained?[46]

The American economy could have had access to the resources it was willing to buy on mutually satisfactory terms, and marketed its own surplus to those countries willing to buy it, without the apparatus of transnational corporate mercantilism. Such a state of affairs would have been genuine free trade. What the American elite really wanted, however, has been ably stated by Thomas Friedman in one of his lapses into frankness:

For globalism to work, America can't be afraid to act like the almighty superpower it is…. The hidden hand of the market will never work without a hidden fist—McDonald's cannot flourish without McDonnell Douglas, the designer of the F-15. And the hidden fist that keeps the world safe for Silicon Valley's technologies is called the United States Army, Air Force, Navy and Marine Corps.[47]

It was not true that the American corporate economy was ever in any real danger of losing access to the raw materials it needed, in the absence of an activist foreign policy to secure access to those resources. As free market advocates often point out, countries with disproportionate mineral wealth—say, large oil reserves—are forced to center a large part of their economic activity on the extraction and sale of those resources. And once they sell them, the commodities enter a world market in which it is virtually impossible to control who eventually buys them. The real issue, according to Baran and Sweezy, is that the American corporate economy depended on access to Third World resources on favorable terms set by the United States, and those favorable terms depended on the survival of pliable regimes.

> *But this* [genuine free trade in resources with the Third World on mutually acceptable terms] *is not what really interests the giant multinational corporations which dominate American policy. What they want is <u>monopolistic control</u> over foreign sources of supply and foreign markets, enabling them to buy and sell on specially privileged terms, to shift orders from one subsidiary to another, to favor this country or that depending on which has the most advantageous tax, labor, and other policies—in a word, they want to do business on their own terms and wherever they choose. And for this what they need is not trading partners but "allies" and clients willing to adjust their laws and policies to the requirements of American Big Business.*[48]

The "system of world order" enforced by the U.S. since World War II, and lauded in Friedman's remarks about the "visible hand," is nearly the reverse of the classical liberal notion of free trade. This new version of "free trade" is aptly characterized in a passage by Christopher Layne and Benjamin Schwarz:

> *The view that economic interdependence compels American global strategic engagement puts an ironic twist on liberal internationalist arguments about the virtues of free trade, which held that removing the state from international transactions would be an antidote to war and imperialism....*
>
> *....Instead of subscribing to the classical liberal view that free trade leads to peace, the foreign policy community looks to American military power to impose harmony so that free trade can take place. Thus, U.S. security commitments are viewed as the indispensable precondition for economic interdependence.*[49]

Oliver MacDonagh pointed out that the modern neoliberal conception, far from agreeing with Cobden's idea of free trade, resembled the "Palmerstonian system" that the Cobdenites so despised. Cobden objected, among other things, to the "*dispatch of a fleet 'to protect British interests' in Portugal,*" to the "*loan-mongering and debt-collecting operations in which our Government engaged either as principal or agent,*" and generally, all "*intervention on behalf of British creditors overseas.*" Cobden favored the "natural" growth of free trade, as opposed to the forcible opening of markets. Genuine free traders opposed the confusion of "free trade" with "*mere increases of commerce or with the forcible 'opening up' of markets.*"[50]

I can't resist quoting Joseph Stromberg's only half tongue-in-cheek prescription "How to Have Free Trade":

> *For many in the US political and foreign policy Establishment, the formula for having free trade would go something like this: 1) Find yourself a global*

superpower; 2) have this superpower knock together the heads of all opponents and skeptics until everyone is playing by the same rules; 3) refer to this new imperial order as "free trade;" 4) talk quite a bit about "democracy." This is the end of the story except for such possible corollaries as 1) never allow rival claimants to arise which might aspire to co-manage the system of "free trade"; 2) the global superpower rightfully in charge of world order must also control the world monetary system....

The formula outlined above was decidedly not the 18th and 19th-century liberal view of free trade. Free traders like Richard Cobden, John Bright, Frederic Bastiat, and Condy Raguet believed that free trade is the absence of barriers to goods crossing borders, most particularly the absence of special taxes—tariffs—which made imported goods artificially dear, often for the benefit of special interests wrapped in the flag under slogans of economic nationalism....

Classical free traders never thought it necessary to draw up thousands of pages of detailed regulations to implement free trade. They saw no need to fine-tune a sort of Gleichschaltung (co-ordination) of different nations labor laws, environmental regulations, and the host of other such issues dealt with by NAFTA, GATT, and so on. Clearly, there is a difference between free trade, considered as the repeal, by treaty or even unilaterally, of existing barriers to trade, and modern "free trade" which seems to require truckloads of regulations pondered over by legions of bureaucrats.

This sea-change in the accepted meaning of free trade neatly parallels other characteristically 20th-century re-definitions of concepts like "war," "peace," "freedom," and "democracy," to name just a few. In the case of free trade I think we can deduce that when, from 1932 on, the Democratic Party—with its traditional rhetoric about free trade in the older sense—took over the Republicans project of neo-mercantilism and economic empire, it was natural for them to carry it forward under the "free trade" slogan. They were not wedded to tariffs, which, in their view, got in the way of implementing Open Door Empire. Like an 18th-century Spanish Bourbon government, they stood for freer trade within an existing or projected mercantilist system. They would have agreed, as well, with Lord Palmerston, who said in 1841, "It is the business of Government to open and secure the roads of the merchant."....

Here, John A. Hobson...was directly in the line of real free-trade thought. Hobson wrote that businessmen ought to take their own risks in investing overseas. They had no right to call on their home governments to "open and secure" their markets.[51]

And by the way, it's doubtful that superpower competition with the Soviets had much to do with the role of the U.S. in shaping the postwar "system of world order," or in acting as "hegemonic power" in maintaining that system of order. Layne and Schwarz cited NSC-68 to the effect that the policy of *"attempting to develop a healthy international community"* was *"a policy which we would probably pursue even if there were no Soviet threat."*

> *Underpinning U.S. world order strategy is the belief that America must maintain what is in essence a military protectorate in economically critical regions to ensure that America's vital trade and financial relations will not be disrupted by political upheaval. This kind of economically determined strategy articulated by the foreign policy elite ironically (perhaps unwittingly) embraces a quasi-Marxist or, more correctly, a Leninist interpretation of American foreign relations.*[52]

The policy planners who designed the Bretton Woods system and the rest of the postwar framework of world order, apparently, paid little or no mind to the issue of Soviet Russia's prospective role in the world. The record that appears, rather, in Shoup and Minter's heavily documented account, is full of references to the U.S. as a successor to Great Britain as guarantor of a global political and economic order, and to U.S. global hegemony as a war aim (even before the U.S. entered the war). As early as 1942, when Soviet Russia's continued existence was very much in doubt, U.S. policy makers were referring to "domination after the war," "Pax Americana," and "world control." To quote G. William Domhoff, "*the definition of the national interest that led to these interventions was conceived in the years 1940-42 by corporate planners in terms of what they saw as the needs of the American capitalist system, well before communism was their primary concern.*"[53]

Considering the continuity in the pattern of U.S. Third World intervention during the Cold War with its gunboat diplomacy of the 20s and 30s, or with its actions as the world's sole superpower since the fall of communism, should also be instructive. Indeed, since the collapse of the USSR, the U.S. has been frantically scrambling to find (or create) another enemy sufficient to justify continuing its role as world policeman.

Despite Chomsky's periodic rhetorical excesses, his characterization of the postwar era was essentially correct: "*Putting second-order complexities to the side, for the USSR the Cold War has been primarily a war against its satellites, and for the US a war against the Third World. For each, it has served to entrench a particular system of domestic privilege and coercion.*"[54]

If anything, the Cold War with the Soviet Union appears almost as an afterthought to American planning for a postwar order. Far from being the cause of the U.S. role as guarantor of a system of world order, the Soviet Empire acted as a spoiler to preexisting U.S. plans for acting as a sole global superpower. Historically, any rival power which has refused to be incorporated into the Grand Area, or which has encouraged other countries (by "defection from within") to withdraw from the Grand Area, has been viewed as an "aggressor." Quoting Domhoff once again,

....I believe that anticommunism became a key aspect of foreign policy only after the Soviet Union, China, and their Communist party allies became the challengers to the Grand Area conception of the national interest. In a certain sense..., they merely replaced the fascists of Germany and Japan as the enemies of the international economic and political system regarded as essential by American leaders.[55]

Likewise, as Domhoff's last sentence in the above quote suggests, any country which has interfered with U.S. attempts to integrate the markets and resources of any region of the world into its international economic order has been viewed as a "threat." The Economic and Financial Group of the CFR/State Department postwar planning project, produced, on July 24, 1941, a document (E-B34), warning of the need for the United States to *"defend the Grand Area,"* not only against external attack by Germany, but against *"defection from within,"* particularly against countries like Japan (which, along with the rest of east Asia, was regarded as part of the Grand Area) bent on *"destroying the area for its own political reasons."*[56] The centrality of this consideration is illustrated by the report of a 1955 study group of the Woodrow Wilson Center, which pointed to the threat of *"a serious reduction in the potential resource base and market opportunities of the West owing to the subtraction of the communist areas and their economic transformation in ways that reduce their willingness and ability to complement the industrial economies of the West."*[57]

One way of defending against "defection from within" is to ensure that Third World countries have the right kind of government. That can be done either by supporting authoritarian regimes, or what neoconservatives call "democracy." The key quality for Third World elites, in either case, is an orientation toward what Thomas Barnett calls "connectivity." The chief danger presented by "outlaw regimes," according to Barnett, lies in their being disconnected *"from the globalizing world, from its rule sets, its norms, and all the ties that bind countries together in mutually assured dependence."*[58]

The neoconservative version of democracy is more or less what Noam Chomsky means by "spectator democracy": a system in which the public engages in periodic legitimation rituals called "elections," choosing from a narrow range of candidates all representing the same elite. Having thus done its democratic duty, the public returns to bowling leagues and church socials, and other examples of "civil society," and leaves the mechanics of policy to its technocratic betters—who immediately proceed to take orders from the World Bank and IMF. This form of democracy is nearly synonymous with what neocons call "the rule of law," which entails a healthy dose of Weberian bureaucratic rationality. The stability and predictability associated with such "democracies" is, from the business standpoint, greatly preferable to the messiness of dictatorship or death squads.

American "pro-democratic" policy in the Third World, traditionally, has identified "democracy" with electoralism, and little else. In Central America, for example, a country is viewed as a "democracy" if its government *"came to power through free and fair elections."* But this policy ignores the vital dimension of popular participation, *"including the free expression of opinions, day-to-day interaction between the government and the citizenry, the mobilization of interest groups,"* etc. The "underlying objective" of pro-democracy policies is *"to maintain the basic order of what...are quite undemocratic societies."* Democracy is a means of *"relieving pressure for more radical change,"* but only through *"limited, top-down forms of democratic change that* [do] *not risk upsetting the traditional structures of power with which the United States has been allied."*[59] Democracy policy in El Salvador, more specifically, promoted a form of "democracy" through the Duarte regime that did not touch the power of the military or the landed elite.[60]

American elites prefer "democracy" whenever possible, but will resort to dictatorship in a pinch. The many, many cases in which the U.S. Assistance Program, the School of the Americas, the CIA, the World Bank and IMF, and others from the list of usual suspects have collaborated in just this expedient are recounted, in brutal detail, by William Blum in *Killing Hope.*[61]

Even an authoritarian communist regime is preferable, as an ultimate last resort, to a democracy that pursues a genuinely populist agenda, like the Arbenz regime in Guatemala. To prevent the latter development, the U.S. will risk a country falling to genuine Marxist-Leninists. It is obvious that the primary concern behind the typical Third World intervention was not the danger of an alliance between that country and Soviet strategic power. Had anti-communism been the U.S. government's main preoccupation, and not economic control, its policy would have been much different.

> *While there were many varieties of capitalism consistent with the anti-Communist politics the United States...sought to advance, what was axiomatic in the American credo was that the form of capitalism it advocated for the world was to be integrated in such a way that its businessmen played an essential part in it. Time and again it was ready to sacrifice the most effective way of opposing Communism in order to advance its own national interests. In this vital sense its world role was not simply one of resisting the left but primarily of imposing its own domination....*

> *....[I]t was its clash with nationalist elements, as diverse as they were, that revealed most about the U.S. global crusade, for had fear of Communism alone been the motivation of its behavior, the number of obstacles to its goals would have been immeasurably smaller.*[62]

An authoritarian communist regime, like the pigs on Animal Farm, can be quite reasonable in dealing with its neighboring farmers. The Chinese "workers' paradise," a favorite haven for foreign sweatshops, is a prime example.

The chief necessity, as we saw above, is that a Third World country's economic policy be made by a domestic elite that is safely insulated from real accountability to the native population, and at the same time amenable to the policy goals and values of transnational elites in such bodies as the World Bank and IMF. In the last couple of years we have seen this to be true of the new regime in Afghanistan, headed by a man noted for his history of collaboration with the latter agencies; of the Iraqi occupation government, or Iraq Provisional Authority, of which a high priority was the adoption of new laws to enforce international copyrights.

C. Export-Dependent Monopoly Capitalism (with Digression on Economy of Scale)

According to Stromberg and the Austrians, the chronic problem of surplus output was not a natural result of the free market, but rather of a cartelized economy. As we saw earlier, J.A. Hobson argued that "*over-saving*" was caused by "*rents, monopoly profits, and other unearned excessive profits*," and called, in proto-Keynesian fashion, for the state to step in and remedy the problem of "*mal-distribution of consuming power.*"[63] Those making such arguments are commonly dismissed, on the libertarian right, as ignorant of Say's Law.

But Say's Law applies only to a free market. As Stromberg points out, a genuine maldistribution of consuming power results from the state's intervention to transfer wealth from its real producers to a politically connected ruling class. And neo-Marxists' work on over-accumulation has shown us that the evils that Keynesianism was designed to remedy, in a state capitalist economy, are quite real. The State promotes the accumulation of capital on a scale beyond which its output can be absorbed (at its cartelized prices) by private demand; and therefore capital relies on the State to dispose of this surplus.

One of the earliest to describe the several aspects of the phenomenon was Hilferding, in *Finance Capital*:

> The curtailment of production means the cessation of all new capital investment, and the maintenance of high prices makes the effects of the crisis more severe for all those industries which are not cartelized, or not fully cartelized. Their profits will fall more sharply, or their losses will be greater, than is the case in the cartelized industries, and in consequence they will be

obliged to make greater cuts in production. As a result, disproportionality will increase, he sales of cartelized industry will suffer more, and it becomes evident that in spite of the severe curtailment of production, "overproduction" persists and has even increased. Any further limitation of production means that more capital will be idle, while overheads remain the same, so that the cost per unit will rise, thus reducing profits still more despite the maintenance of high prices.[64]

All the elements are here, in rough form: the expansion of production facilities to a scale beyond what the market will support; the need to restrict output to keep up prices, conflicting with the simultaneous need to keep output high enough to utilize full capacity and keep unit costs down; the inability of the economy to absorb the full output of cartelized industry at monopoly prices.

But as Hilferding pointed out in the same passage, the natural tendency in such a situation, in the absence of entry barriers, would be for competitors to enter the market and drive down the monopoly price: "*The high prices attract outsiders, who can count on low capital and labor costs, since all other prices have fallen; thus they establish a strong competitive position and begin to undersell the cartel.*"[65] This, Rothbard argued, is what normally happens when cartelizing ventures are not backed up by the state: they are broken either by internal defection or by new entrants. That is, in fact, what Gabriel Kolko described as actually happening to the trust movement at the turn of the century. Therefore, organized capital depends on the state to enforce an artificial monopoly on the domestic market.

By restricting production quotas for domestic consumption the cartel eliminates competition on the domestic market. The suppression of competition sustains the effect of a protective tariff in raising prices even at a stage when production has long since outstripped demand. Thus it becomes a prime interest of cartelized industry to make the protective tariff a permanent institution, which in the first place assures continued existence of the cartel, and second, enables the cartel to sell its product on the domestic market at an extra profit.[66]

And, Hilferding continued, cartelized industry is forced to dispose of the surplus product, which will not sell domestically at the monopoly price, by dumping it on foreign markets.

The increase in prices on the domestic market...tends to reduce the sales of cartelized products, and thus conflicts with the trend towards lowering costs by expanding the scale of production.... But if a cartel is already well established, it will try to compensate for the decline of the domestic market by increasing its exports, in order to continue production as before and if possible on an even larger scale. If the cartel is efficient and capable of exporting...its real price of production...will correspond with the world market price. But a cartel is also in a position to sell below its production price, because it has obtained an extra profit, determined by the level of the protective tariff, from its sales on the domestic market. It is therefore able to use a part of this extra profit to expand its sales abroad by underselling its competitors. If it is successful it can then increase its output, reduce its costs, and thereby, since domestic prices remain unchanged, gain further extra profit.[67]

Further, anticipating the various Marxist theories of imperialism, Hilferding argued that this imperative of disposing of surplus product abroad requires the activist state to seek foreign markets on favorable terms for domestic capital. One such state policy is the promotion or granting of loans abroad, either by direct state loans, or by banking policies that centralize the banking system and thus facilitate the accumulation of large sums of capital for foreign loans. Such loans could be used to increase a country's purchasing power and increase its imports; but more importantly, they could be used for building transportation and power infrastructure that Western capital requires for building production facilities in an underdeveloped country.[68] Of course, such direct foreign capital investment in a country, unlike mere trade, required more direct political influence over the country's internal affairs to protect the investments from expropriation and labor unrest.[69]

The state could also intervene to create a wage-labor force in backward countries by expropriating land, thus recreating the process of primitive accumulation in the West. In addition, heavy taxation could be used to force a peasantry into the money economy, by making them work (or work more) in the capitalist job market to raise tax-money. This was a common pattern, Hilferding wrote: in the Third World as in the West earlier, " *when capital's need for expansion meets obstacles that could only be overcome much too slowly and gradually by purely economic means, it has recourse to the power of the state and uses it for forcible expropriation in order to create the required free wage proletariat.*"[70]

Generally speaking, Third World countries provide numerous advantages for capital seeking a higher rate of return:

The state ensures that human labour in the colonies is available on terms which make possible extra profits.... The natural wealth of the colonies likewise becomes a source of extra profits by lowering the price of raw materials.... The expulsion or annihilation of the native population, or in the most favourable case their transformation from shepherds or hunters into indentured slaves, or their confinement to small, restricted areas as peasant farmers, creates at one stroke free land which has only a nominal price.[71]

In *Imperialism*, Bukharin returned repeatedly to the theme of government policy in promoting monopoly, thorough such devices as tariffs, state loans, etc. In a passage on the effects of foreign loans, Bukharin anticipated today's use of foreign aid and World Bank/IMF credit as coercive weapons on behalf of American corporations:

> *The transaction is usually accompanied by a number of stipulations, in the first place that which imposes upon the borrowing country the duty to place orders with the creditor country (purchase of arms, ammunition, dreadnaughts, railroad equipment, etc), and the duty to grant concessions for the construction of railways, tramways, telegraph and telephone lines, harbours, exploitation of mines, timberlands, etc.*[72]

As Kwame Nkrumah jibed, so-called "foreign aid" under neocolonialism would have been called foreign investment in the days of old-style colonialism.[73]

Schumpeter, the theorist upon whom Stromberg relies most heavily, described the system as *"export-dependent monopoly capitalism"*:

> *Union in a cartel or trust confers various benefits on the entrepreneur—a saving in costs, a stronger position as against the workers—but none of these compares with this one advantage: a monopolistic price policy, possible to any considerable degree <u>only</u> behind an adequate protective tariff. Now the price that bings the maximum monopoly profit is generally far above the price that would be fixed by fluctuating competitive costs, and the volume that can be marketed at that maximum price is generally far below the output that would be technically and economically feasible. Under free competition that output <u>would</u> be produced and offered, but a trust cannot offer it, for it could be sold only at a competitive price. Yet the trust <u>must</u> produce it—or approximately as much—otherwise the advantages of large-scale enterprise remain unexploited and unit costs are likely to be uneconomically high.... [The trust] extricates itself from this dilemma by producing the full output that is economically feasible, thus securing low costs, and offering in the protected domestic market only the quantity corresponding to the monopoly price—insofar as the tariff permits; while the rest is sold, or "dumped," abroad at a lower price....*[74]

This process of "dumping" illustrated "Carnegie's law of surplus": *"every manufacturer preferred to lose one dollar by running full and holding markets by selling at lower prices than to lose two dollars by running less than full or close down and run the risk of losing markets...."*[75]

In describing the advantages of colonies for monopoly capitalism, Schumpeter essentially refuted his own Comtean argument (discussed below in this article) for imperialism's "alien" status in relation to capitalism.

> *In such a struggle among "dumped" products and capitals, it is no longer a matter of indifference who builds a given railroad, who owns a mine or a colony. Now that the law of costs is no longer operative, it becomes necessary to fight over such properties with desperate effort and with every available means, including those that are not economic in character, such as diplomacy....*

> *....In this context, the conquest of colonies takes on an altogether different significance. Non-monopolist countries, especially those adhering to free trade, reap little profit from such a policy. But it is a different matter with countries that function in a monopolistic role vis-a-vis their colonies. There being no competition, they can use cheap native labor without its ceasing to be cheap; they can market their products, even in the colonies, at monopoly prices; they can, finally, invest capital that would only depress the profit rate at home....*[76]

Stromberg explained: "*For American manufacturers to achieve available economies of scale, they had to produce far more of their products than could be sold in the U.S.*"[77]

One point Stromberg does not adequately address here is that economy of scale, at least in terms of internal production costs, requires only thorough utilization of existing facilities. But the size of the facilities was in itself the result of state capitalist policies. The fact that domestic demand was not enough to support the output needed to reach such economies of scale reflects the fact that *the scale of production was too large*. And this, in turn, was the result of state policies that encouraged gigantism and over-investment.

Productive economy of scale is "unlimited" only when the state absorbs the diseconomies of large scale production. Overall economies of scale reflect a package of costs. And those costs are themselves influenced by direct and indirect subsidies that distort price as an accurate signal of the actual cost of providing a service. If the state had not allowed big business to externalize many of its operating costs (especially long-distance shipping) on the public through subsidies (especially subsidized transportation), economy of scale would have been reached at a much lower level of production. The state's subsidies have the effect of artificially shifting the economy of scale upward to higher levels of output than a free market can support. State capitalism enables corporate interests to control elements of the total cost package through political means; but the result is new imbalances, which in turn require further state intervention.

In fairness, Schumpeter touched on this issue in passing, as did Stromberg in quoting him: "*a firm which could not survive in the absence of empire was 'expanded beyond economically justifiable limits'.*"[78] As this quote indicates, Schumpeter dealt, though inadequately, with the extent to which corporate size was the effect of state intervention. He agreed with Rothbard that cartelization or monopoly, as such, could not exist without the state.

> Export monopolism does <u>not</u> grow from the inherent laws of capitalist development. The character of capitalism leads to large-scale production, but with few exceptions large-scale production does <u>not</u> lead to the kind of unlimited concentration that would leave but one or only a few firms in each industry. On the contrary, any plant runs up against limits to its growth in a given location; and the growth of combinations which would make sense under a system of free trade encounters limits of organizational efficiency. Beyond these limits there is no tendency toward combination in the competitive system.[79]

Still, Stromberg greatly overestimates the advantages of large-scale production in a free market. In all but a few forms of production, peak economy of scale is reached at relatively low levels of output. In agriculture, for instance, a USDA study found in 1973 that economy of scale was maximized on a fully-mechanized one-man farm.[80]

Walter Adams and James Brock, two specialists in economy of scale, cited a number of studies showing that "*optimum plant sizes tend to be quite small relative to the national market.*" According to one study, even taking into account the efficiencies of firm size, market shares of the top three firms in nine of twelve industries exceeded maximum efficiency by a factor of anywhere from two to ten. But productive economy of scale was a function primarily of plant size, not the size of multi-plant firms. Any efficiencies of bargaining power provided by large firm size were offset by increased administrative and control costs, and other diseconomies.[81] In fact, Seymour Melman argued that the increased administrative costs of multi-unit and multi-product firms are astronomical. They are prone to many of the same inefficiencies—falsified data from below, and "elaborate, formal systems of control, with accompanying police systems—as state-run industry in the communist countries.[82]

Describing the inefficiencies of large firms, Kenneth Boulding echoed Melman, but in more colorful language:

> There is a great deal of evidence that almost all organizational structures tend to produce false images in the decision-maker, and that the larger and more authoritarian the organization, the better the chance that its top decision-makers will be operating in purely imaginary worlds.[83]

In the most capital-intensive industry, automobiles, peak economy of scale was achieved at a level of production equivalent to 3-6% of market share.[84] And even this level of output is required only because annual model changes (which arguably wouldn't pay for themselves without state capitalist subsidies) require an auto plant to wear out the dies for a run of production in a single year. Otherwise, peak economy of scale would be reached in a plant with an output of only 60,000 per year.[85]

In any case, these figures relate only to productive economy of scale. Increased distribution costs begin to offset increased economies of production, according to Borsodi's law, long before peak productive economy of scale is reached. According to an F.M. Scherer study cited by Adams and Brock, a plant producing at one-third the maximum efficiency level of output would experience only a 5% increase in unit costs.[86] This is more than offset by reduced shipping costs for a smaller market.

The point of this digression is that the size of existing firms reflects the role of the state in subsidizing increased size by underwriting the inefficiencies of corporate gigantism—as Rothbard pointed out, the ways *"our corporate state uses the coercive taxing power either to accumulate corporate capital or to lower corporate costs."*[87] A genuine free market economy would be vastly less centralized, with production primarily for local markets.

Besides the problem of surplus output, the state capitalist economy produces a second problem: that of surplus capital. Not only does monopoly pricing limit domestic demand, and thus restrain the opportunities for expansion at home; but non-cartelized industry is seriously disadvantaged as a source of returns on capital, and therefore opportunities for profitable investment are limited outside the cartelized sectors.

According to Hilferding, *"while the drive to increase production is very strong in the cartelized industries, high cartel prices preclude any growth of the domestic market, so that expansion abroad offers the best chance of meeting the need to increase output."*[88] Bukharin later described the capital surplus as a direct result of cartelization, in quite similar language. In Chapter VII of *Imperialism and World Economy*, he wrote:

> The volumes of capital that seek employment have reached unheard of dimensions. On the other hand, the cartels and trusts, as the modern organisation of capital, tend to put certain limits to the employment of capital by fixing the volume of production. As to the non-trustified sections of industry, it becomes ever more unprofitable to invest capital in them. For

> *monopoly organisations can overcome the tendency towards lowering the rate of profit by receiving monopoly superprofits at the expense of the non-trustified industries. Out of the surplus value created every year, one portion, that which has been created in the nontrustified branches of industry, is being transferred to the co-owners of capitalist monopolies, whereas the share of the outsiders continually decreases. Thus the entire process drives capital beyond the frontiers of the country.*[89]

Monopoly capital theorists have made worthwhile contributions to the issue of capital and output surpluses. For example, the surplus product of cartelized industry drastically increases the importance of the "sales effort"—what Galbraith called "specific demand management" to dispose of the product.[90] This underscores the importance of the state in the problem of surplus disposal: without state intervention to create the national infrastructure of mass media and its attendant mass advertising markets, specific demand management would have been impossible.

One issue Stromberg neglects is the internal role of the state in directly disposing of the surplus. The role of the State's purchases in absorbing surplus output, through both military and domestic spending, was a key part of Baran and Sweezy's "monopoly capitalism" model. Its large "defense" and other expenditures provide a guaranteed internal market for surplus output analogous to that provided by state-guaranteed foreign markets. By providing such an internal market, the state increases the percentage of production capacity that can be used on a consistent basis.[91]

Paul Mattick elaborated on this theme in a 1956 article. The overbuilt corporate economy, he wrote, ran up against the problem that "[p]*rivate capital formation...finds its limitation in diminishing market-demand.*" The State had to absorb part of the surplus output; but it had to do so without competing with corporations in the private market. Instead, "[g]*overnment-induced production is channeled into non-market fields—the production of non-competitive public-works, armaments, superfluities and waste.*[92] As a necessary result of this state of affairs,

> *so long as the principle of competitive capital production prevails, steadily growing production will in increasing measure be a "production for the sake of production," benefiting neither private capital nor the population at large.*

> *This process is somewhat obscured, it is true, by the apparent profitability of capital and the lack of large-scale unemployment. Like the state of prosperity, profitability, too, is now largely government manipulated. Government*

spending and taxation are managed so as to strengthen big business at the expense of the economy as a whole....
In order to increase the scale of production and to accummulate [sic] capital, government creates "demand" by ordering the production of non-marketable goods, financed by government borrowings. This means that the government avails itself of productive resources belonging to private capital which would otherwise be idle.[93]

Such consumption of output, while not always directly profitable to private industry, serves a function analogous to foreign "dumping" below cost, in enabling the corporate economy to achieve economies of large-scale production at levels of output beyond the ability of private consumers to absorb.

It's interesting to consider how many segments of the economy have a guaranteed market for their output, or a "conscript clientele" in place of willing consumers. The "military-industrial complex" is well known. But how about the state's education and penal systems? How about the automobile-trucking-highway complex, or the civil aviation complex? Foreign surplus disposal ("export dependant monopoly capitalism") and domestic surplus disposal (government purchases) are different forms of the same phenomenon.

Marx described major new forms of industry as countervailing influences against the falling rate of profit. Baran and Sweezy, likewise, considered "epoch-making inventions" as partial counterbalances to the ever-increasing surplus. Their chief example of such a phenomenon was the rise of the automobile industry in the 1920s, which (along with the highway program) was to define the American economy for most of the mid-20th century.[94] The high tech boom of the 1990s was a similarly revolutionary event. It is revealing to consider the extent to which both the automobile and computer industries, far more than most industries, were direct products of state capitalism. More recently, in the Bush administration, to consider only one industry (pharmaceuticals), two major policy initiatives benefit it by providing state-funded outlets for its production: the so-called "prescription drug benefit," and the provision of AIDS drugs to destitute African countries. In another industry, Bush's R&D funding for hydrogen fuel engines is enabling the automobile companies to develop the successor technology to the gasoline engine (with patents included) at public expense; this not only subsidizes their transition to viability in a post-fossil fuel world, but gives them monopoly control over the successor technology. "Creative destruction" is our middle name.

NOTES

1. William Appleman Williams, *The Tragedy of American Diplomacy* (New York: Dell Publishing Company, 1959, 1962) 21-2.

2. Ibid. 26.

3. J. A. Hobson, *Imperialism: A Study* (London: Archibald Constable & Co., Ltd, 1905) 66.

4. Ibid. 73.

5. Ibid. 74-5.

6. Ibid. 75-6.

7. Ibid. 76-7.

8. Thomas Hodgskin, *The Natural and Artificial Right of Property Contrasted* (London: B. Steil, 1832) 155-6.

9. Williams, *Tragedy of American Diplomacy* 27.

10. Ibid. 17.

11. Ibid. 17.

12. William Appleman Williams, *The Contours of American History* (Cleveland and New York: The World Publishing Company, 1961) 368.

13. Joseph R. Stromberg, "The Role of State Monopoly Capitalism in the American Empire" *Journal of Libertarian Studies* Volume 15, no. 3 (Summer 2001) 61-3 http://www.mises.org/journals/jls/15_3/15_3_3.pdf Captured October 28, 2003).

14. Williams, *Contours of American History* 363-4.

15. Martin Sklar, *The Corporate Reconstruction of American Capitalism, 1890-1916: The Market, the Law, and Politics* (Cambridge, New York and Melbourne: Cambridge University Press, 1988) 82; Karl Kautsky, "Imperialism and the War," *International Socialist Review* (November 1914), trans. by William E. Bohn http://www.marxists.org/archive/kautsky/works/1910s/war.html Captured September 23, 2002.

16. Williams, *Tragedy of American Diplomacy* 66.

17. Martin J. Sklar, "Woodrow Wilson and the Political Economy of Modern United States Liberalism," in Murray Rothbard and Ronald Radosh, eds., *A New History of Leviathan: Essays on the Rise of the American Corporate State* (New York: E. P. Dutton & Co., Inc., 1972) 27.

18. Ibid. 40.

19. Ibid. 62n.

20. Williams, *Tragedy of American Diplomacy* 179.

21. Ibid. 123.

22. Ibid. 170.

23. Robert Freeman Smith, "American Foreign Relations, 1920-1942," in Barton J. Bledstein, ed., *Towards a New Past: Dissenting Essays in American History* (New York: Vintage Books, 1967, 1968) 247.

24. Ibid. 247.

25. The rest of this paragraph, unless otherwise noted, is based on Laurence H. Shoup and William Minter, "Shaping a New World Order: The Council on Foreign Relations' Blueprint for World Hegemony, 1939-1945," in Holly Sklar, ed., *Trilateralism: The Trilateral Commission and Elite Planning for World Management* (Boston: South End Press, 1980) 135-56.

26. Robert Stinnett, *Day of Deceit: The Truth About FDR and Pearl Harbor* (New York: Free Press, 1999).

27. Williams, *Tragedy of American Diplomacy* 235-6.

28. Gabriel Kolko, *Confronting the Third World: United States Foreign Policy 1945-1980* (New York: Pantheon Books, 1988) 120.

29. *United States Participation in the Multilateral Development Banks in the 1980s.* Department of the Treasury (Washington, DC: 1982) 9.

30. Gabriel Kolko, *The Roots of American Foreign Policy: An Analysis of Power and Purpose* (Boston: Beacon Press, 1969) 72.

31. G. William Domhoff, *The Power Elite and the State: How Policy is Made in America* (New York: Aldine de Gruyter, 1990) 166.

32. Ibid. 271.

33. Leonard P. Liggio, "American Foreign Policy and National Security Management," in Rothbard and Radosh, eds., *New History of Leviathan* 249.

34. Williams, *Tragedy of American Diplomacy* 272.

35. George Orwell, *1984.* Signet Classics reprint (New York: Harcourt Brace Jovanovich, 1949, 1981) 157.

36. Cheryl Payer, *The Debt Trap: The International Monetary Fund and the Third World* (New York: Monthly Review Press, 1974); Walden Bello, "Structural Adjustment Programs: 'Success' for Whom?" in Jerry Mander and Edward Goldsmith, eds., *The Case Against the Global Economy* (San Francisco: Sierra Club Books, 1996); Bruce Franklin. "Debt Peonage: The Highest Form of Imperialism?" *Monthly Review* 33:10 (March 1982) 15-31.

37. Payer, *Debt Trap* 48-9.

38. David Korten, *When Corporations Rule the World* (West Hartford, Conn.: Kumarian Press, 1995; San Francisco, Calif.: Berrett-Koehler, Publishers, Inc., 1995) 166.

39. Bruce Rich, "The Cuckoo in the Nest: Fifty Years of Political Meddling by the World Bank," *The Ecologist* (January/February 1994) 10.

40. Holly Sklar, "Overview," in Holly Sklar, ed., *Trilateralism: The Trilateral Commission and Elite Planning for World Management* (Boston: South End Press, 1980) 28-9.

41. Walden Bello, *Development Debacle: The World Bank in the Philippines* (San Francisco: Institute for Food & Development Policy, 1982).

42. Joseph R. Stromberg, "Experimental Economics, Indeed" Ludwig von Mises Institute, January 6, 2004 http://www.mises.org/fullstory.asp?control=1409 Captured July 25, 2004.

43. Rich, "Cuckoo in the Nest" 9.

44. Ibid. 9-10.

45. Ibid. 10.

46. Sean Corrigan, "You Can't Say That!" August 6, 2002 http://www.lewrockwell.com/corrigan/corrigan13.html Captured August 6, 2002.

47. Thomas Friedman, "What the World Needs Now," *New York Times*, March 28, 1999.

48. Paul Baran and Paul Sweezy, *Monopoly Capitalism: An Essay in the American Economic and Social Order* (New York: Monthly Review Press, 1966) 201.

49. Christopher Layne and Benjamin Shwartz, "American Hegemony Without an Enemy," *Foreign Policy* (Fall 1993) 12-3.

50. Oliver MacDonough, "The Anti-Imperialism of Free Trade," *The Economic History Review* (Second Series) 14:3 (1962) .

51. Joseph R. Stromberg, "Free Trade, Mercantilism and Empire," February 28, 2000 http://www.antiwar.com/stromberg/s022800.html Captured May 1, 2002.

52. Layne and Shwartz, "American Hegemony Without an Enemy" 5, 12.

53. Domhoff, *Power Elite and the State* 113.

54. Noam Chomsky, *Deterring Democracy* (New York: Hill and Wang, 1991, 1992) 28.

55. Domhoff, *Power Elite and the State* 145.

56. Ibid. 160-1.

57. William Yandell Elliot, ed., *The Political Economy of American Foreign Policy* (Holt, Rinehart & Winston, 1955) 42.

58. Thomas Barnett, "The Pentagon's New Map," *Esquire* March 2003 http://www.thomaspmbarnett.com/published/pentagonsnewmap.htm Captured July 26, 2004.

59. Thomas Carothers, "The Reagan Years: The 1980s," in Abraham F. Lowenthal, ed., *Exporting Democracy* (Baltimore: Johns Hopkins, 1991) 117-8.

60. Ibid. 96-7.

61. William Blum. *Killing Hope: U.S. Military and CIA Interventions Since World War II* (Monroe, Maine: Common Courage Press, 1995).

62. Kolko, *Confronting the Third World* 117, 123.

63. Hobson, *Imperialism* 75-6.

64. Rudolf Hilferding, *Finance Capital*, ed. and trans. By Tom Bottomore (London and Boston: Routledge & Kegan Paul, 1910, 1981) 297.

65. Ibid. 297.

66. Ibid. 308.

67. Ibid. 309.

68. Ibid. 317-8.

69. Ibid. 321.

70. Ibid. 319-20.

71. Ibid. 328.

72. Nikolai Bukharin, *Imperialism and World Economy* (International Publishers, 1929 (written 1915-1917) http://www.marxists.org/archive/bukharin/works/1917/imperial/ Captured October 28, 2003 Chapter VII.

73. Kwame Nkrumah, *Neo-Colonialism: The Last Stage of Imperialism* (New York: International Publishers, 1965) 51.

74. Joseph Schumpeter, "Imperialism," in *Imperialism, Social Classes: Two Essays by Joseph Schumpeter.* Translated by Heinz Norden. Introduction by Hert Hoselitz (New York: Meridian Books, 1955) 79-80.

75. Sklar, *Corporate Reconstruction of American Capitalism* 58.

76. Schumpeter, "Imperialism" 82-3.

77. Stromberg, "Role of State Monopoly Capitalism" 65.

78. Ibid. 71.

79. Schumpeter, "Imperialism" 88.

80. W. R. Bailey, *The One-Man Farm*, qt. in L. S. Stavrianos, *The Promise of the Coming Dark Age* (San Francisco: W. H. Freeman and Co., 1976) 38.

81. Walter Adams and James Brock, *The Bigness Complex* (New York: Pantheon Books, 1986) 33-4, 45-6.

82. Seymour Melman, *Profits Without Production* (New York: Alfred A. Knopf, 1983) 80.

83. Qt. in Barry Stein, *Size, Efficiency, and Community Enterprise* (Cambridge, Mass.: Center for Community Economic Development, 1974) 5.

84. Adams and Brock, *Bigness Complex* 38-9.

85. Mark J. Green, et al., eds., *The Closed Enterprise System.* Ralph Nader's Study Group Report on Antitrust Enforcement (New York: Grossman Publishers, 1972) 243-4.

86. Adams and Brock, *The Bigness Complex* 45-6.

87. Murray Rothbard, "Confessions of a Right-Wing Liberal," in Henry J. Silverman, ed., *American Radical Thought: The Libertarian Tradition* (Lexington, Mass.: D.C. Heath and Co., 1970) p. 305.

88. Hilferding, *Finance Capital* 325.

89. Bukharin, *Imperialism and World Economy* Chapter VII.

90. Baran and Sweezy, *Monopoly Capitalism* 112-41.

91. Ibid. 112, 142-77, 207-17.

92. Paul Mattick, "The Economics of War and Peace," *Dissent* (Fall 1956) 377.

93. Ibid. 378-9.

94. Baran and Sweezy, *Monopoly Capitalism* 220.

Chapter Eight
Crisis Tendencies

Introduction.

The underlying crisis tendency of monopoly capitalism, as we saw in Chapters Six and Seven, is over-accumulation. In those chapters, we examined the rise of corporate liberalism as a response to the twin crises of over-accumulation and under-consumption. The inability to dispose of the full product of overbuilt industry, at market prices, is inherent in the system. The primary function of the state, under monopoly capitalism, is to dispose of this surplus product and enable industry to operate at full capacity.

There are, however, secondary crisis tendencies resulting from the state's attempted solutions to the primary crisis tendency of over-accumulation. The state's policies of underwriting the operating costs of the corporate economy and pacifying the underclass lead to increasing expenditures, revenue shortfalls, and a chronic fiscal crisis. But even more fundamental than this fiscal crisis is the accumulation crisis resulting from corporate liberal policies. Keynesian and welfare-state policies, and the social contract with business unions, increase the level of consumption at the expense of accumulation; thus, paradoxically, the state's response to over-accumulation leads directly to a crisis of under-accumulation.

A. Accumulation Crisis

The corporate liberal policies adopted to deal with under-consumption contain the seeds of an opposing crisis tendency: under-accumulation. Labor unionism, Keynesianism, and other means of increasing aggregate demand also reduce the funds available for investment.

Taxation to support the welfare state and other forms of what James O'Connor called "public consumption" reduces the pool of funds available for private investment. At the same time, the increased bargaining power of labor resulting from the corporate liberal social compact increases the portion of the product consumed by workers.

> Worker resistance to wage cuts during crises, labor union implementation of supplemental unemployment benefits which expanded demand, "job creating benefits" which shortened hours of work, expansion of consumer credit, earlier retirement and increased pensions, and rank-and-file resistance to rationalization of production, among other factors, increased employment and working-class demand for wage goods....[1]

To the extent that the value of labor-power is socially determined, the increased bargaining power of labor and the revolution of rising expectations increases the cost of variable capital and reduces the mass of surplus value available for reinvestment. Under the corporate liberal social compact, according to O'Connor,

> the average consumption basket became too big, and its value content too high; the social consumption basket became too great, and its "value content" likewise; class struggles in the individual form within and against the law of value interfered with capitalist processes whereby labor-power was produced and reproduced as variable capital.[2]

The effect of both trends is to increase the overall level of consumption and create a shortfall in new investment.

This is potentially catastrophic for the survival of capitalism. Capitalism, paradoxically, requires constant new accumulation, even when it suffers the consequences of past over-accumulation. One temporary solution to over-accumulation is new investment; the latter is essential to keep previously accumulated capital profitable. As Marx pointed out in Volume Three of *Capital*, the falling rate of profit due to over-accumulation can be offset by increasing the productivity of labor (i.e., the rate of "relative surplus value"). This is accomplished by new investment in improved processes. To paraphrase Al Smith, the solution to the crisis of over-accumulation is more accumulation. The economy is balanced on pinpoint, as in a Ponzi scheme, with further subsidized accumulation necessary to render existing over-accumulated capital profitable. And each such new wave of accumulation, to be profitable, will itself require still further accumulation. So statist solutions to over-accumulation directly impede the further accumulation necessary to keep old investments profitable.

The state may also respond by eating up surplus capital with unproductive outlets like military spending; but this, too, reduces the rate of accumulation which, paradoxically, is necessary to solve the problems of previous over-accumulation.

B. Fiscal and Input Crises

The levels of state expenditure necessary to underwrite the operating costs of capital and render investment productive create a fiscal crisis, parallel to the crisis of accumulation.

Large-scale state capitalist intervention, generally identified with Whigs and Republicans in the mid-nineteenth century, led to a centralization of the economy in the hands of large producers. This system was inherently unstable, and required still further state intervention to solve its contradictions. The result was the full-blown state capitalism of the twentieth century, in which the state played a direct role in subsidizing and cartelizing the corporate economy. Despite such intervention, though, state capitalism was still unstable. As regulatory cartelization advanced from the "Progressive" era on, the problems of overproduction and surplus capital were further intensified by the forces described by Stromberg in the previous two chapters, with the state resorting to ever greater, snowballing foreign expansionism and domestic corporatism to solve them. They eventually led to the New Deal corporate state, to a world war in which the U.S. was established (in Samuel Huntington's words) as "hegemonic power in a system of world order," and an almost totally militarized high tech economy.

A positive rate of profit, under twentieth century state capitalism, was possible only because the state underwrote so much of the cost of reproduction of constant and variable capital, and undertook "social investment" which increased the efficiency of labor and capital and consequently the rate of profit on capital.[3] And monopoly capital's demands on the state are not stable over time, but steadily increase:

> ...the socialization of the costs of social investment and social consumption capital increases over time and increasingly is needed for profitable accumulation by monopoly capital. The general reason is that the increase in the social character of production (specialization, division of labor, interdependency, the growth of new social forms of capital such as education, etc.) either prohibits or renders unprofitable the private accumulation of constant and variable capital.[4]

O'Connor did not adequately deal with a primary reason for the fiscal crisis: the increasing role of the state in performing functions of capital reproduction removes an ever-growing segment of the economy from the market price system. The removal of the price feedback system, which in a free market ties quantity demanded to quantity supplied, leads to ever-increasing demands on state services. When the consumption of some factor is subsidized by the state, the consumer is protected from the real cost of providing it, and unable to make a rational decision about how much to use. So the state capitalist sector tends to add factor inputs extensively, rather than intensively; that is, it uses the factors in larger amounts, rather than using existing amounts more efficiently. The state capitalist system generates demands for new inputs from the state geometrically, while the state's ability to provide new inputs increases only arithmetically. The result is a process of snowballing irrationality, in which the state's interventions further destabilize the system, requiring yet further state intervention, until the system's requirements for stabilizing inputs exceed the state's resources. At that point, the state capitalist system reaches a breaking point.

Probably the best example of this phenomenon is the transportation system. State subsidies to highways, airports, and railroads, by distorting the cost feedback to users, destroy the link between the amount provided and the amount demanded. The result, among other things, is an interstate highway system that generates congestion faster than it can build or expand the system to accommodate congestion. The cost of repairing the most urgent deteriorating roadbeds and bridges is several times greater than the amount appropriated for that purpose. In civil aviation, at least before the September 11 attacks, the result was planes stacked up six high over O'Hare airport. There is simply no way to solve these crises by building more highways or airports. The only solution is to fund transportation with cost-based user fees, so that the user perceives the true cost of providing the services he consumes. But this solution would entail the destruction of the existing centralized corporate economy. For example, when the UK experimented with toll-roads as a method of funding, the attempt to make users pay the full cost of the transportation services they consumed only resulted in truckers being driven onto secondary roads.

> *Truckers [who must pay £10] are not particularly happy with the way they're being charged off the road, and that will come back on the taxpayer because trucks cause massive maintenance problems for the road network.*

> *If the private company running the road—Midland Expressway Ltd—prices those trucks onto our public road network we'll be picking up the bill for that maintenance.*[5]

The same law of excess consumption and shortages manifests itself in the case of energy. When the state subsidizes the consumption of resources like fossil fuels, business tends to add inputs extensively, instead of using existing inputs more intensively. Since the incentives for conservation and economy are artificially distorted, demand outstrips supply. But the energy problem is further complicated by finite reserves of fossil fuels. According to an article in the *Oil and Gas Journal* last year,

> ....*The world is drawing down its oil reserves at an unprecedented rate, with supplies likely to be constrained by global production capacity by 2010, "even assuming no growth in demand," said analysts at Douglas-Westwood Ltd., an energy industry consulting firm based in Canterbury, England.*

> *"Oil will permanently cease to be abundant," said Douglas-Westwood analysts in the World Oil Supply Report issued earlier this month. "Supply and demand will be forced to balance-but at a price."*

> *The resulting economic shocks will rival those of the 1970s, as oil prices "could double and treble within 2 or 3 years as the world changes from oil abundance to oil scarcity. The world is facing a future of major oil price increases, which will occur sooner than many people believe," that report concluded.*

> *"The world's known and estimated 'yet to find' reserves cannot satisfy even the present level of production of some 74 million b/d beyond 2022. Any growth in global economic activity only serves to increase demand and bring forward the peak year," the report said.*

> *A 1% annual growth in world demand for oil could cause global crude production to peak at 83 million b/d in 2016, said Douglas-Westwood analysts. A 2% growth in demand could trigger a production peak of 87 million b/d by 2011, while 3% growth would move that production peak to as early as 2006, they said.*

> *Zero demand growth would delay the world's oil production peak only until 2022, said the Douglas-Westwood report.*

> *However, the International Energy Agency recently forecast that world oil demand would reach 119 million b/d by 2020.*[6]

During the shortages of the late '70s, Warren Johnson predicted that a prolonged energy crisis would lead, through market forces, to a radical decentralization of the economy and a return to localism.[7] Like every other kind of state intervention, subsidies to transportation and energy lead to ever greater irrationality, culminating in collapse.

Other centralized offshoots of the state capitalist system produce similar results. Corporate agribusiness, for example, requires several times as much synthetic pesticide application per acre to produce the same results as in 1950—partly because of insect resistance, and partly because pesticides kill not only insect pests but their natural enemies up the food chain. At the same time, giant monoculture plantations typical of the agribusiness system are especially prone to insects and blights which specialize in particular crops. The use of chemical fertilizers, at least the most common simple N-P-K varieties, strips the soil of trace elements—a phenomenon noted long ago by Max Gerson. The chemical fillers in these fertilizers, as they accumulate, alter the osmotic quality of the soil—or even render it toxic. Reliance on such fertilizers instead of traditional green manures and composts severely degrades the quality of the soil as a living biological system: for example, the depletion of mycorrhizae which function symbiotically with root systems to aid absorption of nutrients. The cumulative effect of all these practices is to push soil to the point of biological collapse. The hardpan clay on many agribusiness plantations is virtually sterile biologically, often with less than a single earthworm per cubic yard of soil. The result, as with chemical pesticides, is ever increasing inputs of fertilizer to produce diminishing results.

In every case, the basic rule is that, whenever the economy deviates from market price as an allocating principle, it deviates to that extent from rationality. In a long series of indices, the state capitalist economy uses resources or factors much more intensively than would be possible if large corporations were paying the cost themselves. The economy is much more transportation-intensive than a free market could support, as we have seen. It is likewise more capital-intensive, and more intensively dependent on scientific-technical labor, than would be economical if all costs were borne by the beneficiaries. The economy is far more centralized, capital intensive, and high-tech than it would otherwise be. Had large corporate firms paid for these inputs themselves, they would have reached the point of zero marginal utility from additional inputs much earlier.

At the same time as the demand for state economic inputs increases, state capitalism also produces all kinds of social pathologies that require "social expenditures" to contain or correct. By subsidizing the most capital-intensive forms of production, it promotes unemployment and the growth of an underclass. But just as important, it undermines the very social structures—family, church, neighborhood, etc.—on which it depends for the reproduction of a healthy social order.

Those who believe the market and commodity production as such inevitably suck all social relations into the "cash nexus," and undermine the stability of autonomous social institutions, are wrong. But this critique, while not valid for the market as such, is valid for state capitalism, where the state is driven into ever new realms in order to stabilize the corporate system. State intervention in the process of reproducing human capital (i.e., public education and tax-supported vocational-technical education), and state aid to forms of economic centralization that atomize society, result in the destruction of civil society and the replacement by direct state intervention of activities previously carried out by autonomous institutions. The destruction of civil society, in turn, leads to still further state intervention to deal with the resulting social pathologies.

The free market criticism of these phenomena closely parallels that of Ivan Illich in *Tools For Conviviality*.[8] Illich argued that the adoption of technologies followed a pattern characterized by two thresholds (or "watersheds"). The first threshold was one of high marginal utility for added increments of the new technology, with large increases in overall quality of life as it was introduced. But eventually a second threshold was reached, at which further increments produced disutilities. Technologies continued to be adopted beyond the level at which they positively harmed society; entire areas of life were subject to increased specialization, professionalization, and bureaucratic control; and older forms of technology that permitted more autonomous, local and individual control, were actively stamped out. In all these areas of life, the effect was to destroy human-scale institutions and ways of doing things, amenable to control by the average person.

In medicine, the first threshold was identified with the introduction of aseptic techniques, antibiotics, and other elementary technologies that drastically reduced the death rates. The second was identified with intensive reliance on extremely expensive medications and procedures with only marginally beneficial results (not to mention iatrogenic diseases), the transformation of medicine into a priesthood governed by "professional" bureaucracies, and the loss by ordinary people of control over their own health. The automobile reached the second threshold when it became impossible for most people to work or shop within walking or bicycle distance of where they lived. The car ceased to be a luxury, and became a necessity for most people; a lifestyle independent of it was no longer an option.

Those who criticize such aspects of our society, or express sympathies for the older, smaller-scale ways of life, are commonly dismissed as nostalgic, romantic—even Luddites. And such critiques are indeed, more often than not, coupled with calls for government regulation of some kind to protect quality of life, by restraining the introduction of disruptive technologies. The worst such critics idealize the "Native American" practice of considering the effects of a technology for "six generations" before allowing it to be adopted. Illich himself fell into this general category, considering these issues to be a proper matter for grass-roots political control ("convivial reconstruction").

But in fact, it is quite possible to lament the loss of human scale society ("Norman Rockwell's America"), and to resent the triumph of professionalization and the automobile, all the while adhering to strictly free market principles. For government, far from being the solution to these evils, has been their cause. Illich went wrong in treating the first and second thresholds, respectively, as watersheds of *social* utility and disutility, without considering the mechanism of coercion that is necessary for social disutility to exist at all. In a society where all transactions are voluntary, no such thing as "social disutility" is possible. Net social disutility can only occur when those who personally benefit from the introduction of new technologies beyond the second threshold, are able to force others to bear the disutilities. As we have already seen in our citations of O'Connor's analysis, this is the case in regard to a great deal of technology. The profit is privatized, while the cost is socialized. Were those who benefited from greater reliance on the car, for example, forced to internalize all the costs, the car would not be introduced beyond the point where overall disutilities equaled overall utilities. As Kaveh Pourvand elegantly put it in a private communication, the state's intervention promotes the adoption of certain technologies beyond Pareto optimality.[9] Coercion, or use of the "political means," is the only way in which one person can impose disutility on another.

The state capitalist system thus demands ever greater state inputs in the form of subsidies to accumulation, and ever greater intervention to contain the ill social effects of state capitalism. Coupled with political pressures to restrain the growth of taxation, these demands lead to (as O'Connor's title indicates) a *"fiscal crisis of the state,"* or *"a tendency for state expenditures to increase faster than the means of financing them."*[10] The *"'structural gap'...between state expenditures and state revenue"* is met by chronic deficit finance, with the inevitable inflationary results. Under state capitalism *"crisis tendencies shift, of course, from the economic into the administrative system..."* This displaced crisis is expressed through *"inflation and a permanent crisis in public finance."*[11]

The problem is intensified by the disproportionate financing of State expenditures by taxes on the competitive sector (including the taxes on the monopoly capital sector which are passed on to the competitive sector), and the promotion of monopoly capital profits at the expense of the competitive sector. This depression of the competitive sector simultaneously reduces its purchasing power and its strength as a tax base, and exacerbates the crises of both state finance and demand shortfall.

The crisis of inputs under state capitalism is further heightened by the state's promotion of the inefficiencies of large size. Most large corporations have been expanded far beyond Pareto-optimal levels by government intervention to subsidize operating expenses and conceal the inefficiency cost of large-scale organization.

In addition, existing firms are forced to be even more hierarchical and authoritarian than they otherwise would be because of past actions of the state. Not only were the producing classes originally robbed of their property in the means of production, but the state has intervened on an ongoing basis to decrease the bargaining power of labor and increase the rate of exploitation. For example, consider the action of the ruling class in the '70s to break the power of organized labor, cap real wages, and shift resources from mass consumption to investment. The result was stagnant wages, increasing work loads (aka "increased productivity), and need for all sorts of internal surveillance and control mechanisms within the corporation to keep the increasingly disgruntled work force in line.

These large corporations have the internal characteristics of a planned economy. Information flow is systematically distorted up the chain of command, by each rung in the hierarchy telling the next one up what it wants to hear. And each rung of management, based on nonsensical data (not to mention absolutely no direct knowledge of the production process) sends irrational and ass-brained decisions back down the chain of command. The only thing that keeps large, hierarchical organizations going is the fact that the productive laborers on the bottom actually know something about their own jobs, and have enough sense to ignore policy and lie about it so that production can stagger along despite the interference of the bosses.

When a senior manager decides to adopt a "reform" or to "improve" the process in some way, he typically bases his decision on the glowing recommendations of senior managers in other organizations who have adopted similar policies. Of course, those senior managers have no real knowledge themselves of the actual results of the policy, because their own information is based on filtered data from below. Not only does the senior management of an organization live in an imaginary world as a result of the distorted information from below; its imaginary world is further cut off from reality by the professional culture it shares with senior management everywhere else. "...*in a rigid hierarchy, nobody questions orders that seem to come from above, and those at the very top are so isolated from the actual work situation that they never see what is going on below."*[12]

The root of the problem, in all such cases, is that individual human beings can only make optimally efficient decisions when they internalize all the costs and benefits of their own decisions. In a large hierarchy, the consequences of the irrational and misinformed decisions of the parasites at the top are borne by the people at the bottom who are actually doing the work. And the people doing the work, who both know what's going on and suffer the ill effects of decisions by those who don't know what's going on, have no direct control over the decision-making.

Robert Anton Wilson described it in grand terms as the workers' burden of nescience confronting management's burden of omniscience:

> *Every authoritarian logogram divides society, as it divides the individual, into alienated halves. Those at the bottom suffer what I shall call the burden of nescience. The natural sensory activity of the biogram—what the person sees, hears, smells, tastes, feels, and, above all, what the organism as a whole, or as a potential whole, wants—is always irrelevant and immaterial. The authoritarian logogram, not the field of sensed experience, determines what is relevant and material.... The person acts, not on personal experience and the evaluations of the nervous system, but on the orders from above....*
>
> *Those at the top of the authoritarian pyramid, however, suffer an equal and opposite burden of omniscience.... They must attempt to do the seeing, hearing, smelling, tasting, feeling and decision-making for the whole society.*
>
> *But a man with a gun is told only that which people assume will not provoke him to pull the trigger. Since all authority and government are based on force, the master class, with its burden of omniscience, faces the servile class, with its burden of nescience, precisely as a highwayman faces his victim.*
>
> *Communication is possible only between equals. The master class never abstracts enough information from the servile class to know what is actually going on in the world where the actual productivity of society occurs.... The result can only be progressive disorientation among the rulers.*[13]

The only thing that keeps the organizations running is the fact that the people on the bottom who know how to do the work have the good sense to ignore directives from above; that, and the fact that each organization is competing against other organizations hobbled by the same institutional culture. The *"genius of our centralized bureaucracies has been,"* as Paul Goodman put it, *"as they interlock, to form a mutually accrediting establishment of decision-makers, with common interests and a common style...."*[14]

In fact, corporations grow to such size and internal complexity that it no longer pays even to attempt to track the costs of such internal transactions. That would be fine in a free market, where a firm as a whole internalized all its own costs and benefits. In that case, the inefficiency costs of internal complexity and lack of cost tracking would be weighed against other offsetting efficiencies, and growth would stop at the point where they cancelled out. But the matter is different when they keep growing because the state protects them from the inefficiencies of their own size. Mises pointed out that large private corporations were prone to the same problems of economic calculation as a planned economy. The larger a corporation, the more of its internal decisions are administrative rather than market transactions, and the further they are removed from actual market prices. An internal corporate planner, allocating resources administratively, relies indirectly on outside market prices as a source of information in the same way as a state planner in a state-managed economy.

In the Spanish workplaces after the revolution of 1936, unit costs were decreased drastically, and output increased. The reason was that power flowed from the bottom up, and the people making the decisions were directly accountable to the people doing the work. As a result, all the consequences of action were much more fully internalized by those making decisions.

This principle applies, not only in for-profit corporations, but in universities, charities, and other large organizations in "civil society." The New Class paradigm of "professional management" has affected the structure of all large organizations in state capitalist society. In every case, the organization is either subject to outside control by a board of trustees, or to a top-down internal management. Paul Goodman has brilliantly described this tendency, as it operates in a wide variety of organizations. Such organizations come under the domination of a professionalized management, and politically selected senior administrators with "prestige salaries." Because the organization distributes the costs and benefits of action among different people, the masses of productive workers within it are no longer motivated by the intrinsic pleasures of work. Instead, personnel must be subject to administrative compulsion or other forms of extrinsic motivation.

In my opinion, the salient cause of ineptitude in promotion and in all hiring practices is that, under centralized conditions, fewer and fewer know what is

> *a good job of work. The appearance of competence may count for more than the reality, and it is a lifework to manufacture appearance or, more usually, to adapt to the common expectation. Just as there is reliance on extrinsic motives, there is heavy reliance on extrinsic earmarks of competence: testing, profiles, publications, hearsay among wives, flashy curricula vitae. Yet there is no alternative method of selection. In decentralized conditions, where a man knows what goes on and engages in the whole enterprise, an applicant can present a masterpiece for examination and he has functional peers who can decide whether they want him in the guild.[15]*

> *....What swells the costs in enterprises carried on in the interlocking centralized systems of society, whether commercial, official, or non-profit institutional, are all the factors of organization, procedure, and motivation that are not directly determined to the function and to the desire to perform it....*

> *But when enterprises can be carried on autonomously by professionals, artists, and workmen intrinsically committed to the job, there are economies all along the line. People make do on means. They spend on value, not convention. They flexibly improvise procedures as opportunity presents and they step in in emergencies. They do not watch the clock. The available skills of each person are put to use. They eschew status and in a pinch accept subsistence wages. Administration and overhead are ad hoc. The task is likely to be seen in its essence rather than abstractly.[16]*

This is the style of organization the overwhelming majority of people work in. Most people have little or no say in their conditions or methods of work, and have no motive for doing it "well" than the need for a paycheck and the fear of being fired. Indeed, the people who evaluate the quality of their work have no clue what quality might actually consist of.

When the prestige-salaried head of a large organization retires, he is never replaced by a production worker from within the organization, who actually understands the process and might make intelligent decisions. Instead, the trustees or directors select from a wide array of resumè carpetbaggers with a history of holding senior management positions in other large organizations. The new head is someone who has thoroughly absorbed the professional culture of senior management, but has never engaged in genuinely productive work in his life.

When the personnel of an organization have no direct interest in its purpose, intrinsic motivation must be replaced by external compulsion. This passage from Ursula LeGuin's *The Dispossessed* is an excellent illustration:

> *Atro had once explained to him how this was managed, how the sergeants could give the privates orders, how the lieutenants could give the privates*

and the sergeants orders, how the captains...and so on and so on up to the generals, who could give everyone else orders and need take them from none, except the commander in chief. Shevek had listened with incredulous disgust. "You call that organization?" he had inquired. "You even call it discipline?

But it is neither. It is a coercive mechanism of extraordinary inefficiency—a kind of seventh-millennium steam engine! With such a rigid and fragile structure what could be done that was worth doing?" This had given Atro a chance to argue the worth of warfare as the breeder of courage and manliness and weeder-out of the unfit, but the very line of his argument had forced him to concede the effectiveness of guerrillas, organized from below, self-disciplined. "But that only works when the people think they're fighting for something of their own—you know, their homes, or some notion or other," the old man had said. Shevek had dropped the argument. He now continued it, in the darkening basement among the stacked crates of unlabeled chemicals.

He explained to Atro that he now understood why the Army was organized as it was. It was indeed quite necessary. No rational form of organization would serve the purpose. He simply had not understood that the purpose was to enable men with machine guns to kill unarmed men and women easily and in great quantities when told to do so.[17]

Paul Goodman used the university to illustrate the principle. Unlike the medieval university, which was a self-organized association of scholars and students, the modern university reflects a purpose imposed from outside. As a result,

the social needs exist in the school as "goals of the administration" and this adds many complications: the scholars must be motivated, disciplined, evaluated. But when students who want to be lawyers or doctors find themselves a faculty, or masters with something important to profess attract disciples, the case is simpler: the goals are implicit and there is no problem of motivation.[18]

In becoming the standard form of organization in the dominant and most influential institutions of our society, the bureaucratic paradigm in industry, education and welfare effectively crowds out or preempts alternative forms of organization based on bottom-up control and decentralism. *"Nobody will be able to imagine such a thing. In brief,...the inevitability of centralism will be self-proving. A system destroys its competitors by pre-empting the means and channels, and then proves that it is the only conceivable mode of operating."*[19]

C. Legitimation Crisis

State capitalism involves *"[r]e-coupling the economic system to the political.... The state apparatus no longer, as in liberal capitalism, merely secures the general conditions of production..., but is now actively engaged in it."*[20] That is, capitalism abandons the "laissez-faire" model of state involvement mainly through the enforcement of a general legal framework, and resorts instead to direct organizational links and direct state inputs into the private sector.

> To the extent that the class relationship has itself been repoliticized and the state has taken over market replacing as well as market supplementing tasks…, class domination can no longer take the anonymous form of the law of value. Instead, it now depends on factual constellations of power whether, and how, production of surplus value can be guaranteed through the public sector, and how the terms of the class compromise look.[21]

The direct intervention of the state on behalf of corporate elites becomes ever greater, and impossible to conceal. This fundamentally contradicts the official ideology of "free market capitalism," in which the state simply acts as a neutral guarantor of a social order in which the most deserving win by their own efforts. Therefore, it undermines the ideological basis on which its popular legitimacy depends. Thus, parallel to the fiscal crisis of the state, state capitalism likewise moves towards what Habermas called a *"legitimation crisis."*

> According to bourgeois conceptions that have remained constant from the beginnings of modern natural law to contemporary election speeches, social rewards should be distributed on the basis of individual achievement…. Since it has been recognized, even among the population at large, that social force is exercised in the forms of economic exchange, the market has lost its credibility as a fair…mechanism for the distribution of life opportunities conforming to the system.[22]

When the state capitalist system finally reaches its limits, the state becomes incapable of further increasing the inputs on which the system depends. The fundamental contradictions of the system, displaced from the political/administrative realm, return with a vengeance in the form of economic crisis. The state capitalist system will reach its breaking point.

D. Neoliberal Reaction and Political Repression

The American corporate elite reacted in the 1970s to the combination of fiscal, accumulation and legitimation crises by adopting a neoliberal agenda of curtailing consumption and subsidizing new accumulation. Along with these new policies, it adopted the forms of political control necessary to force them on a recalcitrant population.

Until the late 1960s, the elite perspective was governed by the New Deal social compact. The corporate state would buy stability and popular acquiescence in imperialist exploitation abroad by guaranteeing a level of prosperity and security to the middle class. In return for higher wages, unions would enforce management control of the workplace. As Richard K. Moore put it, prosperity would guarantee public passivity.[23] But starting in the Vietnam era, the elite's thinking underwent a profound change.

They concluded from the 1960s experience that the social contract had failed. Besides unprecedented levels of activism in the civil rights and antiwar movements, and the general turn toward radicalism among youth, the citizenry at large also became less manageable. There was a proliferation of activist organizations, alternative media, welfare-rights organizations, community activism, etc.

Elite intellectuals like Samuel P. Huntington lamented the drastic decrease in the level of trust of government and other leading institutions among the general public. In *The Crisis of Democracy*, written by Huntington and others as an inaugural paper for the Trilateral Institution (an excellent barometer of elite thinking), the authors argued that the system was collapsing from demand overload, because of an excess of democracy. Huntington's analysis is so illustrative of elite thinking at that time that we will quote it at length.

For Huntington, America's role in maintaining the global state capitalist system depended on a domestic system of power; this system of power, variously referred to in this work as corporate liberalism, Cold War liberalism, and the welfare-warfare state, assumed a general public willingness to stay out of government affairs. For the first two decades or so after WWII, the U.S. had functioned as *"the hegemonic power in a system of world order."*[24] And this was only possible because of a domestic structure of political authority in which the country *"was governed by the president acting with the support and cooperation of key individuals and groups in the Executive office, the federal bureaucracy, Congress, and the more important businesses, banks, law firms, foundations, and media, which constitute the private establishment."*[25]

America's position as defender of global capitalism required that its government have the ability *"to mobilize its citizens for the achievement of social and political goals and to impose discipline and sacrifice upon its citizens in order to achieve these goals."*[26] Most importantly, this ability required that democracy be largely nominal, and that citizens be willing to leave major substantive decisions about the nature of American society to qualified authorities. It required, in other words, *"some measure of apathy and non-involvement on the part of some individuals and groups."*[27]

Unfortunately, these requirements were being gravely undermined by *"a breakdown of traditional means of social control, a delegitimation of political and other means of authority, and an overload of demands on government, exceeding its capacity to respond."*[28]

> The essence of the democratic surge of the 1960s was a general challenge
> to existing systems of authority, public and private…. Within most
> organizations, discipline eased and differences in status became blurred.
> Each group claimed is right to participate equally—and perhaps more than
> equally—in the decisions which affected itself….
>
> The questioning of authority pervaded society. In politics, it manifested itself
> in a decline in public confidence and trust in political leaders and institutions,
> a reduction in the power and effectiveness of political institutions…, a new
> importance for the "adversary" media and "critical" intelligentsia in public
> affairs, and a weakening of the coherence, purpose, and self-confidence of
> political leadership.[29]

The task of traditional state capitalist elites, in the face of this crisis of democracy, was to restore that "measure of apathy and noninvolvement," and thus to render the system once again "governable."[30]

In response to the antiwar protests and race riots, LBJ and Nixon began to create an institutional framework for coordination of police state policy at the highest levels, to make sure that any such disorder in the future could be dealt with differently. This process culminated in *Department of Defense Civil Disturbance Plan 55-2, Garden Plot*, which involved domestic surveillance by the military, contingency plans for military cooperation with local police in suppressing disorder in all fifty states, plans for mass preventive detention, and joint exercises of police and the regular military. Senator Sam Ervin, of the Subcommittee on Constitutional Affairs, claimed that "*Military Intelligence had established an intricate surveillance system covering hundreds of thousands of American citizens. Committee members had seen a master plan—Garden Plot—that gave an eagle eye view of the Army-National Guard-police strategy.*" (Of course, much of the apparatus needed for preventive detention of "subversives" had been in place since the McCarran Internal Security Act of the Truman era.)

> At first, the Garden Plot exercises focused primarily on racial conflict. But
> beginning in 1970, the scenarios took a different twist. The joint teams, made
> up of cops, soldiers and spies, began practicing battle with large groups of
> protesters. California, under the leadership of Ronald Reagan, was among
> the most enthusiastic participants in Garden Plot war games.
>
> …Garden plot [subsequently] evolved into a series of annual training
> exercises based on contingency plans to undercut riots and demonstrations,
> ultimately developed for every major city in the United States. Participants
> in the exercises included key officials from all law enforcement agencies in
> the nation, as well as the National Guard, the military, and representatives
> of the intelligence community. According to the plan, joint teams would react

to a variety of scenarios based on information gathered through political espionage and informants. The object was to quell urban unrest.[31]

The New Deal social compact with organized labor was reassessed in the light of new events. The country was swept by a wave of wildcat strikes in the early 1970s, in coal mining, auto manufacturing, and the post office. These disruptions indicated that the business unions could no longer keep their rank and file under control, and that the Fordist system was no longer serving its purpose of maintaining social control in the workplace.

At the same time, the business press was flooded with articles on the impending "capital shortage," and calls for shifting resources from consumption to capital accumulation, by radically scaling back the welfare state and hamstringing organized labor. This shift was reflected in traditionally corporate liberal think tanks like Brookings and the CED, which both produced studies acknowledging the need to impose limits on consumption in the interest of accumulation; for example, the Brookings Institution's 1976 study *Setting National Priorities: The Next Ten Years.*[32]

Business journals predicted frankly that a cap on real wages would be hard to force on the public in the existing political environment.[33] For example, an article in the October 12, 1974 issue of *Business Week* warned that

> *Some people will obviously have to do with less.... [I]ndeed, cities and states, the home mortgage market, small business and the consumer will all get less than they want.... [I]t will be a hard pill for many Americans to swallow— the idea of doing with less so that big business can have more.... Nothing that this nation, or any other nation has done in modern history compares in difficulty with the selling job that must now be done to make people accept the new reality.*[34]

This only heightened the imperative to curb the excess of democracy and make the state less vulnerable to popular pressure.

Corporations embraced the full range of union-busting possibilities in Taft-Hartley, risking only token fines from the NLRB. They drastically increased management resources devoted to workplace surveillance and control, a necessity because of discontent from stagnant wages and mounting workloads (aka increased "productivity").[35] Not surprisingly, workplace violence ("going postal") escalated along with general levels of employee disgruntlement. The use of internal surveillance systems and personality profiling to detect disgruntlement and weed out those with bad attitudes toward authority, not to mention to track down those guilty of quiet and unobtrusive sabotage, became a central preoccupation with the new Chekists in Human Resources departments.

Wages as a percentage of value added have declined drastically since the 1970s, and real wages have been virtually flat. Virtually all increases in labor productivity have been channeled into profit and investment, rather than wages. The new Cold War military buildup, from the late '70s on, still further transferred public resources to industry.

A series of events like the fall of Saigon, the nonaligned movement, and the New International Economic Order were taken as signs that the transnational corporate empire was losing control. The national security community saw America's "system of world order" coming under increasing pressure from national liberation movements. An excellent example of foreign policy elites' view of the near future is the work of RAND analyst Guy Pauker, who wrote in 1977 of a "possible world order crisis in the 1980s."[36]

Reagan's escalating intervention in Central America was a partial response to this perception. But more importantly, the collapse of the USSR ended all external restraints on the global system designed during WWII, and deprived internal resistance to that system of the Soviet Union's patronage. In the aftermath of this snatching of total victory from the jaws of defeat, the Uruguay Round of GATT ended all barriers to TNCs buying up entire economies, locked the west into monopoly control of modern technology, and created a world government on behalf of global corporations.

This was, in its essentials, the development that James O'Connor had foreseen in 1984—years before the fall of the Berlin Wall and the implosion of the USSR:

> Some who have thought or written about the subject [the global crisis of capitalism] believe that a resolution of the crisis favoring international capitalist interests will require further restructuring of the division of labor and the international economy generally in ways which will permit capital to re-establish social and political control over global labor and key petty bourgeois nation-states (e.g., resolution of the class and national struggles in the Middle East, Southern Africa, and Central America in favor of multinational corporate interests.[37]

In the meantime the U.S. was moving toward radical polarization of income. The general effect of the neoliberal reaction was to blur the lines between imperial core and periphery: the comprador bourgeoisie, living in heavily fortified luxury sectors of Third World cities, coexisted with the gated communities of America as elements of the core; at the same time, something resembling a Third World society has arisen in parts of what was traditionally the First World. The inner city and the depopulated countryside, the seats of urban and rural squalor, respectively, were subject to increasing surveillance and brutality under the guise of the War on Drugs. *"Most of the world has been turned into a periphery; the imperial core has been boiled down to the capitalist elite themselves...."*[38]

As policy elites attempted to transform the country into a two-tier society, a kinder and gentler version of the Third World pattern, the threat of public discontent forced the government to greater and greater levels of authoritarianism.

> *The most obvious means of social control, in a discontented society, is a strong, semi-militarized police force. Most of the periphery has been managed by such means for centuries. This was obvious to elite planners in the West, was adopted as policy, and has now been largely implemented....*
>
> *So that the beefed-up police force could maintain control in conditions of mass unrest, elite planners also realized that much of the Bill of Rights would need to be neutralized.... The rights-neutralization project has been largely implemented, as exemplified by armed midnight raids, outrageous search-and-seizure practices, overly broad conspiracy laws, wholesale invasion of privacy, massive incarceration, and the rise of prison slave labor.*

"The Rubicon," Moore concludes, *"has been crossed—the techniques of oppression long common in the empire's periphery are being imported to the core."*[39]

With the help of the Drug War, and assorted Wars on Gangs, Terrorism, etc., the apparatus of repression continued to grow. The Drug War has turned the Fourth Amendment into toilet paper; civil forfeiture, with the aid of jailhouse snitches, gives police the power to steal property without ever filing charges—a lucrative source of funds for helicopters and kevlar vests. SWAT teams have led to the militarization of local police forces, and cross-training with the military has led many urban police departments to view the local population as an occupied enemy.[40]

Reagan's old California crony Giuffrida resurfaced in the '80s as head of FEMA, where he worked with Oliver North to fine-tune Garden Plot. North, as the NSC liaison with FEMA from 1982-84, developed a plan *"to suspend the constitution in the event of a national crisis, such as nuclear war, violent and widespread internal dissent or national opposition to a U.S. military invasion abroad."*[41] Garden Plot, interestingly, was implemented locally during the Rodney King Riots and perhaps also in recent anti-globalization protests.[42] Delta Force provided intelligence and advice in those places and at Waco.[43]

The apparatus of the police state ratcheted further upward during the Clinton administration, with the passage of the so-called Counter-Terrorism Bill in 1996. The Clinton Bill, arguably more dangerous than anything since done by Ashcroft, gave the President blanket authority to declare any organization "terrorist" by executive fiat, and then to seize its assets without due process of law. Since then, seizing on the opportunity presented by the 9-11 attacks, Ashcroft's Justice Department was able to push through (via the USA Patriot Act) a whole laundry list of police state measures desired by the FBI that Congress had been unwilling to swallow five years earlier.

The post-911 growth of the police state dovetails nicely with the pre-911 reaction against the anti-globalization movement, which since Seattle had replaced the so-called constitutionalist or militia movement as a chief concern of federal law enforcement.[44] John Timoney, Philadelphia Police Commissioner during the August 2000 police riot at the Republican National Convention,[45] has been a close associate of Homeland Security Director Tom Ridge. Before 9-11, Timoney was a vocal enemy of the "international anarchist" conspiracy to disrupt globalization meetings, and advocated the use of RICO statute and harsh federal law enforcement tactics to break the anti-globalization movement. In August 2000, he made what was arguably the most drastic, thorough, and creative use of police spying, harassment, preventive arrest of activists on trumped up charges, of any local police official involved in fighting the post-Seattle movement.[46] As police chief in Miami, he supervised the recent police riots during the FTAA meeting. Timoney's name has periodically surfaced in the mainstream media in connection with Homeland Security, often rumored to be under consideration for a top lieutenancy under Ridge. The "economic terrorism" provisions of USA Patriot, arguably, apply to many of the direct action tactics used by the Wobblies and other radical unions; how long will it be before the "criminal syndicalism" laws of eighty years ago are resurrected under this guise?

An especially creative innovation from the War on Drugs, since applied to all sorts of other areas, is to turn everyone we deal with into a police agent. Banks routinely report "suspicious" movements of cash; under "know your customer" programs, retailers report purchases of items which can conceivably be used in combination to manufacture drugs; libraries come under pressure to report on readers of "subversive" material; DARE programs turn kids into police informers.

The media and popular culture also do their part. In the police drama, *"'rights' are a joke, the accused are despicable sociopaths, and no criminal is ever brought to justice until some noble cop or prosecutor bends the rules a bit."*[47] Meanwhile, the schools, through "peer group socialization" (aka the barracks society), DARE, and "zero tolerance," are molding a public trained from childhood to believe that the way to success is to please authority figures, to avoid making waves, and to do and believe what they are told—and that every problem or perplexing situation should be dealt with by running to someone in authority.

Computer technology and digital media have increased the potential for surveillance to Orwellian levels. The existence of enormous computer databases, surveillance programs like Echelon and Carnivore, and police experimentation with combinations of public cameras, digital face-recognition technology, and databases of digital photos, have between them made a total surveillance state technically feasible. Although trial balloons like Total Information Awareness are occasionally floated, the public still resists final steps toward a universal surveillance database or a national ID card. No doubt Ashcroft already has the draft legislation to implement them handy in his desk drawer, to be produced after the next convenient terror attack restores the properly attitude of servility among the general public.

A common response to those fearing such capability (from the sort of "small government conservative" who is typically full of zeal for the national security state), is to challenge civil libertarians to produce "one example" of how (for example) the USA Patriot Act has been abused. But the powers the government has on paper, and what it could choose to do with them if it ever found it "convenient," are a lot more important than the use it has made of them *so far*. All the rights we have were originally forced on the government from below, not granted by the government out of good will. The only guarantee we have for these rights, in the last resort, is our ability to exercise them *against the will* of the government, and our ability to resist if it attempts to restrict them.

The "slippery slope" argument used against gun control is just as applicable here: the more the exercise of a right is regulated, licensed and monitored, the less credible is the public's ability to exercise that right against the will of the government, and the more that right becomes in practice a privilege *granted by* the government. The federal government has gone a long way to creating the full legal and institutional structure necessary for dictatorship, regardless of whether they choose to exercise it; Ashcroft clearly desires to go most of the rest of the way down that path. The very fact that the government is busily acquiring the ability to track us, and to keep our speech and associations under surveillance, and to suspend them at the stroke of a president's pen, makes those liberties less secure. The effect is to render those liberties a grant from the government, depending on the continuance of its good will.

There are, however, built in limits to these tendencies toward repression and statism; they lie in the potential for legitimation crisis detailed in the previous section. Many aspects of the neoliberal reaction itself, like the politically charged debate over "welfare reform," are examples of the contradictions of capitalism being translated to the administrative realm, as Habermas predicted.

E. Built-In Limits to Effectiveness of Neoliberal Reaction

Even in periods of accumulation crisis and stagnation, like the 1970s, capital is so over-accumulated that industry cannot dispose of its product profitably in a free market, operating at full capacity. Over-accumulation is the underlying and most fundamental crisis tendency at all times.

As we have seen, paradoxically, one solution to the crisis of over-accumulation is even more accumulation to increase the profitability of old investments. The term "accumulation crisis" refers, not to absolute levels of capital accumulation, but to insufficient rates of additional accumulation to make old investments profitable. But this "solution," while staving off disaster in the short run, further exacerbates the long-term problem of over-accumulation, which requires in turn still greater accumulation in the future to keep today's investments profitable. The system becomes ever more over-accumulated, and dependent on greater and greater levels of future accumulation.

Since over-accumulation is chronic and fundamental, even in periods of accumulation crisis, there are limits to the feasibility of neoliberal reaction. The state can only reverse the social and economic gains of labor to a limited extent. So despite the neoliberal hat-tipping to the glories of "free market capitalism," the reaction of the 1970s was not toward less state involvement in the economy. It was only toward less state support for aggregate demand and less accommodation with organized labor. And even so, it was not feasible to reduce the bargaining power of labor to pre-New Deal levels, because it was necessary, in remedying the problems of under-accumulation, to avoid provoking a new crisis of realization.

Thus, the state capitalist system is balanced on the edge of a knife. There is permanent tension between the requirements for realization and full output, and for further accumulation; or, as James O'Connor put it, *"economic (and social and political) contradictions between conditions of value and surplus value production, on the one hand, and effective demand and value realization, on the other."*[48] Corporate liberal solutions to the crisis of over-accumulation impede the further accumulation necessary to make existing investments profitable. But the neoliberal shift of consumption funds to investment threatens the aggregate demand necessary to absorb output at full capacity, and threatens to make active the tendency toward over-accumulation which is always latent in the state capitalist system.

In this state of ongoing tension, something has to give. One way out is severe recession or depression which, by radically devaluing existing accumulations of capital, increases the ratio of surplus value to constant capital and thus restores a healthy rate of profit. After the massive destruction of capital values in depression, those who come out on top are in the position to start a new wave of accumulation. For the capitalists who survive, it is a "solution"; but from the point of view of the capitalist class as a whole, it is a catastrophic one, not to mention dangerous and politically costly. An economic system that "solves" the tension between accumulation and realization by increasingly severe swings of the business cycle sounds dangerously close to the late capitalism predicted by Marx.

The fiscal crisis of the state is also chronic. No matter how much the welfare state is retrenched and unions are emasculated, the economy requires increasing government inputs to render capital profitable. Even during periods of accumulation crisis like the 1970s, capital is nevertheless over-accumulated to the point of being unprofitable without massive state intervention. But such state expenditures, by reducing the pool of private funds available for private investment, also intensify the tendency toward accumulation crisis.

The corporate economy, at its present levels of accumulation and centralization, is simply incapable of operating at full capacity and disposing of its full product without massive state inputs and massive state involvement in the economy. And such interventions, by their very nature, destabilize the corporate economy in such a way as to require still further intervention. As a result, to the danger of accumulation and fiscal crisis is inherent in even the minimal forms of state intervention, which are themselves absolutely necessary to prevent the primary crisis tendency of over-accumulation and under-consumption. It is impossible to stave off accumulation and realization crises without levels of consumption and state spending that imperil adequate levels of new accumulation. And any shift in resources from consumption to investment sufficient to secure adequate levels of new accumulation will threaten the level of demand necessary to absorb the output of industry operating at full capacity. It is virtually impossible to steer a middle course between the two crisis tendencies.

It might not be altogether fanciful to discern in the history of the past hundred years a long-term political cycle of state intervention in the economy: an oscillating political business cycle of alternating reactions to the crises of over-accumulation and under-accumulation. O'Connor seemed to be hinting at such a political cycle when he wrote that "*historical crisis created large-scale capital and the working class/salariat, which created social democratic state forms and contents—all of which were at the root of the modern accumulation crisis.*[49]

The neoliberal reaction of the 1970s, and the subsequent polarization of wealth and income, arguably created new crisis tendencies toward over-accumulation. The impending crisis was concealed in the 1990s by the largely state-created high tech industry. This new industry staved off a new crisis of over-accumulation by providing a large and profitable outlet for surplus capital: a long-wave investment cycle comparable to the auto industry in mid-century. Still, the polarization of income and the channeling of all productivity increases into further investment foreshadowed a new crisis of overproduction and under-consumption.

Richard K. Moore's recent speculations on a quiet anti-neoconservative "coup" currently in progress are quite interesting in this context. Moore suspects, behind the war of a thousand cuts from leaks on the Plame scandal, Abu Ghraib, etc., a movement on the part of the uniformed military and CIA and State Department careerists (not to mention much of the corporate establishment) to remove the Bush clique from power.[50] I myself wonder whether the U.S. policy establishment is reassessing, not only the PNAC foreign policy agenda, but the neoliberal consensus itself. Is there a long-term policy shift in the works, comparable to that of the early '70s—but this time back toward corporate liberalism? It would be interesting, in this regard, to see Thomas Ferguson's assessment of the flow of corporate money to the respective parties.

F. Neoconservatism as Attempted Defense Against Legitimation Crisis

As James O'Connor argued, the individualist ideology is a key part of the accumulation crisis. In its modern form of consumerist individualism (the "revolution of rising expectations"), it increases pressure for higher wages and social spending. Consumerist individualism is at the heart of the legitimizing system of the Taylorist/Fordist social compact of the New Deal. "If they pay us well, we'll let the bosses manage." The worker sacrifices creative work as an expression of individuality, and instead finds his individuality by "pursuing happiness" in the realm of consumption.

More importantly, the older political individualism surviving from the traditional American political culture is an impediment to the authoritarian transformation necessary to transfer resources from consumption to accumulation, and to end excessive demands and democratic pressure on the state. The individualist values of the general population are at the heart of the crisis of legitimacy that limits state action on behalf of organized capital.

The authoritarian ideology of neo-conservatism ("big government conservatism," "national greatness conservatism") is a partial attempt to overcome the traditional American individualism. In place of the inalienable rights of the individual, and the absolute accountability of the state to the citizenry, it emphasizes service and sacrifice to the state. For example, consider Max Boot's lamentation over the easy victory in Operation Enduring Freedom in November 2001, and the inadequate level of casualties for demonstrating the proper martial spirit. Although neoconservatives speak a great deal about "freedom" and "liberty," in the neocon lexicon freedom and liberty are redefined as whatever the individual is asked to sacrifice for. Whatever total war the state is currently fighting is, by definition, to "defend our freedom."

There are, however, built-in contradictions in the neoconservative solution. The concepts of liberty and justice have some residual cultural content that is beyond the ability of court intellectuals to extirpate. Transforming culture and rewriting history are not as easy as Orwell made them out to be. Indeed, neoconservatism appeals to the traditional values and legitimizing symbols of Norman Rockwell America, seeking to graft them onto the new ideology. Neoconservatism frequently appeals to populist values and resentment of elites and parasites, although the targets are carefully chosen (academics, welfare moms, "union bosses," "trial lawyers," etc.) so as not to pose any danger to the real system of power. It is doubtful that the public would swallow the new, authoritarian content of neoconservatism at all, were it not sugar-coated with older populist rhetoric.

There are inherent self-contradictions in neoconservatism, to the extent that its authoritarian strains cannot be adapted to even a heavily redacted version of older American values. Neoconservatism, like older strains of conservatism more genuinely in the American tradition, engages in frequent hat-tipping toward small government, strengthening "civil society," etc. In the 2000 election, Dick Cheney frequently stated that "government never made anyone wealthy" (stadium socialism and the camp followers at Halliburton KBR notwithstanding). The most sycophantic shills for the total warfare state and the domestic police state, like Ann Coulter, pepper their rhetoric with Tenth Amendment appeals for restoring the autonomy of states and localities, and denunciations of government elites' interference with families.

The task is made still harder to the extent that the ideas of justice and fairness have some real content. Neoconservative propaganda cannot invent new values; it can only misdirect existing values to selected targets by distorting or concealing factual evidence. But to the extent that all propaganda must appeal to true values, the audience can isolate those values from the propaganda message and direct the principles to new and more appropriate targets much closer to where the real elites live. To the extent that "elitism" and "parasitism" have real content, there is always a danger that the public will perceive the contradiction between practice and preaching, and decide that the terms can be more appropriately applied to the real power elite. Once the standards of "justice" and "fairness" are used as a propaganda weapon, those weapons may be turned against their previous holders. The populist and libertarian language used against selected academic and welfare-state "elites" possesses objective value content, and appeals to universal norms of fairness; when elite action in other areas of policy violate these objective standards of fairness, the danger is that the public will perceive the opportunistic choice of "elite" targets as inappropriate. The popular term "corporate welfare" is just one example of this.

And the situation is also complicated by the fact that the ruling elite will never be as internally cohesive as Orwell's Inner Party. The state may be the executive committee of the ruling class; but the ruling class has many factions (e.g., the disputes between labor-intensive and capital-intensive industry, domestic- and export-oriented industry, etc., that were at the heart of party alignments in the 20th century). No matter how much one faction of the business elite tries to redefine traditional American values and to suppress their old content, the other faction will have an interest in reinfusing its old value-content and using it as a weapon against their enemies in the elite.

G. The Frankfurt School: Fascism and Abandonment of the Law of Value

One apparent solution is to remove more and more of the cost side of the ledger from the market altogether, with the taxpayers absorbing operating costs and rendering capital more profitable. The overall process, behind the state's oscillating policies of responding to over- and under-accumulation, is a greater and greater involvement, and the movement of ever larger portions of the economy from the realm of the market to the realm of state administration.

Theoretically, there is no limit. The state can continue to solve crises of over- and under-accumulation by shifting costs and revenues from the market to the political sphere indefinitely, until the final result is a privately owned corporate economy in the same position relative to the working and taxpaying population as the ruling class in the Asiatic mode. The role of commodity exchange and realization in the market will steadily decline until the capitalists are the state, and the economy is a single giant, slave-operated latifundium. Owners of the corporate economy operate directly through the state, as in feudalism or Asiatic mode, to exploit population at large through entirely political means.

Some members of the Frankfurt school saw fascism as an attempt to do just that. According to Horkheimer and Adorno, Neumann, and Pollock, Nazism reflected an evolution in which capitalists increasingly acted through the state. They speculated that such a society might, in future, altogether abandon commodity production and the law of value. At some point, in that scenario, the market would be superseded by state administration, and the capitalists would extract a surplus from labor directly through the state. When that point was reached, the market would have been completely transformed into a state-owned and state-managed economy, and the capitalists would no longer be capitalists. Instead, they would be owners of the state economy by virtue of their control of the state.

Frederick Pollock described this phenomenon as the disappearance, with "the autonomous market," of the "so-called economic laws": "*The replacement of the economic means by the political means as the last guarantee for the reproduction of economic life changes the character of the whole historical period. It signifies the transition from a predominantly economic to an essentially political era.*"[51]

Unfortunately for the capitalist ruling class, this possibility is largely theoretical. The stability of all government rests, in the last resort, on public consent. And while the degree to which public opinion can be shaped by the ideological hegemony of a ruling class is indeed remarkable, there are limits in practice to the ability of legitimizing ideology to achieve popular acquiescence.

There are also absolute physical limits. Crises of inputs like transportation and energy would, in all likelihood, be even more acute under post-capitalism. Allocating them entirely by political means, instead of only partially, would simply remove the rationalizing function of market prices altogether. The example of the Soviet economy is instructive. It largely removed the law of value as a consideration in allocating inputs to the economy. Nevertheless, the inherent irrationalities resulting from ignoring the law of value led to ever greater wastage of inputs, and to ever greater inputs to achieve the same results. The state planners had no way of even knowing how many resources they were wasting, because there was no basis for rational economic calculation. The final result was collapse.

Finally, there are political constraints from outside. Even in the event of the post-capitalist class society feared by the Frankfurt School, such a system would surely reach physical limits of expansion short of total military and political control of the planet. Had Nazi Germany succeeded in defeating the Allies militarily and pushing Soviet forces out of European Russia, it is still unlikely that Hitler would have been able to maintain permanent control of subject populations from the

English Channel to the Urals. It is still less likely that a post-capitalist America and its developed world allies, regardless of their degree of military and technical superiority, could hold on to the entire world.

And despite Orwell's cynicism, it is unlikely that America's fellow nuclear powers would act as enablers of global empire, or that the great powers would undertake a tacit obligation not to challenge each others fundamental interests. It is much more likely that the major nuclear powers, Russia and China, would promote their own interests by challenging American/Western dominion, and encouraging defection and insurgency in the Third World.

What's more, Orwell's speculation on the motives of the Inner Party in Oceania is psychologically incredible. It is unlikely if nothing else that any ruling class would be able to maintain the internal cohesion and morale to behave with the ruthlessness necessary, in the long run, to control a hostile world. While the ruling elite no doubt attracts more than its share of sociopaths, ruling classes as a whole cannot maintain stable rule with no legitimizing ideology besides conscious self-interest or the love of power for its own sake.

H. Global Political Crisis of Imperialism

To some extent, as we saw above, a neoliberal policy in the Third World is a solution to both the accumulation crisis and excess of democracy in the First World. The class struggle is transferred from the First to the Third World, and the Third World is used as a base of attack on first. Transnational corporations write off old investments in the First World, use decaying industry there as a cash cow to support new and more profitable investment in the Third World.

As with other aspects of the neoliberal reaction, however, there are built in limits. Neoliberal policies in the Third World contain the seeds of a global political crisis. This is almost certain to be an acute crisis in the medium term. But even in the short term, the dangers to the global capitalist order are very real.

At some point, the effects of neoliberalism (and especially the jacked-up version of the Uruguay Round) are likely to cause political unrest in so many countries of the Third World, and the emergence of so many more populist or national figures like Chavez and Lula, that a coordinated movement among several such countries will emerge.

If several significant TW countries staged a surprise, coordinated repudiation of their national debts, and withdrew from the Bretton Woods agencies, the effects on the neoliberal system would be devastating.

It's interesting that we've seen a near-collapse of central power in Argentina, with the emergence of a variety of grass-roots economic and political organs of self-government; and anti-neoliberal populist regimes in Brazil and Venezuela—all in just a couple years' time. As the impacts of the Uruguay Round and other neoliberal policies make themselves felt in the Third and Fourth world, with the resulting political unrest and emergence of populist and nationalist movements, we can expect more and more such defections. At some point, such countries are likely to stop negotiating with the IMF individually, and attempt a joint action of some kind.

Imagine if several significant Third World countries made such a coordinated withdrawal from the Bretton Woods institutions, and repudiated their international debts. They could combine this with other genuinely free market reforms, like abrogating the intellectual property and industrial property provisions of GATT, so that native-owned competition might emerge to Western corporations, and be allowed to adopt modern production technology without restraint. If the domestic power of feudal oligarchies was broken in these countries, and with it their collusion with Western agribusiness, the land could be deeded to the actual peasant cultivators or agricultural laborers. A number of countries might enter into an accord to legalize mutual banks, LETS, and all other voluntary credit or money systems—and possibly organize a state asset-backed currency of some sort for trade between themselves, as an alternative to dependence on the dollar. They might announce a policy, finally, of ceasing to subsidize from state revenues the infrastructure projects on which Western capital depended to be profitable in their countries: that would mean all electricity, transportation, etc., services would be paid for by western firms on a cost basis. Rather than "privatizing" state enterprises by auctioning them off to kleptocrats and TNCs, they might transform them into either producers' or consumers' cooperatives—at least as genuine a form of privatization as the looting commonly practiced, but one that never seems to be adopted in Jeffrey Sachs' version of "free market" reform.

If this seems overly fanciful, consider Brazil's recent proposal for a free trade area among the G-20 group of developing nations—without the imprimatur of the Usual Suspects. The purpose, said Brazil's president, was "*to fully exploit the potential among us, which does not depend on the concessions of the rich countries....*"[52]

Such a movement might even coordinate with the OPEC countries or China in adopting the Euro as a medium for international trade—the equivalent of a monetary atom bomb on the U.S.

If any one country undertook such measures, the CIA would probably begin immediate destabilization attempts, as it did with Allende's Chile or Chavez's Venezuela; but if several countries made such a withdrawal from the world corporate system simultaneously, pledged each other mutual support, and appealed for support to the people of the rest of the world, it might be more than the U.S. could handle. This latter would include mobilizing popular discontent against non-supportive regimes throughout the Third and Fourth worlds, promoting defaults and withdrawals by even more countries, and radical opposition within the core of the Empire itself.

With the serious political divisions between international capital, such a movement might even attract the support of a great power rival to the U.S. The Europeans, Russians or Chinese would be quite likely to ignore any U.S. attempt to impose trade sanctions. Any would-be rival "Eurasian bloc" of such powers might, indeed, welcome the movement as a form of strategic leverage, the same way the USSR welcomed the old nonaligned movement.

NOTES

1. James O'Connor, *Accumulation Crisis* (Oxford: Basil Blackwell Ltd, 1984) 97.

2. Ibid. 8.

3. See material from James O'Connor, *The Fiscal Crisis of the State* (New York: St. Martin's Press, 1973),in Chapter Six above.

4. O'Connor, *Fiscal Crisis* 8.

5. "Head to Head: M6 Toll Road," BBC News, December 9, 2003 http://news.bbc.co.uk/2/hi/uk_news/3303629.stm   Captured December 10, 2003

6. "World Oil Supplies Running Out Faster than Expected," Oil and Gas Journal, August 12, 2002. See also George Monbiot, "Bottom of the Barrel," the *Guardian*, 2nd December 2003 http://www.monbiot. com/ ; Colin J. Campbell and Jean H. Laherrère, "The End of Cheap Oil," *Scientific American*, March 1998. http://news.bbc.co.uk/1/hi/business/3777413.stm Captured May 15, 2004.

7. Warren Johnson, *Muddling Toward Frugality* (San Francisco: Sierra Club Books, 1978).

8. Ivan Illich, *Tools for Conviviality* (New York: Harper & Row, 1973).

9. Kaveh Pourvand, private email, October 29, 2003.

10. O'Connor, *Fiscal Crisis of the State* 9.

11. Jürgen Habermas, *Legitimation Crisis*. Trans. by Thomas McCarthy (United Kingdom: Polity Press, 1973, 1976) 61, 68.

12. Robert Shea and Robert Anton Wilson, *The Illuminatus! Trilogy* (New York: Dell Publishing Co., Inc., 1975) 388.

13. Ibid. 498.

14. Paul Goodman, *Like a Conquered Province* (New York: Vintage Books, 1965) 357 (published under single cover with *People or Personnel*).

15. Paul Goodman, *People or Personnel* (New York: Vintage Books, 1963) 83-4 (published under single cover with *Like a Conquered Province*).

16. Ibid. 113.

17. Ursula LeGuin, *The Dispossessed* (New York: Harper Paperbacks, 1974) 305-6.

18. Paul Goodman, *The Community of Scholars* (New York: Vintage Books, 1964) 213 (published under single cover with *Compulsory Miseducation*).

19. Goodman, *People or Personnel* 70.

20. Habermas, *Legitimation Crisis* 36.

21. Ibid. 68.

22. Ibid. 81.

23. Richard K. Moore, "Escaping the Matrix," *Whole Earth* (Summer 2000) 53.

24. Samuel P. Huntington, Michael J. Crozier, Joji Watanuki. *The Crisis of Democracy*. Report on the Governability of Democracies to the Trilateral Commission: Triangle Paper 8 (New York: New York University Press, 1975).105-6.

25. Ibid. 92.

26. Ibid. 7-8.

27. Ibid. 113-5.

28. Ibid. 7-8.

29. Ibid. 74-6.

30. Ibid. 113-5.

31. Frank Morales, "U.S. Military Civil Disturbance Planning: The War at Home" *Covert Action Quarterly* 69, Spring-Summer 2000, http://infowar.net/warathome/warathome.html Captured April 15, 2001. The last quote is from Donald Goldberg and Indy Badhwar, "Blueprint for Tyranny," *Penthouse Magazine* August 1985.

32. Harry C. Boyte, *The Backyard Revolution: Understanding the New Citizen Movement* (Philadelphia: Temple University Press, 1980) 226n.

33. Ibid. 13-6, along with notes on 225-9.

34. Ibid. 225-6n.

35. David M. Gordon. *Fat and Mean: The Corporate Squeeze of Working Americans and the Myth of Management Downsizing* (New York: The Free Press, 1996).

36. Guy Pauker, *Military Implications of a Possible World Order Crisis*

in the 1980s R-2003-AF (Santa Monica: Rand Corporation, November 1977); Pauker, *Sources of Instability in Developing Countries* P-5029 (Santa Monica: Rand Corporation, June 1973).

37. O'Connor, *Accumulation Crisis* 1-2.

38. Moore, "Escaping the Matrix" 56.

39. Ibid. 57; See also Sam Smith, "How You Became the Enemy," (*Progressive Review* 1997). http://www.mega.nu:8080/ampp/enemy.html captured April 15, 2001.

40. Diane Cecilia Weber, "Warrior Cops: The Ominous Growth of Paramilitarism in American Police Departments" Cato Briefing Paper No. 50, 26 August 1999. http://www.cato.org/pubs/briefs/bp-050es.html Captured April 15, 2001.

41. Alfonso Chardy, "Reagan Aides and the 'Secret' Government" *Miami Herald* 5 July 1987 http://www.totse.com/en/conspiracy/the_new_world_order/scrtgovt.html Captured April 15, 2001; see also Diana Reynolds, "The Rise of the National Security State: FEMA and the NSC" *Covert Action Information Bulletin* #33 (Winter 1990). Reproduced by The Public Eye http://publiceye.org/liberty/fema/Fema_1.htm Captured April 15, 2001.

42. Morales, "U.S. Military Civil Disturbance Planning"; Paul Rosenberg, *The Empire Strikes Back: Police Repression of Protest From Seattle to L.A.* L.A. Independent Media Center (August 13 2000) http://www.r2kphilly.org/pdf/empire-strikes.pdf Captured April 15, 2001; Alexander Cockburn, "The Jackboot State: The War Came Home and We're Losing It" *Counterpunch* (May 10 2000) http://www.counterpunch.org/jackboot.html Captured April 15, 2001.

43. "US Army Intel Units Spying on Activists" Intelligence Newsletter #381 (April 5, 2000) http://www.infoshop.org/news5/army_intel.html captured March 27, 2001.

44. Jim Redden, "Police State Targets the Left" The Zoh Show: Newsbytes (May 2, 2000) http://www.zohshow.com/News/Newsbytes/tidbits050200b.htm Captured March 25, 2001; Jim Redden, *Snitch Culture: How Citizens are Turned into the Eyes and Ears of the State* (Venice, Calif.: Feral House, 2000).

45. See Rosenberg, *The Empire Strikes Back.*

46. Ibid.

47. Moore, "Escaping the Matrix" 57.

48. O'Connor, *Accumulation Crisis* 58.

49. Ibid. 225.

50. RKM, "about those torture photos..." Cyberjournal, May 19, 2004. http://cyberjournal.org/cj/show_archives/?id='811'&batch='16'&lists='cj' Captured August 8, 2004. Richard K. Moore invites comments on these views; he can be reached by email at richard@cyberjournal.org

51. Pollock, "State Capitalism," *Studies in Philosophy and Social Science*, IX, No. 3 (1941); Franz Neumann, *Behemoth* (1942); Adorno and Horkheimer, *Dialectic of Enlightenment* (1944). All cited in Michael Harrington, *The Twilight of Capitalism* (Simon and Schuster, 1976) 216-18.

52. "Brazil proposes creation of G-20 free trade area," December 13, 2003 www.chinaview.cn 2003-12-13 11:13:39 http://news.xinhuanet.com/english/2003-12-13/content_1229296.htm Captured December 14, 2003.

Part Three
Praxis

Chapter Nine
Ends and Means

A. Organizing Principles.

The Cost Principle. The cost principle is central to mutualist economics. That means that all costs and benefits of an action should be internalized in the actor responsible for it—or in other words, that the person consuming goods and services should pay the full cost of producing them. The cost principle does not require an authoritarian government to apportion costs in accordance with benefits. It requires only a non-coercive marketplace, in which all transactions are voluntary. Given that, the market actors themselves will engage only in transactions where the benefits are sufficient to pay for the real costs. The most important thing is to avoid hidden costs, or externalities, not reflected in price.

Every single evil of capitalism we examined in Part Two of this book can be traced, in a sense, to a violation of the cost principle. In every case, the benefits of the action were divorced from the cost, so that the person benefiting from a particular form of action did not bear the costs associated with it.

Government, in its essence, is a mechanism for externalizing costs. By externalizing costs, government enables the privileged to live at the expense of the non-privileged. But every such intervention leads to irrationality and social cost. For example:

Because labor does not keep its own product, and the disutility and the output of labor are not internalized by the same individual, there is a crisis of overproduction and under-consumption and a need for further state intervention to dispose of the surplus product.

Because labor does not own its means of production, the process of capital accumulation works against labor instead of for it. Instead of investment being the decision of a worker to consume less of his own product today in order to work less or consume more tomorrow, it is the decision of a boss to invest some of the worker's product today so he can receive even less of his product tomorrow. Instead of an improved standard of living for the worker-owner, increased productivity results in unearned wealth for the owner and unemployment for the worker.

Because large corporations do not pay the full cost of the factors they consume, they consume irrationally and inefficiently; because the inefficiency costs of large size are externalized on the taxpayer, they are able to grow beyond the point of maximum efficiency. At the same time that American goods are produced at many times the energy and transportation costs actually needed, the country faces chronic energy shortages and transportation bottlenecks.

It is only through the free market, organized on the basis of voluntary exchange, that the cost principle can be realized. The law of cost operates through the competitive mechanism, by which producers enter the market when price is less than cost and leave it in the opposite case. In a free market, the price of a good or service is a signal of the cost entailed in providing it. Because costs are on the table, reflected in price rather than hidden, people (including business firms) will only consume goods and services that they are willing to pay for.

As Proudhon pointed out, there is no way of knowing the real cost, or exchange value, of anything produced outside the market.

> How much does the tobacco sold by the administration cost? How much is it worth? You can answer the first of these questions: you need only call at the first tobacco shop you see. But you can tell me nothing about the second, because you have no standard of comparison and are forbidden to verify by experiment the items of cost of administration.... Therefore the tobacco business, made into a monopoly, necessarily costs society more than it brings in; it is an industry which, instead of subsisting by its own product, lives by subsidies....[1]

Here's an excellent picture of the functioning of the cost principle in Proudhon's society of voluntary contract:

> Its law...is service for service, product for product, loan for loan, insurance for insurance, credit for credit, security for security, guarantee for guarantee. It is the ancient law of retaliation,...as it were turned upside down and transferred...to economic law, to the tasks of labor and to the good offices of free fraternity. On it depend all the mutualist institutions, mutual credit, mutual aid, mutual education; reciprocal guarantees of openings, exchanges and labor for good quality and fairly priced goods.[2]

As this quote implies, fair exchange is closely bound up with reciprocity, a defining feature of the cost principle.

What really is the Social Contract? An agreement of the citizen with the government? No, that would mean but the continuation of [Rousseau's] *idea. The social contract is an agreement of man with man; an agreement from which must result what we call society. In this, the notion of commutative justice, first brought forward by the primitive fact of exchange,...is substituted for that of distributive justice.... Translating these words, contract, commutative justice, which are the language of the law, into the language of business, and you have commerce, that is to say, in its highest significance, the act by which man and man declare themselves essentially producers, and abdicate all pretension to govern each other.*

Commutative justice, the reign of contract, the industrial or economic system, such are the different synonyms for the idea which by its accession must do away with the old systems of distributive justice, the reign of law, or in more concrete terms, feudal, governmental or military rule....

....The contract is therefore essentially reciprocal, it imposes no obligation upon the parties, except that which results from their personal promise of reciprocal delivery; it is not subject to any central authority....

We may add that the social contract of which we are now speaking has nothing in common with the contract of association by which...the contracting party gives up a portion of his liberty, and submits to an annoying, often dangerous obligation, in the more or less well-founded hope of a benefit. The social contract is of the nature of a contract of exchange: not only does it leave the party free, it adds to his liberty; not only does it leave him all his goods, it adds to his property; it prescribes no labor; it bears only upon exchange.[3]

Voluntary Cooperation and Free Association. As our previous quote from Proudhon suggests, the cost principle and reciprocity in exchange depend on the observance of two other mutualist principles: voluntary cooperation and free association. As we saw in Part One, the law of value works through competition and the free decision of market actors to shift purchasing power and resources among competing alternatives. It is only through such action that price is able to signal the amount of socially necessary labor embodied in goods and services.

Proudhon advocated the abolition of the centralized territorial state and its replacement by a society organized on the basis of contract and federation. These were necessarily implied in the cost principle. In *The Principle of Federation*, Proudhon used some five-dollar words to describe the cost principle: *synallagmatic* (when the contracting parties undertake reciprocal obligations) and *commutative* (when the exchange involves goods or services of equal value). These requirements can be met only under conditions of equal exchange, in which each participant could freely obtain value for value without being compelled to accept something less. And equal exchange is possible only with free market entry and competition.

Social relations organized on this basis of reciprocity required a federation: a "state" that exercised only those revocable powers that the individual conferred upon it, and only to the extent that the individual expressly consented to them. The individual remained sovereign and possessed of all his inalienable rights, voluntarily relinquishing only those courses of action necessary to obtain the object of the contract into which he freely entered.[4]

More recently, most free market anarchists have adopted the "non-aggression principle" as the basis around which to organize a libertarian society.

Most anarcho-capitalists (with some honorable exceptions) automatically imagine a market society based on non-aggression as having the capitalist business firm as the dominant form of organization. But as we will see later in this chapter, this is no necessary reason for this. Mutualists prefer the workers' and consumers' cooperative, the mutual, the commons, and the voluntary collective to the capitalist corporation as a market actor. And except to the kind of vulgar libertarian who instinctively sees big business as the "good guy," there is no reason not to accept these as valid ways of associating freely.

B. Getting There.

Since Proudhon, mutualism has tended to be identified with a gradualist approach. Gradualism involves, at the same time, two kinds of action: 1) creating the institutional basis for a new society within the existing one; and 2) gradually rolling back the state through external pressure, and supplanting it with our alternative forms of organization, until it is entirely abolished.

Proudhon characterized this approach of devolving state functions to voluntary associations as dissolving the state within the social body. It required two simultaneous courses of action: first, to "*organize...the economic forces*"; and second, to

> dissolve, submerge, and cause to disappear the political or government system in the economic system, by reducing, simplifying, decentralizing and suppressing, one after another, all the wheels of the great machine, which is called Government or the State.[5]

The ultimate goal was that the distinction between "public and private" should become meaningless: "*that the masses who are governed should at the same time govern, and that society should be the same thing as the State, and the people the same thing as the government....*"[6] This meant "*the notion of Contract*" would succeed that of government:

> It is industrial organization that we will put in place of government....
> In place of laws, we will put contracts.—No more laws voted by a majority, or even unanimously; each citizen, each town, each industrial union, makes its own laws.
> In place of political powers, we will put economic forces.[7]

The Wobblies use the phrase "building the structure of the new society within the shell of the old" to describe this process. But Proudhon, anticipating them, used this vivid imagery:

> Beneath the governmental machinery, in the shadow of political institutions, out of the sight of statesmen and priests, society is producing its own organism, slowly and silently; and constructing a new order, the expression of its vitality and autonomy....[8]

Brian A. Dominick, in his brilliant "An Introduction to Dual Power Strategy," described it this way:

> Generally speaking, dual power is the revolutionary organization of society in its pre-insurrectionary form. It is the second power—the second society—operating in the shadows of the dominant establishment. It seeks to become an infrastructure in and of itself, the foundations of an alternative future....
>
> The great task of grassroots dual power is to seek out and create social spaces and fill them with liberatory institutions and relationships. Where there is room for us to act for ourselves, we form institutions conducive not only to catalyzing revolution, but also to the present conditions of a fulfilling life, including economic and political self-management to the greatest degree achievable. We seek not to seize power, but to seize opportunity viz a viz the exercise of our power.
>
> Thus, grassroots dual power is a situation wherein a self-defined community has created for itself a political/economic system which is an operating alternative to the dominant state/capitalist establishment. The dual power consists of alternative institutions which provide for the needs of the community, both material and social, including food, clothing, housing, health care, communication, energy, transportation, educational opportunities and political organization. The dual power is necessarily autonomous from, and competitive with, the dominant system, seeking to encroach upon the latter's domain, and, eventually, to replace it.[9]

Such a project requires self-organization at the grassroots level to build "alternative social infrastructure." It entails things like producers' and consumers' co-ops, LETS systems and mutual banks, syndicalist industrial unions, tenant associations and rent strikes, neighborhood associations, (non-police affiliated) crime-watch and cop-watch programs, voluntary courts for civil arbitration, community-supported agriculture, etc. The "libertarian municipalist" project of devolving local government functions to the neighborhood level and mutualizing social services also falls under this heading—but with services being mutualized rather than municipalized.

Peter Staudenmeier, in a workshop on cooperatives at Ann Arbor, referred to such alternative forms of organization as "social counterpower." Social counterpower takes the concrete forms of "prefigurative politics" and "counterinstitutions."

> *Prefigurative politics is a fancy term that just means living your values today, instead of waiting until "after the revolution"—in fact it means beginning the revolution here and now to the extent possible. This might be called the everyday aspect of social counterpower. And counterinstitutions, of which co-ops are often an example, are the structural aspects of social counter-power.*[10]

Jonathan Simcock, on the *Total Liberty* webpage, described a vision of Evolutionary Anarchism that included

> *...Worker Co-operatives, Housing Co-operatives, self-employment, LETS schemes, Alternative Currencies, Mutual Banking, Credit Unions, tenants committees, Food Co-operatives, Allotments, voluntary organizations, peaceful protest and non-violent direct action and a host of similar activities are the means by which people begin to "behave differently", to go beyond Anarchist theory, and begin to build the elements of a new society.*[11]

Since the time of Proudhon, mutualists have taken a gradualist approach to this process:

> *A social revolution, such as that of '89, which working-class democracy is continuing under our eyes, is a spontaneous transformation that takes place throughout the body politic. It is the substitution of one system for another, a new organism replacing one that is outworn. But this change does not take place in a matter of minutes.... It does not happen at the command of one man who has his own pre-established theory, or at the dictate of some prophet. A truly organic revolution is a product of universal life.... It is an idea that is at first very rudimentary and that germinates like a seed; an idea that is at first in no way remarkable since it is based on popular wisdom, but one*

that...suddenly grows in a most unexpected fashion and fills the world with its institution.[12]

Compare this to Landauer's deservedly famous description:

The State is a condition, a certain relationship among human beings, a mode of behavior, we destroy it by contracting other relationships, by behaving differently toward one and other...We are the State and continue to be the State until we have created the institutions that form a real community....[13]

In concrete terms, the working class was organizing the new society

Partly [through] the principle of association, through which all over Europe they are preparing to organize legal workers' companies to compete with bourgeois concerns, and partly [through] the more general and more widespread principle of MUTUALISM, through which working-class Democracy, putting a premium on solidarity and groups, is preparing the way for the political and economic reconstruction of society.[14]

Tucker had his own image of the process. According to James J. Martin, Tucker suggested this "*remedial action*":

That in any given city a sizeable number of anarchists begin a parallel economy within the structure of that around them, attempting to include in their ranks representatives of all trades and professions. Here they might carry on their production and distribution on the cost principle, basing their credit and exchange system upon a mutual bank of their own which would issue a non-interest bearing currency to the members of the group "for the conduct of their commerce," and aid the disposal of their steadily increasing capital in beginning new enterprises. It was Tucker's belief that such a system would prosper within the shell of the old and draw increasing attention and participation from other members of the urban population, gradually turning the whole city into a "great hive of Anarchistic workers."[15]

Gradualism is often falsely identified as "reformist" by revolutionary anarchists. That is not, in most cases, an accurate assessment. Indeed, the very distinction between "reformism" and revolutionary anarchism is in many ways an artificial one. The term "reformist," in strict accuracy, should apply only to those whose end goal is something short of abolition of the state and the class system it upholds. In the nineteenth century, there were various schools of abolitionism, differing on the means by which they intended to abolish slavery and the time scale over which they envisioned accomplishing this. But they were all abolitionists in the sense that they would have been satisfied with no stopping place short of an end to all slavery. A "reformist," strictly speaking, would have been someone who intended to alter slavery to make it more humane, while leaving its exploitative essence intact.

The distinction between reform and revolution is mainly one of emphasis. For example, most revolutionary Marxists agree with Engels that much of the groundwork of socialism will be built within capitalism, until no further progressive development is possible. Only at that point will the transformation of "quantity into quality" take place, and the new society burst out of the older shell that constrains it. And even those who believe the transition from capitalism to socialism can be largely managed peacefully probably recognize that some disruption will occur at the time of the final rupture.

The same is true of anarchists. For example, Brian Dominick rejects the tendency to identify "revolution" solely with the period of insurrection. At least as important, as part of the overall process of revolution, is the years before the final insurrection:

> *The creation and existence of this second power marks the first stage of revolution, that during which there exist two social systems struggling for the support of the people; one for their blind, uncritical allegiance; the second for their active, conscious participation.*[16]

Indeed, the primary process of "revolution" is building the kind of society we want here and now. The insurrection becomes necessary only when, and to the extent that, the state attempts to hinder or halt our revolutionary process of construction.

> *Aside from revolutionary upheaval, the very formation of a dual power system in the present is in fact one of the aims of the dual power strategy—we seek to create a situation of dual power by building alternative political, economic and other social institutions, to fulfill the needs of our communities in an essentially self-sufficient manner. Independence from the state and capital are primary goals of dual power, as is interdependence among community members. The dual power situation, in its pre-insurrectionary status, is also known as "alternative social infrastructure."*

> *And, again, while a post-insurrectionary society which has generally surpassed the contradictions indicated by the term "dual power" is the eventual goal of this strategy, the creation of alternative social infrastructure is a desirable end in itself. Since we have no way of predicting the insurrection, it is important for our own peace of mind and empowerment as activists that we create situations in the present which reflect the principles of our eventual visions. We must make for ourselves now the kinds of institutions and relationships, to the greatest extent possible, on which we'll base further activism. We should liberate space, for us and future generations, in the shadow of the dominant system, not only from which to build a new society, but within which to live freer and more peaceful lives today.*[17]

In other words, mutualism means building the kind of society we want here and now, based on grass-roots organization for voluntary cooperation and mutual aid—instead of waiting for the revolution. A character in Ken MacLeod's *The Star Fraction* gave a description of socialism that might have come from a mutualist:

> ...*what we always meant by socialism wasn't something you forced on people, it was people organizing themselves as they pleased into co-ops, collectives, communes, unions.... And if socialism really is better, more efficient than capitalism, then it can bloody well <u>compete</u> with capitalism. So we decided, forget all the statist s**t and the violence: the best place for socialism is the closest to a free market you can get!*[18]

Rothbard used to quote with approval Leonard Read's claim that, if he had a magic button that would instantly eliminate the government, he would push it without hesitation. But it should be obvious that, regardless of whether or not one recognizes the validity of gradualism, the state will not in fact be abolished overnight. And even if we had a "magic button" that would magically cause all the officials, weapons and buildings of the state to disappear, what would be the result? If the majority of the public still had a statist mindset, and if there were no alternative libertarian institutions in place to take over the functions of the state, an even more authoritarian state would quickly fill the vacuum. As Benjamin Tucker argued,

> *If government should be abruptly and entirely abolished to-morrow, there would probably ensue a series of physical conflicts about land and many other things, ending in reaction and a revival of the old tyranny.*

He called instead for the gradual abolition of government, "*beginning with the downfall of the money and land monopolies and extending thence into one field after another,...accompanied by such a constant acquisition and steady spreading of social truth*," that the public would at last be prepared to accept the final stage of replacing government with free contract even in the area of police protection.[19]

In practice, regardless of semantic arguments over reformism versus revolution, most anarchists agree that our final goal is the abolition of the state, that it is unlikely to happen overnight, and that in the meantime we should do what we can to build a new society starting where we are now. We are therefore faced with the task of pushing the given system in the direction we want, and pushing until we reach our ultimate goal of abolishing the state altogether. That means, to recapitulate: 1) educational work; 2) building counter-institutions; and

3) pressuring the state from outside to retreat from society and scale back its activities.

Our emphasis should be on building this society as much as possible without seeking direct confrontation with the authority of the state. But I am not a political pacifist in the sense of ruling out such confrontation in principle. No matter how industriously we work "within the shell of the old" society, at some point we will have to break out of the shell. At that point either the state will initiate force in order to abort the new society, or it will be so demoralized as to collapse quickly under its own weight, like the Leninist regimes in 1989-91. But either way, the final transition will probably be abrupt and dramatic, rather messy, and will almost certainly involve at least some violence.

On the revolutionary question, I think we should have two guiding principles. The first was formulated by Ed Stamm in his statement on the anti-WTO protests of December 1999: *"any revolutionary activity must have massive popular support."*[20] This will occur of itself if our educational and organizing efforts are successful. It will never be accomplished by vanguardism or "propaganda of the deed." Second, it should not be attempted until we have built as much as we can within the existing structure. The birth pangs do not take place until the gestation is completed. There are some aspects of a stateless society—for example complete workers' control of industry, or land ownership based only on occupancy and use—which cannot be fully accomplished short of final destruction of the present system of power. But we should achieve everything we can short of this before we begin the final push.

But why would the ruling classes allow even a piecemeal rollback of the state apparatus? Why would they not prefer repression to even a partial loss of privilege? The answer is that they will use open, large-scale repression only as a last resort. (Even if we are in the opening phase of such a repression in the aftermath of 9-11, the state will likely keep it low-key and sporadic as long as possible). Such repression is unlikely to succeed beyond the short-term, and could well result in a total loss of power under extremely bloody circumstances. Ruling classes are often willing to make short-term bargains to preserve their long-term power. Even though the ruling elites took the initiative in creating the New Deal welfare state, for example, they did so only as a necessary evil, to prevent the far greater evil of public insurrection. And of course, we cannot underestimate the human failings of denial and shortsightedness, the desire to postpone the inevitable a long as possible. Ruling classes are as prone as anyone else to the "boiled frog syndrome."

Many anarchists oppose in principle such use of the political process for anarchist ends. It is unethical, they say, for anarchists to participate in the political process. Voting entails selecting a representative to exercise coercive force in our name; and appealing to such representatives for action is in effect a recognition of their legitimacy. This is a view shared by many varieties of anarchists. At the left end of the spectrum, anarcho-syndicalists prefer to ignore the state; hence the Wobblies' split with De Leon and the elimination of the "political clause" from the IWW Preamble. Many voluntaryists and anarcho-capitalists (Wendy McElroy, for instance, and the late Samuel Edward Konkin of the Movement of the Libertarian Left) also take this position. Joe Peacott, an individualist anarchist who still embraces the anti-capitalist legacy of that, likewise considers state action morally illegitimate. The only acceptable course is to withdraw all consent and legitimacy from the state, until "the last one out turns off the lights."

The problem with this line of argument is that the state is an instrument of exploitation by a ruling class. And exploiters cannot, as a group, be ethically "educated" into abandoning exploitation, because they have a very rational self-interest in continuing it. Coleman McCarthy can conduct "peace studies" classes, and quote Tolstoy and "the Rabbi Christ" till he's blue in the face, but it isn't likely to persuade a majority of the ruling class that they'd be better off working for a living.

If most ordinary people simply withdraw consent and abandon the political process altogether, the ruling class will just drop the pretense of popular control and resort to open repression. So long as they control the state apparatus, a small minority of dupes from the producing classes, along with well-paid police and military jackboots, will enable them to control the populace through terror. A majority of Italian workers may have supported the factory occupations of 1920, but that didn't stop the blackshirts, paid with capitalist money, from restoring the bosses' control.

In *For Community*, a pamphlet on Gustav Landauer, Larry Gambone argued that it was no longer possible merely to act outside the state framework while treating it as irrelevant. To do so entailed the risk that "you might end up like the folks at Waco." An "anti-political movement to dismantle the state" was necessary.[22]

At some point, before the final dissolution of the state, its mechanism must be seized and it must be formally liquidated.

Even the anarcho-capitalist Murray Rothbard was realistic about the need for the state to play a role in liquidating itself, under some circumstances. This was equally true of his thought at both ends of his long intellectual career. In 1970, at the height of his and Karl Hess' strategic alliance with the New Left, Rothbard was quite receptive to the idea of nationalizing nominally "private" state capitalist industry as a prelude to placing it under syndicalist ownership of worker-homesteaders, issuing pro-rata shares to taxpayers, or some other unspecified procedure.[23]

In 1992, during the paleolibertarian association with Lew Rockwell and the Mises Institute that occupied his last years, he made a similar proposal in the context of post-communist "privatization": post-communist regimes should liquidate state property by returning it to its legitimate owners when possible, or when this was impossible (most of the time in the industrial sector) by transferring ownership to worker-homesteaders. Rothbard was undismayed at complaints that he was proposing to act through the state, and therefore advocating state action. *"In a deep sense, getting rid of the socialist state requires that state to perform one final, swift, glorious act of self-immolation, after which it vanishes from the scene."*[24]

But I'm not calling for "anarchist politicians" to run for office and exercise political power, like those who served in the Catalonian Generalitat. Our involvement in politics should take the form of pressure groups and lobbying, to subject the state to as much pressure as possible from the outside.

A gradualist approach to dismantling and replacing the state and replacing it with new forms of social organization does not mean that we equally welcome any particular reduction in state activity, regardless of its place in the overall strategy of the ruling class. The order in which the state is rolled back is just as important as rolling it back at all.

We must assess the strategic situation and act accordingly. Statism does not exist for its own sake. The state is a means to an end: exploitation. The state is the means by which privileged classes live off the wealth of others. The state and the parties that control it will reflect the interests of those privileged classes. Therefore, any policy proposal coming from the state apparatus and the mainstream political parties, regardless of how convincingly it co-opts libertarian rhetoric, will be intended to serve the interests of some faction of the ruling class, in some way enabling them to live off the labor of the producing classes.

What we call "capitalism" is not even a rough approximation of a free market. It has been a fundamentally statist system of power since its beginnings in the late Middle Ages. From the beginning, it has allowed elements of the market to exist in its interstices, but only to the extent that they served the class interests represented by the state. What market elements have existed under the state capitalism of the past six hundred years or so have been selectively co-opted, distorted, and incorporated into a larger structural framework of statism.

The existing system is a class system, depending on the state for its survival. The policy of the ruling class, as a big picture, combines authoritarian and libertarian aspects, mixing elements of liberty into the overall authoritarian structure when they suit the overall purpose. It stands to reason, therefore, that we cannot evaluate each particular policy in terms of whether it reduces or increases the power of the state in regard to its limited purview alone, without regard to how it serves the overall agenda of power and exploitation. As Chief Justice John Marshall argued, the state's forebearance and inaction reflect its positive interests just as much as do its actions. The state permits greater or lesser latitude in different areas, but only in accordance with an overall strategy aimed at benefiting the interests of the ruling class.

The central function of the state is to enable some people to live at others' expense, through coercion. And both major parties are state capitalist to their very core. So it stands to reason that, in a system defined by its state capitalist nature, every particular facet of tax or regulatory policy is aimed at furthering the interests of the state capitalist elites who enrich themselves by political means. And any particular reduction in taxes or regulations promoted by either party is intended, in the greater context of the state's policy as a whole, to further state capitalist interests.

To say that any particular tax reduction should be welcomed as a victory, outside the context of what it means in the state capitalists' overall strategy, is like the Romans welcoming the withdrawal of Hannibal's center at Cannae as "a step in the right direction," the first step in a general Punic withdrawal from Italy.

I do not advocate the extension of the state in any area of life, even temporarily or for tactical reasons—no exceptions. And I will not be satisfied short of the final goal of eliminating the state altogether. But given the fact that we agree that incrementalism is a viable strategy, it makes a great deal of difference in what order we dismantle the state. Since all its functions are aimed, directly or indirectly, at furthering the political extraction of profits, it stands to reason that the most central, structural supports of subsidy and privilege on which state capitalism depends should be the first to go; those that make it marginally more bearable for the lower classes should be the last to go.

Benjamin Tucker was firmly in favor of this approach. He believed that the staged abolition of government should follow the order least likely to produce dislocation or injustice to labor. Given that abolition of the state meant its gradual dissolution in the economic organism, "[t]*he question before us is not...what measures and means of interference we are justified in instituting, but which ones of those already existing we should first lop off.*"[25] For example, he referred with approval to Proudhon's warning that abolishing the tariff before the money monopoly would be "*a cruel and disastrous policy,*" throwing out of work those employed in protected industry "*without the benefit of the insatiable demand for labor which a competitive money system would create.*"[26]

More recently, Roderick Long makes a similar point in remarks on a gradualist strategy of abolishing the state. In the case of deregulation, he presents the case of a corporation with a government-enforced monopoly that is, at the same time, subject to price controls. The question facing the would-be dismantler of the state is whether to abolish the monopoly and price controls at the same time, and if not, which to abolish first. If they are abolished simultaneously, the newly "deregulated" corporation will be in the position of charging monopoly profits until sufficient time has elapsed for competitors to enter the market and undercut its price. This is an injustice to consumers. Long concludes that the most just alternative is to "*Remove the monopoly privilege now, and the price controls later.*"

> *But is it ethical to continue imposing price controls on what is now a private company, one competitor among others? Perhaps it is. Consider the fact that Amalgamated Widgets' privileged position in the marketplace is the result neither of it own efforts nor of mere chance; rather, it is the result of systematic aggression by government in its favor. It might be argued, then, that a temporary cap on the company's prices could be justified in order to prevent it from taking undue advantage of a position it gained through unjust violence against the innocent.*[27]

This principle is subject to much broader application. Most mutualist and individualist anarchists agree that the main purpose of the state's activities has been to serve the exploitative interests of the ruling class. Most also agree that "bleeding heart" policies like the welfare state have served primarily to moderate (at general taxpayer expense) the most destabilizing results of unequal exchange. The overall effect is to rob the vast majority of the working population, through unequal exchange in the consumer and labor markets, of much of their labor product, and then to spend a small portion of that ill-gotten gain to guarantee a minimum subsistence to those elements of the underclass most likely to cause a ruckus. (Of course, even in the case of the underclass, what they receive in welfare payments is probably not enough to offset what they have lost through the state's policies of reducing the bargaining power of labor and raising the threshold of subsistence).

Arguably, therefore, the plutocracy, as the primary beneficiary of the state's coercion, has no legitimate moral objection to being the last class to stop paying taxes as the state is dismantled. And it likewise has no legitimate moral objection if the working class is the last, in that transition process, to lose the benefits of state action.

A specific policy proposal must be evaluated, not only in terms of its intrinsic libertarianism but, in the context of the overall system of power, how it promotes or hinders the class interests that predominate in that system. We must, as Chris Sciabarra put it in his description of Marx's dialectical method, *"grasp the nature of a part by viewing it systemically— that is, as an extension of the system within which it is embedded."*[28] Individual parts receive their character from the whole of which they are a part.

Arthur Silber, working from Sciabarra's principle of contextual libertarianism, explains the approach quite well:

> ....*there are two basic methods of thinking that we can often see in the way people approach any given issue. One is what we might call a contextual approach: people who use this method look at any particular issue in the overall context in which it arises, or the system in which it is embedded....*
>
> *The other fundamental approach is to focus on the basic principles involved, but with scant (or no) attention paid to the overall context in which the principles are being analyzed. In this manner, this approach treats principles like Plato's Forms....*
>
> ....*[M]any libertarians espouse this "atomist" view of society. For them, it is as if the society in which one lives is completely irrelevant to an analysis of any problem at all. For them, all one must understand are the fundamental political principles involved. For them, that is the entirety of the discussion....*
>
> *And thus, as another example, the alliance between libertarians who use an approach like mine to liberals with regard to the war on terrorism. We tend to focus on the complex systemic issues involved, on the corporate statism, on the unlikely success of any effort to "plan" the development of other countries. Many pro-war libertarians focus only on our right of self-defense, and on our need to destroy our enemies—without considering the system in which those principles will be applied, the nature of the players involved, and how that system itself may render all such efforts unsuccessful, and will likely hasten the growth of an even more destructive and powerful central government here in the United States.....*
>
> *To sum up, then: we can see two very different methods of approaching any problem. We have a method which focuses on contextual, systemic concerns, and always keeps those issues in mind when analyzing any problem and proposing solutions to it. And we also have a method which focuses almost exclusively on principles, but employs principles in the manner of Plato's Forms, unconnected and unmoored to a specific context or culture. As I said,*

my solution is to employ both methods, separately and together, constantly going back and forth—and to endeavor never to forget either.[29]

The enemy of the state must start with a strategic picture of his own. It is not enough to oppose any and all statism, as such, without any conception of how particular examples of statism fit into the overall system of power. Each concrete example of statism must be grasped in its relation to the system of power as a whole, and the way in which the nature of the part is characterized by the whole to which it belongs. That is, we must examine the ways in which it functions together with other elements of the system, both coercive and market, to promote the interests of the class controlling the state.

In forming this strategic picture, we must use class analysis to identify the key interests and groups at the heart of the system of power. As Sciabarra points out, at first glance Rothbard's view of the state might seem to superficially resemble interest group liberalism: although the state is the organized political means, it serves the exploitative interests of whatever collection of political factions happen to seize control of it at any given time. This picture of how the state works does not require any organic relation between the various interest groups controlling the state at any time, or between them and the state. The state might be controlled by a disparate array of interest groups, ranging from licensed professionals, rent-seeking corporations, family farmers, regulated utilities, and labor unions; the only thing they might have in common is the fact that they happen to be currently the best at weaseling their way into the state.

What Roderick Long calls "statocratic" class theory (a class theory that emphasizes the state component of the ruling class at the expense of its plutocratic elements) tends toward this kind of understanding. A good example is the class theory of Adam Smith and his followers:

> *By its nature..., a powerful state attracts special interests who will try to direct its activities, and whichever achieves the most sway...will constitute a ruling class.*[30]

Long pointed to David Friedman as an even more extreme example of this tendency:

> *It seems more reasonable to suppose that there is no ruling class, that we are ruled, rather, by a myriad of quarrelling gangs, constantly engaged in stealing from each other to the great impoverishment of their own members as well as the rest of us.*[31]

But on closer inspection, Rothbard did not see the state as being controlled by a random collection of interest groups. Rather, it was controlled by

> *a primary group that has achieved a position of structural hegemony, a group central to class consolidation and crisis in contemporary political economy. Rothbard's approach to this problem is, in fact, highly dialectical in its comprehension of the historical, political, economic, and social dynamics of class.*[32]

And as we saw in Chapter Four, this "structural hegemony" did not arise in the twentieth or even the late nineteenth century; it was built into capitalism ever since the landed classes and merchant oligarchs created it by a revolution from above, five hundred years ago.

The state is not a neutral, free-standing force that is colonized fortuitously by random assortments of economic interests. It is by nature the *instrument* of the ruling class—or, as the Marxists say, its executive committee. In some class societies, like the bureaucratic collectivist societies of the old Soviet bloc, some portion of the state apparatus itself is the ruling class. In state capitalist societies like the United States, the ruling class is the plutocracy (along with subordinate New Class elements). This is not in any way to assert that economic exploitation or class domination can arise outside of the state; only that the ruling class is the active party that acts through the state. C. Wright Mills, in rejecting the term "ruling class," said that it implied an economic class that held political power. That's right on target.

Not all reductions in state power are equally important, and it could be disastrous to dismantle state functions in the wrong order. The main purpose of every state activity, directly or indirectly, is to benefit the ruling class. The central or structural functions of the state are the subsidies and privileges by which the concentration of wealth and the power to exploit are maintained. The so-called "progressive" functions of the state (despite Arthur Schlesinger's fantasies to the contrary) are created by the ruling class, acting through the government as their executive committee, to stabilize capitalism and clean up their own mess.

Therefore it is essential that the state should be dismantled in sequence, starting with the structural foundations of corporate power and privilege; after a genuine market is allowed to destroy the concentration of power and polarization of wealth, and remove the boot of exploitation from the neck of labor, the superfluous welfare state can next be dismantled. This should not be confused with the social-democratic "anarchism" of Noam Chomsky. I do not advocate a long-term strengthening of the state to break up "private concentrations of power." Capitalist power could not survive without the state. The only issue is what state functions to dismantle first.

The answer, then, is active engagement to dismantle the interventionist state, without which exploitation would be impossible—and to dismantle it in accordance with a strategic plan that identifies the class nature of the present system and an explains how each specific reduction of state activity furthers our own vision of a successor society. This process of dismantling can be accomplished only through broad-based, ad hoc coalitions, formed on an issue-by-issue basis. A good example is the ACLU-NRA alliance against Janet Reno's police state. The congressional opposition to the Reichstag Enabling Act (er, USA Patriot Act) of 2001 and Ashcroft's subsequent agenda includes elements as disparate as Paul Wellstone and Bob Barr.

Keith Preston argues that a viable anti-state movement will have to get beyond obsession with right and left.

> *An entirely new ideological paradigm needs to be developed. One that rejects the traditionalism and economic elitism of the Right and the statism of the Left. One that draws on the best and most enduring elements of classical liberalism, libertarian socialism and classical anarchism but adapts these to contemporary circumstances within a uniquely American cultural framework that appeals to the best within our libertarian and revolutionary traditions. Political and economic decentralization should be our revolutionary battle cry....*
>
> *The original principles of classical anarchism—elimination of the authoritarian state, control of economies of scale by cooperative partnerships of producers, individualism, genuine liberation of outcast groups, resistance to war and imperialism, decentralization, voluntary association, intellectual and cultural freedom, mutual aid and voluntary cooperation—remain as relevant as ever in today's world.*[33]

As David de Leon paraphrased Karl Hess, remarking on libertarians and decentralists of the Left,

> *We should not disregard the perennial flowering of such criticisms of power and idealistic demands for a personal politics of individual fulfillment simply because...the petals appear to be red and black instead of red white and blue.*[34]

And vice versa! The whole of De Leon's wonderful book, *The American as Anarchist* is an homage to the indigenous, genuinely American radical tradition, elements of which are found in libertarian and decentralist movements of both left and right, that finds the Gadsden flag a more appealing symbol than the Red-and-Black. One of the best and most promising attempts at appealing to this indigenous populist tradition was the People's Bicentennial Commission, particularly its small book *Common Sense II*.[35]

We must also remember that "solidarity" is not something we reserve for our ideological clones. Solidarity is not some kind of special favor, but something we are ethically bound to. We must show solidarity for any victim of injustice, when they are in the right, regardless of their overall position. If more of the left had expressed outrage over Ruby Ridge and Waco, it might have been the beginning of a coalition of right and left libertarians against the police state.

But there is a whole cottage industry of obsessive anti-rightists devoted to preventing such cooperation. The attitude of such people toward the libertarian and populist right, it seems, is "I agree with what you say, but I'll fight to the death to stop you from saying it."

There is, among libertarians of both left and right, a tendency to let largely aesthetic considerations stand in the way of cooperation. This is true equally of the libertarian socialists who automatically react with hostility to market anarchists, and of (for example) the right-libertarians who went ballistic over Michael Badnarik's friendly overtures to Green Party presidential candidate David Cobb.[36] In my own polemical career, I have been simultaneously flamed as a "worthless commie looter" in anarcho-capitalist circles, and as a "goose-stepping, Rand-worshipping racist Nazi" in anarchist venues of the Starbucks-vandalizing circle-A variety, for expressing essentially the same ideas.

Roderick Long defines libertarianism as *"any political position that advocates a radical redistribution of power from the coercive state to voluntary associations of free individuals,"*[37] and divides libertarians into socialist, capitalist, and populist camps. In the nineteenth century, "it was fairly common for libertarians in different traditions to recognize a commonality of heritage and concern," a tendency largely lost in the twentieth century.[38] He spends the rest of the article describing the one-sided ideological perspective of each of the three libertarian camps, and calling for dialogue between them to correct these deficiencies.

One reason for the closer affinity between the libertarian traditions in the nineteenth century, perhaps, was that free market liberalism was still closer to its early radical roots. And a much larger segment of the free market movement still regarded itself, at the same time, as part of the working class movement. That Tucker, Labadie, Lum, and the rest of the *Liberty* circle fall into this category, goes without saying. The same goes for the Georgists. Even Herbert Spencer, who at times sounded like a modern-day vulgar apologist for capitalism, was a disciple of Thomas Hodgskin with decidedly squishy ideas on land and credit. The end of this commonality may have been hastened, as Shawn Wilbur has suggested, by the split in the anarchist movement between native American individualists and immigrant collectivists, symbolized by the polemical war between Tucker and Johann Most. In the aftermath of this split, the imported anarchism of Bakunin and Kropotkin became the anarchist mainstream, and the marginalized individualism of the *Liberty* group abandoned its socialist roots and fell under the sway of the capitalist Right.

In building alternative forms of organization, as in rolling back the state, we should remember that our progress doesn't depend on converting a majority of people to anarchism or finding people who agree with us on all issues. We just have to appeal to the values we share with them on particular issues. And we don't have to segregate ourselves into an ideologically pure, separatist movement of "real" anarchists and wait for the other 99 44/100% of society to come around. Progress isn't all or nothing. As Larry Gambone argued in "An Anarchist Strategy Discussion,"

> *...a mass (populist) orientation requires that one search for all the various beliefs and activities that are of a general libertarian and social nature found among ordinary people. These would consist of any form of decentralism, direct democracy, regionalism, opposition to government and regulation, all forms of voluntary association, free exchange and mutual aid.*[39]

In other words, we must approach people where they are, and make our agenda relevant to the things that concern them.[40]

Anarchists belong to countless social and political organizations in which they are a decided minority. We can act within these groups to promote a libertarian agenda. That means making common cause with movements that are not anarchist per se, but aim nonetheless at pushing society in a freer and less exploitative direction. Some may be nominally on the right, like home-schoolers and gun rights people. But the divide between populism and elitism, or between libertarianism and authoritarianism, is a lot more important than the fetishism of left and right. To quote Gambone again, in *What is Anarchism?*

> *The future of anarchism, if there is one, will at best, involve a few thousand people, as individuals or small groups, in larger libertarian-decentralist organizations. (Some will choose to work alone, spreading the anarchist message through writings and publications.) It is imperative that such*

people, so few in number, yet with potential influence, should know what they are talking and writing about.[41]

People who call themselves "anarchists" are probably not even one in a thousand, and may never be. But names aren't important; substance is. Huey Long said that if fascism ever came to America, it would be in the name of "100% Americanism." If anarchy ever comes, it will probably be in the name of "decentralism," "participatory democracy," or "economic justice."

In considering issues of coalition politics, we should also bear in mind that a post-state, post-capitalist society is unlikely to be organized on *anyone's* ideological template. As an example of the latter, Rothbard assumed a stateless society organized around a consensus on the "libertarian law code." Sciabarra rightly criticized Rothbard's totalizing impulse to step outside history and imagine a society organized around the "*totally ahistorical axiom of nonaggression*"—with little regard for how it would emerge from existing society.[42]

The downfall of the present corporate state, almost certainly, will not occur as the result of any single organization or ideology. No mutualist Bolsheviks will storm the Winter Palace of state capitalism and new model society on the basis of the cost principle and voluntary association.

When the existing corporate state falls, it will be a result of two factors. One will be the internal crises of state capitalism itself, and the fact that it is unsustainable. At some point, the demand for inputs like transportation and energy, and government spending to externalize operating costs and make capital artificially profitable, will exceed the ability of the system to provide. The other factor will be pressure from outside; and this pressure is likely to come from a host of movements whose only common denominator is dislike of the centralized state and corporate capitalism.

The most likely outcome is a panarchy in which a wide range of local social and economic systems coexist (at least for a time) with islands of territory under the control of the old state's armed forces, would-be regional successor states, etc.[43] Local communities are likely to experiment with ideologies ranging from syndicalism, mutualism, and Georgism, to racialism and theocracy.

Individualist anarchists, mutualists, and other market socialists, although we belong to a larger free market community and share an affinity with anarcho-capitalists on some issues, must not make the mistake of allowing them to define the strategic picture for us. We must especially avoid the danger of accepting their aesthetic or cultural preferences, like mistakenly identifying the "market" with stereotypically "capitalist" entities like corporations. A voluntary producer cooperative, commune, or mutual aid society is a free market institution. A corporation functioning within the state capitalist system is emphatically not.

If anything, the form of genuinely private property formed by mutualizing openly state-owned property is probably closer to the spirit of a free market than the nominally private corporation whose operating expenses and capital accumulation are subsidized by the state, whose output is guaranteed a market by the state, and which is protected from price competition by the state.

As mentioned above, a recent overture to the Green Party by Libertarian presidential candidate Badnarik produced howls of outrage from some mainstream libertarians. But the Green program of combined nationalization and decentralization is not obviously more "statist" than the version of "free market" privatization advocated by Milton Friedman and Jeffrey Sachs. If anything, it would probably be easier to get to the final goal of a society based on voluntary relations by the route of nationalization and subsequent mutualist devolution, than by the standard vulgar libertarian formula.

One plank in the Green platform commonly selected for special outrage among libertarians is the call for single-payer national health insurance—than which, apparently, nothing could be less libertarian. But, stopping to think about it, what industry is more statist than nominally "private sector" hospitals, staffed by physicians who profit from the "professional" licensing monopoly, dispensing "standards of care" mandated by licensing boards and medical schools under the influence of Big Pharma, prescribing drugs that were developed at taxpayer expense and are under the protection of patent monopolies, and funded largely by Medicare and Medicaid?

This is not to suggest that nationalization and a single payer system, even as preludes to decentralization and cooperative control, are a good thing. I don't think so. The point is simply that a joint free market libertarian-Green project of nationalizing the hospitals and then decentralizing them to mutualist ownership by the patients is no more obviously "un-libertarian" than the standard Rx from Uncle Milty of libertarian action, in cooperation with some giant global corporation, to "privatize" (on quite favorable terms, needless to say) government facilities created from the sweat of working taxpayers. There is at least as much room for cooperation with libertarian socialists of the Green type as there is for cooperation with the usual corporate "good guys" of vulgar libertarianism.

Murray Rothbard, writing in 1969, was quite receptive to Galbraith's proposal to nationalize corporations that got more than 75% of their revenue from government. Indeed, why stop there? *"Fifty percent seems to be a reasonable cutoff point on whether an organization is largely public or largely private."*[44] And once we accept this principle, basing the statist nature of a corporation on the percentage of its revenue that comes from state funds seems somewhat arbitrary. How much of the nominally "private" revenue it receives from taxpayers is artificially inflated by a state-enforced monopoly position? How much of its profit margin derives from paying workers less than they would in a free labor market? The typical Fortune 500 corporation (about as "private" as a feudal landlord) is enmeshed in a network of privilege and coercion of which outright grants of money from the state may be only a minor part.

Our end goal is a society in which all transactions and associations are voluntary. A society of voluntary collectives or cooperatives is at least as much a free market society, in this regard, as one in which all goods and services we consume are produced by Global MegaCorp or the like. Indeed, it is much likelier that the former kinds of organization could survive in a free market society than the latter. And in getting there, we should remember that a voluntary collective is much more legitimate as a free market institution than a "private" corporation that gets most of its profits from the state. The issue is a practical one of how to get there, and we must not allow habitual apologists for Global MegaCorp to determine our loyalties and preferences for us.

In a society where the very structure of the corporate economy is statist to the core, nationalization is by no means the obvious antithesis of a free market reform; as Rothbard saw thirty years ago, it may be a strategic step toward free market reform. If the targets, as integral parts of a statist system, are legitimate, and if the intended stopping point is a society based on voluntary association and exchange, then the issue is one of prudence, not of principle.

In all this talk of a "political" strategy to roll back the state, we must remember that it is only secondary. We are forced to pursue it only because the state actively interferes with our primary activity—what the Wobblies call "building the structure of the new society within the shell of the old." Until the final crisis of statism, in which the state's attempted repression leads to a final rupture with the old system, there's a lot we can do to within the existing society to build a new kind of social order.

And of course, educational work is a key part of this construction process.

> *A major aspect of developing subjective change among people involves reaching out to the population existing outside the dual power, in the throes of the dominant system. For this reason, any dual power community must maintain its own media. Propaganda involves public critique and ideological dismantlement of the dominant social notions and institutions, as well as promotion of revolutionary alternatives. That is, the propagandist's twofold goal includes destroying the perceived legitimacy of mainstream thought and structure, plus advertisement of the benefits of membership in the dual power community.*[45]

Educational work should, if you'll forgive the cliché, start with people where they are and build from there. We must focus on those aspects of the present system that people find most unpleasant or galling in their daily lives, show the role the state's intervention in the market plays in creating those ills, and provide living examples of how those ills can be overcome by different ways of doing things based on voluntary cooperation.

We may also find, in simultaneously building alternative social organizations, and pressuring the state to roll back, that there is a powerful synergy between these two tracks. It is not necessary to pursue one at the expense of the other; our success in one will often strengthen our position in the other struggle.

Whenever it is strategically appropriate, we should coordinate the political program with the non-political program of alternative institution-building. The social movement can be used to mobilize support for the political agenda and to put pressure on the state to retreat strategically. The political movement can provide political cover for the social movement and make mass repression less feasible.

Even when it is imprudent for the social movement to resort to large-scale illegality, it can act as a "shadow government" to publicly challenge every action taken by the state (much like the shadow system of soviets and workers' committees before the October Revolution). Even though such "shadow institutions" may be unable to implement their policies in the face of official opposition, that fact in itself is an opportunity to demand, "Why are you using government coercion to stop us from controlling our own schools, community, etc.?" (This can be especially effective in pointing out the hypocrisy of the Republicans' bogus "populism," with their appeals to decentralism and local control). The objective is to keep the state constantly off-balance, and force it to defend its every move in the court of public opinion.

A good example of this is local attempts to organize against landlords. So long as the state is bound in legal principle to enforce property rights of landlords, any victory won by squatters will be only short-term and local, without permanent results of any significance. But the other side of the coin is that squatters are indigent and homeless people with very little to lose—after all, some people reportedly commit some minor crime around first frost every year just to get three hots and a cot until spring. If every vacant or abandoned housing unit in a city is occupied by the homeless, they will at least have shelter in the short term until they are forcibly removed. And the political constraints against large-scale brutality (if the squatters restrict themselves to non-violent tactics and know how to use the press to advantage) are likely to be insurmountable. In the meantime, the squatters' movement performs a major educative and propaganda service, develops political consciousness among urban residents, draws public attention and sympathy against the predatory character of landlordism, and—most importantly—keeps the state and landlords perpetually on the defensive.

Even within the existing legal framework, tenant unions strengthen the hand of occupiers against absentee owners and reduce landlords' ability to exact rent by monopolizing property. Karl Hess and David Morris, in *Neighborhood Power*, referred to tenant strikes which led to the legal expropriation of the landlords. In some cities, the laws regulating collective bargaining between tenants and landlords required tenants to put their rent into an escrow account during a strike. Some slumlords were eventually forced into bankruptcy by rent strikes, and were then bought out with their tenants' escrow money![46] The legal branches of the movement, like tenant unions and neighborhood assemblies, can also be used to apply pressure and political cover for squatters. The squatters' and tenants' movements can escalate and mutually reinforce pressure on the state.

In pressuring the state to withdraw from society, as well as in the use of political pressure to defend our counter-organization from repression, modern technology has opened up exhilarating possibilities for forms of opposition based on large, decentralized associations of affinity groups.

The potential for such organization is alarming to those in power. A 1998 Rand study by David Ronfeldt (*The Zapatists "Social Netwar" in Mexico*, MR-994-A) warned that internet-based coalitions like the pro-Zapatista support network could overwhelm the government with popular demands and render society "ungovernable."[47] This study was written before the anti-WTO demonstrations, so the post-Seattle movement doubtless has our overlords in a panic. Such forms of organization make it possible to throw together ad hoc coalitions of thousands of affinity groups in a very short time; they can organize mass demonstrations, issue press releases in thousands of venues, and "swarm" the government and press with mass mailings, phone calls and emails. This resembles the "excess of democracy" and "crisis of governability" that Samuel Huntington warned of in the 1970s—but an order of magnitude beyond anything he could have imagined then.

The availability of such decentralized methods of struggle should reinforce our understanding of the need for ad hoc, issue-based alliances with people of many ideological orientations. In the case of dismantling corporate state capitalism, our allies include not only anarchists and the libertarian left, but populists, constitutionalists, and libertarians on the right. Only a minority will agree with us on everything. But on many issues, we are likely to find a majority willing to cooperate on each particular issue. And so long as our strategic vision is not subject to compromise, our victories on particular issues will strengthen our strategic position for pursuing other issues.

One important feature of this decentralized form of organization is its resilience in the face of state attempts at repression or decapitation. We should strengthen this feature by organizing redundant telephone, email and Ham radio trees within each radical organization, with similar redundant communications links between organizations, to warn the entire resistance movement as quickly as possible in the event of mass arrests.

And when the state attempts piecemeal arrests of a few leaders, one organization at a time, we should spread the news not only to "radical" groups and alternative press outlets as quickly as possible, but to the mainstream press. If you belong to an organization whose activists have been targeted in this way, spread the news far and wide on the net and in print, with contact information for the officials involved. If you find such a message in your in-box, take the time to call or email the jackboots with your complaints, and pass the news on to others. For example, I I once called a local police force to protest the illegal arrest of some demonstrators, after I saw a call for action in an email newsgroup; I was told by the harried operator that they were so overwhelmed that they had to refer callers to the state police. Every crackdown on an organization should result in the state being swarmed with phone calls, and the press being saturated with letters and press releases.

The same approach is equally useful in the policy arena. Every attempt at new corporate welfare, or regulatory augmentations of state capitalism, should result in similar swarming of Congressional offices. Every attempt at a piece-meal increase in the police state, many of which we have seen since 9-11, is the state's attempt to test the water of public opinion by putting its foot in. Every such attempt should result in a severe scalding, with phones ringing off the hook and overloaded email in-boxes.

Before we conclude this chapter (and the book), we should briefly consider a few practical issues of mutualist praxis that don't obviously fall under any of our headings so far. As we saw in Chapter Five, examining Bill Orton's analysis on competing theories of property rights, no such theory is self-evidently correct in principle. Free market, libertarian communist, syndicalism, and other kinds of collectivist anarchists must learn to coexist in peace and mutual respect today, in our fight against the corporate state, and tomorrow, in the panarchy that is likely to succeed it. We must learn mutual respect for the legitimacy of our historical claims to the "libertarian" label.

At the same time, as Orton argued, there are prudential reasons for preferring one property rights system over another, insofar as it promotes other commonly accepted ethical values. As mutualists, our preferences in this regard differ from those of both collectivists and capitalists. Unlike capitalists, we prefer occupancy-based property in land and cooperative forms of large-scale production. Unlike collectivists, we prefer market relations between firms to federative relations and planning. We prefer such forms of organization to both the capitalist and collectivist model because they tend to promote social values that, on reflection, capitalists and collectivists may find that they share to some extent.

Mutualists find market competition between individuals and voluntary associations, whenever possible, preferable to unnecessary collectivism.

One of the more ignorant Marxist criticisms of "utopian" and "petty bourgeois" socialism was that it was the reactionary ideology of the artisan and peasant. Instead of building on the progressive achievements of capitalism, which had socialized the production process and laid the foundations for collective control of the economy, it looked backward to a pre-capitalist idyll of petty production. Syndicalists and libertarian communists tend to echo this sentiment: for example, I have heard it numerous times in debates with SPGB members. I suspect, however, that the reason is less technical than aesthetic. Collectivist anarchists generally insist that the collective exists to further the liberty of the sacred individual, and that they have no objection to individual and small group enterprise so long as there is no wage labor. Still, all too often their toleration of such activity carries with it the general air of Ingsoc's distaste for "ownlife."

In fact, Proudhon's writings are full of references to workers' associations and large-scale cooperative production. Proudhon was not ignorant of the requirements of large-scale production and the factory system. But he believed that workers could, if allowed to mobilize capital through large-scale mutual credit systems, organize their own industrial production on a cooperative model. In fact, Proudhon's ideas on association and federation were a major influence on the collectivist anarchism of Bakunin, and on the later French syndicalist movement.

The difference was that Proudhon had no aesthetic affinity for collective forms of production for their own sake.

> ...*mutualism intends men to associate only insofar as this is required by the demands of production, the cheapness of goods, the needs of consumption and the security of the producers themselves, i.e., in those cases where it is not possible for the public to rely on private* [individual] *industry, nor for private industry to accept the responsibilities and risks involved in running the concerns on their own....* [Because the persons concerned] *are acting in accordance with the very nature of things when they associate in this way, they can preserve their liberty without being any the less in an association....*

> *There is undoubtedly a case for association in the large-scale manufacturing, extraction, metallurgical and shipping industries....*[48]

> *The aim of industrial and agricultural cooperatives, including workers' associations where these can usefully be formed, is not to substitute collectivities for individual enterprise.... It is to secure for all small and medium-sized industrial entrepreneurs, as well as for small property owners, the benefit of discovering machines, improvements and processes which would otherwise be beyond the reach of modest firms and fortunes.*[49]

Bakunin ridiculed the Marxists for believing, as demonstrated by their idea of a proletarian dictatorship, that the producing majority could actually control the state in any real sense.

> *What does it mean for the proletariat to be "organized as the ruling class"?... Can it really be that the entire proletariat will stand at the head of the administration?....There are about forty million Germans. Will all forty millions really be members of the government?*[50]

Unfortunately, collectivist anarchism like syndicalism and libertarian communism are prone to the very same problem. A good fictional portrayal of this problem is Ursula LeGuin's novel *The Dispossessed.*[51] In that story, the libertarian communist world of Anarres had fallen under the control of a bureaucratic ruling class. The industrial syndicates and federative planning bodies, over time, inevitably accumulated permanent staffs of planners and experts. Regardless of how nominally democratic those bodies were—being staffed by delegates recallable at will, etc.—in practice the elected members deferred to the expertise of their permanent staffs. The elected syndicates and federations, nominally responsible to the workers, came to function as rubber stamps for the de facto Gosplans. And of course, once the principle of planning is substituted for that of the market, there is no way to avoid such ossification.

Still more unfortunately, we do not have to go to works of fiction to find examples of such managerial degeneration. In a fascinating study of "workers' resistance to work," Michael Seidman described just such a process in the worker-controlled industry of Catalonia. The CNT-UGT gradually adopted a management-like attitude toward the workers toward whom it was formally responsible, and became obsessed with fighting recalcitrance and absenteeism and imposing work-discipline on the labor force in exactly the same way capitalist bosses do. The Technical-Administrative Council of the CNT Building Union, for example, warned that disaster would occur if workers were not "re-educated" to purge them of "bourgeois influences" (apparently preferring leisure to extra work without pay), and work-discipline were not restored. The UGT *told its members not to formulate demands in wartime and urged them to work more.*" Much like the seventeenth-century Puritans, the CNT-UGT found the workers' observance of traditional mid-week religious holidays a major hindrance to "productivity."

> *Faced with sabotage, theft, absenteeism, lateness, fake illness and other forms of working-class resistance to work and workspace, the unions and collectives co-operated to establish strict rules and regulations which equaled* [sic] *or surpassed the controls of capitalist enterprises.*

In some clothing industry collectives, measures adopted included the appointment of a "comrade" to control entrances and exits, and a requirement to accept work assignments and instructions "without comment."[52] It seems Lenin was mistaken: he didn't need to break the workers' councils, after all, to impose his Taylorist ideas on Russian workers.

These developments, both in the fictional world of Anarres and the real world of anarchist Catalonia, reflect what Robert Michels called the "Iron Law of Oligarchy."

> *The technical specialization that inevitably results from all extensive organization renders necessary what is called expert leadership.... Organization implies the tendency toward oligarchy...*
>
> *Every solidly constructed organization...presents a soil eminently favorable for the differentiation of organs and of functions. The more extended and the more ramified the official apparatus of the organization,...the less efficient*

> *becomes the direct control exercised by the rank and file, and the more is this*
> *control replaced by the increasing power of committees.*[53]

Michels was the most famous of a number of sociologists at the turn of the twentieth century, who collectively are sometimes called the "neo-Machiavellians." This group included Vilfredo Pareto, who formulated the theory of circulating elites. Gaetano Mosca argued that in a representative democracy, the public is inevitably relegated to choosing between candidates selected by the ruling elite.

The ideas of the neo-Machiavellians were taken to their gloomiest and most hopeless extreme by Jan Waclaw Machajsky and his disciple Max Nomad, in reaction to the bureaucratic ruling class arising after the Russian revolution. In Nomad's lurid picture, history was a cyclical process. And throughout the process, "*the majority of the human race will always remain the pedestal for the ever changing privileged minorities.*"[54] No matter how many hopeful revolutions the producing classes fought to displace the old elite, no matter how many heady days of freedom were enjoyed in 1917 Petrograd or 1936 Barcelona, the masses were doomed to be ruled (in their name, of course) by a new elite, a Red bureaucracy or party apparat. The labor unions and socialist parties, as Michels had pointed out, were inevitably taken over by a stratum of intellectuals and "professionals" who, if they were successful in using the workers to drive the capitalists out, became the new ruling class.

For Machajsky and Nomad, the problem was inherent in organization. Any representative organization of the working class was destined to become the power base of the intelligentsia.

But things were not as hopeless as they made them out to be. The answer is to minimize reliance on organization itself as much as possible. Part of the problem in Spain was the existence of federal and regional bodies superior to the individual factories. The factory management, although elected by workers, came to identify with the federal bodies rather than the workers to whom they were nominally responsible. Had there been no federal bodies, in which they could meet with their counterparts from other factories to commiserate on the atavism and laziness of "their" workers, the sole source of pressure on them would have come from below—from the workers who could recall them at will.

The free market is made to order for the purpose of avoiding centralized organization and hierarchy. When firms and self-employed individuals deal with each other through market, rather than federal relations, there are no organizations superior to them. Rather than decisions being made by permanent organizations, which will inevitably serve as power bases for managers and "experts," decisions will be made by the invisible hand of the marketplace.

Finally, Marxists and other anti-market socialists are deluded in their belief that the law of value can be superceded by production for "social use." As the Austrians saw, even the actions of solitary individuals are in effect transactions, in which the disutility of labor is exchanged for other utilities. Production can never be undertaken solely with a view to use, without regard to exchange value. The reason goods have value today is that it requires effort or disutility to produce them. With or without formal market exchange, there will still be an implicit exchange involved, labor for consumption, involved in the production process. It implies a judgment, if a tacit one, that the use value of the good is worth the disutility to the worker who produces it. And fairness and unfairness will continue to exist, although concealed (along with the law of value) behind a "collective" planning process. Either the labor entailed in producing the goods consumed by a worker will equal the labor he expends in production, or they will not. If not, somebody is being exploited. The law of value is not simply a description of commodity exchange in a market society; it is a fundamental ethical principle.

Earlier, I wrote that with "honorable exceptions," anarcho-capitalists favor a model of privatization built around the capitalist corporation. Karl Hess was perhaps the first and greatest of these. In 1969 he wrote,

> *Libertarianism is a people's movement and a liberation movement. It seeks the sort of open, non-coercive society in which the people, the living, free distinct people may voluntarily associate, dis-associate, and, as they see fit, participate in the3 decisions affecting their lives. His means a truly free market in everything from ideas to idiosyncrasies. It means people free <u>collectively</u> to organize the resources of their immediate community or individualistically organize them; it means the freedom to have a community-based and supported judiciary when wanted, none where not, or private arbitration services where that is seen as most desirable. The same with police. The same with schools, hospitals, factories, farms, laboratories, parks and pensions. Liberty means the right to shape your own institutions.*[55]

Or as (the lamentably late) Samuel Konkin wrote, "*The Market is the sum of all voluntary human action. If one acts non-coercively, one is part of the Market.*"[56]

Getting into full radical swing, Hess went on in the same article to call for creative thought on revolutionary tactics and goals that would be relevant to poor people, and not just to "the usual suspects." Among the issues to consider was

> —*Worker, share-owner, community roles or rights in productive facilities in terms of libertarian analysis and as specific proposals in a radical and revolutionary context. What, for instance, might happen to General Motors in a liberated society?*[57]

Egad! But isn't General Motors one of the "good guys," an example of the heroic Randian ethic of rugged individualism (snicker)?

More recently, Roderick T. Long wrote a long and carefully reasoned libertarian defense of "public" (as opposed to state) property.[58] And in an article at Antistate.Com last year, Carlton Hobbs defended the traditional idea of the commons as a legitimate form of property in a free market society. By the term "common property," he referred to two different things: first, the joint or collective private property of deliberately formed voluntary associations; and second, "*stateless common property*," to which members of "*a potentially imprecise owning group*" have equal access, "*without any prior formal agreements....*" As examples of the latter, he mentioned forested areas to which the inhabitants of a village had exercised a traditional and non-exclusive right of access for firewood; and a road following a route that has been a public right of way for time out of mind.[59]

Mutualists prefer a method of "privatizing" government functions that places them under social, as opposed to state control. This means decentralizing them to the neighborhood or the smallest local unit, and placing them under the direct control of their clientele. The final stage of this process should see the services funded entirely by voluntary user fees. Larry Gambone refers to the process as "mutualizing" government functions.[60]

This principle of "mutualizing" services was anticipated by Proudhon. Proudhon was ambivalent on the role of the state in establishing mutualism before it "withered away"; at times he proposed action by the existing French state, not only to abolish the legal basis of privilege, but actually to implement mutualist reforms. But although he considered the state necessary to establish public utilities like transportation and communication, and the national bank of exchange, he saw no need "to leave them in the hands of the state once they have been initiated." The only legitimate function of the state was

> *legislating, initiating, creating, beginning, establishing; as little as possible should it be executive....*
>
> *Once a beginning has been made, the machinery established, the state withdraws, leaving the execution of the new task to local authorities and citizens....*[61]

In any case, as we saw above, even an anarcho-capitalist of such impeccable anti-state credentials as Rothbard saw nationalization as a legitimate part of dismantling the state and its "private" adjuncts.

I do not favor an active state role in organizing a new basis of society, even when the ultimate goal is for the state to "wither away." I prefer whatever action the state takes to be part of the immediate process of dismantling itself as quickly as possible. I only wish to point out that the kinds of state action proposed by Proudhon or, say, David Cobb (recall our discussion above) are no different in kind from what Murray Rothbard considered tactically legitimate.

One reason Proudhon preferred mutualizing public services and placing industry under worker control to nationalizing either, was that nationalized firms reproduced the principles of hierarchy and domination inherent in capitalist enterprise. Returning to the example of nationalized tobacco retail outlets, he referred to the "*hierarchical organization of its employees, some of whom are by their salaries made aristocrats as expensive as they are useless, while others, hopeless receivers of petty wages, are kept forever in the position of subalterns.*"[62]

Although anarcho-capitalists tend to take Benjamin Tucker's proposals as forerunners of the kind of capitalist "privatization" they prefer, Tucker's position was by no means that cut and dried. Tucker certainly favored, as do the anarcho-capitalists, the reorganization of all state services on the basis of voluntary cooperation; the state was to be robbed of its ability to force its services on unwilling customers, to tax them for payment, or to prohibit competitors in providing the same services.

At times, however, Tucker used language implying that the state would, while maintaining organizational integrity, lose the character of a state. In regard to protection services, for example, he wrote:

> "But," it will be asked of the Anarchists..., "what shall be done with those individuals who undoubtedly will persist in violating the social law by invading their neighbors?" The Anarchists answer that the abolition of the State will leave in existence a defensive association, resting no longer on a compulsory but on a voluntary basis, which will restrain invaders by any means that may prove necessary.[63]

Protection services would be supplied only to those who desired them, and funded entirely at the cost of voluntary consumers.

Although mutualists do not oppose the creation of competing defense agencies, and certainly would not prohibit them, the likelihood in practice of a number of competing defense firms in a single area is probably exaggerated. The cultural tendency to view defense as a function of community is deeply ingrained, and the habit would probably persist among most people of relying on a common agency, even after membership became voluntary. It would be possible, of course, for dissatisfied customers to attempt to organize competing agencies. But the service approaches so closely to a natural monopoly, between cost of start-up capital and the advantages of size, that it would surely be easier for the dissatisfied to attempt a hostile takeover of the unsatisfactory association. If that association maintained some moral continuity with the old government, say, functioning as a direct democracy with a board of selectmen, this possibility would seem even more obvious to those involved.

At any rate, Tucker was not bound to anything like the anarcho-capitalist idea of "privatized" defense firms. The only requirement was for a government to cease to be such was to stop funding its activities with compulsory taxes: "*....all States, to become non-invasive, must abandon first the primary act of invasion upon which all of them rest,—the collection of taxes by force....*"[64] One plausible scenario is for the old state to lose its coercive character, and become in effect a consumer cooperative owned by the majority of a community who continue to use its services. Smaller competing defense firms might spring up, catering to limited niche markets; and a large minority of the population might prefer not to subscribe to any service, instead relying on informal arrangements with their neighbors and the deterrent effect of an armed populace.

Tucker at times speculated on the functioning of defense associations and agencies in language that suggested their continuity with the state. For example, he repeatedly stressed the preferability of common law procedures like jury trial. In so doing, he expressed an affinity for the old transatlantic Anglo-republican ideal of free juries randomly chosen from the population.[65]

A society organized on these principles would avoid most of the evils we associate with capitalism. Labor would keep most or all of what currently goes into interest, profit and rent. The increased bargaining power of labor would lead, not only to an increased wage, but to much greater control over working conditions.

Without subsidies to centralization and energy consumption, the labor currently wasted on distribution would be unnecessary to maintain the existing standard of living. Production would be on a much smaller, more efficient scale, and closer to home. Population would be dispersed and less mobile, and the extended family and stable local community would be revived.

In addition, the economic cycle would be much less severe in a decentralized economy of production for local use. To see why, let's start at the smallest and most simple level. Imagine a truck farmer who lives next door to a cobbler. The two make an arrangement to exchange shoes for produce. Obviously, the farmer alone can't absorb enough of the cobbler's output to support him; and the cobbler can't eat enough to support the farmer. But the two are at least fairly secure in the knowledge that their future needs for both vegetables and shoes are provided for with a high degree of probability. And they have a fairly predictable market for that portion of their output that is consumed by the other person.

Taking it to the next step, imagine a community of a few dozen people of varying trades, using their own local currency (LETS, mutual banknotes, etc.) to exchange among themselves. Again, because of the limited number of participants, and the high degree of predictability of their future needs (barring any unusual circumstances), it is likely that (so long as each participant produces something needed by most people on a fairly steady basis) each participant will feel secure in his ability to obtain his minimum need of the commodities produced by each of the other participants; and each participant will likewise feel secure in a market for his output, at least to the extent of collective demand for it within the group.

So long as the producers and consumers of different commodities are known to each other in a community, future supply and demand is likely to be relatively stable, and not subject to abrupt or unexpected shocks. So major divergences of supply and demand, and resulting economic crises, are unlikely to occur.

But the further society departs from this decentralist model, and approaches large-scale, anonymous commodity markets serving a wide geographical area, the more unstable and unpredictable markets become.

Some forms of production, by their very nature, require larger and more centralized markets to use certain kinds of productive machinery to full capacity. But in a large portion of cases, the size and instability of markets is a form of irrationality resulting from state policies that externalize the inefficiency costs of large-scale size.

NOTES

1. Pierre Joseph Proudhon, *System of Economical Contradictions or, The Philosophy of Misery*. Translated by Benjamin Tucker (Boston: Benjamin R. Tucker, 1888) 232-3.

2. Pierre Joseph Proudhon, *On the Political Capacity of the Working*

Classes (1865), in *Selected Writings of Proudhon*. Edited by Stewart Edwards. Translated by Elizabeth Fraser (Garden City, N.Y.: Anchor, 1969) 117]

3. Pierre Joseph Proudhon, *General Idea of the Revolution in the Nineteenth Century*. Translated by John Beverly Robinson (New York: Haskell House Publishers, Ltd., 1923, 1969 [1851]) 112-5.

4. Pierre Joseph Proudhon, *The Principle of Federation*. Translated by Richard Vernon (Toronto, Buffalo, London: University of Toronto Press, 1979 [1863]) 37-8.

5. Proudhon, *General Idea of the Revolution* 133.

6. Pierre Joseph Proudhon, *Political Contradictions* (1863-4), in *Selected Writings* 117.

7. Proudhon, *General Idea of the Revolution* 126, 245-6.

8. Ibid. 243.

9. Brian A. Dominick, "An Introduction to Dual Power Strategy," http://www.anarchistcommunitarian.net/articles/theory/bdsdp.shtml Captured Aug. 21, 2004.

10. Peter Staudenmaier, "Anarchism and the Cooperative Ideal," *The Communitarian Anarchist* 1:1.

11. Jonathan Simcock, "Editorial for Current Edition," *Total Liberty* 1:3 (Autumn 1998) http://www.spunk.org/library/pubs/tl/sp001872.html Captured August 22, 2004.

12. Proudhon, *Political Capacity of the Working Class*, in *Selected Writings* 177.

13. Qt. in Larry Gambone, *For Community: The Communitarian Anarchism of Gustav Landauer* (Montreal: Red Lion Press, 2001)

14. Proudhon, *Political Capacity of the Working Class*, in *Selected Writings* 180-1.

15. James J. Martin, *Men Against the State: The Expositors of Individualist Anarchism in America, 1827-1908* (Colorado Springs: Ralph Myles, Publisher, Inc., 1970) 249.

16. Dominick, "Introduction to Dual Power Strategy."

17. Ibid.

18. Ken MacLeod, *The Star Fraction* (published as part of *The Fall Revolution* trilogy) (New York: SFBC, 1995, 2001) 244.

19. Benjamin Tucker, "Protection, and Its Relation to Rent," *Liberty* October 27, 1888, in Benjamin Tucker, *Instead of a Book, By a Man Too Busy to Write One*. Gordon Press facsimile (New York: 1973 [1897]) 329.

20. Ed Stamm. "Anarchists Condemn Anti-WTO Riots," *The Match!* #25 (Spring 2000) 5.

21. I won't get into the ideologically charged and fruitless polemical dispute over whether an anarcho-capitalist can legitimately claim the individualist anarchist label.

22. Gambone, *For Community*.

23. Murray Rothbard, "Confiscation and the Homestead Principle," *The Libertarian Forum* (June 15, 1969) 3.

24. Murray Rothbard, "How and How Not to Desocialize," *The Review of Austrian Economics* 6:1 (1992) 77.

25. Benjamin Tucker, "Voluntary Co-Operation," *Liberty*, May 24, 1890, in Tucker, *Instead of a Book* 104-5.

26. Benjamin Tucker, "State Socialism and Anarchism," in Ibid. 13.

27. Roderick T. Long, "Dismantling Leviathan From Within," Part II: The Process of Reform. *Formulations* 3:1 (Autumn 1995) http://www.libertariannation.org/a/f3ll3.html Captured August 21, 2004.

28. Chris Matthew Sciabarra, *Total Freedom: Toward a Dialectical Libertarianism* (University Park, Penn.: The Pennsylvania State University Press, 2000) 88.

29. Arthur Silber, "In Praise of Contextual Libertarianism," The Light of Reason, November 2, 2003 http://coldfury.com/reason/comments.php?id=P1229_0_1_0_C Captured August 21, 2004.

30. Roderick T. Long, "Toward a Libertarian Theory of Class," *Social Philosophy & Policy* 15:2 (1998) 313.

31. From *The Machinery of Freedom*, qt. in Ibid. 327.

32. Ibid. 287.

33. Keith Preston, "Conservatism is Not Enough: Reclaiming the Legacy of the Anti-State Left," American Revolutionary Vanguard http://www.attackthesystem.com/conservatism.html Captured August 22, 2004.

34. David De Leon, *The American as Anarchist: Reflections on Indigenous Radicalism* (Baltimore and London: The Johns Hopkins University Press, 1978) 131.

35. The People's Bicentennial Commission, *Common Sense II: The Case Against Corporate Tyranny* (New York: Bantam, 1975).

36. Brian Doherty, "Libertarians and Greens: Room for Alliance?" Reason Online Hit & Run, August 2, 2004 http://www.reason.com/hitandrun/006330.shtml Captured August 21, 2004. See especially the comments.

37. Long, "Toward a Libertarian Theory of Class" 304.

38. Ibid. 310.

39. Larry Gambone, "An Anarchist Strategy Discussion," http://www.mutualist.org/id13.html Captured August 22, 2004.

40. See also Larry Gambone, *Sane Anarchy* (Montreal: Red Lion Press, 1995).

41. Gambone. "What is Anarchism?" Total Liberty 1:3 (Autumn 1998) http://www.spunk.org/library/pubs/tl/sp001872.html Captured August 22, 2004.

42. Sciabarra, *Total Freedom* 226.

43. See, for example, "V. Separation of Law and State," in Keith Preston's "Philosophical Anarchism and the Death of Empire" American Revolutionary Vanguard http://www.attackthesystem.com/philo.html Captured August 22, 2004.

44. Rothbard, "Confiscation and the Homestead Principle," 3-4.

45. Dominick, "Introduction to Dual Power Strategy."

46. Karl Hess and David Morris, *Neighborhood Power: The New Localism* (Boston: Beacon Press, 1975) 91-3.

47. David Ronfeldt, *The Zapatists "Social Netwar" in Mexico.* MR-994-A (Santa Monica: Rand, 1998).

48. Proudhon, *The Political Capacity of the Working Classes*, in *Selected Writings* 62.

49. Pierre Joseph Proudhon, *Theory of Property* (1863-4), in *Selected Writings* 63

50. Mikhail Bakunin, "After the Revolution: Marx Debates Bakunin," quoted in Roderick Long, "Toward a Libertarian Theory of Class" 320.

51. Ursula LeGuin, *The Dispossessed* (New York: Harper Paperbacks, 1974).

52. Michael Seidman, "Towards a History of Workers' Resistance to Work: Paris and Barcelona during the French Popular Front and the Spanish Revolution, 1936-38" http://www.geocities.com/CapitolHill/Lobby/2379/seid2.htm Captured August 10, 2001.

53. Robert Michels, *Political Parties.* Translated by Eden Paul and Cedar Paul (New York: The Free Press, 1962) 70-1.

54. Max Nomad, "Karl Marx—Anti-Bourgeois or Neo-Bourgeois?" reproduced at Collective Action Notes http://www.geocities.com/CapitolHill/Lobby/2379/nomad.htm Captured August 10, 2001.

55. Karl Hess, "Where are the Specifics?" *Libertarian Forum* (June 15, 1969) 2.

56. Samuel Edward Konkin, *New Libertarian Manifesto* Second Edition (Koman Publishing, 1983). Unauthorized edition online at Anarchist Library http://flag.blackened.net/daver/anarchism/nlm/nlm1.html Captured February 16, 2002. Chapter I.

57. Karl Hess, "Where Are the Specifics?" 2.

58. Roderick Long, "A Plea for Public Property" *Formulations* 5:3 (Spring 1998) http://www.libertariannation.org/a/f53l1.html Captured August 21, 2004.

59. Carlton Hobbs, "Common Property in Free Market Anarchism: A Missing Link" http://www.anti-state.com/article.php?article_id=362 Captured August 21, 2004.

60. See his website, Mutualize!, at http://www.geocities.com/vcmtalk/mutualize

61. Proudhon, *The Principle of Federation* 45-7.

62. Proudhon, *System of Economical Contradictions* 232-3.

63. Benjamin Tucker, "Relation of the State to the Individual," *Liberty*, November 15, 1890, in Tucker, *Instead of a Book* 25.

64. Benjamin Tucker, "More Questions," *Liberty*, January 28, 1888, in Tucker, *Instead of a Book* 62.

65. Benjamin Tucker, "Tu-Whit! Tu-Whoo!" *Liberty*, October 24, 1885, in Tucker, *Instead of a Book* 55-8; "Rights and Duties Under Anarchy," *Liberty*, December 31, 1887, in Ibid. 58-60; "More Questions," in Ibid. 61-2; "Property Under Anarchism," Liberty, July 12, 1890, in Ibid. 312.

Bibliography

Walter Adams and James Brock. *The Bigness Complex* (New York: Pantheon Books, 1986).

Radley Balko. "Third World Workers Need Western Jobs" May 6, 2004. http://www.foxnews.com/story/0,2933,119125,00.html Captured May 6, 2004.

Paul Baran and Paul Sweezy. *Monopoly Capitalism: An Essay in the American Economic and Social Order.* (New York: Monthly Review Press, 1966).

Morton S. Baratz. "Corporate Giants and the Power Structure," in Richard Gillam, ed., *Power in Postwar America* (Boston: Little, Brown, and Co., 1971).

Thomas Barnett. "The Pentagon's New Map." *Esquire* March 2003. Reproduced online at http://www.thomaspmbarnett.com/published/pentagonsnewmap.htm Captured July 26, 2004.

Walden Bello. *Development Debacle: The World Bank in the Philippines* (San Francisco: Institute for Food & Development Policy, 1982).

Bello. "Structural Adjustment Programs: 'Success' for Whom?" in Mander and Goldsmith, eds., *The Case Against the Global Economy.*

Hilaire Belloc. *The Servile State* (Indianapolis: Liberty Classics, 1913, 1977).

Eugen von Böhm-Bawerk. *Capital and Interest: A Critical History of Economical Theory.* Translated by William Smart (New York: Brentanno's, 1922).

Böhm-Bawerk. *Karl Marx and the Close of His System.* (published in a single volume with Rudolf Hilferding, *Bohm-Bawerk's Criticism of Marx*) (New York: Augustus M. Kelley, 1945).

Böhm-Bawerk. *The Positive Theory of Capital.* Translated by William Smart (London and N.Y.: MacMillan and Co., 1891).

Böhm-Bawerk. "The Ultimate Standard of Value," Annals of the American Academy of Political and Social Science, September, 1894a, in Shorter Classics of Eugen von Böhm Bawerk, South Holland, Ill.: 1962.

William Blum. *Killing Hope: U.S. Military and CIA Interventions Since World War II* (Monroe, Maine: Common Courage Press, 1995).

Harry C. Boyte. *The Backyard Revolution: Understanding the New Citizen Movement* (Philadelphia: Temple University Press, 1980).

Harry Braverman. *Labor and Monopoly Capital: The Degradation of Work in the Twentieth Century.* 25th Anniversary Edition (New York: Monthly Review Press, 1998).

"Brazil proposes creation of G-20 free trade area," December 13, 2003 www.chinaview.cn 2003-12-13 11:13:39 http://news.xinhuanet. com/english/2003-12/13/content_1229296.htm Captured December 14, 2003.

James Buchanan. *Cost and Choice: An Inquiry in Economic Theory. Collected Works,* vol. 6 (Indianapolis: Liberty Fund, 1999).

Nikolai Bukharin. *Imperialism and World Economy.* (International Publishers, 1929 (written 1915-1917). Available online at http://www. marxists.org/archive/bukharin/works/1917/imperial/   Captured October 28, 2003.

Thomas Carothers. "The Reagan Years: The 1980s." In Abraham F. Lowenthal, ed., *Exporting Democracy* (Johns Hopkins, 1991).

Art Carden. "Sweatshops" Mises Economics Blog, May 6, 2004. http://www.mises.org/blog/archives/001956.asp#more Captured May 6, 2004.

Don Carney. "Dwayne's World," at http://www.motherjones.com/ mother_jones/JA95/carney.html Captured April 15, 2001.

Alfonso Chardy. "Reagan Aides and the 'Secret' Government" *Miami Herald* 5 July 1987, at http://www.totse.com/en/conspiracy/the_new_ world_order/scrtgovt.html Captured April 15, 2001.

G. K. Chesterton. *A Short History of England* (New York: John Lane Company, 1917).

Roy A. Childs, "Big Business and the Rise of American Statism." In Joan Kennedy Taylor, ed., *Liberty Against Power: Essays by Roy A. Childs* (San Francisco: Fox & Wilkes, 1994) 15-48.

Noam Chomsky. *Class Warfare: Interviews with David Barsamian* (Monroe, Maine: Common Courage Press, 1996)

Chomsky. *Deterring Democracy* (New York: Hill and Wang, 1991, 1992).

Chomsky. "How Free is the Free Market?" *Resurgence* no. 173. http://www.oneworld.org/second_opinion/chomsky.html Captured April 15, 2001.

Chomsky. *Keeping the Rabble in Line* (Monroe, Maine: Common Courage Press, 1994).

Chomsky. *World Orders Old and New* (New York: Columbia University Press, 1998).

Citizens for Tax Justice. "GOP Leaders Distill Essence of Tax Plan: Surprise! It's Corporate Welfare" 14 September 1999, at http://www.ctj.org/pdf/corp0999.pdf Captured April 15, 2001.

Alexander Cockburn. "The Jackboot State: The War Came Home and We're Losing It" *Counterpunch* 10 May 2000, at http://www.counterpunch.org/jackboot.html Captured April 15, 2001.

Sean Corrigan. "You Can't Say That!" August 6, 2002. http://www.lewrockwell.com/corrigan/corrigan13.html Captured August 7, 2001.

David De Leon. *The American as Anarchist: Reflections on Indigenous Radicalism* (Baltimore and London: The Johns Hopkins University Press, 1978).

"Development as Enclosure: The Establishment of the Global Economy." *The Ecologist* 22:4 (July/August 1992), pp. 131-147.

Maurice Dobb. Introduction to Marx's *A Contribution to the Critique of Political Economy* (New York: International Publishers, 1970).

Dobb. *Political Economy and Capitalism: Some Essays in Economic Tradition*. Second revised edition (London: Routledge & Kegan Paul Ltd, 1940, 1960).

Dobb. *Studies in the Development of Capitalism* (London: Routledge and Kegan Paul, Ltd, 1963).

Dobb. *Theories of Value and Distribution Since Adam Smith: Ideology and Economic Theory* (Cambridge: Cambridge University Press, 1973).

Brian Doherty. "Libertarians and Greens: Room for Alliance?" Reason Online Hit & Run, August 2, 2004 http://www.reason.com/hitandrun/006330.shtml Captured August 21, 2004.

G. William Domhoff. *The Higher Circles: The Governing Class in America* (New York: Vintage Books, 1971).

Domhoff. *The Power Elite and the State: How Policy is Made in America* (New York: Aldine de Gruyter, 1990).

Domhoff. *Who Rules America?* (Englewood Cliffs, N.J.: Prentice-Hall, 1967).

Domhoff. *Who Rules America Now?* (Prospect Heights, Ill.: Waveland Press, 1983, 1997).

Brian A. Dominick. "An Introduction to Dual Power Strategy." Anarchist Communitarian Network http://www.anarchistcommunitarian.net/articles/theory/bdsdp.shtml Captured August 21, 2004.

William M. Dugger. *Corporate Hegemony* (Westport, Conn.: Greenwood Press, 1989).

David W. Eakins. "Business Planners and America's Postwar Expansion," in Horowitz, ed., *Corporations and the Cold War* pp. 143-172.

"Editorial" *International Socialist Review* XIII, No. 6 (December 1912).

A. Roger Ekirch. *Bound for America: The Transportation of British Convicts to the Colonies, 1718-1775* (Oxford, UK: Clarendon Paperbacks, 1987).

Gary Elkin. "Benjamin Tucker—Anarchist or Capitalist?" http://flag. blackened.net/daver/anarchism/tucker/an_or_cap.html (captured October 28, 2003).

Elkin. "Mutual Banking." The original that Elkin posted on the web is down, but it was reproduced in a post at alt.philosophy.debate, Jul 12, 1999. http://groups.google.com/groups?q=%22gary+elkin%22+% 22mutual+banking%22&hl=en&lr=&ie=UTF-8&oe=UTF-8&safe=o ff&selm=37897B99.1B1E%40columbia-center.org&rnum=7&filter=0 Captured July 15, 2004.

William Yandell Elliot, ed. *The Political Economy of American Foreign Policy.* (Holt, Rinehart & Winston, 1955).

Friedrich Engels. *Anti-Dühring.* Marx and Engels, *Collected Works* vol. 25 (New York: International Publishers, 1987).

Engels, "Preface to the First German Edition of *The Poverty of Philosophy* by Karl Marx" (1884), Marx and Engels, *Collected Works* vol. 26 (New York: International Publishers, 1990).

Thomas Ferguson. *Golden Rule: The Investment Theory of Party Competition and the Logic of Money-Driven Political Systems* (Chicago: University of Chicago Press, 1995).

Thomas Ferguson and Joel Rogers. *Right Turn* (New York: Hill and Wang, 1986).

Norman Fischer. "The Ontology of Abstract Labor" *Review of Radical Political Economics* 14:2 (Summer 1982).

Bruce Franklin. "Debt Peonage: The Highest Form of Imperialism?" *Monthly Review* 33:10 (March 1982) pp. 15-31.

Edgar Z. Friedenberg. *The Disposal of Liberty and Other Industrial Wastes* (Garden City, N.Y.: Anchor, 1976).

Thomas Friedman. "What the World Needs Now," *New York Times,* March 28, 1999.

John Kenneth Galbraith. *The New Industrial State* (New York: Signet Books, 1967).

Larry Gambone. "An Anarchist Strategy Discussion." Originally uploaded in three parts on the file page of vcmdiscussion at

YahooGroups. Reproduced with permission at Mutualist.Org. http://www.mutualist.org/id13.html Captured August 22, 2004.

Gambone. *For Community: the Communitarian Anarchism of Gustav Landauer* (Montreal: Red Lion Press, 2001).

Gambone. *Sane Anarchy* (Montreal: Red Lion Press, 1995).

Gambone. "What is Anarchism?" Total Liberty 1:3 (Autumn 1998).

Roger Garrison. "Professor Rothbard and the Theory of Interest," in Walter Block and Llewellyn H. Rockwell, Jr., eds. *Man, Economy and Liberty: Essays in Honor of Murray N. Rothbard* (Auburn, Ala.: Auburn University Press, 1988).

Henry George. *Progress and Poverty* (New York: Walter J. Black, 1942).

Jean Gimpel, *The Medieval Machine: The Industrial Revolution of the Middle Ages* (New York: Penguin, 1977

Robert Goldstein. *Political Repression in America: 1870 to the Present* (Cambridge, New York: Schenkman Publishing Co', 1978).

Paul Goodman. *Compulsory Miseducation* and *The Community of Scholars.* (New York: Vintage Books, 1962; 1964).

Goodman. *People or Personnel* and *Like a Conquered Province.* (New York: Vintage Books, 1963; 1965).

David M. Gordon. *Fat and Mean: The Corporate Squeeze of Working Americans and the Myth of Management Downsizing* (New York: The Free Press, 1996).

Mark J. Green, et al., eds. *The Closed Enterprise System.* Ralph Nader's Study Group Report on Antitrust Enforcement. (New York: Grossman Publishers, 1972).

William B. Greene. *Mutual Banking* (New York: Gordon Press, 1849, 1974).

Daniel Gross. "Socialism, American Style: Why American CEOs covet a massive European-style social-welfare state" *Slate* Aug. 1, 2003 http://slate.msn.com/id/2086511/ (captured October 23, 2003).

Benjamin Grove. "Gibbons Backs Drug Monopoly Bill," *Las Vegas Sun* 18 February 2000, at http://www.ahc.umn.edu/NewsAlert/Feb00/022100NewsAlert/44500.htm Captured April 15, 2001.

Jurgen Habermas. *Legitimation Crisis.* Translated by Thomas McCarthy (United Kingdom: Polity Press, 1973, 1976).

J.L. and Barbara Hammond. *The Town Labourer* (1760-1832) 2 vols. (London: Longmans, Green & Co., 1917)

The Hammonds. *The Village Labourer* (1760-1832) (London: Longmans, Green & Co., 1913).

Michael Harrington. *Socialism* (New York: Bantam, 1970, 1972).

Harrington. *The Twilight of Capitalism* (Simon and Schuster, 1976).

"Head to Head: M6 Toll Road," BBC News, December 9, 2003 http://news.bbc.co.uk/2/hi/uk_news/3303629.stm Captured December 10, 2003.

Hearings on Global and Innovation-Based Competition. FTC, 29 November 1995, at http://www.ftc.gov/opp/gc112195.pdf Captured April 15, 2001.

Eduard Heimann. "Franz Oppenheimer's Economic Ideas" *Social Research* (New York) 11:1 (Feb. 1944) pp. 27-39.

Richard Heinberg. *The Party's Over: Oil, War, and the Fate of Industrial Societies* (New Society Publishers, March 2003).

Karl Hess. "Letter From Washington: Where Are The Specifics?" *The Libertarian Forum* (June 15, 1969). In Henry J. Silverman, ed., *American Radical Thought: The Libertarian Tradition* (Lexington, Mass.: D.C. Heath and Co., 1970).

Karl Hess and David Morris. *Neighborhood Power: The New Localism* (Boston: Beacon Press, 1975).

Rudolf Hilferding. *Finance Capital.* Edited and translated by Tom Bottomore (London and Boston: Routledge & Kegan Paul, 1910 (1981)).

Christopher Hill. *The Century of Revolution: 1603-1714* (New York: W.W. Norton & Co., Inc., 1961).

Hill. *Reformation to the Industrial Revolution, 1530-1780.* Volume II of the Pelican Economic History of Great Britain (London: Penguin Books, 1967).

Carlton Hobbs. "Common Property in Free Market Anarchism: A Missing Link" http://www.anti-state.com/article.php?article_id=362 Captured August 21, 2004.

E. J. Hobsbawm and George Rudé, *Captain Swing* (New York: W.W. Norton & Company Inc., 1968).

J. A. Hobson. *Imperialism: A Study* (London: Archibald Constable & Co. Ltd, 1905).

Thomas Hodgskin. *Labour Defended Against the Claims of Capital* (New York: Augustus M. Kelley, 1963 [1825]).

Hodgskin. *The Natural and Artificial Right of Property Contrasted* (London: B. Steil, 1832).

Michael A. Hoffman II. *They Were White and They Were Slaves: The Untold History of the Enslavement of Whites in Early America.* Fourth edition (Dresden, N.Y.: Wiswell Ruffin House, 1992).

Richard Hofstadter. *America at 1750: A Social Portrait* (New York: Vintage Books, 1973).

David Horowitz, ed. *Corporations and the Cold War.* (New York and London: Monthly Review Press, 1969).

E. K. Hunt. "Marx's Concept of Human Nature and the Labor Theory of Value" *Review of Radical Political Economics* 14:2 (Summer 1982).

Samuel P. Huntington, Michael J. Crozier, Joji Watanuki. *The Crisis of Democracy*. Report on the Governability of Democracies to the Trilateral Commission: Triangle Paper 8 (New York: New York University Press, 1975).

Ivan Illich. *Deschooling Society* (1970). Online version at http://philosophy.la.psu.edu/illich/deschool/intro.html (captured October 28, 2003).

Illich. *Tools for Conviviality* (New York: Harper & Row, 1973).

Joshua King Ingalls. *Social Wealth: The Sole Factors and Exact Ratios in Its Acquirement and Apportionment* (N.Y.: Social Science Publishing Co., 1885).

Bernie Jackson. "The Fine Art of Conservation," *The Freeman: Ideas on Liberty* 48:10 (October 1998).

William Stanley Jevons. *The Theory of Political Economy*. Fifth edition (Kelley & Millman, Inc., 1957).

Leif Johansen. "Labor Theory of Value and Marginal Utilities," *Economics of Planning* 3:2 (September 1963), pp. 89-103.

Johansen. "Marxism and Mathematical Economics," *Monthly Review* January 1963, pp. 505-13.

Warren Johnson. *Muddling Toward Frugality* (San Francisco: Sierra Club Books, 1978).

John Judis. "Bare Minimum: Goodies for the Rich Hidden in Wage Bill," *The New Republic* 28 October 1996, in *Project Censored Yearbook 1997* (New York: Seven Stories Press, 1997).

Karl Kautsky. "Imperialism and the War" *International Socialist Review* November 1914. Trans. by William E. Bohn. http://www.marxists.org/archive/kautsky/works/1910s/war.html captured September 23, 2002.

Frank Kofsky. *Harry Truman and the War Scare of 1948* (New York: St. Martin's Press, 1993).

Gabriel Kolko. *Confronting the Third World: United States Foreign Policy 1945-1980* (New York: Pantheon Books, 1988).

Kolko. *The Roots of American Foreign Policy: An Analysis of Power and Purpose* (Boston: Beacon Press, 1969).

Kolko. *The Triumph of Conservatism: A Reinterpretation of American History 1900-1916* (New York: The Free Press of Glencoe, 1963).

Samuel Edward Konkin III. "Bad Capitalists Good Entrepreneurs." Message 3758 (July 24, 2000), LeftLibertarian@Yahoogroups.com. http://groups.yahoo.com/group/LeftLibertarian/message/3758 Captured August 4, 2004.

Konkin. *New Libertarian Manifesto.* Second Edition (Koman Publishing, 1983). Online at Anarchist Library http://flag.blackened. net/daver/anarchism/nlm/nlm1.html Captured February 16, 2002.

David Korten. *When Corporations Rule the World* (West Hartford, Conn.: Kumarian Press, 1995; San Francisco, Calif.: Berrett-Koehler Publishers, Inc., 1995).

Peter Kropotkin. *Mutual Aid: A Factor of Evolution* (New York: Doubleday, Page & Co., 1909).

Peter Kropotkin. *The State: Its Historic Role.* http://dwardmac.pitzer. edu/Anarchist_Archives/kropotkin/state/state_toc.html   Captured November 12, 2003.

Robert Rives La Monte. "You and Your Vote" *International Socialist Review* XIII, No. 2 (August 1912).

Christopher Layne and Benjamin Shwartz. "American Hegemony Without an Enemy," *Foreign Policy* 92 (Fall 1993).

William Lazonick. *Business Organization and the Myth of the Market Economy* (New York: Cambridge University Press, 1991).

Lazonick. *Competitive Advantage on the Shop Floor* (New York: Cambridge University Press, 1990).

Ursula LeGuin. *The Dispossessed* (New York: Harper Paperbacks, 1974).

Vladimir Lenin. *Imperialism: The Highest Stage of Capitalism* (New York: International Publishers, 1916, 1939).

Chris Lewis. "Public Assets, Private Profits," *Multinational Monitor,* in *Project Censored Yearbook 1994* (New York: Seven Stories Press, 1994).

James G. Leyburn. *The Scotch-Irish: A Social History* (Chapel Hill, N.C.: University of North Carolina Press, 1962).

Leonard P. Liggio. "American Foreign Policy and National Security Management," in Rothbard and Radosh, eds.

Roderick T. Long. "Dismantling Leviathan From Within" Part I: Can We? Should We? *Formulations* 2:4 (Summer 1995) http://www. libertariannation.org/a/f2413.html Part II: The Process of Reform. *Formulations* 3:1 (Autumn 1995) http://www.libertariannation.org/ a/f3113.html Part III: Is Libertarian Political Action Self-Defeating? *Formulations* 3:2 (Winter 1995-6) http://www.libertariannation.org/a/ f3211.html Part IV: The Sons of Brutus. *Formulations* 3:3 (Spring 1996) http://www.libertariannation.org/a/f3313.html Captured August 21, 2004.

Long. "A Plea for Public Property" *Formulations* 5:3 (Spring 1998) http://www.libertariannation.org/a/f5311.html Captured August 21, 2004.

Long. "Toward a Libertarian Theory of Class" *Social Philosophy & Policy* 15:2 (1998).

Oliver MacDonagh. "The Anti-Imperialism of Free Trade," *The Economic History Review* Second Series, vol. XIV, No. 3 (1962) pp. 489-501.

Tibor Machan. "On Airports and Individual Rights," *The Freeman: Ideas on Liberty* (February 1999).

Ken MacLeod. *The Star Fraction* (published as part of *The Fall Revolution* trilogy) (New York: SFBC, 1995, 2001).

Jerry Mander and Edward Goldsmith, eds. *The Case Against the Global Economy (and for a turn toward the local)* (San Francisco: Sierra Club Books, 1996).

Steven A. Marglin. "What Do Bosses Do? The Origins and Functions of Hierarchy in Capitalist Production—Part I" *Review of Radical Political Economics* 6:2 (Summer 1974).

Alfred Marshall. *Principles of Economics: An Introductory Volume.* Eighth edition (New York: The MacMillan Company, 1948).

James J. Martin. *Men Against the State: The Expositors of Individualist Anarchism in America, 1827-1908* (Colorado Springs: Ralph Myles, Publisher, Inc., 1970).

Karl Marx. "Afterword to Second German Edition of Capital" (1873). Marx and Engels, *Collected Works,* vol. 35 (New York: International Publishers, 1996) pp. 12-20.

Marx. *Capital* vol. 1. First English edition (1887). Marx and Engels, *Collected Works,* vol. 35 (N.Y.: International Publishers, 1996).

Marx. *Capital* vol. 3. Marx and Engels, *Collected Works,* vol. 37 (New York: International Publishers, 1998).

Marx. *A Contribution to the Critique of Political Economy.* Marx and Engels, *Collected Works,* vols. 29-30 (New York: International Publishers, 1987-88).

Marx. *The Economic and Philosophical Manuscripts of 1844.* Marx and Engels, *Collected Works,* vol. 3 (New York: International Publishers, 1975).

Marx. *Grundrisse. Collected Works* vols. 28-29 (New York: International Publishers, 1986-87).

Marx. *The Poverty of Philosophy. Collected Works,* vol. 6 (New York: International Publishers, 1976).

Marx. *Theories of Surplus Value.* Marx and Engels, *Collected Works,* vols. 30-32 (New York: International Publishers, 1988-89).

Marx. *Value, Price and Profit.* Marx and Engels, *Collected Works,* vol. 20 (New York: International Publishers, 1985).

Paul Mattick. "The Economics of War and Peace," *Dissent* 111:4 (Fall 1956).

Mattick. *Marx and Keynes: The Limits of the Mixed Economy* (London: Merlin Press, 1969).

Arno Mayer. *The Persistence of the Old Regime.*

John P. McCarthy. *Hilaire Belloc: Edwardian Radical* (Indianapolis: Liberty Press, 1978).

Ronald L. Meek. *Studies in the Labour Theory of Value.* Second edition (New York and London: Monthly Review Press, 1956).

Seymour Melman. *The Permanent War Economy: American Capitalism in Decline* (New York: Simon and Schuster, 1974).

Melman. *Profits without Production.* (New York: Alfred A. Knopf, 1983).

Carl Menger. *Principles of Economics.* Translated by James Dingwall and Bert F. Hoselitz (Grove City, PA: Libertarian Press, Inc., 1976).

Robert Michels. *Political Parties.* Translated by Eden Paul and Cedar Paul (New York: The Free Press, 1962).

John Stuart Mill. *Principles of Political Economy: with Some of Their Applications to Social Philosophy. Collected Works of John Stuart Mill* vols. II-III (University of Toronto Press, 1965).

C. Wright Mills. *The Power Elite.* (Oxford and New York: Oxford University Press, 2000 (1956).

Ludwig von Mises. *Human Action* (Chicago: Regnery, 1949, 1963, 1966).

David Montgomery. *The Fall of the House of Labor* (New York: Cambridge University Press, 1979).

Montgomery. *Workers' Control in America.* (New York: Cambridge University Press, 1979).

Richard K. Moore. "Escaping the Matrix" *Whole Earth* (Summer 2000), pp. 50-59.

Frank Morales. "U.S. Military Civil Disturbance Planning: The War at Home" *Covert Action Quarterly* 69, Spring-Summer 2000, at http://infowar.net/warathome/warathome.html Captured April 15, 2001.

Gustavus Myers. *History of the Great American Fortunes* (Chicago: C. H. Kerr & Company, 1910).

Gary B. Nash. *Class and Society in Early America* (Englewood Cliffs, N.J.: Prentice-Hall, Inc., 1970).

Charles E. Nathanson. "The Militarization of the American Economy" In Horowitz, ed. *Corporations and the Cold War* pp. 205-235.

Kwame Nkrumah. *Neo-Colonialism: The Last Stage of Imperialism* (New York: International Publishers, 1965).

David Noble. *America by Design: Science, Technology, and the Rise of Corporate Capitalism* (New York: Alfred A. Knopf, 1977).

Noble. *Forces of Production: A Social History of Industrial Automation* (New York: Alfred A. Knopf, 1984).

Albert Jay Nock. *Our Enemy, the State* (Delavan, Wisc.: Hallberg Publishing Corp., 1983).

Max Nomad. "Karl Marx—Anti-Bourgeois or Neo-Bourgeois?" reproduced at Collective Action Notes http://www.geocities.com/CapitolHill/Lobby/2379/nomad.htm Captured August 10, 2001.

Robert Nozick. *Anarchy, State, and Utopia* (U.S.A.: Basic Books, 1974)

James O'Connor. *Accumulation Crisis* (Oxford: Basil Blackwell Ltd, 1984).

O'Connor. *Fiscal Crisis of the State* (New York: St. Martin's Press, 1973).

Franz Oppenheimer. "A Post Mortem on Cambridge Economics" *The American Journal of Economics and Sociology.* Part I, 2:3 (1942/43), pp. 369-76; part II, 2:4 (1943), pp. 533-41; part III, 3:1 (1944), pp. 115-24.

Oppenheimer. *The State.* Translated by John Gitterman (San Francisco: Fox & Wilkes, 1997).

George Orwell. *1984.* Signet Classics reprint (New York: Harcourt Brace Jovanovich, 1949, 1981).

Guy Pauker. *Military Implications of a Possible World Order Crisis in the 1980s.* R-2003-AF (Santa Monica: Rand Corporation, November 1977).

Pauker. *Sources of Instability in Developing Countries.* P-5029 (Santa Monica: Rand Corporation, June 1973).

Cheryl Payer. *The Debt Trap: The International Monetary Fund and the Third World* (New York: Monthly Review Press, 1974).

Martin Khor Kok Peng. *The Uruguay Round and Third World Sovereignty* (Penang, Malaysia: Third World Network, 1990).

The People's Bicentennial Commission. *Common Sense II: The Case Against Corporate Tyranny* (New York: Bantam, 1975).

Michael Perelman. *Classical Political Economy: Primitive Accumulation and the Social Division of Labor* (Totowa, N.J.: Rowman & Allanheld; London: F. Pinter, 1984, c 1983).

John S. Pettingill. "Firearms and the Distribution of Income: A Neo-Classical Model" *Review of Radical Political Economics* 13:2 (Summer 1981) pp. 1-10.

Frances Fox Piven and Richard Cloward. *Regulating the Poor* (New York: Vintage Books, 1971, 1993).

Keith Preston. "Conservatism is Not Enough: Reclaiming the Legacy of the Anti-State Left" American Revolutionary Vanguard http://www.attackthesystem.com/conservatism.html Captured August 22, 2004.

Preston. "Philosophical Anarchism and the Death of Empire" American Revolutionary Vanguard http://www.attackthesystem.com/philo.html Captured August 22, 2004.

Pierre Joseph Proudhon. *General Idea of the Revolution in the Nineteenth Century.* Translated by John Beverly Robinson (New York: Haskell House Publishers, Ltd., 1923, 1969 [1851]).

Proudhon. *The Principle of Federation.* Translated by Richard Vernon (Toronto, Buffalo, London: University of Toronto Press, 1979 [1863]).

Proudhon. *Selected Writings of Proudhon.* Edited by Stewart Edwards. Translated by Elizabeth Fraser (Garden City, N.Y.: Anchor, 1969).

Proudhon. *System of Economical Contradictions or, The Philosophy of Misery.* Translated by Benjamin Tucker (Boston: Benjamin R. Tucker, 1888).

Proudhon. *What is Property?* http://dwardmac.pitzer.edu/Anarchist_Archives/proudhon/ProudhonCW.html Captured October 1, 2001.

Ronald Radosh. "The Myth of the New Deal," in Rothbard and Radosh, eds.

Chakravarthi Raghavan. *Recolonization: GATT, the Uruguay Round & the Third World.* (Penang, Malaysia: Third World Network, 1990).

Jim Redden. "Police State Targets the Left" The Zoh Show: Newsbytes, May 2, 2000. http://www.zohshow.com/News/Newsbytes/tidbits050200b.htm captured March 25, 2001.

Redden. *Snitch Culture: How Citizens are Turned into the Eyes and Ears of the State* (Venice, Calif.: Feral House, 2000).

Patrick Renshaw. *The Wobblies* (Garden City, N.Y.: Anchor Books, 1967).

Diana Reynolds. "The Rise of the National Security State: FEMA and the NSC" *Covert Action Information Bulletin* #33 (Winter 1990). Reproduced by The Public Eye, http://publiceye.org/liberty/fema/Fema_1.htm captured April 15, 2001.

David Ricardo. "Absolute Value and Exchangeable Value (A Rough Draft)." Piero Sraffa, ed. *The Works and Correspondence of David Ricardo* vol. 4 (Cambridge: Cambridge University Press, 1951).

Ricardo. *Principles of Political Economy and Taxation.* Third Edition (London: John Murray, Albemarle Street, 1821). *The Works and Correspondence of David Ricardo,* edited by Piero Sraffa, v. 1 (Cambridge University Press, 1951).

Bruce Rich. "The Cuckoo in the Nest: Fifty Years of Political Meddling by the World Bank." *The Ecologist* 24:1 (January/February 1994), pp. 8-13.

J. B. Robertson. *The Economics of Liberty.* (Minneapolis: Herman Kuehn, 1916).

Eric Roll. *A History of Economic Thought.* Third Edition (Englewood, N.J.: Prentice-Hall, Inc., 1956).

David Ronfeldt. *The Zapatists "Social Netwar" in Mexico.* MR-994-A (Santa Monica: Rand, 1998).

Paul Rosenberg. *The Empire Strikes Back: Police Repression of Protest From Seattle to L.A.* L.A. Independent Media Center 13 August 2000 http://www.r2kphilly.org/pdf/empire-strikes.pdf Captured April 15, 2001.

Murray Rothbard. "The Anatomy of the State" *Rampart Journal of Individualist Thought* 1:2 (Summer 1965). Reprinted by Libertarian Alliance. http://www.libertarian.co.uk/lapubs/socin/socin001.pdf Captured August 4, 2004.

Rothbard. "Confessions of a Right-Wing Liberal," in Henry J. Silverman, ed., *American Radical Thought: The Libertarian Tradition* (Lexington, Mass.: D.C. Heath and Co., 1970).

Rothbard. "Confiscation and the Homestead Principle" *The Libertarian Forum* (June 15, 1969).

Rothbard. "How and How Not to Desocialize," *The Review of Austrian Economics* 6:1 (1992).

Rothbard. *Man, Economy and State: A Treatise on Economic Principles* (Auburn University, Alabama: Ludwig von Mises Institute, 1993).

Rothbard. *Power and Market: Government and the Economy.* (Kansas City: Sheed Andrews and Mcmeel, Inc., 1970, 1977).

Rothbard. "The Student Revolution" *The Libertarian* (soon renamed *The Libertarian Forum*) (May 1, 1969).

Rothbard. "War Collectivism in World War I" in Rothbard and Radosh, eds., pp. 66-110.

Murray Rothbard and Ronald Radosh, eds. *A New History of Leviathan: Essays on the Rise of the American Corporate State* (New York: E.P. Dutton & Co., Inc., 1972).

Kirkpatrick Sale. *Human Scale* (New York: Coward, McCann & Geoghegan, 1980).

John-Baptiste Say. *A Treatise on Political Economy.* Translated by C. R. Prinsep from Fourth French Edition (Philadelphia: John Grigg, 1827).

Arthur Schlesinger, Jr. *The Age of Jackson* (Boston: Houghton-Mifflin, 1946).

Joseph Schumpeter. "Imperialism." *Imperialism, Social Classes: Two Essays by Joseph Schumpeter.* Translated by Heinz Norden. Introduction by Hert Hoselitz. (New York: Meridian Books, 1955).

Schumpeter. *Ten Great Economists From Marx to Keynes* (New York: Oxford University Press, 1965).

Chris Matthew Sciabarra. *Total Freedom: Toward a Dialectical Libertarianism* (University Park, Penn.: The Pennsylvania State University Press, 2000).

Michael Seidman. "Towards a History of Workers' Resistance to Work: Paris and Barcelona during the French Popular Front and the Spanish Revolution, 1936-38" Collective Action Notes http://www.geocities.com/CapitolHill/Lobby/2379/seid2.htm Captured August 10, 2001.

Laurence H. Shoup and William Minter. "Shaping a New World Order: The Council on Foreign Relations' Blueprint for World

Hegemony, 1939-1945" in Holly Sklar, ed., *Trilateralism: The Trilateral Commission and Elite Planning for World Management* (Boston: South End Press, 1980) pp. 135-156.

Arthur Silber. "In Praise of Contextual Libertarianism" The Light of Reason, November 2, 2003 http://coldfury.com/reason/comments.php?id=P1229_0_1_0_C Captured August 21, 2004.

Jonathan Simcock. "Editorial for Current Edition" *Total Liberty* 1:3 (Autumn 1998) http://www.spunk.org/library/pubs/tl/sp001872.html Captured August 22, 2004.

Holly Sklar, ed. *Trilateralism: The Trilateral Commission and Elite Planning for World Management* (Boston: South End Press, 1980).

Martin J. Sklar. *The Corporate Reconstruction of American Capitalism, 1890-1916: The Market, the Law, and Politics* (Cambridge, New York and Melbourne: Cambridge University Press, 1988)

Martin J. Sklar. "Woodrow Wilson and the Political Economy of Modern United States Liberalism." In Rothbard and Radosh, eds., pp. 7-65.

Adam Smith. *An Inquiry Into the Nature and Causes of the Wealth of Nations* (Chicago, London, Toronto: Encyclopedia Britannica, Inc., 1952).

Robert Freeman Smith. "American Foreign Relations, 1920-1942" in Barton J. Bledstein, ed., *Towards a New Past: Dissenting Essays in American History* (New York: Vintage Books, 1967, 1968).

Sam Smith. "How You Became the Enemy (Progressive Review, 1997). http://www.mega.nu:8080/ampp/enemy.html captured April 15, 2001.

Ed Stamm. "Anarchists Condemn Anti-WTO Riots" *The Match!* Spring 2000.

Peter Staudenmaier. "Anarchism and the Cooperative Ideal" *The Communitarian Anarchist* vol. 1 no. 1.

L. S. Stavrianos. *The Promise of the Coming Dark Age* (San Francisco: W. H. Freeman and Co., 1976).

Barry Stein. *Size, Efficiency, and Community Enterprise* (Cambridge, Mass.: Center for Community Economic Development, 1974).

Robert Stinnett. *Day of Deceit: The Truth About FDR and Pearl Harbor* (New York: Free Press, 1999).

Joseph R. Stromberg. "Experimental Economics, Indeed." Ludwig von Mises Institute, January 6, 2004. http://www.mises.org/fullstory.asp?control=1409 captured July 25, 2004.

Stromberg. "Free Trade, Mercantilism and Empire." February 28, 2000. At http://www.antiwar.com/stromberg/s022800.html (captured October 28, 2003).

Stromberg. *The Political Economy of Liberal Corporatism*. (Center for Libertarian Studies, 1977). Available online at http://www.blancmange. net/tmh/articles/stromberg.html (captured Sept. 23, 2002).

Stromberg. "The Role of State Monopoly Capitalism in the American Empire" *Journal of Libertarian Studies* Volume 15, no. 3 (Summer 2001), pp. 57-93. Available online at http://www.mises.org/journals/jls/15_ 3/15_3_3.pdf (captured October 28, 2003).

Dirk J. Struik. "Introduction" to Karl Marx, *The Economic & Philosophical Manuscripts of 1844* (New York: International Publishers, 1964).

Paul M. Sweezy. "Competition and Monopoly" *Monthly Review* 33:1 (May 1981) pp. 1-16.

R. H. Tawney. *Religion and the Rise of Capitalism* (New York: Harcourt, Brace and Company, Inc., 1926).

"Testimony of Chairman Alan Greenspan". U. S. Senate Committee on Banking, Housing, and Urban Affairs. 26 February 1997, at http:// www.federalreserve.gov//boarddocs/hh/1997/february/testimony. htm

E. P. Thompson. *The Making of the English Working Class* (New York: Vintage, 1963, 1966).

Leo Tolstoy. "Parable" wysiwyg://partner.87/http://www.geocities. com/glasgowbranch/parable.html Captured June 5, 2002.

Jerome Tuccille. "Bits and Pieces" *The Libertarian Forum* (November 1, 1970).

Benjamin R. Tucker. *Instead of a Book, By a Man Too Busy to Write One.* Gordon Press facsimile (New York: 1973 [1897]).

United States Participation in the Multilateral Development Banks in the 1980s. Department of the Treasury, Washington, DC, 1982.

"US Army Intel Units Spying on Activists" Intelligence Newsletter #381 (April 5, 2000) http://www.infoshop.org/news5/army_intel.html captured March 27, 2001.

Wakefield. *A View of the Art of Colonization*. Reprints of Economic Classics (New York: Augustus M. Kelley, 1849, 1969).

Immanuel Wallerstein. *The Capitalist World-Economy: Essays* (Cambridge University Press, 1979).

Wallerstein. *Historical Capitalism* (London, New York: Verso, 1983).

Wallerstein. *The Modern World System*. Part I: Capitalist Agriculture and the Origins of the European World-Economy in the Sixteenth Century (New York: Academic Press, 1974); Part II: Mercantilism and the Consolidation of the European World-Economy, 1600-1750 (New York: Academic Press, 1980).

William English Walling. *Socialism as it Is: A Survey of the World-Wide Revolutionary Movement* (New York: MacMillan & Co., Ltd., 1912).

Diane Cecilia Weber. "Warrior Cops: The Ominous Growth of Paramilitarism in American Police Departments" Cato Briefing Paper No. 50, 26 August 1999, at http://www.cato.org/pubs/briefs/bp-050es.html captured April 15, 2001.

James Weinstein. *The Corporate Ideal in the Liberal State: 1900-1918* (Boston: Beacon Press, 1968).

Thomas J. Wertenbaker. *The First Americans: 1607-1690* (Chicago: Quadrangle Books, 1971).

Friedrich von Wieser. *Natural Value.* Ed. by William Smart. Trans. by Christian A. Malloch (London and New York: MacMillan and Co., 1893).

William Appleman Williams. *The Contours of American History* (Cleveland and New York: The World Publishing Company, 1961).

Williams. *The Tragedy of American Diplomacy.* (New York: Dell Publishing Company, 1959, 1962).

"World Oil Supplies Running Out Faster than Expected" *Oil and Gas Journal,* August 12, 2002.

Mark Zepezauer and Arthur Naiman. *Take the Rich Off Welfare* (Odonian Press/Common Courage Press, 1996).

Individualist/Mutualist Resources

After:All blog
http://afterallblog.blogspot.com/
Any Time Now: Anarchist-Decentralist Newsletter
Affinity Place, Argenta B.C. VOG 1BO CANADA
http://www.atnzine.net/
Bad Press/Boston Anarchist Drinking Brigade
PO Box 230332, Anchorage, AK 99523-0332, USA
http://world.std.com/~bbrigade/
The Black Cr0ayon
http://www.blackcrayon.com/
Devize's Melting Pot
http://devizesmeltingpot.blogspot.com/
Joel's Humanistic Blog
http://joelschlosberg.blogspot.com/
A Libertarian Labyrinth
http://libertarian-labyrinth.org/
In the Libertarian Labyrinth blog
http://libertarian-labyrinth.blogspot.com/
Listen Liberty!
http://www.geocities.com/listen_liberty/
The Match!
P.O. Box 3012, Tucson AZ 85702, USA
Mutualist Blog
http://mutualist.blogspot.com
Mutualist.Org: Free Market Anti-Capitalism
http://www.mutualist.org/

Mutualists Yahoogroup
http://groups.yahoo.com/group/mutualists/
Mutualist Journal Club
http://mutualist-jc.blogspot.com/
Mutualize!
http://www.geocities.com/vcmtalk/mutualize
The Portal
http://www.the-portal.org/
Porcupine Blog
http://porkupineblog.blogspot.com/
Red Lion Press
Box 297 Station A Nanaimo BC V9R5K9 CANADA(do not mention Red
Lion Press on envelope)
Total Liberty Magazine
The Owl Press, 47 High Street, Belper, Derby DE56 1GF
http://mysite.wanadoo-members.co.uk/total_liberty1/
Upaya: Skilful means to Liberation
http://upaya.blogspot.com/
Voluntary Cooperation Movement
http://www.geocities.com/voluntary_cooperation_movement/
start.html
Note: These sources are limited almost entirely to explicitly individualist
or mutualist links (especially of the socialist Tuckerite strand). I have,
for reasons of space and time, omitted many valuable resources on
cooperative and decentralist economics, as well as a great deal of valuable
analysis by both libertarian socialists and free market libertarians. Had
I taken time to list them systematically, it would have amounted to
several days' more work and increased the cost of a lengthy book with
the equivalent of an added chapter.
For a wealth of material in these categories, check the sidebar at my
Mutualist Blog.
In addition, in my rush to finish the minimal changes necessary
to prepare this text for the BookSurge edition, I have (aside from a
very few new resources that immediately came to my sleep-deprived
mind) limited myself largely to updating the addresses and URLs for
those listed in the original edition. I have no doubt that many other
important resources will come to mind as soon as I send this off. My
sincere apologies, for my ingratitude for great benefits received, to all
whom I have missed or forgotten.